ROUTLEDGE LIBRARY EDITIONS: THE AUTOMOBILE INDUSTRY

Volume 10

LABOUR RELATIONS IN THE MOTOR INDUSTRY

LABOUR RELATIONS IN THE MOTOR INDUSTRY

A Study of Industrial Unrest and an International Comparison

H. A. TURNER, GARFIELD CLACK
AND GEOFFREY ROBERTS

LONDON AND NEW YORK

First published in 1967 by George Allen & Unwin Ltd

This edition first published in 2018
by Routledge
2 Park Square, Milton Park, Abingdon, Oxon OX14 4RN

and by Routledge
711 Third Avenue, New York, NY 10017

Routledge is an imprint of the Taylor & Francis Group, an informa business

© 1967 George Allen & Unwin Ltd

All rights reserved. No part of this book may be reprinted or reproduced or utilised in any form or by any electronic, mechanical, or other means, now known or hereafter invented, including photocopying and recording, or in any information storage or retrieval system, without permission in writing from the publishers.

Trademark notice: Product or corporate names may be trademarks or registered trademarks, and are used only for identification and explanation without intent to infringe.

British Library Cataloguing in Publication Data
A catalogue record for this book is available from the British Library

ISBN: 978-1-138-73855-3 (Set)
ISBN: 978-1-315-16182-2 (Set) (ebk)
ISBN: 978-1-138-06080-7 (Volume 10) (hbk)
ISBN: 978-1-138-06086-9 (Volume 10) (pbk)
ISBN: 978-1-315-16284-3 (Volume 10) (ebk)

Publisher's Note
The publisher has gone to great lengths to ensure the quality of this reprint but points out that some imperfections in the original copies may be apparent.

Disclaimer
The publisher has made every effort to trace copyright holders and would welcome correspondence from those they have been unable to trace.

LABOUR RELATIONS
IN THE MOTOR INDUSTRY

A STUDY OF INDUSTRIAL UNREST
AND AN INTERNATIONAL COMPARISON

BY

H. A. TURNER

GARFIELD CLACK AND GEOFFREY ROBERTS

London
GEORGE ALLEN & UNWIN LTD
RUSKIN HOUSE MUSEUM STREET

FIRST PUBLISHED IN 1967

This book is copyright under the Berne Convention. Apart from any fair dealing for the purpose of private study, research, criticism or review, as permitted under the Copyright Act, 1956, no portion may be reproduced by any process without written permission. Enquiries should be addressed to the Publishers.

© *George Allen & Unwin Ltd, 1967*

PRINTED IN GREAT BRITAIN
in 10 on 11 point Times Roman type
BY SIMSON SHAND LTD
LONDON, HERTFORD AND HARLOW

PREFACE

AND A NOTE ON RECENT EVENTS

This preface, for once, is meant to be read. The study that follows had its origin in two articles published in 1961 by Mr John Bescoby, now of Newcastle University, and the present writer, which made some analysis of post-war industrial disputes in the British car manufacturing firms. One or two of the conclusions then reached, the authors of the present study see no particular reason to change. But the articles led to some discussion, which suggested two things. First, that even at that time, the motor industry was becoming—not merely among social scientists of several kinds but within the industry itself—a standard illustration of various (and divergent) 'theories of strikes'. But secondly, that it was an advanced example of certain new, or only recently-emergent trends, not only in labour disputes in Britain, but (more important and enduring in their effects) in collective organization and industrial attitudes in general. These things seemed to merit a wider study. We did not quite appreciate, however, just how wide it would have to become.

It had originally been intended to make the study in two ways: on the one hand, to examine the conduct of labour relations within each of the major firms or plants—as illustrating what might be called the 'normal' situation; on the other, to follow through a selection of major disputes as examples of deviation from normality. But this approach soon ran into difficulties. For one thing, in this case normality and abnormality could not be quite so sharply distinguished—nor did such big strikes as occurred represent the typical content of disputes. Particularly, there were difficulties in establishing —in either the 'normal' or 'abnormal' situation—what actually happened, as opposed to what was generally supposed to happen. For instance, some car firms belong to an employers' association which has agreements specifying the way disputes should be handled at the plant level. But even in the firms concerned, the 'procedure' which is theoretically to be followed hardly ever corresponds to this model. While in practice, there are large differences of view between management and union representatives as to how the individual firm's *own* formal procedure actually operates: in the same plant, for instance, one may be told by the shop stewards that real problems are always taken straight to the works superintendent, and by the management that nearly all disputes are settled at lower levels.

Such statements are not necessarily incompatible. But they

involved a problem which is even more pronounced in attempting to study strikes. In such affairs, there are almost always large differences of opinion between the parties (of which there are usually far from being only two) not merely—as is inevitable—on the rights and wrongs of the matter, but on what is actually happening, and on the significance and order of particular incidents. The Press does its best, and labour correspondents in general have an almost academic identification with their subject, fascination for its detail and desire to generalize about it. They have, unbeknown, been invaluable to us. But they have to work fast, and what they or their editors think it important to report about a strike while it is on was not necessarily its significant feature for our purposes. The summary official records of reported industrial stoppages—of which a selection is published anyway, and the rest condensed in official statistics—were available to us, but these are very brief. Some disputes are the subject of detailed reports by the Ministry of Labour's conciliation officers, but these files sometimes contain confidential observations, and it was thought inadvisable to consult them. Some big disputes had been the subject of Courts of Inquiry, which represented at least examinations made by detached people in an atmosphere of deliberation, and one or two others we were able to follow through 'on the spot'. But these, again, were only a small part of the picture.

The only way to overcome these difficulties of establishing the nature of situations seemed to be to participate in them oneself; and this one of us at least has done. Dr Clack lived for two years in a large car manufacturing centre, passing the best part of a year as an operative in a car plant, attending meetings of shop stewards and spending some time in the plant's personnel office, and working shorter periods again—for comparative purposes—in general engineering establishments. This experience has informed this study in general, one aspect of it is reported summarily in the appendix to our Chapter VII, and we gratefully acknowledge here the management and trade unionist co-operation which enabled us to secure it—as well as the grant from the Human Sciences Committee of the Department of Scientific and Industrial Research towards the separate inquiry of which it formed part. A more detailed account and interpretation of it is being published separately as an Occasional Paper for the Department of Applied Economics (by the Cambridge University Press), as 'Industrial Relations in a British Car Factory'. But this method, too, involves a problem: how typical is the experience in which the observer 'participates'? Other material we were accumulating already indicated that patterns of labour relations in the motor industry were richly (if not sometimes appallingly) complex—and were also changing quite fast. One still had, in other

PREFACE

words, to try and determine the general picture, and the directions in which it was changing.

One method of doing this, of course, is to secure facts, interpretations and opinions from the picture's human occupants themselves. Dr Clack and Mr Roberts have between them interviewed very many people who are responsible, in one way and another, for the conduct of the motor industry's labour affairs—particularly (where it seemed to us most important) at local and plant level. These include the labour relations and personnel managers, local union officers and officials of employers' associations, and leading shop stewards concerned, we think, with all the major car factories in the main centres of production—and again we express our appreciation to those busy persons, too many to name, who gave us their time, experience, and much valuable information (as well, often, as their patience with our many supplementary questions). But here, too, there were problems. Industrial relations constitute a subject with many aspects, which continually suggested themselves as inseparable from one another and improper to neglect—and in our study's subject this was also a time of increasing public interest: *and* of controversy. On many questions there was a lack of concrete or precise information, and on others there were strong differences of opinion. Moreover, those who were most closely involved in particular situations would sometimes themselves say that they were not best placed to judge the broader movement of events.

One needed measurements and indicators, in short. We make some use of officially-published data. More was supplied by firms, or made available to us with their permission from returns they made to other bodies, and much supplied by union officers; and for these courtesies we again express our thanks. On several things, however, —some aspects of wages, for instance, and of the dispersal of union membership—we had to compile our own data from such raw material as was to hand. In particular, the construction of a separate series of strike-statistics for car-manufacturing—though here we had the work previously done by Mr Bescoby and myself to build on—involved the detailed examination and analysis of the summary official records of some thousand separate disputes, in the motor industry and allied sectors of the economy—as well, frequently, as their matching-up with press reports, because the summary or classification was inadequate for our purposes. Here, certain press libraries have been most helpful: but we should particularly thank those statistical officers of the Ministry of Labour who bore so kindly with our shufflings of their treasured basic material and with our cross-examinations of their own results.

Figures, indeed, provide much of the framework on which this study is hung. For this we make no apologies: statistical analysis both deals with the hardest kinds of facts available and provides a means to analyse their inter-relationships. But some things are not amenable to this kind of treatment, and we also make much use of another scientific technique, comparison. Particularly, because the motor industry is a major international one, but because—except on its American branch—there seems little written about its labour aspects, we have compared countries. Dr Clack and myself have between us visited nearly all the major European car plants, and the most important American ones; we owe much to the information, interest—and hospitality—we received from managements, trade unionists and officers of employers' organizations in other countries.

We are, nevertheless, very conscious of this study's inadequacies. Our chapter on trade union organization, for instance, hardly does justice to the fascinating development of workplace union representation, and Mr Roberts is producing from our material a more detailed study for separate publication—which will also include some reference to the way firms themselves are organized to deal with labour questions. The structure of management in this connection is a topic in itself, which we have deliberately excluded as a separate question—beyond such references to it as necessarily arise in other connections. It seemed impossible, in practice, and except in a very formal sense (and sometimes not even then), to separate a firm's treatment of labour relations from other aspects of its management. And here, there is again the problem of the difference between what is supposed to happen—or even what the people concerned may themselves think happens—and what actually happens. The difference between forms and realities or, to use the now-conventional terminology, between the formal and the informal. At this stage, we make only two comments. One, that we rather think it would be more appropriate—so far as management at least is concerned—to speak of 'the culture of the firm' than 'the culture of the factory'. And two (more specific to our subject), it seems to us that several of the British motor industry's problems, including its apparent labour difficulties but extending to others, in part arise because its managements were often formed around brilliant design and production engineers, whose great technical success itself involved them in an embarrassment of human organization—constructs in materials of which their own expertise was impatient, and which it often found unpredictable and inconsistent.

Nevertheless, empiricism is in general a virtue of both engineers and of trade unionists. One aspect of this study is the way in which, within a now quite long-established formal system of collective relationships, a new system is emerging—still, in part, informally.

Preface

In our first Chapter, we give some brief account of recent developments in organized industrial relations in the motor industry (so recent, in fact, that several inquiries into particular disputes made under the new Motor Industry Joint Labour Council's aegis were reported after this book was already mostly written). And in our last Chapter we indicated that—though different views of what organization of industrial relations is most appropriate to contemporary society are highly tenable—we ourselves think these new developments are in the right direction. Indeed, it is not at all impossible that they may have matured to a much more organized and coherent form by the time this book appears. In that sense, this study could also be a historical one. Our essential purpose, however, is to take the motor industry—as the case in which several contemporary questions of industrial relations seem sharpest—as a stand for wider exploration of those questions, not merely in a policy sense but in the sense of the social scientist's concern for the causation of human events.

Here, events since our text was printed give us at least the consolation that they support its predictive potential. A new recession in the car trade induced by government deflationary measures in mid-1966 has led to substantial strikes (see our Chapter IV). Our reluctance to forecast that the relative freedom of Vauxhall from strikes would continue (Chapters VII and XI) has been justified. For labour relations, some consequences of Jaguar's merger into the British Motor Corporation (B.M.C.) may be implied from Chapters VII and VIII. The car firms' 'wage drift' (Chapter V) seems likely to evade the statutory 'wages standstill' introduced in mid-1966. On individual disputes, reports now come from the new Joint Council (Chapter I): we exchanged our draft with Mr Scamp for one of these prepublication, but have not otherwise compared impressions; if any general report is issued under his aegis, our study's readers should consult it as a parallel, conciliator's analysis.

To the firms and organizations, and the many individuals who have helped us by discussion, the supply of organizable fact, or by comment on our use of it, we have already indicated our very great obligation. Those who read our various drafts in whole or part and sent us many detailed comments we should thank more specifically. They include the labour relations directors or managers of Citroën, Daimler-Benz, Fiat, Ford of Germany, Opel, Peugeot, Renault, Simca, Volkswagen and Volvo, officers of the International Metalworkers' Federation, the German Metalworkers' Industrial Trade Union (I.G. Metall), the Swedish Trade Union Centre (L.O.) and the Swedish Engineering Employers' Federation (S.V.), and Professor Kazutoshi Koshiro of Yokohama University: who all replied to us so promptly—and so often in English. Mr Robert E. Cole of Tokyo University, Professors M. S. Ryder and R. B. McKersie, respectively of Michigan and Chicago Universities, Mr W. B. Gould, formerly of the U.S. National Labour Relations Board, and Mr Charles Levinson, now General Secretary of the International Chemical and General Workers' Federation, also sent us valuable comment on our international comparisons. The Director of Statistics of the Ministry of Labour commented most usefully on our statistical drafts. Mr R. Hopkins, Personnel Director of Vauxhall Motors, and Mr Richard O'Brien, former Director of Industrial Relations of B.M.C., gave us detailed and thoughtful remarks on our Chapters on wages and the 'work situation'. Mr G. H. B. Cattell, Managing Director of Humber Ltd, and Mr Maurice Platt, former head of Vauxhall Motors' engineering department, sent us most informative notes on the motor industry's technology and wage systems, as did certain consultants who preferred to remain nameless. Mr Jack Jones, then Acting Assistant General Secretary of the Transport and General Workers' Union and that union's former West Midlands Regional Secretary, gave us on a personal basis, many incisive comments on our first draft as a whole, as did Mr Hugh Clegg of Nuffield College, Oxford. Dr Paul O'Higgins, of Christ's College, Cambridge, sent us helpful and subtle notes on our final draft. Mr L. J. Handy, of the Cambridge University Department of Applied Economics most patiently read our sundry drafts in succession and saved us from not a few inconsistencies.

Together, these gentlemen have prevented us from committing many errors. For this study's opinions and interpretations—and for those errors that remain—they have no responsibility whatever. And that some errors of interpretation—or even, despite our best efforts, of fact—will transpire is highly possible. This is a large book, but also a condensed one, and it is not unlikely that some few of the very busy people to whom it refers will have their attention caught by just those summary lines that have an application to their particular circumstances, and feel that we have got them wrong. If so, the chance is implicit in an attempt to grasp a very large and complex human situation as a whole, and we hope they may forgive us in understanding of our effort to do so. It is possible, too, that we may still be found guilty of residual inconsistencies: this risk is also inevitable in the attempt to form a collective assessment of a controversial, complicated and developing situation. But the situation and the people involved in it, we have ourselves found of absorbing interest: we leave it at the point where we at least agree with each other.

H. A. TURNER
Cambridge, October 1966

CONTENTS

PREFACE: and a note on recent events   *page* 7

I. STRIKES: AND THE CAR INDUSTRY

   A. The general trend of strikes: and post-war disputes in the car firms   19

   B. The industry and workers   26

   C. Collective organization: unions, employers and joint arrangements   33

   D. The work and working environment   38

APPENDIX: The effects of strikes in car factories   45

II. THE ISSUES IN DISPUTE

   A. What is a strike? And some other problems   51

   B. The car firms' strike-record: preliminary analysis   58

   C. The 'causes' of strikes: a reconsideration, and post-war trends   62

   D. New issues—and new plants. Questions arising   67

APPENDICES: A. The car manufacturers' strike statistics   72

            B. Causation of car firm disputes, 1921–64   76

III. PRODUCTIVITY GROWTH AND TECHNICAL CHANGE

   A. 'Automation' and productivity trends   77

   B. Technical change and labour displacement   82

   C. Production stresses, 'effort bargaining', and management   88

   D. Wage problems, and a conclusion   96

APPENDIX: Output, employment and productivity indices for motor vehicles, 1948–64   103

IV. STRIKES AND THE LEVEL OF ACTIVITY

   A. Output fluctuations and disputes   104

   B. Factors in the 'severity' of strikes   113

   C. Seasonal patterns; insecurity and the strike-liability   121

APPENDIX: What happened in 1965?   129

LABOUR RELATIONS IN THE MOTOR INDUSTRY

V. WAGES IN THE MOTOR INDUSTRY

   A. Wage-levels and trends — 133

   B. Inter-firm and inter-plant differentials — 138

   C. Plant wage-structures, and 'anomalies' — 145

   D. The instability of earnings — 155

VI. THE WORK, WORKERS AND WORK SITUATION

   A. Some 'theories of strike-proneness'; the work, work organization and work situation — 165

   B. The workers and working hours; 'ageing' and 'green labour' — 171

   C. 'Solidarity', 'size' and 'supervision' — 178

   D. Withdrawals from the work situation: absenteeism, accidents, labour turnover—and strikes — 184

VII. TRADE UNIONS AND SHOP STEWARDS

   A. The pattern of union organization — 192

   B. Multiple unionism, and internal structures — 198

   C. Shop stewards: the new 'establishment' — 205

   D. Stewards, strikes and managements — 211

   E. The 'combines', weaknesses of the steward organization—and 'parallel unionism' — 216

APPENDIX: Some smaller strikes: from the inside — 224

VIII. THE FIRMS COMPARED: AND THE EMPLOYERS' ORGANIZATION

   A. Big firms and smaller ones — 230

   B. Strike-experience of individual companies — 235

   C. The 'cycle' theory: and dispute-causation at the plant level — 241

   D. Institutional factors: the Employers' Federation, and 'procedure' — 247

   E. The results of 'procedure' — 251

APPENDIX: The strike-liability of individual firms — 259

IX. THE BIGGEST STRIKES: AND THE ROLE OF INDIVIDUALS

   A. 'Sizeable strikes': an analysis — 265

   B. Austin, 1953 — 271

Contents

    c. Ford, 1957–63   275
    d. 'The firm line': Pressed Steel and Rootes, 1961   282
    e. The 'agitator theory'   287

X. INDUSTRIAL RELATIONS IN FOREIGN CAR FIRMS

    a. General considerations: and the U.S. industry, union and strike-liability   293
    b. Bargaining in the U.S. industry: system and results   300
    c. Germany   306
    d. France   311
    e. Italy—Fiat   314
    f. Sweden, Japan, some others—and a comparative note   318

XI. SUMMARIES AND CONCLUSIONS

    a. Theories of strikes again: background factors, insecurity, and the functional role of strikes   326
    b. Causes of strikes: 'fair wages' and 'job rights'   333
    c. Obsolescence in institutions   339
    d. The firms again—and exceptions to strike-proneness   344
    e. Three approaches: and a summing-up   350

INDEX   357

LIST OF TABLES AND DIAGRAMS
(*Roman Number refers to Chapter*)

TABLES

I/1. Post-war Industrial Disputes in the Car Firms *page*	23
I/2. Manual Employment in the Car Firms: 1963	31
I/3. Employees by Occupational Groups: May 1963	32
App. Fulfilment of Production Schedules in a Large Assembly Plant	48
II/1. Strikes in British Car Firms, 1921–64	59
II/2. Strikes in Car Firms: Distribution by Causes (official classification)	61
II/3. Strikes in Car Firms: Distribution by Causes (re-classified)	65
II/4. Strikes in Car Firms: Post-War Developments	66
II/5. Post-War Strikes in Car Firms: Subsidiary Issues	67
II/6. Strikes in New Plants	68
App. A. Strikes and 'Man-Hours Lost': as reported by the Manufacturers	74
B. Causation of Car Firm Disputes, 1921–64 (by official classification and as re-classified)	76
III/1. Output, Employment and Productivity of the Three Largest Car Producers, 1952–63	81
III/2. Changes in the Proportion of Administrative, Technical and Clerical Employees in the Motor Industry, 1924–58	94
App. Output, Employment and Productivity Indices for Motor Vehicles, 1948–64	103
IV/1. Annual Frequency of Strikes by Cause (re-classified)	115
IV/2. 'Severity' of Car Firm Strikes	116
IV/3. Number of Strikes beginning in each Month, by Period	122
IV/4. Number of Strikes beginning in each Month, by Cause	125
App. IV A. Car Market Developments, Production and Labour stoppages, 1962–65	131
IV B. Stoppages known to be 'Wholly Official' in the Motor Vehicle Industry	132

TABLES

v/1. Percentage Ratio of Average Hourly Earnings (including overtime), Average of January and June 1963, for Skilled to Other Workers, Motor Vehicles & Engineering — 158

vi/1. Percentage of Male Employees in each Age Group, Motor Vehicles and Other Industries, 1950 and 1964 — 172
vi/2. Percentage of Employees by Age Group in Two Car Firms — 173
vi/3. Percentage of Workers on Shift Systems, Vehicles and Other Industries — 176
vi/4. (a and b) Short-time and Overtime Variations, Motor Industry and Others — 178
vi/5. Strikes in Car Firms 1960–63 according to the Number of Workers Directly Involved — 180
vi/6. Percentage of Administrative, Technical and Clerical Employees in some Car Plants and Firms, 1955 and 1961 — 183
vi/7. Annual Accident Frequency Rates for Various Car Factories, 1958–62 — 187
vi/8. Estimated Annual Labour Turnover for all Male Employees, Motor Vehicles and Other Industries, 1960–65 — 189

vii/1. Estimated Trade Union Strengths in the Car Firms, 1965–66 — 195
vii/2. Distribution of Trade Union Membership in the Assembly Division of a Car Plant — 197

viii/1. Strike Liability of the Car Firms: by Groups — 232
viii/2. Percentage of Strikes by Cause and Groups of Firms — 232
viii/3. Percentage of Striker-days by Cause and Groups of Firms — 233
viii/4. Strike-liability of the Individual Firms: 1946–64 — 235
viii/5. Annual Average Strike-Liability of Individual Firms — 239
viii/6. Causes of Post-War Strikes, by Firm — 242
viii/7. Results of Conferences under Federation Conciliation Procedure, Car Firms and All Engineering, 1964–65 — 252

VIII/8. Typical Outcomes of References to Federation Conciliation Procedure, Car Firms and All Engineering, 1964–65   254

IX/1. Sizeable Strikes   266

X/1. Ratio of Manual Workers' Average Hourly Receipts: October 1961 (automobile industry to all engineering, 3 countries)   324

XI/1. Car Firm Striker-Days by Cause (inter-war and post-war compared)   334

DIAGRAMS

IV/1. Strikes and Output, 1921–39   108
IV/2. Strikes and Output, 1946–64   110
IV/3. Monthly Output and Strike Trends, De-seasonalized, 1957–62   112
IV/4. Strikes in Major and Minor Firms, 1946–64   120
IV/5. Strikes and Production (in each calendar month), 1946–62   123

V/1. Car Firm: Adult Male Average Hourly Earnings, (trend by firm), 1948–62   139
V/2. (a–d) Percentages of Adult Male Operatives at Different Pay Levels (by industry, individual firms, and certain plants, October 1960)   148
V/3. Average Hours Per Head Worked by Full-Time Operatives (vehicles and engineering), 1956–64   161
V/4. Variations in Weekly Earnings in Particular Sections of a Car Plant: 1960–63, and 1962–63   163

VIII. (x) Post-War Strike-Liability of Car Firms: By Firm and Cause   260

X/1. Strikes, Striker-Days and Output in the U.S. Automobile Industry   296

CHAPTER I

STRIKES AND THE CAR INDUSTRY

(A) THE GENERAL TREND OF STRIKES: AND POST-WAR DISPUTES IN THE CAR FIRMS

Strikes are a display of industrial relations at their points of tension. They provide a sharp, if spectacular, focus for a wider study of either particular industrial situations or of industrial discontent in general. Like all conflicts, strikes attract an audience, which sees them from different angles. Strikes are the best available indicators of a sum of specific dissatisfactions—or are, at least, the only unambiguous ones. But to single them out in this way is not to emphasize the importance of strikes as such, nor to imply anything at all about what attitudes or public policy should be appropriate to them. There seems currently, for instance, an almost universal assumption that strikes are bad, that they are necessarily manifestations of darkness rather than light in the process of industrial adaptation and change. While an opposed, but very much minority opinion holds practically all strikes justifiable. Here, we try to exclude automatic judgments of this kind, or emotional overtones which parallel them.

The disclaimer needs making because the British motor industry has become in recent years a popular sounding-board for opinion and speculation about almost all aspects of strikes. That the industry attracts this comment is not difficult to understand. Cars are widely-desired and aggressively-visible products whose makers are relatively few, are concentrated in few areas, and are thought to be highly paid. Strikes by car workers seem frequent, and quite small ones may lead readily to large consequences in terms of men laid off work for lack of the bits and pieces to work with. The important role of the industry in the country's balance of payments accounting encourages alarm about the alleged effects of strikes on the economy, while people who like to think in terms of conspiracies have not found it difficult to see the more publicized of car workers' strikes as skirmishes in a wider and colder war. The publicity which the industry attracts may itself be a part of the armoury of those actually engaged in its battles. And it has even been suggested that these have sometimes not been without an incidental utility to trade union officials facing an election, or to harassed managers explaining their failure to meet production deadlines in an otherwise watertight control system[1]; they have certainly been so to politicians—in both the 1964 and 1966 general elections, motor industry disputes provided ammunition for rival contestants for office.

Strikes by car workers, however, provide only one instance of a more general rise in the strike-liability of British employees during recent years. But this rise itself represents a reversal of a longer, and more universal trend. During the last generation, strike-liability in the United Kingdom, in concert with that of many other industrial countries, 'withered away'.[2] Even if strikes multiplied in number, they on the whole individually involved many fewer workers than at one time, and became on the average much briefer. For example, the average annual number of striker-days[3] in all British industries in the period from 1900 to the early 1930s was over seventeen million a year. Even excluding 1926, the year of the General Strike, the average was some thirteen million. But taking the years from 1932 to 1955, the average fell to just under two million striker-days—and in the post-war part of this period the actual total each year deviated very little from this average. The much higher average up to 1932 was largely the product of the high incidence of major industrial disputes during the half-dozen years before and half-dozen years after the First World War. In fact, in Britain the 'withering away' was a rather sudden process of the early 1930s. However, the relative stability in our strike-incidence since the 1930s has been fairly sharply disturbed over the past decade.[4]

There are currently some 2,500 strikes publicly recorded each year in Britain. The average strike (supposing for the moment such a creature to exist) apparently involves five or six hundred workers

---

[1] See Joan Woodward, 'Industrial Behaviour—is there a Science', in *New Society*, October 8, 1964. Reference to the motor industry is implicit: for example, 'to a harassed middle manager or foreman, aware that he is not going to get the new model off the line at the specified time, a stoppage of work can be a godsend ... It might be found that line management in a strike-prone industry have a vested interest in perpetuating the industry's reputation.'

[2] See A. M. Ross and P. T. Hartman, *Changing Patterns of Industrial Conflict* (New York: Wiley, 1960).

[3] We generally use 'striker-days' in preference to the official term 'working days lost'. The reason for this is discussed in Chapter II.

[4] For a more detailed discussion than the following see H. A. Turner, *The Trend of Strikes*, Leeds University Press, 1963.

and lasts two or three days. The number of striker-days is thus running at rather over three million a year. The average for the ten years to 1964 was actually just under four million; however, the annual average for the previous decade, to 1954, was only just over two million. Taking again that ten-year period to 1964, the number of workers reported to have been involved in strikes is comparable with that in the years of unrest up to and including 1926, and the number of separate strikes is very much higher than for any comparable period since figures first began to be systematically collected, in the 1890s. Moreover, very many minor stoppages (to say nothing of go-slows, overtime bans, and cases of work-to-rule) are not included in the official statistics because they are too small, or have simply escaped the Ministry of Labour's notice; and this understatement is likely to be greater when—as at present—the typical strike is small and short.

The extent of this rising movement of industrial unrest in recent years is to some degree masked by events in the mining industry. The official record of British industrial unrest has for fifty years and more been dominated by the collieries, and in seventeen of the past twenty years, miners were responsible for the majority of separate strikes reported. The number of miners' strikes, however, reached a climax in 1957 and since then has fallen sharply—a movement which has masked the broader national trend. But setting mining aside as having many special features, the frequency of strikes for all other industries is worth listing year-by-year for the recent period. For ten years up to 1956, the annual number of industrial stoppages fluctuated around 550 (which was also very similar to the rate for the immediate pre-war years). In 1956 it was 570. But thereafter, it rose each year: first to 640, then to 670, to 790, to 1,170, to 1,230, and in 1962 to 1,240. In 1963 it dropped back slightly to 1,080, but in 1964 rose to 1,470. In 1965 it was 1,610. In effect, the frequency of strikes outside of mining has almost trebled in ten years—despite an overall economic and employment situation which has been rather more discouraging to such a movement than in the immediate post-war decade.

How important is the increased incidence of disputes in comparison with other forms of 'lost time' in industry? Even in 1962, for example, when striker-days rose to nearly six million (due largely to two one-day national engineering stoppages), the time spent on strike still averaged only two hours per employee—perhaps a tenth of the working time lost to the common cold. Even making a generous allowance for various forms of understatement in the official figures, the average number of workers idle at any one time because of industrial disputes is currently unlikely to be much above

30,000—which is about half the number normally incapacitated by industrial accidents, and contrasts with an unemployed population numbered in hundreds of thousands. Nor is the public statisticians' 'loss of working days' an unqualified measure: amongst at least some groups of workers it has been noted that lost output and earnings from disputes are recovered by extra effort and overtime working. A case has even been made to show that an occasional strike may sometimes help to maintain productivity.[1]

It may, however, be held that our strike-incidence focuses on certain trades the economic importance of which is such as to make the effect disproportionate. And this raises questions about the distribution of the strike-liability. Strikes are heavily concentrated in certain industrial groups: coal miners (of course), dockers, building workers, and workers in the rather heterogeneous 'metals' trades (Metals, Engineering, Shipbuilding and Vehicles). Taking the period from 1960, for example, for each year mining and 'metals' workers alone have accounted for three out of every four strikes, and for nearly three-quarters of all striker-days. Reasons which have been suggested to account for this kind of concentration of strike-liability are numerous, and include such things as insecurity of employment, rapidly changing work or working conditions, the nature of the work itself, and the relative social isolation of particular working communities. These are rather blunt—and in some cases debatable—propositions which we take up again later in the book.

The 'metals' group of industries taken together account for an especially large part of the increase in strike-liability of recent years. This group represents in large part the sector directly affected by collective agreements between the Confederation of Shipbuilding and Engineering Unions and various employers' associations (particularly, the Engineering Employers' Federation itself), and has in the last five years become responsible for over 60 per cent of all 'working days lost' from labour disputes. The increase has been particularly marked in certain categories of the vehicles trades. There is no official series for industrial disputes in the motor industry over most of the post-war period. Ministry of Labour strike statistics up to 1948 included the motor trades in the general 'Engineering' industry. From 1949 to 1958 they were grouped in a vehicle industries category which included aircraft manufacturing. It is only since 1959 that the published figures relate to a 'motor vehicle and cycle' industry group which embraces not merely the car assembly factories but the specialist makers of heavy road vehicles, of two-wheelers, three-wheelers, and other perambulatory devices plus a good number (but not all) of the component and accessory manu-

[1] See T. T. Paterson, *Glasgow Limited* (Cambridge, C.U.P., 1960).

facturers as well as various repairers and other establishments which are included on technical grounds. We have had, therefore, to compile our own series for disputes in the motor trades.[1] And these show labour unrest within the vehicles industry to have been again increasingly concentrated, in the car firms proper.

For example, on our private estimates, at the end of the 1940s the strike frequency in the car firms was about one quarter of the total of the vehicles group as a whole, and these firms accounted for about one-tenth of the vehicles group's strike-incidence. By the late 1950s, these proportions had both increased to between one-half and two-thirds: thus accounting very largely for the more than trebling of the strike-liability—i.e. both frequency and incidence of stoppages—of the vehicles industry as a whole over the same period (changes in industrial classification notwithstanding). It is, indeed, notable that until the mid-1950s the car firms (which have provided about half the total employment of the 'motor industry' as officially defined during the post-war period) were not particularly strike-prone. Up to that turning-point, most of the motor industry's post-war strike-liability appears to have been concentrated in its commercial vehicle and component sectors. But in those sectors industrial unrest has maintained—until very recently, at least—a fairly constant level. It is this special channelling of heightened labour disturbance through an alternative group of enterprises which has determined this study's focus.

From the data we have collected, it is possible to trace this rising movement of industrial unrest in the motor industry summarily:

Table I/1—POST-WAR INDUSTRIAL DISPUTES IN THE CAR FIRMS*

Annual averages of 3-year period	Number of separate strikes traced	Workers 'directly and indirectly involved'	'Working days lost'
1947–49	10	9,000	25,000
1950–52	14	25,000	131,000
1953–55	14	42,000	137,000
1956–58	31	82,000	322,000
1959–61	75	116,000	307,000
1962–64	86	141,000	321,000

* Although the figures represent the product of our own researches, they are arranged to follow the statistical definitions and canons of the Ministry of Labour. Thus, workers involved in more than one strike in any period are counted more than once accordingly—so that the particularly high figure of workers involved for 1962–64 somewhat reflects the fact that there were two general engineering strikes which affected several car firms during this period. Even without such stoppages, however, the figure would still have been about the same as for 1959–61, and more than twice as big as that for 1956–58.

[1] The method of these estimates is explained in Chapter II.

Labour Relations in the Motor Industry

The current labour force of the car firms is about a quarter-million employees, having risen from a probable 150,000 or so just after the war. Measured in customary terms of the ratio of 'lost' working days to the total of employees, therefore, the strike-incidence of the car firms has risen from about twice the national average in the early post-war years (a proportion by no means remarkable for manufacturing industry) to about six times the national average during the 1960s—thus contributing substantially to the rise in the national incidence itself. The car workers, in fact, had become at least as dispute-liable as such traditionally strike-prone groups as miners, shipbuilders and dockers—a phenomenon which led the Minister of Labour to pick out the motor industry from early 1961 as appropriate for a series of special joint meetings of employers' and union representatives to reform the industry's labour relations. No impact of that initiative apparently emerges in the above table.

However, it is again as well to keep matters in perspective. Even during the decade from 1955 to 1964 inclusive, the average car-assembly firm operative or machinist has been involved in only seven disputes which caused a stoppage of work big enough, say, to have been officially recorded, and has lost a total of less than three weeks' work on their account. Even making a fairly generous allowance for unreported stoppages, and for workers laid off on account of disputes at other establishments than their own (who are not included in the table above), the average time 'lost' works out at about two days a year for each worker employed by the car firms, or only a little over that figure if the 'loss' is assumed to affect manual workers alone. Even during the decade from the mid-1950s the average American automobile operative—who is, in his own country, no longer reckoned to be outstandingly strike-prone—almost certainly lost more working time from strikes than his British equivalent. It is difficult to be more definitive because of differences in the data available for the two countries; but it *is* clear that the time involved in individual absences from work by British car workers remained several times greater than that committed to strikes. Even the car firms, in fact, despite both their high strike-incidence and comparatively low accident rate, might well gain as much by a substantial reduction in industrial casualties as by one in industrial disputes, While there is some doubt as to how much of the work-time reported as 'lost' from disputes would in fact have been used: the car firms' strike-incidence has been generally higher (as we shall show) in periods of slack demand.

This implies, of course, a considerably smaller economic impact for labour unrest than would be gathered from many observations on these matters by public personalities. The car manufacturers themselves have made, separately or collectively, statements about the effect of labour disputes on output in sundry terms—number of vehicles lost, percentage of total production, shortfall on capacity utilization, cash loss on turnover, and working hours lost. But these various estimates are not very obviously compatible with each other. For 1965—a year for which such estimates were particularly common—they range from an effect of 2 per cent for the principal car producers, up to one of over 11 per cent for the whole motor industry. On the other hand, 'working days lost' so far officially reported by the Ministry of Labour—which were in 1965 quite abnormally high even for this industrial group—ran at under 1 per cent of total work-time in the motor vehicle and cycle sector. We have been sufficiently interested by these discrepancies as to attempt some more direct examination of the effect of disputes—and other kinds of stoppages—on car production, and the result is contained in this Chapter's Appendix; some later discussion (particularly that of Chapter IV) is also relevant to the problem. Suffice it to say here that we do not think an adequate calculation of 'working time lost' substantially underestimates the economic effect of strikes, and that there is some reason to believe it, on the average, an overstatement.

This is not to say that a big strike—or a run of minor stoppages concentrated in one department or plant of a concern like B.M.C., in which technical integration is already a major prestidigitatory problem—may not have a palpable impact on the firm's output (if the effect on production as a whole is offset by its competitors' gain). But in general, we rather suspect that the increasing irritation displayed by prominent motor industry spokesmen in the 1960s at the phenomenon of active industrial unrest—an irritation which overflowed into the Press—was provoked as much by the frustration induced in these technically-minded people by their apparent inability to predict and control their human instruments' behaviour as by any dramatic impact of that behaviour on production. We have not, indeed, even been able to trace—what one might well have expected to find—any connection between apparent labour discontent and poor workmanship. If either the number of defects found in new cars on delivery or—less precisely—those developed in subsequent service are compared for models surveyed and tested by the Consumers' Association, no consistent difference between the products of the various British manufacturers emerges, despite the wide disparities in their respective strike-liabilities.[1] There *does*

---

[1] Vauxhall cars tested and surveyed by C.A. in the last year or two do appear to show fewer defects on delivery than those of other British manufacturers reported on—including some of much more expensive cars. But since this is a very recent development it seems difficult to link it with Vauxhall's generally peaceable

appear to have been a difference in these respects between British cars as a whole and certain foreign models, and the models concerned also come from countries with a very low strike-incidence. But the difference may arise simply because imported cars often undergo an extra stage of inspection before final delivery.

Our interest in motor industry disputes, therefore, arises not from any special economic importance they may possess but from the light they may shed on the general movement of industrial relations to which we have referred, and from the broader problems they illuminate and illustrate. For instance, this increase in the car firms' strike-liability was hardly to have been expected, had one been examining their situation in the early 1950s, say. Another index of industrial discontent, labour turnover, has remained distinctly lower for the motor vehicle industry than for manufacturing generally— with only two-thirds the latter's ratio of terminated engagements, for men in a normal year.[1] And the car workers in particular have no such inter-war history of long-term under-employment and wage-depression as that which may have confirmed the strike-habit in some older industries. In recent years, pay-packets in the car factories have become a common subject of envious popular reference. But wages in several car firms, at least, have apparently always been relatively high. The motor industry has, of course, been one of the more dramatic growth centres of the present century's economy.

(B) THE INDUSTRY AND WORKERS

This seems an appropriate point to outline briefly the growth and structure of the car firms themselves.[2] Cars are a twentieth-century product. The early years of the motor industry, to 1920, were times of experimentation which saw the slow growth of many small-scale producers. Output rose from only 4,000 vehicles in 1905 to 34,000 by 1914, and by 1922 it was still less than 75,000—produced then by seventy-five firms. Despite the limitations imposed by a components industry which was developing only slowly, the car firms were even then becoming primarily assemblers of bits and pieces, and during the 1920s the industry changed over to mass production methods. By 1929 the output of cars had reached 182,000; there had been few new entrants since 1920, and over sixty firms had stopped making

labour relations: except, perhaps, by inverse! It is also within that period that the firm has had several sizeable disputes.

[1] Estimated from the *Ministry of Labour Gazette's* quarterly returns of labour turnover in manufacturing industries.

[2] This outline draws heavily on G. Maxcy and A. Silberston, *The Motor Industry* (London: Allen and Unwin, 1959).

cars despite this rapid expansion. Car production was becoming oligopolistic.

At the beginning of the 1930s, three firms were producing three-quarters of the total output of finished cars: Morris (35 per cent), Austin (25 per cent), and Ford (15 per cent). During this decade, popular models became the prerogative of only six firms. In 1925, General Motors of America had acquired Vauxhall, and Hillman and Humber had later merged to form the basis of the Rootes Group. Standard was the other member of the 'Big Six' of the 1930s —years marked by intense price, quality, and model competition, by frequent model changes, and by growth through internal expansion. Most mergers in the industry involved the purchase of bankrupt firms with good names at bargain prices. The Big Six remained until the 1950s, when the merger of Morris and Austin reduced them to what were then commonly called the Big Five—though the growth in Ford's share of total output, and the development of certain 'quality' firms, made it more realistic to speak of the Big Two and Lesser Five: i.e. B.M.C. and Ford on the one hand, and Vauxhall, Rootes, Standard, Rover and Jaguar on the other. From 1937 the car firms had changed over to armaments production, and the war years resulted in expanded and more scattered plant. But the new facilities—in the form often of 'shadow factories' first leased and later sometimes acquired from the State—were modern, and were ready replacements for war-damaged sites. The rapid reconversion to peace-time production was based partly on these new facilities and partly on the old pre-war designs and tools: new models did not appear until 1947. There were few market problems—the world was hungry for cars of any kind—and the industry's main difficulties arose out of shortages of materials and components. It was not until 1949 that the output of cars exceeded the pre-war annual record of 1937, and not until 1950 that the number rose above half a million.

There were a number of important mergers during the early 1950s, the best-known of which was the formation of B.M.C.—undertaken ostensibly to exploit the economies of large-scale production, and also as a defensive movement. The two American-controlled firms had been increasing their share of the market since 1929, mainly at the expense of Austin and Morris. Other mergers were related at least partially to a fear of shortages of sheet steel parts: Fisher and Ludlow, and Briggs Bodies, were absorbed into B.M.C. and Ford respectively in 1953, leaving Pressed Steel as the only large independent car-body maker (until 1965—when it, too, was acquired by B.M.C.). And the long-established firm of Jowett ceased production in 1954, pleading a consequent inability to obtain bodies. In 1955, Singer was absorbed in the Rootes group. By this year, five of the seven main producers of finished cars were each turning out over 100,000 cars a year, with Jaguar and Rover a considerable way behind—catering for a more specialist, high-priced, market. But this 'rationalization' did not introduce a period of organizational stability.

Two other pressures may be singled out as making for changes during the 1950s. There was the more rapid technical development inseparable from a competitively changing product with a doubled output—to one million cars in the eight years to 1958. The emotional impact of the technical changes has been perhaps inflated by the car firms' particular identification with 'automation', but these changes did at least extend mechanization from skilled operations to many unskilled jobs like materials-handling, so that up to the expansion of the 1960s growth in the manual labour force reflected little of the growth in output. The other pressure arose from the re-appearance of substantial foreign competition in world markets during the mid-1950s, and the resultant change from sellers' to buyers' market conditions. Cost and quality now became more important factors than they had been since the onset of the Second World War.

In 1964 the output of cars rose above one-and-threequarter million, and the 1960s have witnessed further concentration in the industry. In 1960 Armstrong Siddeley stopped producing cars under their own marque. Between 1957 and 1960, Standard had sold its tractor-producing facilities and acquired body and other plants. The firm now called itself Standard-Triumph International, but had marketing difficulties, and was taken over by the Leyland Group in 1961. Rootes—by this time probably the most marginally profitable of the firms—virtually staked its future on a single new model, and has recently qualified its independent existence by the sale of a minority though considerable shareholding to the Chrysler Corporation of the U.S.A. In 1965 Rootes bought the Linwood body plant from Pressed Steel. Rover has for many years produced more utility vehicles—Landrovers—than passenger cars, and the medium-sized Rover 2000 model was a major break with the firm's more conservative styling and appeal. And Rover acquired the firm of Alvis in 1965. Jaguar, the other semi-mass producer, extended its interests into the commercial vehicle field with the purchase of Daimler from the B.S.A. company in 1960 (cars, buses, and fighting vehicles), Guy Motors in 1961 (trucks), and Coventry Climax Engines in 1963. In 1965 B.M.C. took over Pressed Steel, and in 1966 'rationalized' its body-building facilities by the formation of Pressed Steel-Fisher. But the viability of these re-arrangements of the 1960s have yet to prove themselves under continuing competition.

The motor industry is, of course, more than just seven or eight firms: from the 1920s, at least, the car firms have been primarily final assemblers of a series of end-products. The major component of a car—in terms of cost—is the painted and trimmed body, and this can account for up to half of the bought-out expenditure for a typical mass-produced vehicle. B.M.C. and Ford produce most of their own bodies, but Pressed Steel supplies bodies to all the firms. Pressed Steel had other interests before its recent merger, but car bodies were nine-tenths of its business, and two out of every five British cars have Pressed Steel bodies. Electrical equipment, tyres and rubber parts, may together account for up to one-fifth of a firm's expenditure on bought-out parts, and are produced by a few firms with interests spreading across several industries. Brakes, wheels, and suspension units are also produced largely by independent suppliers to the industry as a whole, as are the host of other accessories such as instruments, steering and transmission units, fuel pumps, sparking plugs, windshields, locks, and doorhandles. In short, to define the motor industry with any precision soon exposes one to the problems of arbitrary industrial classification.

But these problems of classification may be side-stepped here as unfruitful: again, labour unrest is highly concentrated in the assembly firms. In 1963 and 1964, for example—and on our estimates again—the major car manufacturers experienced two-thirds of the working days lost through disputes in the motor vehicle and cycle industry as officially defined (although they were responsible for only half its total employment). In 1965 this proportion rose to over four-fifths. Outside the car firms, in other words, the motor industry's incidence of industrial unrest—though it has shown some tendency to rise in very recent years—is not particularly remarkable. This study is therefore concerned only with firms which actually assemble cars, car bodies, and light vans, together with their owned and associated foundries, engine, transmission and component plants.

The heavy commercial vehicle firms, in particular, are thus omitted; but their markets and techniques of production differ substantially from the car assemblers'. Their sector is in fact dominated by one large firm—Leyland acquired A.C.V. by share exchange in 1962. The division between cars and light vans on the one hand, and heavy commercial vehicles on the other, is basically tidy despite some increasingly rough edges: Standard-Triumph still remains a distinctive part of the Leyland organization, and similarly identifiable is Jaguar's heavy commercial vehicle activity. Also, the car firms have been slow to enter the really heavy vehicle field, while body-making for this type of vehicle is still scattered amongst many small coach-building works. We are dealing, that is, with a coherent group of large establishments, organized in a small number of big or very big firms, which are very similar in their technology, the operatives they employ, and market circumstances.

Two features of the car firms already touched upon are worth further mention: their concentration in a few areas, and the concentration of their processes of manufacture in separate establishments. B.M.C. is understandably the most dispersed group—as well as being the biggest. The Austin side has remained largely a single-site complex at Longbridge, but Morris cars were made in more scattered plants—one result perhaps of the more commercial interest of the firm's founder. Before the Pressed Steel 'takeover' there were already sixteen main manufacturing establishments in the B.M.C. empire, including those in Wales and Scotland. Of the sixteen, ten are in the Midlands—six in Birmingham, three in Coventry, and a foundry at Wellingborough. Three other B.M.C. plants are in Oxford, which, because Pressed Steel production is concentrated there (that company's Swindon works being very much smaller), may be thought of as a car-making town. Rootes, again probably because of the commercial leanings of its founders, is scattered about—in London, Dunstable, the Midlands and Scotland. But the main Rootes assembly plants are in Coventry (although its venture into the smaller-car market is being assembled at Linwood). Standard (now Triumph) cars have always been produced in Coventry, and Rover and Jaguar are also primarily Midlands firms—with their main facilities around Birmingham and Coventry, respectively. Of the American-owned firms, Vauxhall has been the more compact geographically—concentrated in and near Luton. Although Ford has had a number of plants scattered as far apart as Doncaster, Leamington Spa, and Southampton, the major complex is at Dagenham. While both the American firms are expanding facilities on Merseyside, Ford is at the same time disposing of some of its more isolated outposts and drawing facilities closer to the main centre.

The separation, between establishments, of engineering processes from more specifically assembly operations, and the related separation by product, is very noticeable in the more widely-dispersed B.M.C. Of its plants, two at Coventry make engines; two in the Midlands make bodies; one in Oxford makes mainly radiators; one in Birmingham makes carburettors. B.M.C.'s big assembly plants are in Birmingham and Oxford. The Ford complex at Dagenham has, of course, similar divisions, with machining concentrated in one factory, body assembly in another, and final assembly in a third. Even the smaller firms, such as Jaguar and Rover, divide machining from final assembly in separate establishments.

There are no official or comprehensive figures available of the number of persons who work in the car industry as we define it for our purposes, although, with the use of the Press and the assistance of some of the firms, a fairly precise estimate is possible for manual employment in 1963. For some earlier years guesstimates may be based on the official Censuses of Production. In 1924, for example, about 177,000 persons were employed on the manufacture of cars, commercial vehicles, motor cycles and cycles, together with all their components and accessories. In 1935, a more detailed classification was made: about 130,000 persons were employed on making cars, car bodies, and commercial vehicles alone. By 1948, this number had risen to about 180,000, and in the Census of 1958, the number was between 205,000 and 210,000.

The estimated employment of hourly-paid workers towards the end of 1963 is best put in the form of a table:

Table I/2—MANUAL EMPLOYMENT IN THE CAR FIRMS: 1963

Firm (all plants)	*Hourly-paid adults*
B.M.C.	63,500
Ford	47,000
Vauxhall	24,000
Pressed Steel	21,400
Rootes	11,000
Rover	8,400
Standard-Triumph International	8,100
Jaguar	6,200
All others (say)	10,000
	199,600

From figures issued by the Ministry of Labour for the official 'Motor Vehicle Manufacturing' category, it would seem reasonable to expect about one-fifth of total employment in the car firms to be in white-collar grades—i.e. as administrative, technical and clerical employees. These would thus form about 50,000 of a total of employed persons in the car firms of about 250,000. About this time and for a year or two after, employment seems to have been growing at around 1 per cent yearly, though with differences between firms—Ford and Vauxhall, at least, apparently contracting their operative labour force.

There are interesting differences in the proportion of women amongst the hourly-paid workers in the various plants, the major reasons for which seem to be the traditions of particular regions as well as the type of process involved. Both of the American-owned firms—since at least the early 1950s—seem to have employed women for only about 2 per cent of their manual labour, and it is possible to suggest that these firms operate in 'company' areas where the post-war shortages of labour have been less acute than elsewhere. Union pressure would be an unlikely explanation: these firms have been less well-organized than most others, and by implication the firms seem to have preferred male employment. On the other hand, firms in the Midlands employ women to the extent of from 5-10 per cent of the labour force (with the exception of the engine plants where the proportion is much lower). The Midlands is, of course, the traditional labour shortage area. In Oxford the position is more mixed: Morris employs 5 per cent while Pressed Steel—across the road—employs only 2 per cent. Union pressure seems a more likely explanation than process in this case, as Pressed Steel has long been tightly organized, and the comparable Fisher and Ludlow plant in Birmingham employs 5 per cent of women. Women often work on sewing seats and interior trim for the bodies, and on inspection, but are sometimes found in more unlikely places. There are some on lathes and in the press shops in Birmingham plants. They are also sometimes on the tracks, often as polishers but sometimes fitting soft components. In two plants where women form more than half the total employment—S.U. Carburettors in Birmingham and Morris Motors at Llanelly—there has been as persistent labour unrest as in some where women are a small minority; and the plants with the lowest proportions of women operatives have been by no means the most strike-prone.

Compared with other manufacturing industries—and with the rest of the metal-using group of industries—employees in motor vehicle manufacture are concentrated in the skilled and operative occupational categories. There are relatively fewer white-collar workers and labourers. The following summary table—taken from a Ministry of Labour survey of May 1963—shows the extent of this variation:

Table I/3—EMPLOYEES BY OCCUPATIONAL GROUP: MAY 1963

Industry:	Number (000)	*Percentage of total employees*			
		White-collar	Skilled	Semi-skilled	Other
Motor vehicle mnf.	437	20.6	29.1	33.3	17.0
Metals group	3,912	26.8	28.7	22.9	21.7
Rest of manufacturing	3,918	21.2	21.3	31.0	26.4

Assuming that the figures for motor vehicle manufacturing do not differ much from those for the car firms proper, the low proportion of labourers is scarcely surprising: car making does not involve heavy manual work, and materials-handling is highly mechanized. A little surprising is the relatively high proportion of skilled operatives. But to some extent, this may be an inflated figure; some employers—including two at least of the car firms—were only able to supply information to the Ministry according to the wages paid rather than the degree of skill, and their trackmen and some other non-craft production operatives earned skilled rates.

Of more interest is the lower proportion of white-collar workers—i.e., of administrative, technical and clerical employees. Census of Production returns indicate what seems to be no sharp rise in the proportion of these workers in motor manufacturing until the 1930s, but a distinct increase to around 16 per cent by the late 1940s, and a sharper rise since. Ministry of Labour returns seem to be calculated on a different basis, giving a generally higher proportion, but they also reflect a considerable rise for the vehicles group as a whole in the post-war years (apart from a drop between 1961 and 1963). The various series must clearly be used with considerable caution, but what each on its own does indicate—assuming internal consistency—is that the car firms do have a lower proportion of white-collar workers than the whole vehicles group, which again has a lower proportion than engineering generally. The implications are taken up in later chapters.

(c) COLLECTIVE ORGANIZATION: UNIONS, EMPLOYERS AND JOINT ARRANGEMENTS

A word on the collective organization of the car makers—men and managements. This is perhaps best described as on the whole strong, but patchy and disjointed. On neither side is there a widely-recognized organization specifically and independently concerned with collective bargaining and negotiation for the car or even the motor vehicles industry as such. On the workers' side, all the unions, except one or two of doubtful membership (like the Toolmakers) which have been regarded by others as 'breakaways', have long been affiliated to the Confederation of Shipbuilding and Engineering Unions (C.S.E.U.). Conversely, most of the 'Confed's' thirty-one affiliates have members in the car firms, though only one of them is primarily concerned with the vehicle trades—the National Union of Vehicle Builders (N.U.V.B.). All firms now have a strong union membership, with a 'union shop' in most of the Midlands plants. Though at Vauxhall, until quite recently, perhaps not very much more than half of those eligible were union members.

There is no systematic division of interests between the unions, but the four which are largely concerned with assembly workers are the two 'general' unions—the Transport and General Workers' Union (T. & G.W.U.) and the National Union of General and Municipal Workers (N.U.G.M.W.)—the Amalgamated Engineering Union (A.E.U.), and the N.U.V.B. But there are also several craft or near-craft unions, such as the Sheet Metal Workers, the Electrical Trades Union (E.T.U.), the Draughtsmen (D.A.T.A.), and so on, which have important memberships in the car plants. One feature of recent years has been the increasing unionization of clerical workers —in the Clerical and Administrative Workers' Union and the National Association of Clerical and Supervisory Staffs, in particular. The only strict closed shop for operative labour in the industry —i.e. where the employers recruit all manual labour only through the union offices—is at Standard-Triumph (though individual plants or sections in one or two other companies have similar arrangements); and at this firm the clerical workers also achieved a union shop at the end of 1963.

The shop stewards of the various unions have joint organizations amongst themselves which are approved or tolerated by the unions in roughly inverse proportion to their coverage: for example, the T.U.C. General Council reported on such organizations to its 1960 Congress, justifying joint shop stewards committees at the plant level but condemning general shop stewards' movements of the industry-wide or national type. The toleration at works and departmental level arises out of necessity: with few clear-cut spheres of interest between the unions, and a need to maintain the maximum flexibility in transferring workers from one area or job to another, shop floor representation which does not provide for co-ordination between unions is largely unworkable. It is recognized by stewards, unions, and managements, that there is need for joint discussion and control by the stewards from at least the main unions over many matters which, in the absence of a concerted approach, could rapidly disrupt a whole plant.

On the management side, all but the two American-owned firms belong to the Engineering Employers' Federation. So far as wages go, this means little more than that their workers benefit by the national advances conceded for the general engineering industry and by its minimum guaranteed week. Most of the production workers are paid piece-rates or other bonuses far above the basic rates agreed upon by the Federation. But the federated firms are bound also by the engineering industry's 'disputes procedure' and certain other engineering rules such as those reserving 'managerial functions'.[1] Rootes and one

[1] A detailed account of engineering 'procedure' is now available in A. Marsh's *Industrial Relations in Engineering* (Pergamon Press, 1965).

or two other firms also recognize certain agreements of the Joint Wages Board for the Vehicle Industry—which deals mainly with conditions in non-car establishments. Ford and Vauxhall belong to no employers' association or external negotiating body, but each have separate negotiating and 'grievance' procedures of their own.

This last statement, however, needs two qualifications. Since about 1950, there have been informal and more or less regular meetings between the major firms' senior labour relations or personnel managers, and which did not until recently include any production management. The group grew quietly and gathered in members by the way, until by 1960 there were about a dozen persons—including some from the commercial vehicle manufacturers. Membership was irrespective of Employers' Federation commitments, and in fact the association is believed to have been started by a manager at Ford. One of the most important functions of this informal group has been an exchange of information—for example, on earnings in each other's plants. The group was absorbed into a more formal body which arose out of the joint talks convened by the Minister of Labour in 1961. Membership was now thickened with additions from line management—some of whom are believed to have been unaware of the group's prior existence. Quarterly meetings now became formal, and minutes were kept. This new Motor Industry Industrial Relations Panel (M.I.I.R.P. for short) was, however, felt by some of the longer-established members to have been too formal and hence restricted in its exchange of information, but informality was said to be returning to its meetings.

What is potentially a much more radical addition to the car manufacturing industry's collective arrangements has developed out of successive government initiatives. In late 1960 the strike-incidence of the car firms soared to an apparent peak (the nature of which is explored later in this study). Leading representatives of the employers and of the principal unions concerned in the industry were called together under the Minister of Labour's chairmanship to examine its situation, and reached a measure of agreement which was outlined in a joint statement of April 19, 1961.[1] The statement '... agreed a number of points on which action should be taken in our respective fields to assist individual companies, workpeople and trade unions in their day to day relations', including a stricter observance of established procedures for handling disputes, improvements in the selection and training of shop stewards and supervisors, examination of the adequacy and sufficiency of firms' and unions' professional staff to deal with 'matters arising' in labour relations, and improve-

[1] The Statement is reproduced in full in the *Ministry of Labour Gazette* for May 1961 (as well as by way of an Appendix to Marsh, *op. cit.*)

ments in 'communications' and 'the circulation of information'—including, particularly, an examination of 'our methods of joint consultation'. A number of other matters were also specified as subjects for further study or review: these included the application of 'work study' (or time-and-motion study, as it is perhaps more widely known), wage-structures, inter-union relations, and the general training of young workers.

Of these various agreements, perhaps the only one to be of substantial immediate influence was the representatives' statement that 'We have fully and candidly considered the various procedures for handling disputes and we have satisfied ourselves that these procedures are generally adequate if operated in the right spirit. . . . Accordingly both sides will act in accordance with their respective constitutions to secure observance of those procedures by employers and union members.' This declaration, the terms of which were again persistently urged on firms and unions by the Minister of Labour and his officers, materially influenced the handling of certain major disputes in the next year or two. Otherwise, the meetings' most obvious consequences were some re-arrangements and recruitment among the labour relations staffs of firms, and an increased provision of courses for shop stewards by University extra-mural departments, technical colleges and so on (a national development which was also being urged by the T.U.C., and which later received encouragement from a joint T.U.C. and British Employers' Confederation committee). But if the apparent strike-wave of 1960–61 did not altogether recede, its pressure seemingly became less urgent or critical. A smallish Motor Industry Joint Study Group of labour relations directors and managers and of national union officials was formed as a continuing body: at least on the surface, however, no significant further initiatives emerged from it for two or three years.

By 1964, however, the 'firm line' towards unofficial strikes which was implied in the 1961 Statement had apparently yielded only limited results. Early in that year the Ministry of Labour began to canvass, with growing publicity, devices to supplement official and 'constitutional' disputes procedures, with their formal inability to operate whilst unofficial stoppages are in progress; suggestions included one for 'flying squads' of professional conciliators to inquire into, and report on, such affairs. The proposal for such 'fact-finding' inquiries was rejected by the T.U.C. and B.E.C. as likely—though they would have no such formal powers of examination and recommendation as a legal Court of Inquiry—to encourage unofficial action; and it was converted by those bodies into a scheme for a retrospective joint examination (reporting to themselves) of a selected group of unofficial strikes. These moves had no specific reference to the motor industry. But the principle involved was taken up by the Joint Study Group, which in the autumn set up from its sub-committee a 'fact-finding commission' to 'identify the underlying causes' of a series of disputes which had occurred at the Morris assembly plant in Cowley; the commission produced a number of recommendations for 'the achievement of improved relationships'. And the experiment was thought sufficiently successful for the commission to be established as a permanent body with the C.S.E.U.'s agreement; but it undertook no further inquiries on its original basis.

In 1965 there was a new jump in the car firms' strike-incidence, with several biggish stoppages before the summer. Members of the new Labour government made irritated, if not angry, condemnations of unofficial strikes, and in September the Prime Minister called a meeting of leading car firm employers and national union leaders at Downing Street. The meeting was apparently presented by the Minister of Labour with a virtual ultimatum: either the industry 'put its own house in order' or the government would feel obliged to take action itself (the possibility of a form of compulsory arbitration seems to have been referred to). Various proposals were aired, including an offer of a general 'union shop' if the unions would undertake the responsibility of disciplining their own members. This, the unions ultimately rejected (understandably, since—other considerations apart—they already had at least 90 per cent membership of manual workers); and in the upshot the joint representatives settled upon what they perhaps found the least disturbing proposal, to strengthen the existing 'fact-finding commission'. It was converted to a new Motor Industry Joint Labour Council, with Mr Jack Scamp as government-appointed chairman and legal powers to act as a Court of Inquiry in appropriate circumstances. While these arrangements were being completed, a series of inquiries into particular strike-situations were launched by the commission.[1] Apart from the investigation of individual disputes, the new Council was also allocated responsibility for reviewing labour relations generally in individual companies, and for studying and promoting the improvement of industrial relations in the industry as a whole—its chairman being required to report progress to the Minister of Labour. To date, however, the Council's formal role remains an investigatory one. Whether its existence will modify the previously-established negotiating and disputes procedures remains to be seen.

---

[1] At time of going to press, six reports on particular dispute-situations have been issued under Mr Scamp's chairmanship.

LABOUR RELATIONS IN THE MOTOR INDUSTRY

(D) THE WORK AND WORKING ENVIRONMENT

The picture of the car factories themselves which can be drawn from the information presented up to this point is rather abstract. It is of the sort which anyone with time and energy could produce without ever approaching within hooting distance of any of the establishments. The framework needs to be filled with detail and atmosphere: what is it like to be in a car factory, and to work there? The rest of this chapter gives one view of what could be a typical assembly plant (and there are, of course, many points in common with other kinds of factory). The information was gathered while touring around most of the main car assembly establishments in the country, as well as during seven months spent by one of the writers in one particular plant in the Midlands. These months were spent mostly on the shop floor as an 'ordinary' worker, but included a period as 'silent member' of the car firm's shop steward organization, and a similar period in its employment office. The picture is thus a composite of many impressions. Nor is it more than a limited canvas: experience of the management and labour organizations, and the attitudes and actions of workers and supervisors, for example, are not here treated explicitly. Such information has mostly been built into more appropriate sections in the book.

First impressions of the plant—from the outside—are forbidding: there is a security system of juxtaposed high fences, few gates, and uniformed custodians. Through the gates pass almost unbroken streams of trucks bringing supplies, car-transporters carrying bodyshells in and finished vehicles out, and a two-way stream of the new cars themselves—bearing red licence plates and mostly on short road tests. Once inside the gates, several features cannot help but strike the visitor: with few exceptions, the premises are neat, tidy, clean and well-kept—they are often relatively newly-developed. Nor, at closer quarters, is the factory excessively noisy, although there are the obviously noisy areas where parts are stamped out, where there are large power-presses, and the sections where 'dingmen' knock small dents out of the body shells. Once under the main roofs, there is a low-volume but high-pitched and characteristic noise—the weird, intermittent shriek of pneumatic spanners and drills, which is a constant accompaniment of car assembly work. The low rumble of the moving tracks themselves is seldom audible. The dominant smell of assembly areas is not of paint or swarf but of rubber and plastics and oil—with an occasional tang of exhaust fumes from passing traffic.

The shop floor has a network of freeways for wheeled traffic, and a wary eye and ear must always be kept open for this mechanical handling equipment. Assembly areas actually look not unlike those stylized flow charts drawn by work study men. The activities taking place can be easily seen and comprehended—functions both of the size and familiarity of the product under construction. The flow of work is logical and perceptible, even though most tracks move fairly slowly—from three to six feet a minute is a good average range of line-speeds. From one direction come body shells—pressed or stamped out in sections and welded together in an adjacent plant—moving through the processes of washing and degreasing, sealing and priming, rubbing and flatting, then painting again. They are oven-dried, and then move out on to conveyors which are lined on both sides with work stations for the addition of hard components and soft trim. These tracks then merge with another major flow line: engine and transmission units have been travelling along similar conveyors. The trimmed bodies are now hoisted and then lowered on to the power-transmission skeletons—an operation of ponderous delicacy, suggesting a brooding ostrich settling on its eggs, perhaps. The 'mounting track' now continues for accretion of the remaining bits and pieces, for wheels, washing, tuning, testing, and final inspection.

Inspection and documentary checks are made at many points along the lines: pieces of card and paper accumulate as an essential part of the assembly process. The rest of the production layout is supplementary to this main flow: sub-assembly lines for such items as gearboxes or doors, stores for the thousands of separate parts, endless-chain overhead conveyors carrying finished seats and doors, or areas where wheels are fitted with tyres by an automatic machine. There are trim shops for making the seats and other sewn items of interior trim; brass, polishing and plating shops for making radiator grilles, window frames, and other chromed parts; and a sawmill for wooden parts, if any. Taken together, the assembly processes make for neither boring incomprehensibility nor esoteric mystique in the making of cars.

The range of actual jobs is, of course, wide, despite the fact that there is almost none of the fine and intricate work typical, for example, of the assembly of instruments. This kind of part—like speedometer clocks and other dashboard fittings—is bought from suppliers fully assembled. Nor is there much heavy physical work of the kind associated with, for instance, foundries—except in those few plants where casting is carried out. Even the sweeping and cleaning of the premises is often mechanized. Fetching, carrying, lifting and stacking is carried out mainly by fork-lift trucks, and this work is facilitated by the use of more or less standardized bins or stillages. The most numerous worker is the assembler: fitters, finishers, and trimmers. The traditional 'craftsmen' are relatively few in number, and are found most often in experimental and development departments, in the toolrooms, and in maintenance gangs. In addition to office workers, the factory 'staff' include chargehands and foremen, and, together with junior departmental managers, these persons are somewhat loosely called 'supervision'. Other staff are estimators or ratefixers, and 'progress chasers'—i.e. those who keep the documentary records and the production lines integrated and who check on the stocks of supplies. Some inspectors may also have staff status.

Tracks are the symbol of car plants, and a word must be said about the organization of track-work. The jobs vary from sticking cloth or plastic pieces with adhesives, to fitting and bolting bumpers. Most of them involve drilling holes and screwing, bolting, riveting, or clipping small parts together and to the body shells. A planned number of operations must be completed within a fixed length of track, physical working and storage space being the major determinants. The way the work is actually done is the result of a number of interrelated variables. How long is the track—i.e., how many work stations are possible? How many models must it be capable of handling? How many men fit in a body shell without interfering with each others' tasks? How many operations can each perform for given track speeds?

Despite these imperatives, the time cycles of sets of operations vary in practice from track to track and plant to plant: few are completed within three minutes or outside of half an hour. But however the sets of operations are apportioned, there are inevitable differences in the effort required: there are 'loose' and 'tight' jobs. A work station 'team' will sometimes shuffle operations about between themselves for reasons of both equity and convenience. Generally, however, trackmen work not so much fast as steadily, and breaks for personal needs are planned for. Other breaks can be 'earned' by speeding up the pace of work, 'working back down the line' where this is possible, or by having other members of the gang 'pull the job in' during temporary absences. Longer absences are covered by having a corps of utilitymen, floaters, or slipmen (the term varies from plant to plant)—operatives with considerable experience of the particular models who can fill in for an absentee for an hour or a week. Floater gangs vary in strength from summer to winter: they are often about 5 per cent of a track complement, but seldom as much as 10 per cent.

The pace of work in the factory seems to cluster about three rough norms. Individual piece-workers, such as welders on body-making, trimmers on seat or console making, lathe or press operators and so on, tend to move observably faster than both the trackmen and those who 'service' the tracks, for example, storemen. The difference is expected, imposed, and standardized: at least in theory, jobs paid by the piece are planned to exhibit a 'piece-work effort' considerably greater (about 30 per cent in one plant) than 'day-work effort'—and with higher rates of pay. The trackmen work less speedily than individual piece-workers, but their pace is relatively closely governed. However, line-speeds are sometimes varied slightly during the day to adjust for bottlenecks or shortages, and to maintain earnings. And some trackmen—like individual piece-workers—do have the opportunity to build 'banks' of sub-assemblies which they can draw on when they wish to slow their pace. The mechanical pacing of the tracks also partly governs the overall pacing of the day-workers who service the track areas. But the nature and expected pace of day-work allows greater variability in effort: work can usually be 'banked', while backlogs can be cleared by working harder (though not excessively so). 'Indirect' workers are thus seldom rushed, even allowing for different patterns in individual self-pacing. In short, individual piece-work is highly-paced and fairly continuous, track work is slower but more constant, while day-work need seldom raise a sweat although it may often by choice be done in short bursts of intensive effort.

Pay, of course, is the major focus of working interest, and while wage-systems may differ between firms, the procedures for paying wages seem to be fairly similar (at least for the hourly-paid workers). Payslips specifying the amounts which go to make up gross earnings, and the deductions made, are distributed through foremen and chargehands on a Thursday or Friday in respect of the previous week's work. Bonus additions may sometimes be over a fortnight in arrears because of the time required for their calculation. Queries about the payslips may be made either before or after the pay packets themselves are distributed. The cash is paid in sealed envelopes, transparent and with the bank notes folded to allow the contents to be checked before the seal is broken. The envelopes contain also duplicates of the payslips already distributed, while these latter are signed and serve as receipts when returned to the wages clerks at the handing-over ceremony. Supervisors are usually careful to handle the payslips so that privacy of earnings is possible for those who wish it. But there are few who are shy of talking in specific terms about their earnings. Differences in earnings within a department are slight anyway, while details of earnings, and of the extent of tax and other deductions—and payslips themselves—are often exchanged.[1] But it did seem that paydays had a slight aura of

[1] Payslips were gathered from individuals in various departments as part of an

expectancy about them, although not always. Fluctuations in earnings could be considerable, and the resultant dissatisfaction was at its peak on paydays.

Working hours in the factory can be said to have a number of different kinds of 'punctuation'. There is no surge into workplaces as there is out of them. Men drift into the plant for anything up to half an hour before work starts. Even so, day and night shifts seldom meet. The firm's time starts with the hooter, although it is usual to provide three minutes grace for clocking-in. Each worker has a factory number, and a corresponding clock-card placed in racks adjacent to the departmental time-clocks each week. Lateness in excess of three minutes bears a penalty calculated in quarter-hours of pay, while consistently erratic time-keeping does not go unchecked. Queues form around time-clocks only where clocking-off at the end of the day is required. Between them, clock-cards and the factory hooter clearly delimit the working day.

Working time is broken-up in different ways. There are formal and regular breaks, such as for the mid-day meal, and for morning and afternoon tea. Specific work tasks amongst indirect workers become related to these formal breaks: a worker may regard a particular task as a 'steady job' to be made to last, or be squeezed into, the time preceding the next such break (always allowing for those minutes formally allocated to the purpose of 'washing up'). It would seem that time passes more easily when allocated to the achievement of a small number of short-term goals. Regular 'music while you work' programmes seem to have a similar effect on the passage of working time. But the formal breaks can always be supplemented by informal ones: the ten minutes per hour smoking time in certain stores; 'working back the line' or having the job 'pulled in by a mate' enables a trackman to conduct ten or fifteen minutes' private business with a friend in another section; while trips to the lavatories (armed with the day's newspaper) are planned for in the allocation of work-loads.

Sanctions and discipline intrude themselves perhaps less in the car plants than in other kinds of factory: moving tracks enforce their own supervision—of workpace if not of work-quality. But in situations where every operation can be attributed to a particular individual, and where succeeding operations often depend on the satisfactory completion of work only a short distance 'back the line', inspection and quality are partially ensured by the technology as well as by the informal supervision men may exercise over each other. It is not uncommon for one foreman to supervise the work of over a

assessment of the extent of weekly fluctuations in earnings: there was little reluctance to make these slips available to a researcher. It was more difficult to find workers who retained their payslips at all.

hundred trackmen; and his task is largely made up of problems of labour-loading due to absenteeism and transfers, changes in cycles of operations, sudden crises due to non-standard parts, mechanical failures, and so on. Constant surveillance and 'bossing about' is neither necessary, salutory, nor much in evidence.

But lines of command are closely observed. For example, workers who 'feed' the tracks with components and other supplies, and who may spend most of their time with trackmen, are seldom instructed and cannot be disciplined other than by their 'home' supervision. Complaints about inventories—or behaviour—have to be passed to the correct line of command for action to result. Within a department, the division between managers and men, and lines of authority generally, are less sharp than might be imagined. For chargehands are drawn from the floor, have long service, sometimes have to 'clock-on' like workers, and have only mild supervisory functions over the small working groups of which they are members. And for most of the time, anyway, men are their own managers, there being considerable scope for personal discretion to be used in doing even the simplest and most menial of jobs.

Direct contact with higher levels of supervision is, for most workers, infrequent: even within a department there is seldom direct contact with the superintendent or departmental manager. And outside the immediate area of work, status and authority is diffused by problems of personal identification. There is latitude in the choice of factory uniform—although less for supervision than for workers. For example, storemen may voluntarily wear brown dustcoats, usually made available by the firm at cost price and on credit. Blue boiler suits are common in engine assembly areas and paint shops. Trackmen usually wear no uniform: many do not use protective clothing at all as the work is clean. Military characteristics are more mandatory in the dress of lower management. Supervisors wear brown or white coats with different colours edging the collars to denote specific status. But inspectors also wear white coats, as do rate-fixers. Superintendents wear suits—the unambiguous working dress of middle and higher management. Because age and facial qualities are no guide to status (unless the individuals are known), and because uniforms of supervision are not foolproof guides, authority is highly localized.

The most common sanctions are worth specifying. Chargehands or foremen may deliver verbal admonitions—or 'bollickings'—*in situ*, and there is normally no record of these. Nor is it expected that they should remain in memory in personal terms. But continued incompetence or breaches of regulations may land a worker 'in the office': he reports to the departmental manager, who warns him in the presence of the foreman and his own shop steward, while the warning is recorded. These records are essential evidence where the final sanction of dismissal may be resorted to, or where a case may be appealed to the Personnel Office. However, the interpretation of works rules generally—like that of standards of inspection—is fairly flexible, and this creates a certain insecurity. Some regulations —like restrictions on smoking in stores and around paintshops—are obviously rigidly enforced and observed. Others, like works' speed limits, restrictions on personal movements, clocking-in for other workers, and the length of work-breaks, may be subject to abrupt changes arising from decisions (sometimes from bad temper) at higher levels. And notice of the new (although perhaps temporary) standards of entitlement or tolerance may not always be sufficiently widely or rapidly communicated to prevent inadvertent breaches. However, discipline generally—although real—is often handled superficially and cynically, as a kind of game by both sides.

The ability to move about the works has already been mentioned: it is one measure of a worker's 'induction'. Free movement is almost invariably a specific breach of works regulations, but the rigidity of enforcement varies from time to time and from area to area. Successful circumvention thus requires considerable knowledge of local conditions, customs and practices. The regulations may require the formal acquisition of movement passes which may be quite elaborate —specifying dates, times, departments and persons. But unlike 'exit' passes which allow workers to leave the factory premises during working hours, movement passes are not widely applied in practice in car factories. Trackmen are, by virtue of their work, fairly restricted geographically, while many indirect workers are required to move about outside the areas of effective supervision. The most important factor in setting the level of geographical freedom for those at a fixed workplace is just this necessary coming and going by others—including the more permanent changes resulting from labour turnover. In factories of several thousand workers, personal anonymity is achieved at quite a short distance from the workplace. An inducted worker knows and uses the jargon of the industry and the firm; he walks about decisively and 'with intent'—often carrying something; he will have ready answers. A 'foreigner' is recognized by his clothes, his grasp of the jargon, and by the manner in which he picks his way about. For the researcher in a participant-observer role, full 'induction' is necessary to gain information or insights of a more than superficial or parochial kind.

APPENDIX

THE EFFECTS OF STRIKES IN CAR FACTORIES

Various statements have been made about the effect of labour stoppages on output. In their oral evidence to the Royal Commission on Trade Unions on February 15, 1966, the motor manufacturers themselves attributed the difference during 1964–65 between a 5 per cent increase in motor vehicle production capacity and a 6.7 per cent decline in production largely to strikes. Individual firms have published calculations for various periods between 1964 and early 1966 of the 'output of vehicles lost', or 'loss on turnover', which approximate to 10 per cent or more. Other statements by manufacturers have, however, been made in terms of 'working hours (or days) lost' at particular plants, and for the industry as a whole. Thus other evidence submitted by the manufacturers collectively to the Royal Commission showed rather over 10 million man-hours as 'lost . . . in 1965' from all types of dispute: if this figure related to the employees of the car firms alone, it was equal to some 2 per cent of all working time—the figure for B.M.C. alone working out at under 4 per cent. On the other hand, the proportion on Ministry of Labour figures was very much lower—less than 1 per cent of working days for the whole motor vehicle industry—and 'working time lost' in 1965 was quite exceptionally high: two to four times the 1964 figures (depending on whose estimates are taken). So the different statements are not easy to reconcile with each other.

Some of the discrepancies presumably arise from different methods of reckoning the effect of strikes. One way is to take the 'planned output' or 'planned capacity', as estimated in advance for a given period (say, a calendar or financial year), and to allocate the difference between either of those figures and actual production to various causes. The 'planned' figure, however, is one that depends on several concealed assumptions—for instance, about the dates at which new plant will actually be available and obsolescent capacity replaced. It makes assumptions about the number of shifts which will be worked, the amount of overtime, and the rate at which track speeds and expenditure (maintenance, etc.) related to what one might call 'the intensity of utilization' will be held. It assumes a particular mixture of product models and types—which implies a sales forecast. And this in turn implies an assumption as to the general level of demand. All these elements are in fact subject to significant variation

—especially those involving demand factors. The car industry's collective estimate of future home demand for the *National Plan* involved a rise to 1.6 million in 1970: the government's estimate was 1.8 million; but the sum of individual firms' estimates was higher than the government's. In one major car plant in 1964 actual weekly production schedules (which reflect adjustments to current supply and demand factors) averaged under 85 per cent of the plant's 'capacity rate'—taking this as indicated by the rate it was capable of achieving (and did for several consecutive weeks achieve) under conditions of intensive utilization, with moderate overtime. Moreover, average production was only 75 per cent of this rate, which in any case was based on two-shift working only.

'Planned' figures are thus purely conceptual ones. An alternative is to work from the actual production schedules themselves. We have been given access to the daily and weekly records of the production manager and sectional supervision of a large assembly plant, which has certainly not had a below-average strike-proneness. These records include current production schedules and actual outputs, together with stated reasons for failures to achieve the former (though not for over-achievements, which also sometimes occurred). We have analysed them over a period of three years, 1962–64 (during which sales were generally increasing), and discussed them with the principal recorders.

One thing that immediately appears is that most short interruptions to production have no significant effect on output, so that many fewer incidents are deemed worthy of notation at the works level than at the sectional. Despite mechanization and flow production, there is apparently some flexibility in the system: track speeds or output rates in particular sections can be increased temporarily within varying limits, and units in transit between two sections sometimes represent a 'stock which can be drawn on to keep production going for a while if the prior section stops. There seems to be a threshold which a sizeable stoppage—or an accumulation of small stoppages (which will then usually be of a kind, like persistent paint defects)—has to reach before it affects production. Its effect may then, however, be disproportionate to its length—presumably because of secondary disorganization and delays. Nevertheless, if one adds up all the percentage shortfalls on sectional output schedules, one apparently gets a daily average shortfall substantially greater than that on the week's schedule for the plant.

A second problem is that even in the production manager's record it is not always possible to separate the effect of different incidents. For instance, in one week one may find both 'green labour' and component shortages reported, or have a breakdown on one part of the line at the same time as a 'downer' on another. One might attempt to weight each incident in terms of estimated hours lost in each section affected, but the length of stoppage is not invariably recorded, except in the case of labour disputes or actions (these records apparently constitute the raw material of the manufacturers' estimates of 'working hours lost'). And if one could make the calculation, there would still be the problem that all stoppages are not reflected in the same proportion in output. In any case, the separation could only be arbitrary in many instances. For instance, this is a piece-work plant, and a run of hold-ups due to breakdowns or component rejections may lead into 'downers' in protest against lost earnings: how much of any resultant shortfall on schedule is due to which cause? So one can only properly reckon in rather broad groups, representing causes or combinations of causes which can be isolated from each other: we have done this from the works records (these things—quite apart from the first problem mentioned—make it quite impracticable to do it from the sectional ones).

In the table on p. 48:

1. *Labour action* includes strikes, meetings and stewards' meetings, go-slows, 'piece-rate negotiations', effects of strikes at other factories, and lay-offs associated with these things.

2. *Breakdowns, technical, etc.* includes breakdowns, supply shortages or rejections, technical changes and adjustments, component failures and defects, untenable working conditions (e.g. fumes), together with associated lay-offs.

3. *Combined incidents* includes stoppages as described above, in which items from 1 and 2 cannot be separated from each other—again with associated lay-offs.

4. *Lay-offs* covers stoppages because of temporary excess production (e.g. as 'all car parks full').

5. *Miscellaneous and unstated* includes exceptional absence rates, public transport difficulties, labour shortages, severe weather conditions, and 'Acts of God' generally—as well as short-falls against which no explanation has been noted. (This may sometimes happen because the explanation is self-evident—e.g. absenteeism after New Year's Day; but in a factory schedules are also statements with 'morale' implications, and managements may occasionally prefer to effect a small temporary change in output without formally changing targets.)

It will be seen that here the current schedules are themselves also 'perfectionist' statements which assume no interruptions of the product flow. It will also be noted that the short-fall under item 3. is high when that under 2. is also high, and that the contribution of 1. is higher when lay-offs are up. The percentage under item 1. seems a

Labour Relations in the Motor Industry

FULFILMENT OF PRODUCTION SCHEDULES IN A LARGE ASSEMBLY PLANT

	1	2	3	4	5	
Av. short-fall on weekly schedules: % due to:	Labour action	Break-downs, tech-nical	Com-bined incidents	Lay-offs	Misc., & unstated	Overall %
1962	1.1	3.0*	3.4	0.7	2.9*	11.1
1963	1.9	3.5	6.6	1.1	2.4	15.5
1964	4.8	2.2	1.6	2.9	2.3	13.8
Av. 1962/4	2.6	2.9	3.9	1.6	2.5	13.5

* Three weeks in 1962 with both 'breakdowns' and 'labour shortages' have been split between 2 and 5.

little more than the firm's *per capita* 'loss of working time' for the period, when this 'loss' is estimated (from other records) on the Ministry of Labour basis, but appears less than two-thirds that which would result from adding to the 'Ministry figure' the effect of strikes at other plants and of small disputes which the Ministry would not count. The Table thus seems consistent with alternative data (since on the 'working time' basis the 'loss' from labour disputes was between 4 per cent and 5 per cent while the short-fall on production schedules from this cause could not have been less than 2.6 per cent or as much as 6.5 per cent).

Two general comments should be made. First, the average short-fall on schedules does *not* necessarily represent a 'loss of production': each week's schedule is in a sense a correction to the previous week's target and result, so that orders are met. The plant's operation is adapted to short-falls of this order, and if they suddenly stopped there would be excess capacity; the table only indicates the broad relation between different kinds of interruption which the plant's capacity allows for. Secondly, the short-falls under heads 2. and 3. certainly do not necessarily indicate managerial inefficiency. Costs of reducing these items further (extra maintenance and repair men, more progress chasers and inspectors, more contract supervisors, etc.) may be disproportionately high. On the other side, workers are paid mainly on output, and 'waiting time' payment is relatively low (about 40 per cent on tracks). But one would, therefore, probably find a lower average short-fall in a time-rate plant, where delays cost management more: one would also certainly find a lower percentage under item 1.

For another comparative indication of the effect of strikes, just after the gas supply breakdowns of winter 1965–66 we asked the major car firms to estimate the effect on them in terms of 'working

Strikes and the Car Industry

days lost'. All replied, but one of the bigger firms could not separate the effect from that of a strike it was experiencing coincidentally. After making some allowance for this, the car firms' 'lost working days' came to 170,000 in the two cuts, or less than ½ per cent of the industry's full work-year. One of the bigger companies also gave us its estimate in terms of the number of vehicles (of all types) involved. If its ratios could be assumed typical of the industry, the total 'output lost' would be rather over ½ per cent of the annual production rate then current. Which fits in with the preceding point about big stoppages having proportionately larger effects than small ones.

We conclude that the 'loss of working time' gives the most meaningful and consistent approximation to the effect of strikes, provided that all stoppages due to strikes are included (so that in this sense, and for the present purpose, the motor manufacturers' figures—equal to 2 per cent in 1965 but less than 1 per cent in the three previous years—give a better picture than the Ministry of Labour's); and subject to the—unexpected—condition that in this industry a number of very small dispersed stoppages apparently has less effect on production than one big one involving the same total striker-days.

Just what 'cost' can be attached to this measurement is another question. In the plant referred to above, for instance, one might say that since 'man-hours of idleness' from disputes averaged 4 per cent to 5 per cent of total work-time its capacity was to that extent excessive and its overhead costs (but not its total costs) per car proportionately increased. But, as we have shown 'capacity' is a rather elastic figure: this plant was normally operating at not much more than half of its theoretical maximum capacity (with three shifts) anyway, so the potential saving from the abolition of strikes would be much less than 4 per cent to 5 per cent of overheads. On the other hand, a very large proportion of all 'time lost' is attributable to the disputes arising from the piece-rate system which the management applies to encourage productivity. One could reduce this loss by abolishing piece-work, but what would be the effect on output—or the cost of maintaining output without this 'incentive'? Similarly, in this plant, some part of the 'loss of working time' from disputes was clearly linked with 'lay-offs' because of temporary sales difficulties, which raises the question whether all the time thus 'lost' would in fact otherwise have been worked?

The 'loss of working hours (or days)' thus seems only meaningful as an index of *delays* to production. The extent to which these delays have an economic consequence depends on two things. First, whether the product affected is actually saleable at the time (most of the car output 'lost' from strikes in 1960–61 and 1965 was not wanted by the market). Secondly, on whether—and at what cost—the delays can be made up. The typical motor firm's strike is comparatively short and the output rate seems rather flexible—though extra costs may be involved where temporary output increases involve overtime (indeed, the average overtime premium, taken on the 'working time lost', might not be a bad approximation to the 'cost' of strikes). When there *are* shortages of particular cars, firms seem to give priority to the ultra-competitive export markets (the home market is highly protected) so export effects are not proportionate. Even at home, however, consumers may buy another firm's cars rather than wait when a strike does drag on (if strikes did not threaten some loss to the employer, there would not *usually* be much point in striking).

CHAPTER II

THE ISSUES IN DISPUTE

(A) WHAT IS A STRIKE? AND SOME OTHER PROBLEMS

In this Chapter we propose to analyse in more detail the general trend of the car-assembly firms' dispute-liability and its development, and especially to attempt at least a superficial assessment of the sources of those firms' particular strike-proneness. Any such analysis must be largely statistical in character, but figures are perhaps both more frequently quoted, and most open to challenge, where vested interest is evidently involved and where issues are highly charged with emotion—as in most industrial disputes. For instance, how does one reconcile the Ministry of Labour's report of some 100 industrial stoppages in the whole motor vehicle industry group in the first half of 1965 with the statement of a leading car manufacturers' spokesman, on the eve of that year's Motor Show, that there had been four to five hundred such disputes in the same period. Or again, just what significance is to be attached to the report—in the *Financial Times* of December 15, 1964—that 'in the twelve months ended August there were 254 unofficial strikes, resulting in the loss of about 750,000 man-hours' at the Morris Motors plant at Cowley, Oxford? On the face of it, there was on average a separate all-day stoppage by 400 men every working day of the year. Particularly, therefore, since—for reasons already explained—we have had to construct our own series for disputes in the car plants, we had best begin by some explanation of, and comment upon, their nature.

This study has drawn on the several available sources to compile its figures on strikes: from individual firms, from the Press, and from official sources such as the Ministry of Labour and the reports of Courts of Inquiry into disputes. We lean most heavily on the Ministry, not only for the summary accounts of 'Principal Stoppages' published monthly in the *Gazette*, but also for the records of lesser disputes which are otherwise included only in the Ministry's statistical tables. The other main source of information has been the Press, on which we have had to rely for detailed accounts of individual strikes and thus, because official assistance does not permit this identification, for assessment of the position of individual firms and plants. But the level of public interest in motor industry disputes, and the fact that the Ministry also uses Press coverage to check its own records, give a high degree of identity between Press and official reportage—at least for the important post-war period.

But there is no obligation on employers or trade unions to report disputes, and it is necessary to say something about the nature and adequacy of the official figures, or of figures compiled (like ours) wholly or partially from official records. Excluded from the public records are those stoppages which the Ministry's men know about, but which involve 'fewer than ten workers and those which last for less than one day, except any in which the aggregate number of working days lost exceeded 100'. Also excluded, of course, are those stoppages—of all sizes—which escape the Ministry's notice altogether. It is possible to say something about the significance of these exclusions.

Taking first the number of stoppages (which for practical purposes means strikes—lockouts being these days almost unheard of), there is reason to believe that this is grossly understated, on account both of official definition and lack of knowledge. The official net sweeps imperfectly and its mesh is not too fine. It is known that there are many stoppages which last less than a day or shift. An embracing definition of a strike would include lunch-break shop-floor meetings which fortuitously overrun into working hours, as well as full-scale walkouts of several hundred men who go home an hour or so before the end of a normal shift (but who return the next day). In between, there are the many 'downers', or mid-shift stoppages, which may involve a department or section of several scores of men and last for several hours. These are a normal feature of the day-to-day conduct of industrial relations at most of the car plants, deliberately undertaken for aggressive or defensive reasons, to express protests, back up claims, achieve action, demonstrate the genuineness of a grievance, and so on. The call in these cases is still 'all out'—but not out of the factory gates, only out into the yard or nearest open space to await immediate developments. It is 'downers' in particular which are least likely to become public knowledge.

But we have some indicators of the extent of 'downers'. One example comes from the report of the Court of Inquiry which examined a dispute at the Ford-owned plant of Briggs Motor Bodies in 1957: in the eighteen months between August 1955, and March 1957, the Inquiry was told, there had been 234 stoppages which together involved approximately half-a-million man-hours of idleness. Of these stoppages, only thirteen were reported in the

THE ISSUES IN DISPUTE

Press, or were included in the Ministry's records. These thirteen, however, can be estimated to have accounted for 90 per cent of the half-million man-hours stated to have been lost. Similarly, Ford protested to the trade unions early in December 1960, that its Dagenham plants had had fifty-seven strikes during the year. Of these, only ten appear to have been publicly recorded. Nor is this a Ford peculiarity: B.M.C.'s Bathgate plant is reported to have had some sixty stoppages over a two-year period, of which only about a dozen were recorded in the *Ministry of Labour Gazette* or the Press; and the Rootes Linwood plant had twenty-two stoppages in a three-month period in 1964, of which only four were so recorded.[1] Strikes recorded over a recent twelve-month period by B.M.C. at all its plants totalled 226—as against thirty-seven publicly recorded. In this case it seems that the reported stoppages accounted for less than half of the actual idle time attributable to them, in strong contrast to the Ford example which was first quoted. But this is probably mainly because the firm's record—unlike the reports of the Ministry of Labour—includes time lost at plants other than those at which particular disputes occurred. And similar figures for the same firm for a later period showed less discrepancy between publicly and privately recorded idleness from disputes.

However, the reserve such discrepancies place on the usefulness of the official record must not in any case be overstressed. For none of the sources of information usually include alternative forms of worker protest to strikes, such as go-slows and overtime bans, except in so far as they become unusually extensive or develop into open stoppages of work. But in one firm which has a recent record, overtime bans were actually a more frequent incident to disputes than actual stoppages of work—although they were estimated to have caused less than 5 per cent of the lost working time attributed to the latter. Comparative use of the private information is, moreover, bedevilled by definitions: 'strikes' at one establishment may be 'pauses for discussion' at another. None of the unions concerned collect systematic data—otherwise further interesting classificatory dissensions might emerge. Nor are the private records available for all firms for any extensive periods, and we make no further use of them here.[2] If public reportage of strikes represents only a large

[1] The B.M.C. and Rootes data are taken from the *Financial Times* of April 21 and 23, 1964. No source is given, but the figures seem to have come from the firms.

[2] After this Chapter was written, the motor manufacturers themselves collected some data on disputes for a recent period, and presented this as evidence to the Royal Commission on Trade Unions, etc. The data is too incomplete to be of much relevance to this study, except as general verification of the writers' estimates, and suffers from definitional vaguenesses. But it has considerable intrinsic interest and is, therefore, discussed in an Appendix to this Chapter. If

sample of actual 'dispute incidents', it almost certainly covers the greater part of idle time due to disputes—because of the concentration of that measure in the larger stoppages which are always widely reported: thus of the more than 700 post-war stoppages at individual car plants examined later in this study, some thirty biggish ones accounted for well over half the total resultant idle time at the establishments where all these disputes occurred. And in other respects, the criteria and standards of the official record-keeping are sufficiently rigid and consistent to allow the data to be used for comparisons over extended periods.

Given agreed definitions, the frequency of stoppages is a reasonably objective measure, but the official terminology which refers to 'loss of working days' raises a question of meaning. The word 'loss' is, of course, loaded. We have noted that output held up through disputes may be regained through overtime working or increased effort afterwards (particularly in piece-work trades, which in Britain are broadly speaking the most strike-prone); and we have also remarked that when disputes occur in a recession, what has been 'lost' as a result of a strike may not have been wanted anyway, so had the strike not occurred the workers affected might instead have been involved in short-time working or lay-offs. Unqualified use of the official terminology bolsters the belief that strikes generally have serious economic consequences—although few studies support this view, and some indicate the reverse. The American terminology in this regard is perhaps rather better: 'man days of idleness'—though even here the term may convey a certain image of sloth (if softened by overtones of envy). In general, we prefer the strictly neutral term 'striker-days'.

However, there are three possible measurements of the relevant striker-days. In any stoppage one can take the 'loss' or 'idleness' on the part of the workers who actually strike in the first place. Alternatively and secondly, there is the loss by the establishment or plants actually struck, including that on account of employees laid off because no work is now available for them. Or thirdly, there is the loss by all the workers stopped in consequence of the dispute at all the establishments in some way affected by it, however indirectly. Because of the elaborate division of labour and integration of production in the motor industry (so that very small disputes may occasionally cause large interruptions of the work flow) the differences between these three measurements may be particularly great there. One B.M.C. strike of less than 200 hoist operators, for instance, stopped 6,000 other workers in the same plant, and was

continued and improved it may be of substantial value; it may then be linked with the writers' estimates for years up to the early 1960s.

The Issues in Dispute

then reported to have led to 8,000 operatives in other B.M.C. factories alone being laid off.

In theory, the first of these three measurements is most useful if an index of 'industrial militancy' is required. The third should be the best measure for deriving an index of strikes' economic effects. In practice, the first measurement may be misleading because workers only 'indirectly involved'—whose lost time it would exclude—might have been laid off to put pressure on the original strikers, or to forestall a refusal to handle 'black' work or materials. Alternatively, having been laid off, they may be told by their leaders to consider themselves on strike—we refer to an instance in our Chapter VIII—so that they will refuse to return to work on the management's request alone. If they had not been laid off, they might in any case have struck in sympathy; they might even (as in the cases of certain day-shift workers in Pressed Steel and B.M.C. during the protracted 'four-night week' dispute of the summer of 1960, and of production operatives in a more recent Morris Bodies dispute) have otherwise struck against having their work interrupted by strikes!

Official reports of stoppages make no distinction in any case between 'days lost' by workers 'directly' and 'indirectly' involved in disputes at particular establishments. And our own study suggests that there are, for the vehicle industries at least, many years in which not much statistical significance can be attached to the official records' distinction between the *numbers* of workers 'directly' and 'indirectly' involved in stoppages. For what it is worth, rather under half of workers recorded as involved in car plant strikes in very recent years were noted as 'directly' so.[1] But one cannot therefore assume that over half the recorded 'working days lost' was on the part of operatives indirectly involved, because workers other than the original strikers may only be laid off after a dispute has continued for some time. We make a qualified use of the distinction between workers 'directly and indirectly involved' in certain later connections, but it is not safe to do so over any long period.

In practice again, the third measurement—aside from the objections to its validity as a 'wastage' index—is rarely available.[2] From a

---

[1] On the other hand, just about four-fifths of all the workers reported to have been involved in some forty 'principal stoppages' in car firms since 1921 were said to have been 'directly involved'. The difference probably arises in part because in big strikes the workers indirectly affected were mostly in other establishments than those in dispute, and thus not recorded.

[2] Mr F. Beswick, M.P., stated in *The Autocar* of April 21, 1961 (presumably from an official source) that for half-a-million days reported lost by the whole 'motor industry' in 1960 at establishments involved in disputes, a further 300,000 were lost in consequence at other establishments. In the last two or three years the Ministry of Labour has published estimates of this 'secondary idleness', for the

variety of sources, we would estimate that the total 'lost working time' experienced by the car firms during the past decade or so *may* have been on average anything up to some 50 to 60 per cent above their striker-days as recorded by the Ministry of Labour. This difference being largely due to two effects (in not very different proportions) which the Ministry could not take into account: lay-offs which a strike at one plant may cause at other plants of the same firm; and lay-offs caused by stoppages at other companies (e.g. body or component suppliers). But this 'secondary loss' can only be estimated in very round terms. Its actual incidence will vary from firm to firm, according to company organization and other factors, and particularly from time to time, according to whether there are many small strikes or a few big ones. We, therefore, normally use the second measurement—corresponding to the official 'loss of working days by workers directly and indirectly involved'—which in any case usually seems the one most precisely reported.

Finally, we make no attempt at a breakdown between 'official' and 'unofficial' strikes. The distinction here is usually between those strikes which are called or supported by the unions, and during which participants receive strike pay, and those which are not. Certainly, the overwhelming majority of strikes (at least 90 per cent of those publicly recorded, and an even larger proportion of all labour stoppages) start by being unofficial—and remain so, if only because most of them are over before the unions whose members are concerned could, under their respective rules, have decided whether to support them financially or not. A very large proportion of stoppages are not even notified to the local union officers: on the other hand, it is not at all unknown for a strike to be declared official some time after it is concluded, so that those concerned may receive strike pay in arrears; a strike may thus be unofficial while it is on but official in retrospect. Except in the comparatively rare case where a union has specifically declared itself against a particular stoppage therefore, the term 'unofficial' has little real meaning.

The description of a strike as unofficial in any case tells one little about the attitude of the local union officers—or the attitude they would take up if they knew about it—and it is difficult to make much sense of a distinction where trade union support may be given in every way short of the financial, or short of a public statement to that effect. The rules of individual unions vary widely in the facility they

'motor industry' alone. Thus in each of 1963 and 1964 100,000 working days were reported in the *Gazette* as lost through disputes by establishments other than those at which they occurred, compared with 315,000 and 429,000, respectively, at the establishments actually involved. But no such estimates were apparently made before 1960, and their approximate nature seems obvious.

The Issues in Dispute

provide for declaring a dispute official, and under British trade union structure (particularly in the metal-working industries) it is not at all unusual for a strike to be official for some of the workers involved and unofficial for others. Under some union constitutions, where the power to authorize strikes is shared between local and national bodies, it is not inconceivable that a dispute may be declared, even for the same group of workers, official and unofficial at the same time. Some issues, like victimization and union recognition or representative rights, are clearly more likely to attract official trade union support; and the bigger and more long-lasting a stoppage, the greater the likelihood that it will have formal union cognizance and (though this is not, of course, at all the same thing) blessing. But no more rigorous analysis is feasible in practice. In any case, there is no consistent available record of whether—and to what extent in each case—strikes are official or unofficial.

The term 'unconstitutional' is often used interchangeably with 'unofficial', although it should refer to stoppages in breach of the agreed disputes procedure rather than of trade union constitutions. For *all* firms affiliated to the Engineering Employers' Federation, it has been stated that there were forty-four strikes in 1964 which took place after all the prescribed stages of conciliation had been completed, and that the number had been rising in recent years. But no long-run separation of vehicle firms is available, and there is no parallel figure for 'non-federated' concerns. Clearly, the great majority of motor industry stoppages have also been 'unconstitutional' in this sense. However, the term seems as loaded as the 'loss of working days', in that it apparently appropriates a legalistic term to compound the iniquity of irregular strikers—and at that, irrespective of the appropriateness or efficiency of particular procedures, or of the perishability or pressures of particular issues.

But since this Chapter is concerned to make at least a preliminary survey of the 'causes' of disputes, a word might also be said on this point. Some people think that the explicit causes of strikes are unimportant—mere accidents that spark off a situation created by deeper factors. Explanations for strikes parade in the jargons of many disciplines, and in this deeper sense causes can be assigned almost according to personal biases and predilections (a sample of such explanations is given in the Chapter on working environment). But the differences in the distribution and trend of strikes, when classified under the Ministry of Labour's 'principal causes', between industries, firms, and periods are too systematic for the immediate issues in disputes to be considered anything else but highly significant. For the list of 'principal causes' is perhaps misleadingly named: it is not a definitive grouping of stoppages according to the ultimate causes of industrial unrest, but a classification according to the main reasons given by those most closely involved at the time.[1] Background conditions to a high or low strike-propensity cannot be ignored—indeed much of the rest of this study is concerned just with the examination of such factors. But the immediate issues in strikes usually seem of a kind that might very well represent to the people concerned grievances which are sufficiently real to explain their stopping work about them—and losing wages in consequence (strike pay, if afforded, notwithstanding).

(B) THE CAR FIRMS' STRIKE RECORD: PRELIMINARY ANALYSIS

After all these preliminaries and reservations, here are some facts, as closely as we can estimate them. Table II/1 summarises the car firms' strike-liability and its reported causation over the whole period from 1921 to 1964.[2] It has not been possible to get earlier figures, as it is only from 1921 that individual plants were sufficiently described in the official record books, and it thus becomes possible to separate car manufacturing establishments from other engineering works. The distribution of causes follows the Ministry's classification (only a little re-arranged, since some types of stoppage, like pure 'sympathy' strikes, have not been sufficiently numerous in the car firms to justify separating them from strikes on trade union status).

All the pre-war years together account for well under 10 per cent of the total strike-liability, whether measured in terms of the frequency of stoppages or the total of striker-days involved in them. There is a sharp increase in the strike-liability during the War, followed by a temporary decline in the late 1940s (about half the striker-days shown for 1945–49 is concentrated into 1946, when there were several biggish stoppages). What otherwise stands out about the post-war period is again the progressive increase in the liability, even allowing for the expansion of employment: more than two-fifths of all the strikes and workers involved, and over a third of striker-days, fall in the five years from the beginning of 1960 (and this effect would have been more marked still had a six-year interval to include 1959 been taken). And this concentration is not substantially affected by the exclusion of the general engineering stoppages from the table—in any event two of these fall in the 1960s.

Nor has the average size or length of car-industry strikes changed greatly over the whole period, except for two or three exceptional years (such as 1952 and 1953, when very large strikes at Ford and

---

[1] W. E. J. McCarthy usefully discusses 'The Reasons given for Striking' in the *Bulletin of the Oxford University Institute of Statistics*, XXI, 1, February 1959.
[2] A more detailed statement is attached to this Chapter as an Appendix.

Table II/1—STRIKES* IN BRITISH CAR FIRMS† 1921-64

Frequency by 'Principal Causes' (Official Classification)‡

Years	No. of strikes	Workers involved (000s)	Striker-days (000s)	Claims for wage increases	Other wage disputes	Hours of work	Dis-missals	Other employment questions	Other working arrange-ments, etc.	Trade union status, etc.
1921–30	27	22	84	2	13	—	3	6	1	2
1931–39	37	56	226	10	13	1	4	4	1	4
1940–44	121	98	276	26	61	—	10	7	12	5
1945–49	78	61	302	15	23	1	13	13	5	8
1950–54	59	104	684	13	9	—	14	5	7	11
1955–59	197	288	821	76	32	2	26	14	29	18
1960–64	401	533	1,340	152	72	13	38	27	88	11
Total										
1921–64	920	1,161	3,733	294	223	17	108	76	143	59

* Excluding general engineering stoppages involving federated firms. There have been five of these altogether since the War—a one-day strike in 1953, the week's stoppage of 1957, an apprentices' strike of 1960, and two one-day stoppages of 1962. Altogether, they are estimated to have accounted for about 800,000 striker-days in the car plants. Pre-war general stoppages are the engineering lock-out of 1922, the partial involvement of engineering (including the Coventry vehicle plants) in the General Strike of 1926, and the quite widespread strike of engineering apprentices in 1937. No estimate of these stoppages' effect on car firms is possible.

† The car firms as we define them would include or have included Alvis, Armstrong-Siddeley (Motors Division), B.M.C. constituents, Carbodies, Citroen, Chrysler, Daimler, Ford and Briggs Bodies, Jowett, Jensen, Jaguar, Lagonda, Pressed Steel, Rootes constituents, Rolls-Royce (Motors Division), Reliant, Renault, Rover, Standard-Triumph International, Vauxhall, Vulcan.

‡ The classification referred to is that of the monthly *Ministry of Labour Gazette*'s report, except that 'dismissals' are separated from other issues of 'employment, etc.' The *Gazette*'s annual article on industrial disputes also separates demarcation disputes from these issues, but this again is not worth doing for the car firms.

Austin raised the average length of strike and average number of workers involved considerably). The average reported strike (again, supposing there to be such a thing) involved about 1,400 men and lasted three to four days. The average length is surprisingly steady over the whole period (considering the great change in employers' attitudes), but there are two spells when the average number of strikers per strike was significantly lower than the norm: in the 1920s, when the industry had not yet settled into its mass-production pattern and was still largely scattered about in smaller establishments, and during the War, when the pressures to settle disputes and prevent their spreading were understandably greater (and when strikes were mostly illegal anyway). Otherwise, there is a certain tendency—especially marked since the early 1950s—for the average strike to get smaller and shorter as the number of disputes rises: which is to say, of course, that there has been a disproportionate increase in the frequency of small, short disputes.

There is not a great deal that is worth noting here about the changes in the distribution of strikes by 'principal causes' over the years—at least, in terms of the number of strikes. That there were few strikes for general wage-increases during the 1920s is not surprising; and there were several largish strikes during this period against reductions in wages which are included here in 'other wage disputes'. The relatively high proportion of war-time strikes for 'wage-increases' is—on closer examination—more concerned with matters of wage-structure; but this category of dispute has shown a particularly rapid post-war increase, so that wage-increase demands now seem by far the most important cause of strikes. However, disputes about 'other working arrangements, rules and discipline' have multiplied fastest of all (though this is a general industrial trend) and now rank second in frequency. While the number of strikes over trade union issues (which include such matters as the 'closed shop' and union recognition or 'jurisdiction'), having risen up to the late 1950s, has fallen off during very recent years.

Table II/2 below summarizes information about the distribution of strikes and strike-incidence by causes in three periods from 1921, to permit comparison with what is known of strike-causation in industry generally. So far as the frequency of different kinds of dispute is concerned, the proportions of strikes attributable to the various causes do not in recent years seem very different from the distribution in manufacturing generally—except that dismissal disputes seem, surprisingly, less frequent in car firms than in other industries, and stoppages on trade union issues are also less frequent than might be expected. But comparing the causation of disputes in terms of striker-days, not only trade union issues but dismissals

The Issues in Dispute

emerge as a more substantial source of 'lost' time, relative to other causes of strikes, than in other industries—from which one can infer something about the size of car plant stoppages on these questions. And these two causes of dispute are often in fact associated: several of the biggest post-war strikes, for example, have arisen from the dismissal of individual shop stewards or from their inclusion among groups of workers discharged.

Table II/2—STRIKES IN CAR FIRMS: DISTRIBUTION BY CAUSES (OFFICIAL CLASSIFICATION)

Percentage attributed to:	1921–39		1940–45		1946–64	
	Of strikes	Of striker-days	Of strikes	Of striker-days	Of strikes	Of striker-days
Claims for increases in wages	19	45	24	39	34	29
Other wage disputes	40	37	46	28	18	13
Hours of work	2	*	1	*	2	2
Dismissals	11	5	8	7	13	22
Other employment issues	16	8	8	6	8	6
Other working arrangements, rules and discipline	3	*	9	13	18	14
Trade union status and sympathetic action	9	5	5	7	6	15
	100	100	100	100	100	100

* Less than 1.

The size or obstinacy of the different kinds of strike appears from a comparison between the two sets of figures in each of Table II/2's three periods. Thus, strikes for wage increases, which once tended to be substantially bigger than the average, have since the War become markedly smaller. But this is partly because we have excluded from these figures the effect of the general engineering stoppages in which 'federated' motor firms have been involved, since we cannot estimate this for the inter-war period; with such stoppages in, however, the percentage of post-war striker-days attributable to wage-increase disputes would rise to forty-four. While strikes about dismissals have become big since the War, those about 'other wage issues', though apparently quite frequent, are generally smallish throughout the record. These are strikes about systems of payment, allowances for work under non-standard conditions, earnings guarantees and the like (as well as those against wage reductions in the inter-war years). The other types of strike which are generally smaller than the norm are those over employment issues (which are mostly 'demarcation' or 'dilution' disputes), and those about 'other working arrangements, rules and discipline'. This last has become virtually a miscellaneous category, but one which includes an apparently growing proportion of disputes on issues which cannot be fitted into the official classification elsewhere.

Disputes over trade union questions in the car firms have been particularly important for the period from the end of the War (or from 1944) to 1960. This importance is not hard to explain in general terms. The structure of the engineering unions involves implicit rivalries of two kinds: between unions for membership and bargaining strength; and, within unions, between the national or even district officials and the shop stewards as alternative foci of leadership. In the fields of engineering union interest which were established in the nineteenth and early twentieth centuries, these rivalries have become more contained; but the rapidly-expanding motor industry's influx of new workers represented potential recruits to competitive unions and leaderships. On the other hand, the industry's managements have numbered several forcible 'personalities' who, if not quite technocratic in outlook, have been sometimes impatient of the human paraphernalia of production and inclined to regard the workplace union organization in particular as a challenge to their authority and competence. As an example, the absence of these factors might well be thought significant, at the very least, in explaining the freedom of Vauxhall from disputes for the bulk of the period under consideration. This firm, from quite early days, took trouble to provide its own form of workplace consultation, while only one major union was for long predominant amongst its workers.[1]

(C) THE 'CAUSES' OF STRIKES:
A RECONSIDERATION, AND POST-WAR TRENDS

But the analysis of Table II/2 involves certain confusions. The official strike category which corresponds to dismissals as a cause of dispute includes not merely the discharge of individuals on disciplinary or similar grounds, but the block dismissal of operatives for whom work is no longer available. On the other hand, a strike around a demand for 'work spreading' *instead* of a threatened redundancy might come

[1] During the 1960s this firm has been becoming statistically rather more normal, and its (still few) stoppages have become somewhat larger and more intractable. Rapid expansion, changes in key management and union personnel, and even publicity are factors which have been suggested to account for this, but the problem is discussed further in our concluding Chapter.

to be officially classified as one about either working hours or 'other working arrangements' according to the method proposed—or even, if that method included an 'earnings floor'—as being about 'other wage questions'.[1] A similar problem arises in regard to wage disputes themselves. In most industries, demands for wage-increases appear to represent the biggest single source of days lost from disputes: but it is not easy to understand why this factor should be quite so prominent in the car firms' strike record. Car workers' earnings seem to have been—on the average—relatively high even in the inter-war years, and for a large part at least of the post-war period wages for normal hours in the major car plants have probably been about a third above those ruling in engineering (wage rates and earnings are discussed extensively in Chapter V). Yet even excluding the national engineering strikes' effect, stoppages in support of wage-increase demands would—according to Table II/2—seem to account for nearly one-third of the car firms' post-war strike-liability.

From the more detailed records available to us, however, it becomes clear that very many of the strikes officially classified as due to demands for wage-increases in fact spring from differences in rates or earnings between related jobs in the same plant or firm. B.M.C workers at Llanelly have struck because they thought their wages were lower than those in the firm's main plants, and Pressed Steel operatives at Swindon because they thought their earnings lower than at the firm's main plant at Oxford. Within individual plants, claims arising from differences in piece-workers' earnings, or between those of production operatives and auxiliary workers, are a very common cause of disputes. Such disputes, in fact, seem more concerned with the *structure* of wages than their absolute levels.

Inevitably, classifying strike causes is an exercise in arbitrariness. For example, at B.M.C.'s Tractor and Transmissions plant, 120 toolroom workers struck because fourteen fitters had been suspended for refusing to work an extra shift when other operatives were on short time. Is this a strike about hours, discipline, or employment—or a 'solidarity' stoppage? But arbitrariness can be more or less relevant. It is not a criticism of the Ministry of Labour's method of classifying strikes to say that it has been historically established, in the light of the experience of older industries and antique strike movements. It does not appear to be the most revealing way of analysing the car firms' strike-causation.

---

[1] Since 1960 the official category concerned with dismissals has included, in subsequent records, a sub-group of strikes 'for increased security against redundancy'. But this cause is not distinguished in the published statistics and does not in any case include all disputes directly related to labour surplus—nor could it do so without creating an inconsistency with the earlier records.

It has been possible to re-classify disputes so as to group together, on the one hand, all those originating primarily from a state of work-shortage or labour surplus (thus distinguishing them from purely individual dismissals or questions about shop stewards' status) and, on the other hand, to separate strikes for 'straight' wage-demands from those arising from the structure, system, or composition of wages. It is often said, however, that some firms (particularly Ford and Vauxhall) avoid the disputes associated with piece-rates by paying only a time-based wage: but among time-workers an analogous source of trouble exists in the work-load to be accepted in return for the fixed hourly wage (expressed, for instance, in the not infrequent stoppages about the size of time-paid working gangs). So again, these disputes are grouped together with those about piece-rates and wage differentials as being over 'wage-structure' or related questions.[1]

When these changes are made, all that is left in the official category of disputes about 'other working arrangements' are two distinct types of stoppage, which can again be separated: these are strikes about the rights of management—to transfer workers, for instance, or determine their supervision and working methods—and strikes against physical working conditions, such as heat and ventilation in paintshops (this particular issue being a hardy annual). Strikes about hours similarly boil down to some fairly recent ones about shift work (like the 'four-night week' stoppages of the 1960s, or those against three-shift working at Ford) which are too few to justify separating out from other conditions of work. While the official group 'other employment questions' has little left in it but a recurrent disagreement on work-allocation between members of the N.U.V.B. and the Sheet Metal Workers, which can be grouped under 'trade union relations' with other types of inter-union dispute and stoppages over union status. The result of all this regrouping is shown below in Table II/3; and the overall picture is immediately rather different from that presented in Table II/2.

The most important part of this table lies in the section dealing with the post-war period.[2] Too much could be made of the shifts in the proportionate distribution of disputes between causes for the earlier periods, over which there were (as Table II/2 suggests) very considerable changes in the absolute frequency and incidence of

---

[1] Where piece-workers are concerned it is in any case difficult to separate disputes about comparatively low earnings from those about allegedly excessive work-loads, since either condition may produce a demand for increased rates.

[2] The distribution of disputes and dispute-incidence for the whole period 1921-64 is summarized in an Appendix, so that the effect of the alternative classifications of causes can be compared.

The Issues in Dispute

Table II/3—STRIKES* IN CAR FIRMS: DISTRIBUTION BY CAUSES (RE-CLASSIFIED)

Percentage attributable to:	1921–39 Of strikes	1921–39 Of striker-days	1940–45 Of strikes	1940–45 Of striker-days	1946–64 Of strikes	1946–64 Of striker-days
Straight wage-increase demands or wage reductions	12	36	3	½	13	14
Wage-structure and work-loads	47½	46½	64	69	39	30
Working hours and conditions	5	½	2	1½	9	3
Individual dismissals	8	2	8	4	9	8
Redundancy, short-time, etc.	10	8	3	½	12	18
Management questions	1½	3	6	12	6	6
Trade union relations, etc.	16	4½	14	12½	12	21½
	100	100	100	100	100	100

* Excluding general engineering stoppages.

stoppages. Though fairly obvious general pressures can perhaps be called to account for these shifts—for example, the relatively high proportion of wage-structure disputes in the early years may suggest that the pressures of the inter-war economic situation led to a concentration on minor wage improvements, an impression which seems confirmed by the comparative obstinacy of the stoppages for straight wage-increases (and against some general wage reductions, which had also to be classified in this category). An even greater concentration on such disputes in the war period was probably encouraged by the virtually automatic granting of general wage-increases (often through compulsory arbitration) on 'cost of living' grounds. There is also the obvious falling away of redundancy and short-time disputes during the war. Nevertheless, there remains another explanation for the rather abrupt changes in distribution: the figures for the inter-war period are based on much smaller numbers, and are hence much more heavily influenced by the few large stoppages that occurred. But it is still worth noting also how strikes over trade union issues have become proportionately less numerous but more weighty. Over the whole post-war period, they are the second largest single contributor to 'lost' time after wage-structure issues (notwithstanding the most recent tendency for the category to decline in relative importance, a tendency which is here masked by the bulking together of the post-war years). Some of this phenomenon is attributable to war-time and early post-war struggles for recognition, not necessarily of unions as such, but of particular unions or of shop stewards.

Table II/3 does not include the effect of the general engineering stoppages, but even if it had (in which case 'straight' wage-demands would account for a third of post-war striker-days) wage-structure remains responsible for nearly a quarter of time lost, and with redundancy and trade union questions still accounts for over 55 per cent of all idle time due to disputes. Again, the comparison with Table II/2 says nothing about the *general* validity of the official method of classifying the causes of strikes. But in the particular circumstances of the car firms, its effect is not merely to understate the impact of a major internal source of dispute—trade union relations—but to very largely conceal that of two others: redundancy, and the industry's wage-structure and system (or rather, perhaps, in view of the car firms' negotiating arrangements, its general lack of this last attribute as far as wages are concerned). It is in fact these three issues—but particularly wage-structure and redundancy—that have been most responsible for the marked increase in the car firms' strike-incidence over the post-war period. In absolute terms, the contribution of each of these categories to the post-war total of striker-days alone has been considerable: of a total of just over three million days apart from those due to general engineering stoppages, redundancy accounts for nearly 600,000; trade union relations for 660,000; and wage-structure and related matters for over 900,000. This last category, indeed, substantially exceeds in effect the impact on the car firms of the national stoppages called by the engineering unions in recent years.

Table II/4—STRIKES IN THE CAR FIRMS: POST-WAR DEVELOPMENTS

Annual average:	Number of strikes attributable to:			Striker-days (000s) attributable to:	
	Wage-structure, etc.	Redundancy, etc.	Trade union relations		Other issues
1946–55	4 (17)	2 (15)	3 (34)		4 (29)
1956–60	21 (73)	8 (65)	7 (37)		16 (32)
1961–64	31 (96)	6 (23)	6 (33)		35 (94)

The Issues in Dispute

However, the contribution of the three major causes of car strikes during the post-war period is analysed further in Table II/4. Again, the striker-days estimate here does not include the effect of general engineering stoppages: with these in, the annual average loss from 'other' causes would probably be about 40,000 days up to 1955, about 150,000 from 1956 to 1960, and about 150,000 from 1961–64. But one must in any case note the sharp increase, within the post-war period, in the strike-liability attributable to 'other issues' than the three main ones. And this increase has been especially marked in the 1960s, when the strike-liability on account of these secondary sources of dispute has risen quite disproportionately—so that whereas before 1960 they accounted for 25 to 30 per cent of striker-days and stoppages, in more recent years they have contributed from 40 to 45 per cent. In effect, the causation of car firm strikes has also shown a marked recent tendency to become more dispersed, and to involve a wider network of grievances—so that under certain categories of contention the impact, whether in terms of striker-days or strike-frequency, has begun to compare with the three dominant issues already described.

(D) NEW ISSUES—AND NEW PLANTS. QUESTIONS ARISING

It is perhaps worth pursuing this subsidiary movement a little more closely, if only because of its possible significance for the future pattern of labour demands and protest, in the motor industry or others:

Table II/5—POST-WAR STRIKES IN CAR FIRMS: SUBSIDIARY ISSUES

Annual average:	Number of strikes attributable to:				Striker-days (000s) attributable to:			
	Straight wage-increase demands*		Individual dismissals		Management questions		Working hours and conditions	
1946–55	1	(21)	1	(4)	1	(3)	1	(†)
1956–60	7	(23)	4	(12)	3	(8)	2	(9)
1961–64	10	(24)	8	(36)	6	(26)	11	(8)

* Excludes general engineering stoppages.
† = less than 1,000.

Comparing this with the preceding Table, and the 1960s with the earlier post-war years, it seems apparent that disputes involving trade union relationships, and to a secondary extent stoppages over 'straight' wage-demands (mostly arising from claims against non-federated car firms), have settled down to a steady annual source of 'man-days of idleness'. Since the 1960 recession, disputes arising from redundancy have continued at not much below the frequency they reached in the late 1950s, but in the industry's more recent period of prosperity became much less severe and substantial. Disputes about working hours or conditions of work have risen very sharply in frequency, but also contribute very little to the total of 'working days lost' (and have also, as may appear subsequently, been fairly localized). But stoppages in protest against the dismissal or suspension of individual workers have not only doubled or more than doubled in frequency but have also become considerably more obdurate. And so have disputes over other rights of management—particularly in this case, to engage and transfer workers as it thinks fit: so that the rise in the strike-liability from these last two causes of disagreement has more than offset the recent decline in the impact of redundancy disputes. The most recent strike-movement, in other words, is treading very closely into the area of traditional 'managerial functions'. However, quarrels over wage-structure and related matters have also continued to increase, so that whether in terms of the resultant number of strikes or of striker-days, this factor still ranks in effect with that of all the subsidiary issues of grievance together.

It is perhaps of relevance to note here the pattern of strikes which has been developing at the new car plants built during the 1960s in Scotland, on the Mersey, and in Wales. There have been no large strikes: they remain small but fairly frequent. All the firms concerned have shared in this liability—including even Vauxhall. The overall figures are as follows:

Table II/6—STRIKES IN NEW PLANTS

Year	Number of strikes	Striker-days (000s)
1961	5	2.3
1962	11	4.2
1963	28	32.7
1964	22	14.9

Whether the major car firms expected the new areas to be free of the dispute-proneness of the older car-producing districts is not clear. It might perhaps have been anticipated that new plants, with problems of settling down, would lead to an initial wider spread of the dispute-liability in terms of the stated issues, and this is certainly so. Dismissals and working conditions figure prominently: but the bulk of dispute-causation is again wage-structure issues, and eight of the reported strikes have been about trade union issues. However, if the

The Issues in Dispute

1963 performance is to become typical of the new plants, then there is going to be little to choose between the strike performances of the older as against the newer factories. In 1963, strikes in the new plants were almost a third of the total recorded for all the firms, and days lost were one-eighth of the total—almost exactly the fraction which the new plants' labour force forms of the total labour force of all the firms. But there is still some experimentation taking place— particularly in Scotland and in respect of wage-systems—and it is perhaps too soon to reach firm conclusions about the success of the 'decentralised' expansion, at least in terms of labour relations.

Identification of the major issues in car firm strikes, and of how these issues have been changing in relative importance, gives some guidance for further examination of the industry and its labour relations. The industry has been one of the economy's outstanding growth sectors: to take only recent years, output rose from half-a-million units in 1949, to over one million in 1955, to one and a half million in 1960, and to nearly one and three-quarters of a million in 1964. It would be tempting to associate strikes simply with rapid expansion and the strains of increasing productivity. There is also the car firms' popular identification with 'automation'—and widespread feelings of unease about the process which make the rarity of disputes specifically about technological changes somewhat surprising. A closer examination of productivity and technological change in the industry is reserved for the next chapter.

But why should redundancy have been so outstanding a cause of strikes in just the industry where growth has been swiftest? Motor manufacture has always been marked by change and concentration, but such structural changes have been accelerated in the post-war period by the short but severe slumps that have interrupted the otherwise rapid growth. The recession of late 1960, in which output fell by a half in a few months, was the third in a decade, so that the industry's progression had begun to assume an abrupt cyclical pattern. In the immediate post-war years, output rose particularly rapidly and was at least half based on exports—in which the British industry had a temporary special advantage. Since the recession of 1956, overseas competition has become intense, and the annual output growth has slowed, although it still remains high. Against this background it is perhaps understandable that insecurity should emerge as a major theme in car strikes. But it is not so much the increased frequency of 'redundancy' strikes that accounts for their importance—as Table II/4 demonstrates. The remarkable thing about them is that whereas other kinds of strike have tended to get smaller as they become more frequent, stoppages on redundancy became—for a while at least— very much bigger. A more detailed examination of the relation between strikes and production fluctuations is undertaken in Chapter IV.

However, 'wage-structure and work-load' disputes not only exceed redundancy issues as a source of lost time over the post-war period; they constitute by far the biggest single cause of individual strikes—nearly two-fifths of which have been attributable to them. And wage-structure issues are especially responsible for the remarkable rise in the frequency of disputes, from an average of fourteen annually in the decade to 1954, to one of thirty-nine for the five years to 1959, and to eighty during the 1960s. While unlike the redundancy disputes, which become more important in slumps in the car industry's activity, 'wage-structure and work-load' strikes become more frequent in booms and are thus considerably more disruptive of production.

Moreover, even our own classification may somewhat understate the impact of 'wage-structure' as a factor in disputes, since included in strikes about 'straight wage-demands' are not only those explicitly and primarily based on the prosperity or productivity of the car trade or particular firms, on the cost of living, and the like, but also wage disputes about which we have no detailed information. Even some of those we have deliberately included in this group might well be argued to be in fact about wage relativities. For instance, the first substantial strike after the war's end was for a wage-increase at the 'non-federated' Dagenham plants, and we have classified it as such; but it in fact arose from an arbitration award to workers in 'federated' concerns, and might equally well be regarded as a dispute about wage-structure.

But the general pattern of wage-structure disputes seems to be connected with changes on the side of the car firms themselves: from the end of the war up to 1953, the annual frequency of such strikes was remarkably regular, at just about four each year. In 1953 however, at the time of the main mergers of the 1950s, they virtually ceased. The following year they re-appeared, and, with a brief interruption by the 1956 recession, their frequency increased until in the 1960s they were responsible for two-fifths of all stoppages and striker-days. This increase is in spite of the fact that they include disproportionately few big disputes having substantial trade union backing—which suggests an almost wholly spontaneous movement on the operatives' part. The peculiarities of wage-structure in the industry are therefore taken up at some length in a separate chapter.

The importance of managerial and trade union structures and practices has already been suggested, but the whole pattern of strikes in the car plants is in any case heavily influenced by events in particular firms. For instance, the fact that even excluding the general

The Issues in Dispute

engineering stoppages, strikes for 'straight wage-demands' remain slightly larger than the average (see Table II/3) is mainly due to their concentration in certain big 'non-federated' establishments; while it is well established that some firms, including Ford, Pressed Steel, Standard-Triumph, and more recently, Morris Motors at Cowley, have had 'runs' of heavy strike-liability between periods of relative quiescence. And this suggests an examination of the strike-liability of particular firms, and closer acquaintance with the sizeable stoppages which contribute so overwhelmingly to the total strike-incidence. These things, too, have their place in subsequent chapters.

APPENDIX A

THE CAR MANUFACTURERS' STRIKE-STATISTICS

In their Memorandum of Evidence to the Royal Commission on Trade Unions, etc. the motor firms presented some figures of strikes experienced, and 'man-hours lost' in consequence, for a period from January 1962 to end-October 1965. We reproduce these in the accompanying Table, only a little simplified—to make them more readily comprehensible—by rounding off the man-hours to the nearest 1,000 and eliminating some redundant data. For comparison, we have also converted their total 'man-hours' figure to days on the assumption of an eight-hour working day as the average (which possibly produces a slight over-estimate for the period in question). And we give our own figures, on Ministry of Labour definitions, for the same years. The statistics in the manufacturers' printed evidence were to some extent apparently contradicted by some other figures they circulated at the Commission's public hearing—which showed, for instance, over 200,000 fewer 'man-hours lost' from strikes within the companies involved in 1964. However, we assume the printed figures to be definitive so far as the firms are concerned.

The manufacturers' figures of the total numbers of strikes are of little use in their present form except as giving some indication of to what extent the frequency with which sanctions are applied in industrial disputes exceeds official recording of stoppages. As such, however, they only give one side of the picture: sanctions may be applied by managements as well as workers, and in many forms short of an open lockout—for instance, by the 'withdrawal of privileges' from shop stewards or by laying-off uninvolved operatives immediately a dispute occurs. But the major defect of the figures is that they have no definitional basis. They clearly include a large number of very small incidents—refusals of small groups of men to start a new job until the piece-rate is settled or working conditions improved, or to obey an order they consider improper, delays of shop stewards in returning from meetings, and so on. (Vauxhall's one recorded strike in 1962 involved only seventeen man-hours, and some one-fifth of the stoppages reported by Rover to an inquiring commission were lunch-hour meetings that ran over time.) But different companies have different practices in recording these things, so one does not really know what the figures mean. Moreover, their trend is clearly affected by increasing reportage of such events. In the 1960s there has been a

A. STRIKES AND 'MAN-HOURS LOST' AS REPORTED BY THE MANUFACTURERS

Firm		1962† Strikes	1962† Man-hours (000s)	1963 Strikes	1963 Man-hours (000s)	1964 Strikes	1964 Man-hours (000s)	Total 1962-64 Strikes	Total 1962-64 Man-hours (000s)	1965 to end Oct. Strikes	1965 to end Oct. Man-hours (000s)
B.M.C.	a	263	2,943	302	1,685	387	1,943	952	6,571	340	5,004
	b	—	78	—	283	—	223	—	584	—	985
Ford	a	58	793	7	34	22	77	87	904	25	186
	b	—	0	—	0	—	0	—	0	—	0
Jaguar	a	n/a	n/a	n/a	n/a	n/a	53	n/a	(53)	4	15
	b	n/a	n/a	n/a	n/a	n/a	123	n/a	(123)	—	8
Pressed Steel	a	74	455	89	200	116	76	279	731	148	881
	b	—	121	—	198	—	252	—	571	—	453
Rootes	a	41	223	58	46	79	89	178	358	96	86
	b	—	6	—	49	—	11	—	66	—	402
Rover	a	33	246	45	141	92	283	170	670	126	412
	b	—	30	—	27	—	77	—	134	—	103
Standard	a	n/a	n/a	n/a	238	n/a	200	n/a	(438)	107	1,268
	b	n/a	n/a	n/a	74	n/a	176	n/a	(250)	—	0
Vauxhall	a	1	*	4	5	24	36	29	41	17	203
	b	—	0	—	0	—	0	—	0	—	0
Totals	a	470	4,660	505	2,348	720	2,757	(1,695)	(9,765)	863	8,055
	b	—	235	—	631	—	861	—	(1,728)	—	1,950
Man-hours under (a) converted to 'striker-days' (000s):		—	583	—	294	—	345	—	1,222	—	1,007
Writers' Estimates										whole year	
Number of 'recordable' strikes:		66	—	88	—	103	—	257	—	96	—
'Striker-days' at plants actually involved (000s):		—	482	—	226	—	255	—	963	—	719

a = 'strikes within the company'; b = 'effect of strikes outside the company'; * = less than 1,000 man-hours; ( ) = incomplete data
† Includes effect of general engineering stoppages.

tendency for firms which formerly attached so little importance to disputes that they kept no record of them, to collect supervisors' reports in increasing detail, and this is reflected in the Table.

The 'man-hours lost' figures for 'strikes within the company' are, however, reasonably consistent with our own data—the difference for 1962–64 between our own estimates and the manufacturers' when converted to a 'striker-day' basis being clearly overwhelmingly due to the firms' inclusion of 'lost time' at plants other than those at which the strikes occurred. (It is, indeed, one indication of the miniscule character and effects of most of the incidents included in the firms' tally of strikes that their inevitable exclusion from our estimates makes so little difference to the total of striker-days.) The difference does, however, seem rather oddly distributed between firms. It is possible to allocate the 'loss of working days' recorded by Ministry of Labour criteria between firms by identifying, from Press and geographical evidence, the motor companies involved in reported strikes, as summarized monthly in the *Gazette*'s 'Principal Stoppages'. When this is done, there is a very close correspondence between our estimates of striker-days and the individual firm's record of 'man-hours lost'—no discrepancies appearing which are not attributable to such things as minor differences in dating, the absence of information for S.T.I. in 1962, or the necessarily approximate nature of our allocation of the incidence of the 1962 general engineering strikes. So that it looks as if the 'secondary' effect of disputes at the plant level on other plants of the same company is in general rather small.

There are, however, two exceptions to this correspondence. The Jaguar figures (only given for 1964–65) appear to be very incomplete: one stoppage alone at this firm in 1964 was reported by the *Gazette* to have involved some 30,000 striker-days. On the other hand, B.M.C. (which will be observed to account for some two-thirds of all 'man-hours lost' on the manufacturers' figures) shows a very large discrepancy, averaging some 75 per cent above our estimate for 1962–64 and increasing over the period—whereas for other firms discrepancies between the two sets of data diminish as time goes on. The particularly dispersed organization of B.M.C. is certainly one reason why its apparent 'secondary loss' should be so very much higher than other firms'. But as we showed in our Appendix to Chapter I, it is often very difficult in practice to determine how much of a particular 'loss of working time' is due to disputes and how much to other factors. There are also apparent differences in the extent to which individual companies are anxious to have their respective dispute-liabilities annotated. We cannot say how far the above contrasts reflect differences in the recording practices of firms.

The Issues in Dispute

The correspondence between ours and the manufacturers' estimates is best for 1964, and would apparently not be so good (had either they or we been able to complete the year's analysis properly) for 1965. This raises a point of some general interest on the nature of strike-statistics. The reports accepted by the Ministry of Labour (and by ourselves, in this study's various estimates) are usually based on the number of workers absent from work on each day of a dispute. But a percentage (about five, in the motor industry) is normally absent from work for various reasons anyway, and may thus be counted as 'on strike' on the days in question. Two major disputes in 1965 occurred on issues which may have encouraged exceptional absenteeism anyway—the widespread and protracted refusals to work the short Friday night shifts provided for by the 1964 national engineering agreement, and the resistance to a change in Coventry car firms from the traditional local summer holiday weeks. It would be understandable if the firms affected had found difficulty in distinguishing organized from individual absentees.

The 'man-hours lost' reported as an 'effect of strikes outside the company' are distributed about as one would expect—Ford and Vauxhall making nil returns because of their highly integrated organization, but Pressed Steel having a relatively high loss because of cuts in requirements for bodies when other companies are struck. The totals, however, would be more useful had not the alternative data circulated by the manufacturers for 1965 again showed a very much lower figure for the whole year on account of 'disputes at suppliers' than that recorded by their Table as due to 'outside strikes' in the year's first ten months—a discrepancy which would be only partially eliminated by adding the whole of Pressed Steel's stated loss under the latter head to the former figure.

APPENDIX B

CAUSATION OF CAR FIRM DISPUTES, 1921–64*
By Official Classification and as Re-classified

By 'Principal Cause', Ministry of Labour Classification			As Re-classified		
Percentage:	Of all strikes	Of striker-days	Percentage:	Of all strikes	Of striker-days
Claims for wage increases	32	32	Straight wage-demands, or wage-reductions	11	15
Other wage-disputes	24	16	Wage-structure and workloads	44	35
Hours of work	2	1	Working hours and conditions	7	2
Dismissals	12	19	Individual dismissals	9	7
Other employment issues	8	6	Redundancy, short-time, etc.	10	16
Other working arrangements, rules and discipline	16	12	Management questions	6	6
Trade union status and sympathetic action	6	13	Trade union relations	13	19
	100	100		100	100

* Excluding general engineering stoppages.

CHAPTER III

PRODUCTIVITY GROWTH AND TECHNICAL CHANGE

(A) 'AUTOMATION' AND PRODUCTIVITY TRENDS

Perhaps the most obvious background circumstance to the car workers' condition since the war has been the rapid growth of production. So it seems reasonable to inquire how far the strains of increasing output, and especially the demands or effects of fast-rising productivity, have themselves contributed to labour unrest in the car firms. And because a major part in these developments has been played by mechanization and technical change, this particularly involves some enquiry into the effect of these things on labour relations.

Since the adoption of assembly-line production in the 1920s, the outstanding changes in car making have probably been automatic machining and materials handling. Some indication of the impact of these new techniques, nowadays often lumped together and called 'automation', can be obtained by comparing movements in output, employment and productivity following their introduction in the late 1940s. Between 1948 and 1959, for example, the output of motor vehicles (cars, commercial vehicles and motor cycles) in the U.K. grew by 180 per cent, but the motor vehicle industry's labour force increased by a mere 18 per cent, so productivity (crudely measured) rose by 138 per cent. The labour-saving potential of automation immediately caught the imagination of both the public and the workers in the industry, and caused many to forecast that its introduction would create widespread redundancies and consequent unrest. There was also concern about its effects on skills, job satisfaction and wages; and here again many expected the process of adjustment to lead to conflict.

The most important processes involved in manufacturing motor cars are casting, forging, machining, pressing, the welding or assembly of parts into sub-components and vehicles, and painting. In fact these processes have experienced widely differing rates of technical change and are spread out at very different stages on the road to 'full automation'—in which, with a handful of planners, repairmen and monitors, the process runs itself.[1] Pressing, for instance, is very highly mechanized, there is considerable automation in welding, and even in inspection. But the 'direct labour' content of most body and assembly work is high, and little headway has been made in the casting and forging processes which are still largely carried out in traditional ways. Even though foundries have become more mechanized, progress towards full automation is limited by the current methods of making moulds and cores, and by the caution of managements in taking up the more advanced shell and carbon dioxide moulding techniques. Similarly, further mechanization of the forging process cannot be expected until such new techniques as cold forming, powdered metallurgy and investment casting have been further developed, because the current methods are so inaccurate that they need to be carefully supervised.

The closest approach to full automation has been made in machining technology. Here it stemmed from the invention of transfer machines, which consist of a number of operating stations linked together by a mechanism which automatically transfers the workpiece from station to station. These were first introduced in 1923 by Morris, which, however, discarded them because of their unreliability; and they were not seriously adopted until 1946 when U.S. Ford installed them in large numbers in its Cleveland engine plant. The early American machines were specially built to machine a particular component, and often had to be scrapped when models were changed. Because of the expense involved they were unsuitable for European needs, but French, British and German engineers developed flexible, unit-based, standardized machines which could be more readily altered and re-shuffled to fit in with current needs.

This type of equipment was introduced by British car firms in the late 1940s, and by 1957 formed the backbone of the larger producers' machine shops. In 1948, for example, Vauxhall installed twelve transfer stations into its cylinder block line, and Ford introduced twenty-four transfer stations into its block line in 1950. In contrast, by 1955 Austin was operating seventy in-line transfer machines and 120 rotary machines in its machine shops at Long-

[1] There is a useful short survey of automation in the car industry by Mr F. Griffiths, the Chief Production Development Engineer at B.M.C., 'Automation in motors calls for much re-thinking', *'Financial Times' Survey of Electronics and Automation* (January 23, 1961), p.37.

bridge. But Ford and Vauxhall had both commenced ambitious expansion programmes in that year (Ford spent £75m. in this way between 1955 and 1959, and by 1964 this expenditure had risen to £140m.) and the rapidity of automation in machining can be gathered from the increase in the number of stations on their cylinder block lines. At Ford these had by 1960 grown to 722, and at Vauxhall to 459. Rootes and Standard were also introducing automatic equipment at about the same time, but lower turnover and less money to spare meant that they could not go as far. The quality car firms, such as Rover and Jaguar, had even less reason to change over to transfer machining. However, automation has not been confined to the machine shop, though because the transfer machine is the most dramatic of the new techniques it has received the most attention. Those press shops which make use of the best modern practice are now laid out according to flow principles, and include a high proportion of automatic machines, automatic handling mechanisms and linking conveyor belts. Further progress here depends on the innovation of techniques of loading presses automatically, and the development of cheaper large presses to enable them to be turned over from batch to full flow production.

In the assembly process, of course, the major innovation was the introduction of the flow-line system before the First World War. This has gradually been developed over the years, most extensively by the larger manufacturers. Under the earliest systems of large-scale production, groups of workers moved along a line of cars carrying out their allotted tasks; but then Ford saw the benefits to be gained by keeping the workers in one place and moving the cars instead. Apart from the immediate economic advantages of this system—savings in skilled manpower through greater subdivision of tasks, increased productivity, reductions in stocks, less handling—its chief virtue was to open up opportunities for making greater use of mechanical handling methods (by sub-conveyors and so on). The basic technique of making cars on flow principles has altered little since those days. But over the course of time the system has become more streamlined, more sophisticated and more capable of maintaining an uninterrupted flow of production. Since the end of the last war there has been a great extension of the use of power-driven conveyor belts, of mechanized handling by fork-lift trucks and standardized containers, and of electrically or pneumatically powered hand tools. And at its most sophisticated the whole assembly process is now directed and controlled by a computer.

As with transfer machining, the extent to which the car firms have embraced these developments has depended on their scale of operation. But if any further major breakthrough in production methods is to occur, it will stem from the search for ways and means of automatically assembling components. A certain amount of success has already been achieved, chiefly with welded assemblies, but a cheap and adequate substitute for human eyes and fingers has yet to be found. Thus, such progress as the car firms have made towards *full* automation has come mainly from the innovation of automatic handling devices. Both the transfer machine and the flow line enable automatic clamping, transfer and conveying devices to take over functions that were previously done by hand; while the various types of control mechanism, including the computer, drastically reduce the need for the handling process to be directly guided and regulated by people.

In fact, while the motor industry has been an outstanding 'high-growth sector' since the war, there is little evidence that this recent advance represents anything new in the industry's experience. Its general rate of growth in output from the mid-1920s through the 1930s was apparently of much the same order as in the post-war period, though employment in the vehicle industries was rising rather faster in the inter-war years. This was, however, offset in its effect on output by a slightly lower rate of capital investment. So far as the impact of technological progress proper on vehicle production can be estimated, this seems to have proceeded at just about the same pace in the post-war years as during the inter-war period, factors other than increased inputs of labour and capital accounting at each time for just about 3 per cent annual increase in vehicle production.[1] In total, however, mechanization—rather than increased employment of labour—has probably made an even greater contribution to the growth of the motor industry's output since the war than it did before it.

Some further impression of the impact of automation on output, employment and productivity in the motor vehicle industry as a whole can be obtained from this Chapter's Appendix.[2] We have said that between 1948 and 1959 productivity for all motor vehicles increased by 138 per cent, and it seems very probable that productivity growth in the car firms proper was even faster. Of course, we were there comparing the year that the industry regained its feet after the war with the year in which output reached its peak during the 1950s.

[1] See the estimates of Messrs C. H. Feinstein, J. Odling-Smee and R. C. O. Matthews reported by R. C. O. Matthews in 'Some Aspects of Post-War Growth in the British Economy in Relation to Historical Experience' (particularly their Table VI), *Manchester Statistical Society*, November 1964.

[2] To provide a measure of comparability to our own calculations, we have included in the Appendix the much more refined index of productivity published by Professor Lomax, and some estimates from Censuses of Production. All these estimates indicate a high (if somewhat decelerating) productivity growth.

PRODUCTIVITY GROWTH AND TECHNICAL CHANGE

If, for example, we compare 1959 with 1964, it will be seen that the further expansion of output—by some 50 per cent for motor vehicles other than cycles—owed rather more to a growth in the labour force, of about a quarter. But over the whole post-war period, the rapid growth of output and productivity stands in sharp contrast with a modest increase in employment; and there can be little doubt that the innovation of new techniques, and particularly automatic machining and materials handling, is substantially responsible. The improvements in methods of managerial control which have taken place, together with the less obvious economies of a generally increasing scale of production, have probably played the major supporting role in the development of the industry's productive efficiency.

Because official employment statistics do not contain a separate series for car manufacturing, we must either infer the experience of the car sector from that of the industry as a whole or gather our own information. Accordingly, we examined the rates of growth of employment, output and productivity in the three biggest producers —responsible for some four-fifths of all car output—and our results are summarized in Table III/1. They do not contradict our surmise that, for the major car manufacturers at least, productivity rises even faster than in the motor industry as a whole:

Table III/1—OUTPUT, EMPLOYMENT AND PRODUCTIVITY OF THE THREE LARGEST CAR PRODUCERS, 1952–63 (INDICES, 1954=100)

	Output of cars	Employment on cars	Productivity
1952	59	95	63
1953	83	97	85
1954	*100*	*100*	*100*
1955	105	109	96
1956	93	98	95
1957	119	93	128
1958	129	102	126
1959	159	116	138
1960	173	130	132
1961	128	121	106
1962	156	126	122
1963	205	141	145

Source: Calculated from data supplied by the manufacturers.

Over the whole period, it will be seen that output was rising at an average rate of nearly 14 per cent annually, to which the growth of employment contributed only 4 per cent a year. This rate of growth is perhaps a little exaggerated by the series starting at the low point of the 1951–52 recession, but they are also interesting as demonstrating the sharp fluctuations to which the industry's growth in employment, output, and therefore productivity has been liable (a point to which we shall return in the next Chapter).

(B) TECHNICAL CHANGE AND LABOUR DISPLACEMENT

The introduction of transfer lines may dispense with up to 90 per cent of the manpower employed beforehand (both directly and indirectly) although the average reduction is about 60 per cent; and it can at the same time double the level of output from the section converted. Typical of modern transfer lines was the one introduced into the Morris gearbox plant during the late 1940s. This was manned by four workers who produced 1,600 gearboxes in forty-four hours, and it replaced eighteen semi-automatic lathes which were operated by thirteen workers who had produced 750 gearboxes in a similar time. So it was not surprising, when this equipment was being widely installed by the British car firms during the mid-1950s, that many people both inside and outside the industry should conclude from such examples that automation was bound to cause unemployment. In fact, as Table III/1 shows, because of the expanding demand for cars total employment has risen despite the growth of productivity. Moreover, the car firms have to keep abreast of their competitors in techniques of production, and so they have tried to avoid giving their employees cause to resent the introduction of new equipment. Managers are well aware that if their workers saw that automation was bringing unemployment they would be unable to introduce it without serious resistance, if not bitter industrial conflict.

In fact the introduction of automation into a British car plant has been associated with serious unemployment (and a consequent strike) on only one occasion. This case occurred at Standard in 1956 when the company planned to absorb its tractor workers into the car plant whilst a major re-tooling was taking place in its tractor plant. The change was timed to coincide with the usual summer peak in car sales and the arrangements had been previously discussed with the shop stewards over a period of eighteen months. Unfortunately, in 1956 there was a credit squeeze at home, competition stiffened abroad and the market for Standard's cars collapsed. The management then declared 3,500 workers redundant and the workers reacted by staging a fifteen-day strike. A number of factors seem to have contributed to this mishap: sheer bad luck; over-optimism, perhaps, on the management's part; and the high proportion of the company's activities affected by the change. But two points are worth emphasizing; first, the downturn in sales which occurred in 1956 caused most car firms to discharge men—including B.M.C., whose decision to declare one in eight of its work people redundant also caused a major strike; and, second, Standard was the only firm caught in the middle of an important technical change.

In other words, automation has only been a direct cause of conflict where it has led to redundancy: and redundancy has caused conflict whether or not it has been associated with automation. But although automation has in fact seldom caused unemployment, fear of its labour-saving potential may well have added, during the middle 1950s at any rate, to feelings of insecurity originally derived from the pre-war pattern of large seasonal variations in employment. Before the war men were regularly laid off during the winter lull in sales, and while the demand for cars since the war has been so high that these seasonal variations largely disappeared for a time, periodic recessions have still occurred—considerable numbers of workers being discharged in 1953, 1956 and 1961. It is, therefore, not surprising that many were still inclined to subscribe to the view that automation leads to redundancy. Their anxiety over security has led many workers to reason that since they have no way of knowing how long either their high boom-time earnings or their jobs will last, their best policy is simply to go all out for what they can get while the companies' profits are high. In our view, this outlook has been a circumstance of fundamental relevance to the car firms' dispute-proneness, and the contribution of automation to the industry's strike record is largely dependent on the part it has played in developing it.

Apart from such contributions as they may have made—and this is very difficult to assess—to a general sense of insecurity, mechanization and technological innovation may have more specific effects which, while they fall short of redundancy, may yet induce industrial unrest. For instance, in America the car firms often lay workers off during changes of product or technique. In Britain, however, the introduction of new models or methods has caused very little interruption of employment in recent years because the car firms have adopted the practice of 'phasing new models in and old models out' and of running the new equipment in while the old is still working (the longer annual holiday shut-down has been particularly useful for this purpose). Thus, managements avoid the risks of losing experienced workers or of conflicts with work people that temporary lay-offs would involve.

However, without the high degree of occupational mobility common to the car factories it would be difficult to avoid such dislocations of employment. Because roughly 80 per cent of the jobs in the car plants are 'semi-skilled' and quickly learned, it is fairly easy to move workers between departments to facilitate technical changes, and the workers have generally been quite prepared to take on new jobs as automation (or other technical changes) have wiped out their old ones. This does not mean that men can always in fact be transferred quite so easily. Even though all the car firms have agreements with the trade unions which specify that semi-skilled and unskilled men must be prepared to move between jobs, there has been considerable resistance to transfers in cases—for instance—when workers on time-rates consider a reduction in the size of their section will oblige them to do more work for the same pay (to accept a 'stretch-out'); when piece-workers believe that bringing more men on to their job will reduce piece or bonus earnings; and when members of one union refuse to work alongside workers from other unions. We have no evidence, however, that things of this kind have been any more associated with technological development than with the other changes to which the motor industry is liable.

Nor would workers willingly accept new jobs if the change meant they would be downgraded. But, as it happens, the men displaced by recent automation have almost invariably been in the semi-skilled grade; so the most extreme form of personal downgrading—from a 'skilled' job to a 'semi-skilled' one—has seldom occurred. Even so, car managements—no doubt aware of the dangers—have usually taken care to ensure that technical changes cause a minimum of overt downgrading of this kind. However, downgrading can take other forms, and in our observation both workers and managers generally think of a reduction in earnings when the subject is mentioned to them. In those firms which pay by results, when an operator moves to a new job he is expected to accept the existing rate for that job—regardless of whether it is higher or lower than the one he received on his previous job. If, of course, the task is a new one—as most are after a major technical change—then a rate will be fixed by the usual bargaining process. To avoid dissatisfaction with piece-prices which would jeopardize the success of a technical change, managements try to keep transfers to a minimum in any case, and when men have to be moved care is usually taken to allocate them to jobs carrying rates which will yield earnings at least as high as those they have been accustomed to.

In the piece-rate firms, then, where new prices have to be fixed the question of whether or not automation is involved has made little difference to the manner of the negotiations. If disputes occur they develop, as always, from differences of opinion over the 'effort-bargain' implied in a proposed rate. It is true that unions and stewards have made some point of insisting that the men should share in the benefits of automation, but the effect of this attitude differs little from that of their general determination to improve the economic lot of their members. Where the more striking examples of automation are concerned, however—such as transfer machines—managements have often been prepared to concede distinctively higher-yielding rates to ease the new equipment's acceptance.

The firms which pay straight time-rates also expect their workers to change their jobs as required. At Ford, for example, adult male workers are, at the time of writing, still recruited into one of three standard pay-grades, which roughly coincide with the traditional skilled, semi-skilled and unskilled categories, and are paid the appropriate hourly rate. When they are transferred from one job to another they usually remain within the same grade, and the main problem which occurs is the men's reluctance to leave jobs which are better-favoured—either because they are easier and more congenial or because they provide more overtime. For example, on July 30, 1962, 149 workers in Ford's preparation-for-sale department struck because the management moved forty-five men from the department. One of the reasons for the strike was a protest against an alleged 'stretch-out', and another was the reluctance of the men to leave a popular job which provided plentiful overtime. Even so, movements of labour occasioned by automation have been largely effected in Ford without strikes.

Vauxhall, of course, operates a more elaborate time-rate and grading system than Ford. There are six occupational groups for workers directly engaged on production, ten for indirect workers and further groups for stokers, women and boys. Within each group there are up to five grades, and a man's hourly rate depends on his occupational group and his grade. Workers are assigned to occupational groups according to their previous industrial experience and the vacancies available. They start in the lowest grade, and after six months' probation the satisfactory ones are promoted to the next grade; further promotion depends on the judgement of the departmental manager concerned, but everyone has the right to appeal to their department's Grading Appeals Committee. (These bodies consist of three workmen, one of whom is usually a shop steward, and are appointed by senior management.) Like the other firms, Vauxhall moves men between jobs as the work situation demands, but the grouping and grading system acts as a disincentive to casual transfers of labour. Even though all the semi-skilled workers are in one occupational group, when a man is moved to a new job there is still his grade to consider. The firm's practice is to allow him to hold his existing grade for two months during which he must prove he is worthy of it in his new job. Usually he is successful; but the Company must, before moving men, give some thought to their abilities and grades, and to the alternative jobs available, to make sure that transfers are affected without bitterness.

In general, then, direct personal downgrading has rarely been a consequence of recent automation, so this can be ruled out as a source of the car industry's labour troubles. In fact, such technical changes in car manufacture as may have been held to have brought about mass downgrading were largely completed before the War. In the early days of the industry, of course, cars were made by skilled machinists, fitters and coachbuilders. But, with the widespread adoption of flow-line production methods during the 1920s and 1930s, the larger manufacturers—Austin, Ford, Morris, Rootes, Standard and Vauxhall—gradually ceased to employ craftsmen on direct production, and by the end of the 1930s these had almost disappeared from productive operations. The smaller, quality car manufacturers, on the other hand, made a more modest use of flow techniques because of the smaller scale of their operations, and even in the 1950s some 15 per cent of direct production workers at Rover and Jaguar were skilled men (or, at least, were rated and regarded as such). But in both groups of firms, the replacement of craftsmen on direct production work by semi-skilled operators was brought about by the mass-production techniques of the 1930s. Consequently, the subsequent mechanization has had little further effect on the composition of the direct labour force. The introduction of transfer machines, for example, has meant that fewer semi-skilled machine operators are required to produce any output desired; but the machines are still tended by semi-skilled operators.

On the other hand, the adoption of automatic techniques has made a significant contribution to the increase in the ratio of ancillary to direct production workers, which has gathered speed since the War. This it has done in a number of ways. First, because automatic equipment requires fewer operators, the number of direct production workers demanded by any given level of output is reduced. Second, the complex nature of, for example, transfer machines, automatic handling equipment and automatic paint sprayers has increased the need for skilled maintenance and repairmen, whilst toolmakers are also in greater demand. And third, the installation of automatic techniques of production control (together with the increase in the scale of operations with which it is associated) has made it necessary for firms to employ more planning staff. Some idea of the size of these changes can be gained from Vauxhall's experience. Between 1950 and 1960 the ratio of ancillary to direct production workers changed from 40/60 to 60/40, and while its total work force grew by 60 per cent the number of skilled men employed (all on maintenance and repair work) increased by 70 per cent.

On the whole, therefore, recent technological change—unlike

that of the inter-war period—has produced an increase in the proportion of skilled workers, as well as certain other net upgradings. Moreover, one possible effect of automation on skilled work in the car industry—an effect which has already led to labour disputes in the U.S.A.—has not so far been much experienced in this country (indeed, it may well be that the possibility of disputes has itself inhibited the development concerned). Broadly speaking, the craftsmen responsible for maintaining and repairing transfer machines and other types of automatic equipment have adjusted smoothly—or at least, without conflict—to the changes in technique demanded from them. But if British firms follow the example of U.S. Ford or certain French firms, disputes in this area may be hard to avoid. Recently, American motor manufacturers have been arguing that the installation and maintenance of automatic machinery 'requires unusual combinations of skills and some new skills, and such requirements have come into conflict with the established lines of demarcation in some instances'.[1] In fact, U.S. Ford has attempted to establish in several of its plants what is—according to Mr Crossman's account[2]—'a new skilled-trade classification identified as "Automation Equipment Maker and Maintenance", which combines some of the duties of several different skilled trades'. American Ford introduced this grade into one new plant before it was organized by the United Automobile Workers (U.A.W.), and despite objection by the union have succeeded in retaining it. The company has, however, failed to introduce this innovation into any of its old-established plants.

Crossman also considers that the traditional division between mechanic and electrician is becoming a hindrance in servicing some modern equipment. 'For example,' (he says) 'in the unit head used on transfer lines in the motor car industry, the electrical and mechanical parts are closely interlocked, and the craftsman servicing it needs a grasp of both electrical and mechanical practice. Conventional craft-apprenticeship provides a man with one skill or the other but not with both. Apprenticed electricians can be trained in the mechanical side, or vice versa, but for a proper balance a mixed or electro-mechanical training will probably be found essential'.[3] He further suggests that a new trade of servo-technician should also be established to take over the maintenance of all servo-mechanisms from instrument mechanics. It does not take much

---

[1] C. C. Killingsworth, 'Industrial Relations and Automation', in 'Automation', *The Annals of the American Academy of Political and Social Science* (March 1962), p. 73.
[2] E. F. R. W. Crossman, in *Automation and Skill*, H.M.S.O. (London), 1960.
[3] *Op. cit.*

imagination to visualize the difficulties (given the craft organization and training of the British motor industry's skilled maintenance workers) which may arise in implementing such changes; local difficulties between the A.E.U. and E.T.U. have already occurred in Scotland and Coventry on the problem.

(C) PRODUCTION STRESSES, 'EFFORT BARGAINING', AND MANAGEMENT

So far, however, we have largely considered what fairly specific causes of labour conflict the high rate of productivity growth and technological change in the motor industry might have involved. There remains the much broader question of how far technical change may have altered the character of the average operative's work so as—for instance, by increasing strain or reducing 'job satisfaction'—to have created a general background of tension or discontent. Again, the outstanding recent impact of technological change on work content has occurred in the machine shop. In certain other major processes, such as painting, there have also been important changes in job content since the introduction of mass production methods, but assembly work has been scarcely altered by the introduction of the automatic marshalling systems which are the contribution of automation to this part of car manufacturing. The greater use of power tools, power and roller conveyors, and mechanical handling equipment has certainly (to the appreciation of the workers) reduced manual effort, but these developments are hardly comparable with the change in machining.

A report on automation published by the Department of Scientific and Industrial Research contains a number of observations which are relevant to the impact of automatic production methods on operative skills in the car industry. Drawing conclusions from an examination of the introduction of transfer machines, its writers state that '... the job of the machine operator in engineering remains semi-skilled but appears to be more responsible and interesting'.[1] They also consider that in general on automated processes '... there is ... a switch from "motor" or manual elements to "perceptual" and "conceptual" elements in skill, that is to say to the ability to take in information and the ability to organize it or interpret it for action'. The contrast that is being drawn here is between the operator of an automatic lathe who is responsible for loading, unloading, checking the correctness of the cut, the wear on the tools, and the general performance of the machining station; and the man with a mainly monitoring function over a line of a score or so machining

[1] *Automation* (H.M.S.O.) 1956, p. 73.

stations and over the automatic transfer of workpieces between these stations. Clearly, the transfer machine operator, if he has to exert less physical effort, has more to think about, more ground to cover, more points to watch and needs to react more swiftly; moreover, the relative outputs and costs of the equipments at risk mean that he has far more responsibility.

Transfer machine operators, however, receive about a fortnight's training on the job by supervisors and experienced workmen, and are then closely supervised for another two weeks; at the end of this period they are usually sufficiently competent to work under normal supervisory arrangements. In the words of the D.S.I.R. report, '... operators on present day automatic processes need no advanced technical training but they must learn to understand their machines and processes. They may need more skill or less than formerly ... but there is rarely a sharp break with existing skills. The evidence suggests that the new operative skills can be acquired through a moderate degree of training on the job.' After a more detailed examination Crossman reached similar conclusions in 1960, although in his view the methods used by the firms to select and train the men most able to shoulder the added responsibility of transfer line work left something to be desired.[1] However, from our point of view the important consideration is that acquiring competence in these new jobs presents no special difficulty, and contains no suggestion that the work is especially demanding or onerous by comparison with normal machine shop tasks.

It is, moreover, interesting to note that the few surveys which have been carried out of the attitude of operatives to work on automated plant conclude that the majority prefer employment on automatic equipment. An American study of the attitudes of workers moved to transfer lines reports that three-quarters of them preferred their new jobs to their old ones on conventional machines.[2] Their main reason, apparently, was the substantial reduction in handling which went with their new jobs. Our own inquiries reveal a few cases of machinists preferring conventional equipment to transfer machinery of the earlier type, while confirming that in general operatives have welcomed the opportunity to move to automatic equipment. Since their appearance in the 1940s, transfer machines themselves and the layout of transfer lines have both been improved considerably. The early machines needed a great deal of attention; the operator often had to load a workpiece every minute or so as well as inspect the quality of the product and the functioning of his machining

[1] *Op. cit.*
[2] W. A. Faunce 'Automation and the Automobile Worker' in *Social Problems*, Vol. VI, Summer 1958, pp. 68–78.

stations. Moreover the layout of many of these lines did not include automatic linking between all of the machines and men were employed to hand workpieces from one machine to another. On both these jobs the degree of mechanical pacing was greater than in work either on semi-automatic individual machines or on the assembly lines. And, in consequence, there was a considerable amount of dissatisfaction with the new tasks. The major complaint that men at Vauxhall, for example, had against them was that they were unable to regulate their pace of work to obtain periodic rest pauses.[1] But most of the transfer machines now in use were installed between 1955 and 1960 and are a considerable improvement on the early ones. They need less attention and, because they are more reliable, they can be arranged in longer continuously-linked lines. Thus the job of the men operating them is mainly concerned with quality control and looking for mechanical faults; and nowadays there is apparently considerable competition amongst operatives to be selected for this employment.

Modern transfer lines have, in fact, a number of attractions. To begin with, the operators often have more opportunities to work overtime—which are still appreciated in some plants, if not so much in the Midlands—than other machinists because the higher initial cost of their equipment means that it is more intensively worked. They also exercise greater discretion in how they go about their various tasks than is available to the men on conventional plant. Pride in the imposing size of their equipment and in being responsible for its large number of machining stations is another attraction. Furthermore, there is a significant change in the supervisory relationship, from one in which the supervisor tries to induce the operator to maintain a given rate of physical effort to one where the two meet on more equal terms to discuss how a complex and important piece of machinery is working. While physical conditions are usually very much better than in the old machine-shops.

The major drawbacks of work on transfer lines are mental strain and isolation. Both Touraine[2] in France and Faunce[3] in U.S.A. found that this aspect of the work was the one which operators disliked most. Indeed, Faunce found that the 25 per cent of his sample of workers who preferred their old jobs did so for this reason. Touraine says that transfer machine operators feel lonely because

[1] In their book, *Man on the Assembly Line*, C. R. Walker and R. H. Guest, found '... that the mass production characteristic disliked most by a majority of workers in our sample was mechanical pacing'; (Harvard University Press, 1952) p. 175.

[2] A Touraine, *L'Evolution du Travail Ouvrier aux Usines Renaults*, Paris (Centre National de la Recherche Scientifique), 1955.

[3] W. A. Faunce, *loc. sit.*

their only contacts are infrequent ones with technicians and supervisors. In contrast, Crossman points out that on modern lines the operator can leave his post for brief periods to talk to his fellows, so that he is not so seriously isolated as is sometimes supposed, even though he is not in continuous contact with his workmates; and the arrangement of lines is now sometimes more sophisticated in its treatment of the human factor. The other major complaint that operators have against transfer-line work is that their monitoring function places them under considerable strain. They have to move around their machines, patiently alert, watching and waiting for something to go wrong, and they may find this very wearing on their nerves.

Even so, on balance it seems that operators find work on transfer lines gives more satisfaction than the work on conventional machines that most of them have done before. But this enhanced satisfaction—and since the introduction of transfer machines is the extreme example of recent trends in the car operative's work content, it must represent an enhanced average satisfaction—can hardly be associated with the car workers' increased post-war willingness to strike. May Smith argued that '... the worker on repetitive processes may be repeating a very limited number of movements, but his emotional life may be quite varied; he has to adjust to supervisors, to equals, to subordinates; if he fails to please the first he may find sympathy and support from the others; ... when such situations arise—and they are not rare—the focus of interest would go from the monotony of the work to the emotion aroused'.[1] And pursuing this, one would expect to find that the more repetitive, monotonous and dissatisfying the job the greater the dispute-proneness of the workers affected. But this relationship does not, it appears, hold true for the car industry, at least. And apart from the machinists' case, one might add that some strike-prone occupational groups (such as the internal transport drivers) lead quiet varied working lives.

By itself, then, it does not seem that the increasing mechanization of production processes can be held significantly liable for the British car industry's recent dispute-proneness. But a development which it has both facilitated and in one sense demanded could have played a more direct role in that tendency. This is the increased managerial control over the arrangement and intensity of work, by techniques which have themselves made a perceptible contribution to the industry's high productivity growth. Both the American-owned firms base their task allocations on elaborate and refined systems of 'work measurement', and similar techniques are widely applied by

[1] May Smith, Industrial Fatigue Research Board, *Fourth Annual Report*, 1924, p. 26.

the British firms. Time study is, of course, extensively used as a basis for piece-rate fixing, and more sophisticated forms of work study and job analysis are also applied in the 'federated' plants to a degree which varies with the capital intensity of individual firms and (inversely) with some traditional local resistances which have not fully dissolved. The manufacturers apparently considered these sufficiently important for acceptance of work study to be urged by their Joint Statement with the national unions of April 1961,[1] though union official policy everywhere advocates it, instruction on work study methods is a usual ingredient of shop stewards' training courses, and we have ourselves found no disputes in the post-war records which arose from opposition to work-study (or even the use of the stop-watch) as such.

Under the less mechanized and integrated production systems, however, these superficially scientific methods of labour measurement still allow considerable room for shop-floor negotiation: the 'allowances' to be added to the 'elements' of which particular operations are composed, the 'effort-rating' of the workers studied, and even the 'elements' themselves, may all be adjusted to make a specified work-load acceptable. The mechanization of handling, however, combined particularly with the use of automatic data processing and other control devices, has very much reduced the margin of managerial uncertainty in work-load assessment—and thus also reduced the area within which the 'effort bargaining' which is a major function of union workplace organization can operate. At the same time, the high capital costs of the new equipments puts a considerable pressure on management to work it as intensively as possible, so that its own front in such bargaining is likely to be stiffened.

In the piece-work firms, of course, the 'effort bargaining' is more implicit, since the agreement of higher earnings in price negotiation usually avoids a direct confrontation on the problem; though it is possible that increasing managerial awareness of the disturbing consequences for internal wage-structures that rate-fixing miscalculations may have given the high productivity potentials of new equipments is a background factor in the very large contribution of wage-structure disputes to the increased strike-frequency since the mid-1950s. But in British Ford—the only company which formally maintains an insistence that work-loads are beyond the reach of negotiation—conflict over them appears to have been recurrent. In practice, the company's attitude seems to have been perceptibly compromised by informal understandings at the workplace level, but fluctuations in the degree of tolerance which higher management extends to such arrangements also seem to have played a large part

[1] Summarized in Chapter I.

in its intermittently-disturbed labour relations.

Another effect of recent technological progress which may have produced some strain in management-labour relations is the increased demands it involves on management itself. The introduction of automation in particular has presented managements with a number of problems. The main ones stem from increases in the technical complexity of production, in technical integration and in capitalization. As the authors of the D.S.I.R. report comment, '... these trends result from any kind of mechanization, but they are strikingly intensified by automation. They increase the responsibility of management by requiring a heavy investment of capital and a high rate of output, and by making plants more flexible in terms of what can be produced. They increase, in fact, the need for planning and control of a very high order.'[1] Management must '... maintain a high output by devising suitable programmes of operation and changing them when necessary. Three organizational tasks are essential; to overcome the technical inflexibility that occurs in automatic plants ... where processes and machines are linked together; to find an adequate system for the maintenance of automatic equipment; and to arrange, where appropriate, that automatic processes run continuously.'

Increased technical integration raises one of the most difficult problems managements have to face. In a modern car plant an interruption of the flow of any one of a host of components may soon bring production to a halt. And on a transfer line a failure of one of the twenty or so stations will stop the whole line. Thus, because of the weight of capital investment involved in such processes, managers must try their utmost to avoid breakdowns and minimize their effect. A number of methods are commonly employed: stocks of key components are maintained; spare machines are kept; transfer lines are not allowed to grow too long; cutting tools are watched for wear; and careful thought is given to preventive maintenance. This managerial concern about 'down-time' has an impact on the men in that they too feel under constant pressure to avoid breakdowns.[2] The men we spoke to consider that this built up mental fatigue and added to tension. We are, of course, not able to measure this factor, nor were we able to trace its influence on dispute-liability but if operators and managers are working under such a stress then problems which might otherwise be settled easily could possibly lead to strikes.

One way of reducing pressure on the work-force is to employ more (and better) managers so that the other methods of avoiding inter-

[1] *Op. cit.*, p. 55.
[2] Cf. Faunce, *loc. sit.*, p. 63.

ruptions to the flow of production can be exploited more effectively. Indeed, the authors of the D.S.I.R. report thought that '... it is reasonably certain that the ratio of managers, supervisors and technicians to operatives will be greater in automatic than in non-automatic plants, because processes will be more complex technically and managerial control will have to be stricter. This trend already exists and evidence of it, though fragmentary, is consistent. For example, at the Ford engine plant in Cleveland, Ohio, where automation has been pretty extensively applied, there is one foreman to eighteen operatives; at the Detroit plant, where less modern techniques are used, the ratio is one in thirty-one.'[1] But this does not seem to have happened so strikingly in the British car industry where there were only modest increases in the proportion of administrative, technical and clerical workers employed in the motor firms between 1948 and 1958. This is the last date at which data is currently available from the Censuses of Production, but the decade was also that in which productivity was rising fastest. More recent data available from Ministry of Labour and other sources is not quite comparable, but does not suggest the 'A.T.C. ratio' to have risen by more than 1 per cent to 2 per cent since the last date in the following table:

Table III/2—CHANGES IN THE PROPORTION OF ADMINISTRATIVE, TECHNICAL AND CLERICAL EMPLOYEES IN THE MOTOR INDUSTRY, 1924-58

Employment* (000s)

Year	Total	A.T.C.	Per cent A.T.C.
1924	169	21	12.5
1930	195	27	14.0
1935	217	27	13.2
1948	316	51	16.1
1950	354	57	16.1
1954†	307	54	17.7
1958†	335	64	19.2

Source: Census of Production.
 * Based on average employment.
 † Excludes motor cycles and cycles.

The ratio of 'staff' employees to operatives does not respond conclusively to the introduction of mass production in the late 1920s, but does show an accelerated rise after 1950 which is presumably in part an effect of automation. But between 1948 and 1958 the proportion of administrative, technical and clerical employees in manufacturing

[1] *Op. cit.*, p. 66.

industry as a whole increased from 16.0 per cent to 21.2 per cent, and is still (see our Table I/3) notably above that in the motor sector. And yet the use of automatic techniques has undoubtedly been more extensive in the car industry; while a large proportion of the increase in its 'A.T.C. ratio' after 1950 must be due to the consequent rise in its employment of technicians and planners. Does this mean that the car firms have been penny-pinching on their managerial services? This is not a question which can be answered by any objective data available, and the connection between the 'A.T.C. ratio' of particular firms and their respective states of labour relations is one on which the evidence is ambiguous, anyway—we have more to say on this in Chapter VI. But there are at least suggestions that the combination of rapid output and capacity growth with frequent technical and other changes has imposed severe strains on the industry's managerial and supervisory cadres—as well as that even its most technically-skilled production managers are often not so well equipped or provided to deal with the human issues these things repeatedly thrust upon them.[1] Some of the piece-work plants, in particular, may well have allowed their payment system—and the insistences of the productive process itself—to assume an unduly large part of the supervisory function.

It might, incidentally, be thought that the increasing technical integration of car manufacturing would itself have implications for the character of labour disputes. Over 15,000 parts go into the average car; and, unless stocks are kept, the failure of many of these parts to arrive at the right place at the right time will eventually bring the whole manufacturing process to a halt. Moreover, because of the expense, reserves are not normally kept for more than a few days. This means that any action which holds up production any-

[1] We quote, on this, comments received from two of the industry's very experienced and senior technologists. On the difficulties of finding a satisfactory basis for the payment system: '... the real problem is to produce the management strength and management services which are capable of maintaining continuity in the supply of material to the track sides and of ensuring that standards are maintained and methods are sound. I think the one great need of the industry now is to introduce more brains and better disciplines into the management teams. We have too much practical shop floor experience and too few people who can grasp the essentials of management accounting or control systems. Very few works managers or workshop superintendents are equipped with anything more than an apprenticeship and practical experience of workshop problems associated with batch production.' And on the general problems of adjustment to frequent changes: '... the points ... regarding the excessive load placed on departmental managers and supervisors are most important. ... It is also true that many good technical shop managers, who will cheerfully work excessively long hours to solve a manufacturing problem, find it much less to their liking to spend much precious time in explaining forward intentions and policies to disbelieving shop stewards.'

where in the process will sooner or later have far-reaching effects, and apparently places a potent weapon in the hands of strikers. It is curious, in view of this, that there has been no observable long-run tendency for strikes to involve more people. The average number of workers reported as directly and indirectly involved[1] in individual strikes in car firms in the pre-war decade was 1,200; in the three years 1946–48 it was 1,250: but this was also about the figure for the years 1961–63. The average involvement in strikes rose somewhat in some intervening years, but this was evidently associated with occasional trade depression or the circumstances of particular big disputes. Apparently the degree of technical integration has been a comparatively minor influence on the extent of the stoppages caused by motor industry disputes, and this may be largely due to the precautions manufacturers have taken—by establishing alternative suppliers and parallel processes, for instance—to reduce the effect of interruptions to production in general.

(D) WAGE PROBLEMS, AND A CONCLUSION

That, however, is by the way. We can now turn from the rather speculative considerations which preceded that interjection to examine some more concrete effects of technological change. The adoption of automatic techniques has certainly raised a number of wage problems in the car industry. For instance, it has accentuated the pressures the piece-work firms have found to arise from the tendency of the earnings of direct labour to outstrip those of ancillary workers. The consequent gaps in relative wages have been a recurrent cause of disputes, and by increasing the proportion of ancillary workers and thus swelling the ranks of those liable to feel disadvantaged by such effects, automation must have made matters worse. Or again, because labour costs per unit are radically reduced on highly mechanized processes, there is a temptation for firms to buy acceptance of change by the operatives affected. This is certainly not an unreasonable way of obtaining the workers' goodwill, but the risk is that unless the firm is very careful indeed, this will build illogicalities into its wages-structure which may later become a source of conflict.

The wage-structures and systems operative in the car firms are, as we have already shown, a major cause of disputes. And we shall again have something to say on them at length in our chapter on

---

[1] For reasons given in Chapter II, we do not think too much significance can be attached to the distinction in official statistics between workers directly and indirectly involved in disputes, at least so far as the motor industry is concerned. But in any event, no long-term trend in this ratio emerges from the data.

wage-questions. For the moment, however, we can note that the major overt difficulties created by re-equipment and technological change have arisen in this area of labour relations. And the central problem appears to be that of finding a wage system appropriate to highly mechanized—but far from fully automated—technology. Except for Ford, car firms on both sides of the Atlantic traditionally used some form of payment-by-results scheme—frequently one based on the output of the individual worker—in the belief that such incentives maximize effort. But since the general effect of increased mechanization—and especially of automation—is apparently to transfer control over the rate of output from the workers to the management, this reason for incentive payment seems correspondingly weakened.[1] Furthermore, technical changes are seldom introduced at the same rate for all the different processes within a large plant (or at each of a firm's plants), nor need they have a similar impact on output. So that, in firms where payment is by results, even if great care is exercised in the initial negotiation of piece-rates when new techniques are introduced, earnings on similar jobs may well *increase* at different rates—with distorting effects on the wages-structure. In the U.S.A. all the larger car firms have now abandoned incentive schemes, and though the earlier moves in this direction (such as Ford's adoption of time-rates) were determined by the managements' desire to reserve the allocation of rising productivity's rewards to their own discretion, this cannot be said of more recent arrangements: the U.A.W., for instance, is also opposed to piece-work.

The British car firms have produced several attempts to escape from the problems created by traditional piece-work systems. British Ford, of course, has always insisted on time-rates and its present very simple structure of three wage-grades for men and one for women has already been referred to. In 1948, after two years of negotiation with its shop stewards, Standard (which was at that time not affiliated to the engineering employers' federation) introduced its so-called 'large gang' system under an agreement with the Coventry C.S.E.U. District Committee. The essentials of the Standard scheme were the division of its manual labour force into a few very large gangs of workers, and the provision of production bonuses payable to each gang in proportion to fulfilment of its estimated output, and to be shared amongst its members; output bonuses were also devised for those operatives who could not be included in gangs. At the same time there was a drastic reduction in the number of payment grades;

[1] This argument has been widely presented. See, for instance, the D.S.I.R. Report, p. 78, Killingworth (*loc. cit.*) p. 77, Crossman (*op. cit.*), p. 55, and the I.L.O., *Automation* (Geneva, 1957), p. 72.

while all production workers were upgraded into the skilled category.[1]

The management hoped that the new system would make it easier to introduce new production methods—partly by eliminating the difficulties of individual piece-rate revision—and would stimulate the work-people in each gang to pull together and to protect their earnings by co-operating to prevent losses in production. An American student, Melman, argues that the system fulfilled management's initial hopes, but so many other factors were involved that it is very difficult to judge its success. In particular, it was accompanied by a high-wage policy which, between 1949 and 1956, pushed average earnings at Standard substantially above the average for the industry.

This position of 'wage leadership' became increasingly embarrassing to the company in the late 1950s. And after the climactic events of 1956 at Standard's, Mr Alec Dick, who had recently been appointed Managing Director, argued that by their strike the men had broken their agreement with the company and that it was free to rejoin the employers' federation. In the context, this involved a revision of the company's bonus payments (to which the federation had objected) and there was a reversion to a much more dispersed system of small-group output bonuses for production operatives and so-called 'lieu' bonuses for indirect workers. It is perhaps interesting that while the 'large gang' system was in operation there were few strikes at Standard's (beyond a fair-sized one in 1954 against the dismissal of some shop stewards) before the large redundancy strike of 1956, and that the frequency of stoppages at the company has since risen somewhat. However, S.T.I.'s recent strike-liability is still quite modest, and several of its post-1956 disputes were confined to white-collar employees. And in any case, its previously low dispute-liability does not necessarily demonstrate the 'large gang' system's efficiency in avoiding the wage difficulties which spring from technical change; the company may simply have been buying industrial peace with its high-wage policy. It was certainly said at the time that the 1949 arrangements involved in large measure the management's abdication from control of shop-floor working arrangements in favour of the shop stewards.

From the late 1920s (when it was taken over by General Motors) until 1956, Vauxhall also operated a group payment-by-results scheme. The management found that the system worked well where the operators controlled their own working speed, but during the early 1950s it became concerned about the impact on its wage-

[1] For a detailed description see S. Melman, *Decision-Making and Productivity* (Blackwell, 1958).

structure of the adoption of automatic equipment which made jobs machine-paced. Since operators would thus be deprived of the possibility of earning bonuses for exceeding output norms, the firm was sure that the outcome would be an overwhelming pressure for 'lieu' bonuses in compensation, which it feared would import anomalies into the plant wage-structure.[1] Accordingly, the management decided to change to straight time-rates, before a large new plant was opened in 1957. Several months were spent discussing its proposals with the shop stewards and district officers of the A.E.U. and N.U.V.B.—the management emphasizing that time-rates would cut out losses of earnings due to breakdowns and the like, and would bring a new element of stability into the workers' incomes. Eventually the hourly time-rate was set at a point two-thirds of the way up the range of current hourly piece-work earnings for each main occupational group, and the operating times required to achieve such a wage were taken as standard times. At the same time the grading scheme already sketched was introduced, the object of this being not merely to satisfy the desire for traditional job differentials to be maintained, but to provide a 'ladder' within each occupational group up which the operative can (and normally does) advance, thus providing some reward to competence and application.

Most experiments with new wage-systems have thus been conducted in non-federated plants. However, federated firms have experimented with wage-systems in their new Scottish plants which depart from those they operate in the Midlands. Pressed Steel, for instance, adopted a variant of the 'Scanlon Plan', under which workers are paid time-rates plus a bonus based on the plant's savings on estimated production cost during any period. This 'Linwood Scheme' was later held to have contributed to the round of disputes at Pressed Steel's Scottish plant in 1965, when the plant bonus (which was largely determined by current sales) fell sharply following a fall in Rootes' demand for bodies: though it is also said that there were even more disputes under the former piece-work system. At any rate, the scheme is currently under revision—reportedly to a more normal arrangement of bonuses paid on production by department, but with very large departmental groupings, rather like S.T.I.'s former 'big gangs'.[2] But both Rootes and B.M.C. also started their new plants on novel systems. In the B.M.C. case, at least, these took the form of 'work-measured day-wages', in which different time-wages are set for different levels of output up to that which is estimated to

[1] Sir Reginald Pearson, 'From Group Bonus to Straight Time Pay', *Journal of Industrial Economics*, March 1960.
[2] This plant's subsequent acquisition by Rootes may, of course, involve further changes in wage-arrangements.

represent full proficiency. And Rootes, too, used a variant of the 'Scanlon' Plan. In both firms, however, base-rates are supplemented by what are effectively individual 'merit-rates' (though neither of them use that term, because of some traditional suspicion amongst engineering operatives of the merit-rating system).

It has, of course, been questioned whether any system of payment-by-results is appropriate to an industry where the pace of work is so much mechanically determined as in the car plants, and where automation is so advanced. But if the target speed of equipment is technically or managerially determined, it is still substantially conditioned by the capacity of the plant's human attendants, and their effort or attention may still determine whether or not the target is reached. Absence of a positive earnings incentive may involve high supervisory costs; even with the modified day-wages in Rootes' Linwood plant, the ratio of supervisors to operatives had to be three times as high as in its Coventry works, which are on more traditional piece-rate systems. And the American-owned firms themselves still retain some 'incentive' element in their pay system; apart from Vauxhall's grading system, both Ford and Vauxhall have a 'merit-rating' payment which may (and probably does in most cases) add a few pence to their operatives' hourly wages, and Vauxhall has a profit-sharing scheme which distributes £500,000 or so annually. And piece-work is not totally without advantages to the worker.

Moreover, a simple time-rate system, even if supplemented by a grading and merit-payment scheme, makes it difficult to discriminate at all finely between the responsibilities or capacities involved in the different jobs men of a particular occupational group are expected to tackle. (For example, on transfer lines designed to machine large workpieces—like cylinder blocks—the rough boring and drilling is carried out under one operator and the finishing work is carried out under another operator on the second half of the line. The first man's job is much easier than the second's, but at both Vauxhall and Ford the men are in the same grade and paid the same rate; this has been a source of dissatisfaction for some time in these firms.) So that at time of writing Ford has secured union agreement to a review of its hitherto exceedingly simple wage-structure. And if a time-work system avoids the problems of settling detailed individual piece-rates it may imply an almost equal area of conflict in the setting of detailed work-loads. Indeed, the customary earnings differential between piece-worker and time-worker also generally implies a parallel effort differential, and the existence of this might well raise an obstacle to the conversion of existing payment systems to a time basis. At any rate, these experiments seem far from having produced a perfect payment system for car production.

Productivity Growth and Technical Change

These problems of wage-policy are not, of course, exclusively identified with technological change, though they reach a particular acuteness where techniques approaching automation are concerned. They are, rather, connected with the car industry's high rate of change in general—since all changes, in the piece-work firms at least, involve problems of wage-adjustment—and particularly with a high rate of productivity growth (to which the rapid rise in demand for cars and the consequent economies of scale have contributed, as well as technical progress). However, one final problem of labour relations which is associated with car industry mechanization can be reported. We mentioned earlier that one of the attractions of transfer machines to operators is the opportunity they offer for additional overtime work. But the high capitalization involved in such machines frequently calls for more intensive working than overtime can provide and from the 1950s on there has been a growing demand by management that operatives accept three-shift working. This seems to have been universally unpopular with car workers and, together with the associated question of night work, has been the principal cause of such strikes as have occurred since the War over hours of work. The workers claim that three-shift working is psychologically and physiologically unnatural and socially upsetting. Generally, it is only in communities where such working arrangements have been in existence for many years—like those of steel and chemical workers on continuous processes—that they are readily accepted. But continuous working of this kind involves a stability and continuity of demand and activity which the car firms have so far been unable to achieve.

However, the main fears that the car firm's progress towards automation at first engendered—that this would lead to widespread redundancy, job dislocation, or downgrading of labour—have clearly not been realized. These fears were partly based on overestimates of the extent to which the car industry could utilize automatic techniques, and underestimates of the potential growth in demand for cars. They also somewhat misjudged the effect of mechanization on skills, and failed to reckon that the economic importance of the new technology would lead managements to make considerable efforts to secure their workers' acceptance of the changes it involved. They particularly overlooked the experience in handling changes at the workshop level which managements and men have gained from having to deal with the stream of major and minor alterations to their products which the car firms have always made to attract buyers.

On the other hand, technological change has certainly complicated the wage-structure problems which bulk so large in the motor industry's dispute-causation, and has produced one specific (if minor) cause of conflict in the pressure it creates for extended shift working. It may well have intensified the 'effort bargaining' process which is in the background to so many car firm disputes—and led to particular tension in Ford, where that process is formally (if not always consistently) rejected by the management. Otherwise, we are left with a number of intangibles. Progress towards automation has probably not increased the monotony of work or reduced job-satisfaction, and it has certainly lightened the physical burdens of employment in the car industry. But it may have intensified the mental strains involved— either directly, by the increased concentration and responsibility demanded of operatives on certain new equipments, or indirectly, through the growing pressure on managements arising from the more elaborate integration of processes. And it has probably contributed to the general sense of insecurity which many in the industry think an important background factor in its recent dispute-proneness. But against these things, the industry's rapid rate of productivity growth has clearly permitted it to maintain a high-wage position which might be thought somewhat to compensate for these possible sources of discontent. At the least, automation cannot be a central factor in the car firms' labour troubles.

APPENDIX

OUTPUT, EMPLOYMENT AND PRODUCTIVITY INDICES FOR MOTOR VEHICLES, 1948-64

	Output		Employment			Productivity			Cars and commercial vehicles, indices [Census of production]	
	Cars and all commercial vehicles		Motor vehicles* (1948 and 1958) S.I.C.s		Cars and commercial vehicles (output per man)		Motor vehicle manufacturing [K. S. Lomax's indices]			
	000s	Index	000s	Index	Vehicles per man	Index	Output per man	Output per man-hour	Vehicles per man	Value added per man
1948	512	49	279	89	1.8	55	—	—	—	—
1949	630	61	292	94	2.2	67	—	—	—	—
1950	785	76	300	96	2.6	79	—	—	—	—
1951	735	71	302	97	2.4	73	—	—	—	—
1952	690	66	305	98	2.3	70	—	—	—	—
1953	835	80	298	96	2.8	85	—	—	—	—
1954	1,039	100	312	100	3.3	100	100	100	100	100
1955	1,238	119	331	106	3.7	112	108	108	—	—
1956	1,006	97	329	105	3.1	94	98	102	—	—
1957	1,151	111	311	100	3.7	112	113	115	—	—
1958	1,364	131	319	102	4.3	130	121	125	121	126
1959	1,560	150 / 100	330 / 385	106 / 100	4.7 / 4.1	142 / 100	134 / 100	133 / 100	—	—
1960	1,811	116	437	114	4.1	102	101	109	—	—
1961	1,464	94	415	108	3.5	87	99	109	—	—
1962	1,675	107	430	112	3.9	96	—	(114)†	—	—
1963	2,012	129	453	118	4.4	109	—	(124)	—	—
1964	2,333	149	482	125	4.8	119	—	(128)	—	—

Sources: Output, employment, etc., Ministry of Labour, Board of Trade and Society of Motor Manufacturers and Traders. Productivity calculations for cars and commercial vehicles, from a combination of this data (motor-cycles being excluded because, without proper weighting, they would distort the trend unduly).
Professor Lomax's indices, quarterly in *The Guardian*.

Notes: 1954 and 1959 are taken as base years (100) to facilitate comparison with Professor Lomax's Productivity Index, and to fit changes in the employment classification.
* Up to 1959 motor-cycle and cycle workers are included; after 1959, by a change in the Standard Industrial Classification, these are excluded and workers employed in a number of component and accessory trades are included for the first time.
† Linked with revised index as from 1961.

CHAPTER IV

STRIKES AND THE LEVEL OF ACTIVITY

(A) OUTPUT FLUCTUATIONS AND DISPUTES

In this Chapter we discuss the connexion between the car industry's strike-liability and the fluctuations in its output—both cyclical and seasonal.[1] For all countries for which statistics exist, strikes in general can be shown to be in some measure sensitive both to the trade cycle and to seasonal variations in economic activity.[2] This sensitivity may be demonstrated in different ways: various measures of strike-liability may be plotted against one or more of several measures of economic activity, such as prices, cost-of-living indices, wage-rates, employment and production. Choice of series for correlation depends on the purpose of the exercise, but in general the limitations of this kind of analysis of strike lies in the heavy effect of influences which cannot be gauged statistically. How does one measure a political climate, or the quality of union leadership, for example? But despite the masking effect of such influences, the sensitivity of strikes to the general level of economic activity remains observable.

In particular, broad comparison of strike movements on an international basis, as well as those treating more limited localities, show a tendency for the number of strikes to be very sensitive to changes in economic activity. The frequency of strikes increases in boom years and in seasonal periods of high activity, and conversely, falls off in slumps or quiet periods (in winter, for many industries). The rationale of this direct relationship is that in boom years and high production periods, workers are readier to strike spontaneously and employers are equally more willing to make concessions. Workers are earning more and fear unemployment less, whilst employers

---

[1] In part, this chapter revises, brings up-to-date and extends a paper by H. A. Turner and J. Bescoby in the *Bulletin of the Oxford University Institute of Statistics*, May 1961.

[2] See discussion by K. G. J. C. Knowles, *Strikes*, pp. 145–160.

are optimistic about recovering increases in costs when faced with buoyant markets. In slumps and quiet periods, on the other hand, strikes occur only against what workers may regard as attacks on their basic standards, so that they naturally tend to be fewer.

The number of workers involved in strikes is sometimes taken as an indication of the extent of labour militancy, but the relationship between this measure and the level of economic activity is in general little more than haphazard. For the number of workers involved is heavily influenced both by the attitudes of trade union leaders in particular disputes and by the kind of jobs done by the actual strikers—which affects the numbers of those laid-off work in consequence. The other common measure of strike-liability, namely striker-days, is held to reveal also something of the stubbornness or persistence of strikers. But when comparing international, or even composite national statistics, there seems to be no consistent relation between this measure and most indices of economic activity.[1] This is again scarcely surprising, because the size and length of strikes depends very largely not only on the kind of issues involved and on the strategy and resources of trade unions, but also on the attitudes of employers—not to speak of the pressures brought to bear on both parties by 'outsiders' in particular situations. Which is not to say that trends in either workers involved or striker-days are not subject to plausible explanation when dealing with more limited coverage and more specific circumstances. And what the general failure of these trends to reflect economic movements does imply is that in depressions strikes (perhaps just because they are more likely to be concerned with the defence of basic standards) tend also to be more massive and obdurate, thus offsetting the decline in strike-frequency.

In the case of the car firms, the clearest single measure of the level of economic activity is production. Shop-floor activity is quite immediately and unambiguously connected with demand, for the stock-piling of motorcars is limited by reason of their high costs, their relative perishability, and their sheer requirements of space. And a distinguishing feature of the car industry's general history has been that its rapid expansion of output has been interrupted by regular and often violent fluctuations. Thus, the annual production

---

[1] H. A. Clegg and Rex Adams have shown, in *The Employers' Challenge* (Blackwell, Oxford 1959), that in Britain there appears an inverse historical association between the strike-incidence and retail price-movements, the annual total of striker-days increasing, on average, when prices were falling. However, this phenomenon seems of little relevance to a period like that since 1939 when prices have risen continuously. Moreover, no such association appears for the number of workers involved in disputes; the implication being that strikes last longer when prices are declining. Which may reflect the attitudes of employers more than that of workers.

of cars and light vans in Britain fell by nearly a quarter of a million units between 1955 and 1956—that is, by more than one-fifth of the 1955 total. Production during 1961 fell by a similar proportion of the previous year's total, and in this instance the change in the industry's fortunes was even sharper than the figure suggests, as boom and slump both featured in 1960s record: production in the first quarter of 1961 was only 63 per cent of what it had been in the first quarter of 1960. On the other hand, the British industry suffered less than others during the depression of the early 1930s. Whereas the output of motor vehicles (cars and commercial vehicles) fell in America and Germany by about three-quarters between 1929 and 1932, and in France by about a third, production in the United Kingdom fell by less than one-sixth. In Britain, non-seasonal fluctuations in car production have been felt mainly in the post-war period.

It would be out of place to attempt here to account in detail for cycles in the car industry's output: for our purpose the booms and slumps are taken as data. But some of the major factors which have influenced the post-war pattern of British production may be briefly mentioned. The role of export markets is particularly important. In the immediate post-war years the British industry was the only one in a position to resume production quickly which did not also demand scarce dollars for its products, and the government allocation of sheet steel (then in short supply, too) was also used as a lever to raise the level of car exports. Large overseas markets were built up for British cars—particularly in Commonwealth countries. Some of these countries later began to develop motor industries of their own, and tariff and other restrictions on imports combined with the re-appearance of competition from other countries to make these markets unreliable. While the fickleness of the American market was an important factor in the 1960 slump. At home, fiscal policy has had sharp effects on the demand for cars, through changes in credit policy, hire purchase regulations and the level of purchase tax. Hire purchase minimum deposits were raised and credit tightened in 1955 and 1956, with important effects on the car industry (though the consequences of the Suez affair were also important in the recession). And it was the reduction of purchase tax on cars at the end of 1962 which was mainly responsible for masking the effects of seasonal factors during the succeeding two years.

However, the seasonal fluctuations in production, which seem to have been very severe before the war, were to some extent attenuated in the 1950s by the development of export markets where climatic effects on demand were either unimportant or reversed (as in Australia) and by the concentration of 'fleet' and other non-personal purchases of cars in winter months. The British climate, apart from aggravating the problems of storage or stockpiling, nevertheless imposes a marked surge in home demand in the spring and early summer, and a corresponding falling off during the winter. That sturdily reiterative British institution, the October Motor Show, originated as an avowed attempt to iron out these climatic effects, and it is still the manufacturers' general practice to introduce basically new models to the public at the Show, in the hope that 'one-upmanship' will induce many purchasers to advance their orders forward from the spring to the winter months. The partial re-orientation of the British firms' export drive towards Europe, the recently increasing relative importance of the home market, and the growing absolute share of personal buyers in that market, are all likely to make seasonal fluctuations in output more important in future.

But the continuing and underlying source of instability in the car firms' market is probably the character of basic consumer demand.[1] This is really not for new cars but for vehicle ownership: a large number of those who become car owners for the first time do so by buying second-hand cars. The demand for new cars is thus largely a replacement demand, which—apart from complicating the lives of forecasters—implies a special sensitivity to the general economic climate, because purchases can be easily deferred. In the long run the level of consumer income would seem to be the most important single factor affecting the demand for cars, whether new or second-hand. But if this demand rises (as it does) disproportionately to increases in average real income, it is also likely to be disproportionately responsive to such short-term influences as anticipated price changes, the incipience of new models, or the general availability of money. As with other commodities with a relatively long production period, but whose purchase is readily postponed, these things may combine to produce a regular cycle in demand and output.

Even the most cursory examination suggests some connection between strikes in the motor industry and the output of vehicles. Of course, the trends of strike-liability and production in the car firms rise together, but we have already concluded the possible inference, that increasing industrial unrest arises from the strains of increasing output, to be misleading. In fact, the main peculiarity of the pattern lies in its fluctuations. Diagrams IV/1 and IV/2 show the annual totals of strikes and striker-days plotted against production. Together, the diagrams cover the period from 1921 to 1964, omitting only the war years (for which there is no comparable measure of output). Production figures are taken from returns made by the firms to the Board of Trade, and the strike data is compiled

[1] On the demand for vehicles, see Maxcy and Silberston, *op. cit.*, Chapter III.

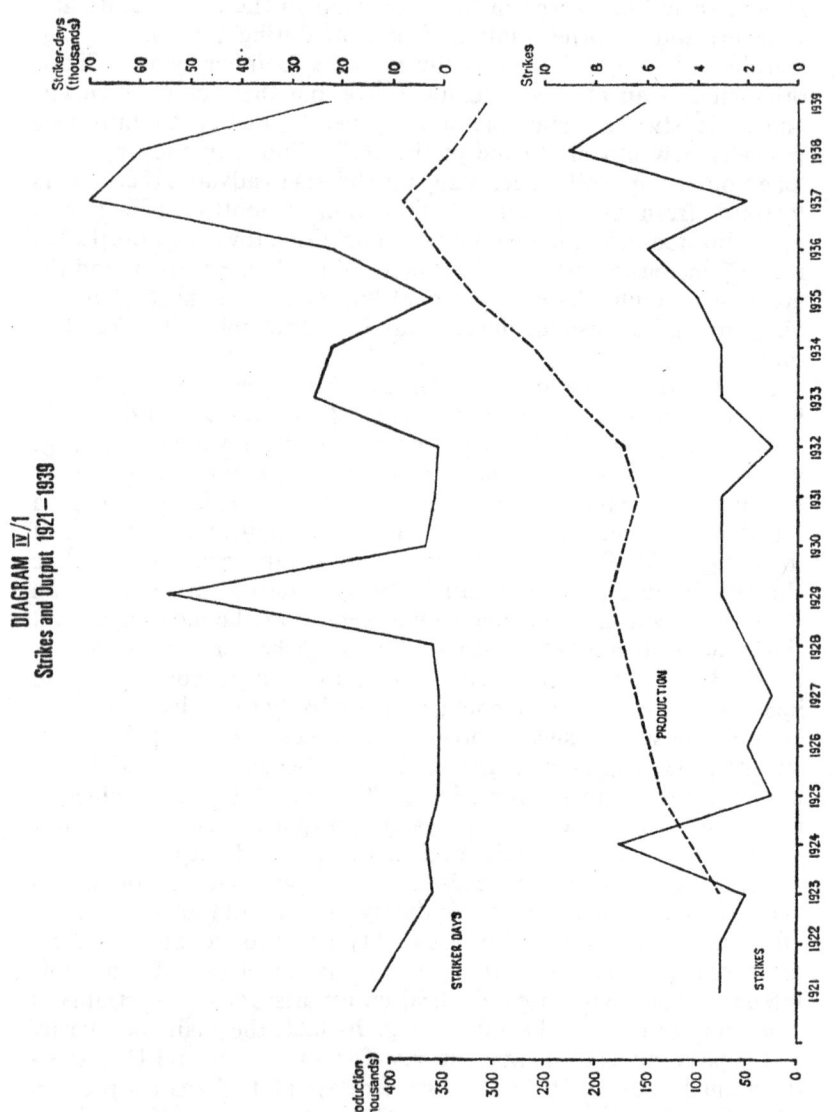

DIAGRAM IV/1
Strikes and Output 1921–1939

Strikes and the Level of Activity

as described in Chapter II. (The 'production' line for the pre-war years shows the output of passenger cars only, as there is no way of separating out light vans—made almost exclusively by the car firms—from total commercial vehicle output until after the War. This presents no real problems, as the graph of total light motor production would closely follow that of passenger cars.)

Taking first the pre-war years, for more than three-quarters of the period reported strikes numbered fewer than four a year: under these circumstances there is little significance to be attached to variations in this measure. Overall, of course, the frequency of strikes increases with the trend of output, but it would be remarkable if this did not appear to be the case in an industry at such an early stage of its growth curve. Striker-days remain at a low and steady level through most of the 1920s, but the shape of the curve is dominated from 1929 onwards by individual sizeable stoppages. For example, strikes at Austin accounted for the 'peaks' of 1929 and 1938, whilst the 1937 total is due almost entirely to one strike at Rolls-Royce. The hump in 1933 and 1934 is also the result of two strikes—at Ford and Pressed Steel, respectively. Moreover, the curve takes no account of such effects as general 'outside' stoppages—particularly the engineering lockout of 1922 and the General Strike—may have had on motor firms.

However, Diagram IV/1 does show interesting features. Although no regular annual production totals are available before 1929, the expansion of output seems to have been almost continuous—at least, the effect of the 1929-31 depression appears very slight. Expansion was particularly rapid for the years from 1932 to 1937. And the downturn of production from 1938 onwards is almost certainly not attributable to any substantial downturn of activity (in contrast with a fairly sharp recession in the American industry in this year). For by 1938, many of the British car workers were engaged on aircraft manufacture under re-armament policy: workers in six of the nine car firm strikes of 1938 were recorded as being so employed. Nor do the issues they were striking over in 1938 and 1939 indicate a decline in economic activity. There were strikes against time-study, against the employment of non-union labour, against overtime working and disciplinary action by managements, as well as over the perennial piece-work price problems—all suggesting the frictions arising from a redirection of, and emphasis upon, output.

In Diagram IV/2—for the post-war period—production is now measured by the combined annual outputs of passenger cars and light vans.[1] The 'production' line shows immediately the rapid

[1] In 1963, commercial vehicles were statistically reclassified by gross weight rather than as previously by carrying capacity. This is the reason for the 'produc-

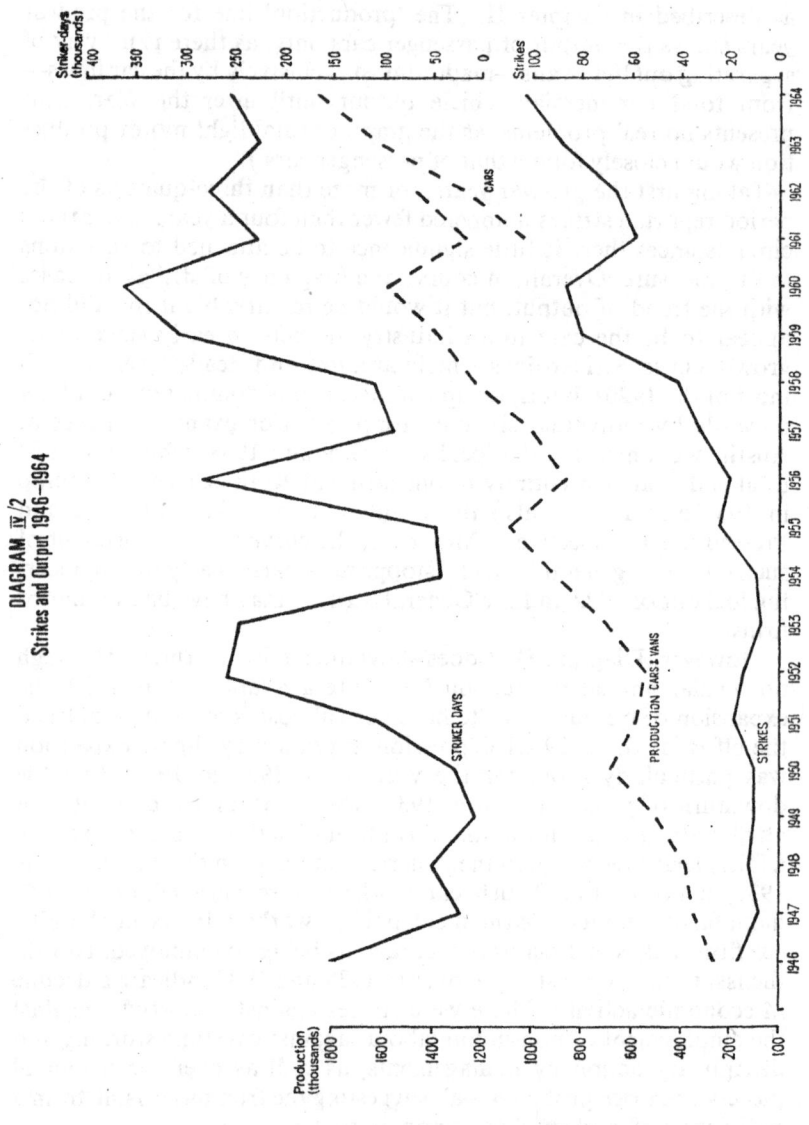

tion' line's discontinuity about this point: its latter part is for passenger cars only. The strike-trends, as in other Diagrams in this chapter, exclude general engineering stoppages.

conversion to peace-time production: output more than doubled in the three years to 1950, although the first post-war models were not in series assembly until 1947. And the high rate of increase is emphasized by the appearance of marked and sharply-defined 'displacements' of the output trend. Strike-frequency varied pretty directly with output: while rising generally over the whole period, the annual number of disputes seems to have become increasingly sensitive to the recessions. It fell, with something of a lag, in the 1951–52 slump; again but less steeply in 1956; and even more sharply than would appear from the graph in the sudden slump which appeared in late 1960. So far, this is in line with the historical experience of industry at large, with a tendency for the number of stoppages to rise in booms and fall in slumps.

The really interesting feature is the movement of striker-days. During the 1950s, this incidence clearly varied almost inversely with the number of strikes—so that it actually tended to reach a very pronounced peak during the industry's recessions, just when the strike-frequency was falling off. In the 1960s, this clear inversion seems broken on Diagram IV/2, but this appearance is mainly due to the timing of 1960s trend changes which, being concentrated into the same year, are largely concealed by the use of annual totals. In fact, output reached a record peak in the first half of the year, when over 900,000 cars and vans were produced, but fell sharply to some 70 per cent of that figure in the year's second half. At the same time the level of striker-days rose abruptly—from less than 150,000 for 1960s first six months to over 210,000 for the second half of the year. This is quite contrary to the car industry's normal seasonal pattern of strike-incidence, in which—as we shall show later—the annual total of striker-days is heavily concentrated in the year's early months.

The events of 1960—as well as the general rhythm of labour unrest in the car firms—become clearer if seasonal influences are (for the moment) eliminated. This can be done by taking a twelve-month moving average from the *monthly* figures—as in Diagram IV/3—instead of annual totals. The result is too detailed for the whole post-war period to be depicted in a single diagram, so Diagram IV/3 picks out the months from 1957 to mid-1962 inclusive which embrace the recovery from the 1956 recession, the 1960 boom and slump, and the subsequent recuperation. It then appears, for instance, that the 1960 recession was already under way in the early part of the year, but the downturn was largely concealed, in the actual production trend, by the normal spring surge of domestic demand. Which suggests that if the industry's forecasting services were more adequate it might be better prepared for such events as those of 1960 than it apparently was. However, the important thing is the trend of striker-days over this period.

Diagram IV/3 shows how 'working days lost' fell off at the beginning of the period selected, as production recovered from the 1956 recession. They then rose gently, as the frequency of disputes increased with rising output, but jumped quite abruptly in late 1958 when the growth of production hesitated. They fell off again when

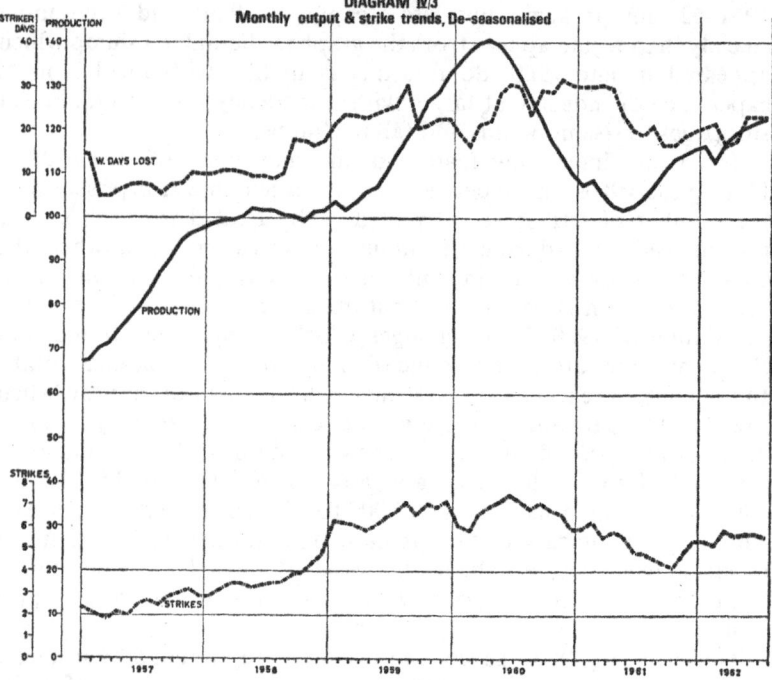

production soared through late 1959 and early 1960. But when output fell sharply, in mid-1960, the level of striker-days again jumped up, remaining high until the first signs of a production recovery appeared in early 1961. At the same time, the frequency of strikes, having fallen off in the 1960 recession, increased as output growth was resumed, and by early 1962 was again beginning to pull up the level of striker-days.

What abstracting seasonal factors from the output and strike trends shows, in fact, is that there are two influences on the level of striker-days in the car firms. In part, this level is a function of the frequency of strikes, which in turn reflects the rate of production, but with some lag. So that to some small extent total 'man-days of

Strikes and the Level of Activity

idleness' do vary with output, but with a certain delay. But secondly, there is a strong, direct, but *inverse* connection between striker-days and production, so that in each of the recessions of 1952, 1956 and 1960, the monthly total of striker-days has tended to rise abruptly to a figure of 25,000 to 30,000—and has stayed at that level until output recovered. It has then fallen sharply to—since the frequency of strikes only responds to production with a lag—an unusually low figure, from which it begins to climb again as the number of strikes rises. This pattern has been repeated in each of the three major post-war slumps analysed.[1] At the same time, however, the contrast between the depression level of striker-days and the 'normal' level has become progressively less sharp because the longer-run increase in the frequency of disputes has been pushing up the car industry's basic monthly 'loss of working days'.

(B) FACTORS IN THE 'SEVERITY' OF STRIKES

The pronounced negative association between the number of strikes and total striker-days does, of course, bear one similar implication to that of historical strike-experience in general: stoppages tend to be frequent and small in booms, while in slumps they become fewer but bigger or more protracted. However, in the car firms this last effect is much more pronounced than for industry in general. And so the usual interpretation of the historical pattern hardly explains the fluctuations in their case. Firstly, even the decline in the frequency of strikes during recessions is not symptomatic of a general tendency but—as will be shown later in the contrast between 'major' and 'minor' firms—affects only a distinguishable minority of car workers. Secondly, and as we have just noted, striker-days have not varied *quite* inversely with production. They have in fact risen (even if only moderately) together with the frequency of strikes in the middle stage of the booms—but have gone on rising for a while after production (and with production, the number of strikes) has turned down. But thirdly, it would hardly be possible to argue that car workers' strikes have been especially severe in recessions because they occurred in resistance to attacks on basic wage-standards or other analogous conditions, as was true of some of the industry's big disputes in the inter-war period. For out of more than seven hundred post-war strikes in the car firms, we have found not a single one against a reduction in basic wage-rates (even Standard's proposal to its shop stewards in 1960 to reduce disproportionate bonuses was abandoned after inconclusive discussions). However, this raises the

[1] Data on the 1965 recession only became available as this study was going to press. It is discussed in the appendix to this chapter, however.

question of the relation between the issues in dispute and the motor industry's trade cycle.

The table on the next page allocates the annual frequency of strikes in the car firms according to their causes. Here only four groups of causation are distinguished because—difficulties of classification apart—little significance can be attached to annual variations within the framework of a more detailed breakdown. Included in this table also are some war-time figures—to show the development of, and issues involved in, the strike wave which rose to its climax near the end of the War. The number of strikes under each head do not, of course, give any indication of the contribution of the various issues to the total number of striker-days: for example, some of those on trade union matters such as the status of shop stewards have been particularly big, whilst most wage-disputes have been fairly small.

There have clearly been changes in the causation of car strikes over time. Thus the relatively high frequency—and incidence—of strikes towards the end of the War was due to a crop of disputes about trade union issues, and over managerial questions like, for example 'objection to Works Manager's attitude', 'for removal of a foreman', and 'against disciplinary measures'. The imminent return of peace-time conditions could perhaps have been expected to lead to such disputes. On the other hand, the very marked increase in the frequency of strikes from about 1957 on has been largely due to disputes about wages and related issues, which appear to have multiplied remarkably since the big car firm mergers of 1952–53. Although stoppages on other issues have all increased 'sympathetically' to some extent, it is disputes about wages that have been responsible for most of the annual *fluctuations* in the frequency of strikes—with the exception of 1963 and 1964, when other questions contributed more to the increase in disputes.[1]

In the pre-war years, just less than one-fifth of all car strikes were about redundancy and related employment matters, and the proportion climbed to only just over one-fifth for the post-war period. But whereas these stoppages accounted for a mere one-tenth of striker-days before the War, their contribution rose to well over a quarter for the period after the War (see Table II/3, in Chapter II). And in both periods the bulk of the striker-days concerned is attributable to disputes specifically about redundancy, rather than

[1] Trade union issues proliferated in 1963 disputes, which seemed to reflect a growth of sensitivity over transfers of labour and the 'maintenance of membership'. In 1964, strikes about 'working conditions' multiplied: this is partly only a statistical feature, in that some stoppages were classified thus by the Ministry of Labour summaries without more specific mention of the actual content of the disputes. It was also partly due to a much-publicised series of strikes over working conditions in an old paint-shop at the Cowley works of Morris Motors.

individual dismissals or other employment matters. Which implies that since pre-war days, workers' feelings about job-security have become much more intense—sufficiently so, at any rate, to induce much more sizeable or more protracted disputes on this question. If redundancy strikes have not been notably more numerous in recessions, their frequency seems (as might be expected) to be very sensitive to the *onset* of a slump—increasing in 1951, 1956, and particularly in 1960 (when they were the only kind of strike to grow

Table IV/1—ANNUAL FREQUENCY OF STRIKES BY CAUSE (RE-CLASSIFIED)

		NUMBER ATTRIBUTABLE TO:			
Year	Total number of 'reportable' strikes	Wages, wage-structure and work-loads	Redundancy, dismissals, etc.	Trade union relationships, etc.	Managerial arrangements, working conditions, etc.
1940	9	6	1	2	—
1941	10	6	1½	1½	1
1942	24	21	1½	½	1
1943	34	24½	4½	3	2
1944	44	25½	5½	7	6
1945	31	19	2½	2½	7
1946	17	5	3	7	2
1947	8	4	4	—	—
1948	12	4	2½	1½	4
1949	10	4	4	2	—
1950	11	5	2	2	2
1951	18	6	5½	3½	3
1952	13	6½	2½	3	1
1953	7	1	3	3	—
1954	10	5	½	3	1½
1955	24	13	5	5	1
1956	20	5	8	4	3
1957	32	14	8½	6½	3
1958	41	20½	10½	5	5
1959	80	53	8	12	7
1960	86	48	24½	6	7½
1961	58	26½	13½	2	16
1962	66	40½	12½	3½	9½
1963	88	48	15½	13	11½
1964	103	53½	14½	6	29

Notes:
1. National strikes in the engineering industry (which in fact affected certain car firms) are not included.
2. A strike involving two major issues is counted as a half-strike under each of the relevant groups of causes.

significantly in number). But this alone hardly explains the comparative severity of strikes in recessions, because redundancy stoppages have become more common in years of recovery and boom also. What is important is that strikes specifically about redundancy were the outstanding contributors to the increased level of striker-days in both 1951 and 1956, and made a major contribution to the increased strike-incidence of 1960.

What has happened, in effect, is that although strikes in support of straightforward wage demands have fallen off sharply during recessions, most other kinds of dispute—but particularly those concerning employment—have become *individually* more severe; and this is an effect which seems to have lasted (sometimes even into succeeding years) until the fact of recovery became widely apparent. The table below on the 'severity' of strikes (a term which may be regarded as applying to their comparative length, or the average number of workers they involve, or these two things in combination) demonstrates this tendency fairly clearly. The evidence is perhaps somewhat exaggerated by the effect of a few particularly large strikes, such as those of 1952, 1953 and 1956: but even discounting this effect the only really odd year out is 1959—a year in which the average severity was raised by three big stoppages over trade union issues.

Table IV/2—'SEVERITY' OF CAR FIRM STRIKES

Year	Average length of strikes (days)	Average no. of workers involved (000s)	Average striker-days per strike (000s)
1950	2.4	0.9	2.3
1951	2.7	2.1	5.7
1952	9.8	2.1	20.9
1953	18.1	1.9	34.4
1954	2.8	1.5	4.3
1955	2.1	0.9	1.9
1956	4.9	2.9	14.0
1957	2.2	1.2	2.6
1958	2.1	1.2	2.6
1959	2.6	1.5	3.8
1960	2.4	1.7	4.1
1961	3.4	1.2	4.0
1962	2.9	1.4	4.1
1963	2.1	1.3	2.6
1964	2.3	1.1	2.5

But the apparent trend for car-workers' stoppages to become, not merely more severe in recessions, but unusually so, does give a clue to the special strike-pattern of the car firms. One determinant of the severity of any strike, for instance, is the extent of support (or sometimes more negatively, the lack of condemnation) it receives from the unions. The overwhelming majority of car workers' strikes have certainly started by being unofficial. Taking for the moment the annual number of strikes as an indicator, the general militancy of car workers has been rising almost continuously since the mid-1950s. Thus, in the presence of an active shop stewards' movement and some degree of inter-union competition, union leaders have been under mounting pressure from their followers, and this seems to have been to some extent reflected in an increased tendency of unions, if not to organize strikes, at least to reserve their disapproval, to pay strike benefit after the event, or even to declare strikes official once they have started.

No satisfactory statistical index of the degree of union support for strikes is available for the post-war period, but the increasing tendency was signalled when the N.U.V.B. authorized the Austin strike of 1953 (which originated from a shop steward's dismissal arising out of a threatened redundancy[1]) and became rather more emphatic with the encouragement by the T. & G.W.U. of strike action against B.M.C.'s dismissal of several thousand workers at very short notice and without 'redundancy compensation' in 1956. The trend was perhaps inhibited by the Minister of Labour's approach to the motor industry unions in 1961, and the subsequent official emphasis on the observance of due procedure. But it was the threats of an official strike at Ford at the end of 1962 and beginning of 1963 —also over redundancy, in direct origin—which led to the 'Jack' Court of Inquiry.[1] And during 1964 and early 1965 there were official stoppages at Standard, Rover, Austin—and even Vauxhall.

The suggestion that the policy considerations of union leadership have been a factor in the car industry's special pattern of striker-days could be graphically supported if the annual number of workers involved in strikes had been included in Diagram IV/2 (it was omitted to keep the diagram simple). The number who come out on strike in any dispute is, of course, influenced by official trade union attitudes: up to the beginning of the 1950s, the curve of 'workers involved' follows that of the frequency of strikes; but from then on, when some strikes (at least) became bigger because they were officially or semi-officially supported, it follows that of striker-days.[2] Union leaders have to consider more than the immediate impulses of pressures of their rank and file. They are obviously concerned to

[1] See Chapter IX for detailed accounts.
[2] Since this section was written, some more direct statistical evidence has become available, which is cited in this chapter's Appendix (Table IV/B).

maintain good negotiating relations with employers; they are fully aware of the delicate position of the British car industry in foreign markets; and they have become sensitive to a public opinion which they suspect of hostility. It can hardly be thought that they became more willing to support strikes in recessions because they thought them more likely to succeed at such times. Indeed, the cuts in output required by market conditions have often been so sharp that the firms have been hard put to it to adjust to them by short-time working alone. Yet the firms have been increasingly reluctant to dismiss their workers, for fear of being unable to recoup their labour requirements later on. Thus an official strike during a recession is likely to do less damage to union-employer relations than one at other times—much of the output 'lost' would not have been needed anyway; and the strike can take place on issues and in circumstances more likely to attract public sympathy.

It seems at least significant that the proportion of workers 'directly involved' in stoppages appears, if anything, rather higher in recessions. The attitudes of union members themselves are also involved in this pattern of strike-incidence. Operatives are keenly aware—from production schedules and their company's park of cars awaiting distribution—of the state of trade. Many of them have now a long experience of the latter's fluctuations, and know that it commonly recovers. A stoppage on a narrow group-interest issue at time of recession might expose the few participants to managerial reprisal; but at such times car workers may be more than usually willing to join a stoppage with a broader basis of appeal because they will probably lose no work by doing so, but may actually avoid the necessity of lay-offs or redundancy.

In particular, of course, firms themselves are in much less of a hurry to settle disputes during recessions. Indeed, it is not impossible that during the most recent periods of bad trade, the attitude of firms has become much more crucial than that of union officers or members to the tendency for strikes to increase in severity at such times. One can readily imagine that a management which has reached the limits of its ability to stock finished cars or persuade its dealers to take more, and is afraid that sufficient short-time will be difficult to organize but that lay-offs will result—if not in official strikes or public criticism—in a labour shortage when trade recovers, may accept an unofficial dispute as a heaven-sent occasion to suspend production temporarily. It will at least be much less inclined to improvise to maintain output than it would when demand is high.

In these circumstances, the strike becomes almost a form of 'work-spreading'. To have a strike is not perhaps the most rational way to fill in a slump, but it is more interesting and sociable than some other forms of idleness, and helps to keep workers from drifting away to other jobs. This is not, of course, by any means to say that the particular severity of every big strike that has occurred in the British motor firms since 1951 is attributable to such reactions to recession; nor that such occasions may not have been used by one or other of the parties to pursue incidental objectives. But as a general explanation of the car industry's unusual pattern of strike-incidence, these reactions—and perhaps especially the suggestion that workers' responses have had something to do with that pattern—become even more plausible when the examination is taken further.

There is, in fact, a very marked difference in the experience of major and minor firms. Necessarily arbitrary though the separation between the two groups must be, it has been possible to apportion the strikes in the industry fairly precisely between them. Diagram IV/4 shows the trends, both in numbers of strikes and in striker-days, for each group separately. 'Major' firms are the Big Five—B.M.C., Ford, Rootes, Vauxhall, Standard, together with their subsidiaries and all the concerns that have merged with them;[1] and 'minor' firms represents the Independents such as Pressed Steel, Jaguar, Rover, Rolls-Royce, Jensen, Alvis and others, as well as some (such as Jowett) which have ceased car production in the course of the period.

It is at once evident that the Independents' strike-frequency has been far the more sensitive to the state of trade; for them, for instance, strikes fell to zero during the recession of 1951–52. For the major firms, however, strikes did not fall off until 1953. The frequency of strikes in the minor firms again fell sharply in the slump of 1956; in the Big Five it continued to rise uninterruptedly. In the 1960–61 slump it once more declined sharply for the Independents; for the Big Five, it fell to a much lesser extent. This picture is no doubt a reflection of the marginal competitive position which several of the smaller firms have occupied: workers in them may well have been afraid that to strike in a recession would not postpone unemployment, but perhaps accelerate it by pushing their firm over the competitive brink. This view seems to be confirmed by the experience of Standard and Daimler. These firms—at least from the mid-1950s—were the most insecurely 'marginal' members of the major and minor firms respectively, and were eventually absorbed into larger groups. But over the intervening period, the readiness to strike in both firms declined remarkably.

In contradistinction to the general car industry pattern, which tends to be dominated by the major firms' experience in this respect,

[1] Except Pressed Steel, which merged into B.M.C. only after this analysis was made.

DIAGRAM IV/4
Strikes in major and minor firms

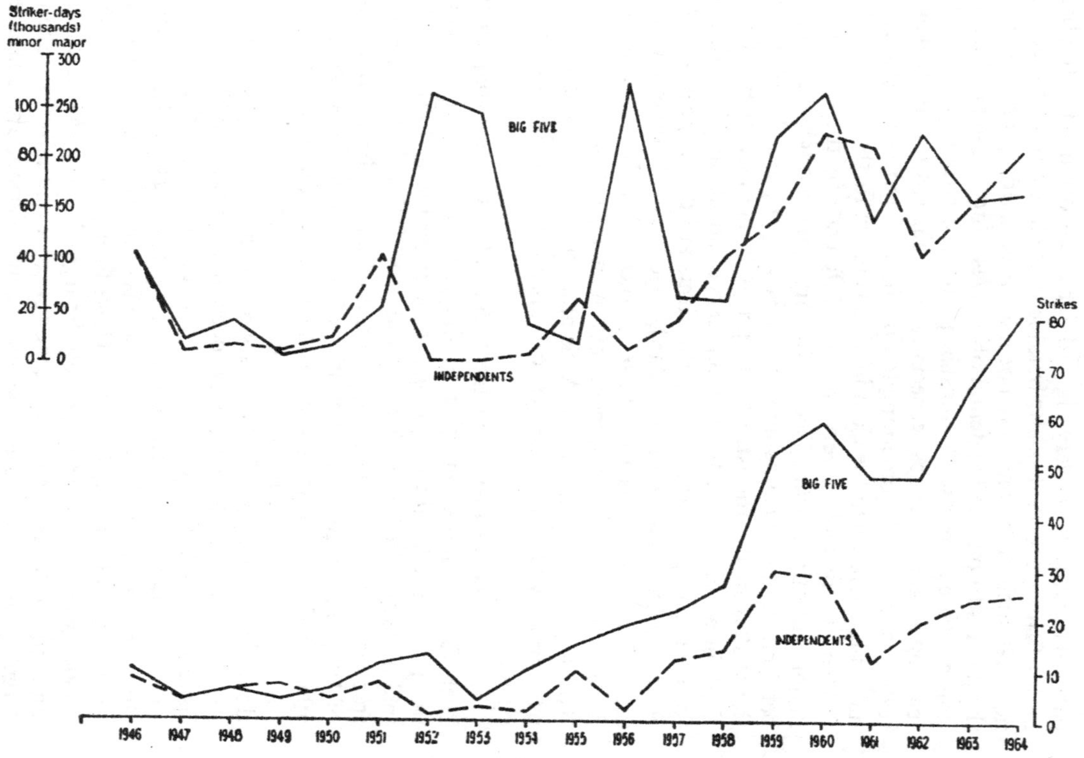

the fluctuation of striker-days for the Independents follows that of their strike-frequency almost exactly. The main exceptions are 1960, when some of the surviving Independents no longer looked quite so marginal, and became involved in substantial disputes over dismissals or redundancy; and 1962, when the home market boom sparked off by the purchase tax reductions had not yet begun and there was some hesitation in the demand for quality cars (so that while strikes were on the increase in some of these firms, striker-days were heavily down in others). Indeed, in the minor firms there appears to be actually a tendency for strikes to get bigger at the top of a boom rather than at the bottom of a slump; and even for the Big Five, the frequency of strikes and the number of striker-days vary together up to 1953. It is thus the addition of something else to this last pattern which explains the fact that, after this date, striker-days reach their peaks in recessions for the industry as a whole. The 'addition' is apparently the large (and sometimes official) strike in non-marginal firms.

(C) SEASONAL PATTERNS; INSECURITY AND THE STRIKE-LIABILITY

Having abstracted from seasonal patterns earlier in this Chapter we can now look at them separately. Seasonal variations in output are not susceptible to particularly refined measurement. There are problems in assessing the significance of the officially-published monthly production figures, because reporting firms count their output at different points in the process of finishing and despatching cars, and have different counting periods. Output is also affected by variations in the number of working days in each month. Obviously, low production in the months of July and to a lesser extent August results from the annual holiday shut-down in the industry; and isolated public holidays—especially in March, April, and December—can affect those months' totals considerably. We hope that taking runs of years together will suppress the less obvious variations which these things may cause. Large—or long—strikes in major firms, while they may not affect annual production substantially, do affect monthly outputs considerably: we mention particular instances where it seems relevant. In the analysis of strike data, where strikes spread over from one month to the next we have allocated the effect to the months in which such strikes began (as, incidentally, elsewhere in this study). The next table (IV/3) shows the frequency of strikes in each month, for pre-war, wartime, and two post-war periods.

One obvious point is the considerable variation between months despite the grouping of years, and even when the sample is fairly

Table IV/3—NUMBER OF STRIKES BEGINNING IN EACH MONTH, BY PERIOD

Period	Jan	Feb	Mar	Apr	May	Jun	Jul	Aug	Sept	Oct	Nov	Dec
1921–39	6	9	8	3	5	4	3	7	6	4	7	2
1940–45	17	8	16	13	12	7	5	18	7	19	14	16
1946–55	17	10	8	9	13	18	6	9	9	14	9	8
1956–64	46	57	38	50	68	44	31	62	44	52	46	36

large—as in the later periods. There are also differences between the 'patterns' of the four periods. So climatic factors are clearly not a dominating influence on strike frequency here.[1] But to look more closely at the pre-war period first—the third, and particularly the first, quarters of those years were most strike-liable. The probable explanation for this pattern is mainly the discontent of the winter lay-offs: not surprisingly, of seven redundancy strikes in this period, one was in December and five were in the first three months of the year (strikes over trade union matters were also concentrated in these months). And the pre-war strikes in August and September may support a view which was at one time quite widely held—that the October Motor Shows led to strikes because of the greater pressure for production, the changes involved, and the leverage which display deadlines gave to union negotiators. In contrast to the pre-war period, however, the war years saw a heavy concentration of strikes in the year's last quarter, which carried over into the first quarter as well. There is little to be said about this pattern's origin for our purpose: whatever explanations could be suggested would be dominated by specifically wartime conditions—for instance, that wartime winters were simply hard to live through.

The post-war years are more interesting. In both the periods distinguished, there are relatively few strikes in December (the reason seems obvious). In both again, the peak frequency occurs in the quarter April to June (in the years from 1956 most markedly in May), but with subsidiary peaks—in October for the earlier years and in August for the more recent period. Looking at the strike frequency pattern another way, half a dozen of the Decembers—but also of the Augusts—had no strikes at all. Five Marches and five Junes had no strikes. Only one January in the whole post-war period was strike-free. But the two post-war decades seem sufficiently similar in pattern to warrant closer examination as a whole.

Diagram IV/5 shows strikes, striker-days, and production in each month for the years 1946–62 (1963–64 is here omitted as there is no

[1] See Knowles, *op. cit.*, p. 157 ff, for some observations on the seasonality of strikes in general.

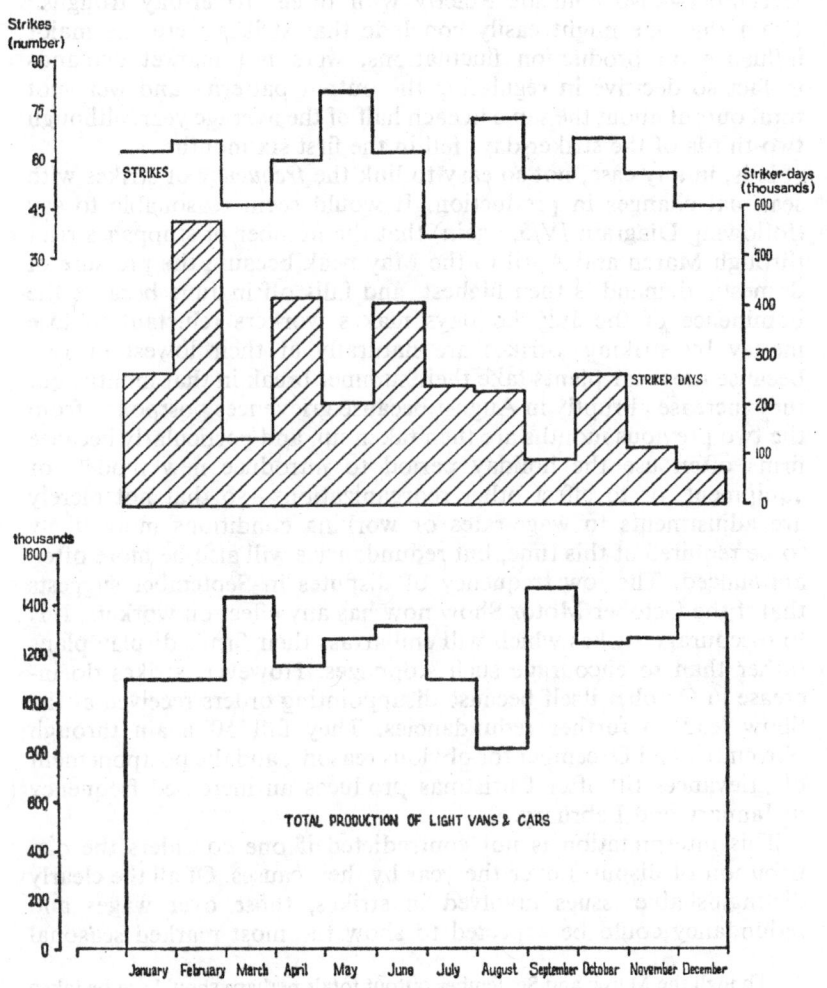

DIAGRAM IV/5
Strikes and Production
1946-1962

comparable production figure which includes light vans). The inverse relation between striker-days and output discussed earlier in the chapter is immediately apparent: striker-days are generally highest in months when production is below peak level, and tail off as output rises through the year's last quarter, reaching their nadir in December. Three production peaks—in March, September, and December—also coincide exactly with three striker-day troughs.[1] From this one might easily conclude that strikes were the major influence on production fluctuations, were not market demands in fact so decisive in regulating the output pattern—and were not total output about the same in each half of the average year, although two-thirds of the striker-days fell in the first six months.

It is, in any case, not so easy to link the *frequency* of strikes with seasonal changes in production. It would seem reasonable to say (following Diagram IV/5, again) that the number of stoppages rises through March and April to the May peak because the pressure of domestic demand is then highest, and falls off in June because the imminence of the July holidays makes workers reluctant to lose money by striking. Strikes are naturally at their lowest in July because most car plants take their summer break in that month; but they increase abruptly in August because grievances postponed from the two previous months are then taken up, and particularly because firms often use the holiday period to introduce new models or equipment, or to effect other reorganizations—so that not merely are adjustments to wage-rates or working conditions more likely to be required at this time, but redundancies will also be more often announced. The low frequency of disputes in September suggests that if the October Motor Show now has any effect on workers, it is to discourage strikes which will embarrass their firm's display plans rather than to encourage such stoppages. However, strikes do increase in October itself because disappointing orders received at the Show lead to further redundancies. They fall off again through November and December for obvious reasons, and the postponement of grievances till after Christmas produces an increased frequency in January and February.

This interpretation is not contradicted if one considers the distribution of disputes over the year by their causes. Of all the clearly distinguishable issues involved in strikes, those over wages and redundancy could be expected to show the most marked seasonal

---

[1] Though the March and September output totals perhaps should not be taken at quite face value: they may partly reflect the build-up of sub-assemblies and working stock during the quiet months of January and February, and during the shut-down period of July and August (when those not entitled to leave, and some others, remain at work).

variation. The following table shows the seasonal distribution of these two kinds of strike for the years 1946–64:

Table IV/4—NUMBER OF STRIKES BEGINNING IN EACH MONTH, BY CAUSE

Cause	Jan	Feb	Mar	Apr	May	Jun	Jul	Aug	Sep	Oct	Nov	Dec
Wages, workloads	28½	28¼	28	29	49	33½	17½	40	25	32	32	19¼
Redundancy	9	4¼	2½	5	3½	7½	6	13	5	8	12	6

In so far as wage strikes are concerned, their peak frequency clearly falls in May and August, and they are at their lowest in July and December. Otherwise they seem—as could be expected—to be fairly evenly spread over the year. Nor has there been any significant change from this pattern during the course of the post-war period. And inasmuch as the figures justify any inference, it is that wage-related disputes build up during the spring expansion of production, and again in the weeks after the summer holiday, when Christmas is still far off, and when changes of job-rates and working conditions are most likely to be confronted.

Redundancy strikes also have a clear seasonal pattern: they have occurred most frequently in August—presumably in reaction to the labour casualties entailed by reorganization of work during the annual shutdown. Firms might prefer this occasion to announce redundancies because, its convenience to them apart, it could also possibly be regarded as one least likely to cause hardship or unrest: it would be still early enough in the year for workers to look optimistically on the prospects of alternative jobs, and holiday money could also be viewed as a kind of severance payment. (These considerations would probably have had less force in the pre-war period, and redundancy strikes were then at their peak in February.) At any rate, redundancy strikes in the summer have been, on the average, smaller than those at other times, and the incidence of striker-days due to redundancy disputes comes most heavily in the other peak months for such stoppages—just after the Motor Show in November, and in January, which is a low point for domestic sales of cars. There are relatively few redundancy strikes in the months from February to May. None of which is surprising, or raises problems of interpretation in itself.

However, this view of the changing monthly frequency of disputes in general does carry some suppositions about the underlying pattern of output which are not borne out by the latter's apparent actual course. Whatever reservation one puts upon the production figures,

May does not—in fact, and on the average—seem to have been the peak month, for instance. Indeed, the monthly frequency of stoppages, unlike their longer-term cyclical variation, seems virtually inverse to the fluctuation of output: so that it rather resembles the pattern of striker-days. The numbers of strikes and of 'working days lost' clearly move closely together in the last five months of the year, and even in the first seven their fluctuation is not too dissimilar—except in May, when disputes are frequent but lost working days rather few (which may simply mean that firms are particularly anxious to settle conflicts at that time, thus making their workers' choice of May as the best month to strike in look quite rational). But the *general* level of striker-days is much higher in the year's early months than in its latter ones. Not only are stoppages more frequent in the first part of the year: they are, on the average, notably bigger or longer.[1]

Thus the seasonal pattern of the car firms' strike-movements seems to reflect some of the same influences as the latters' longer-run variation. Striker-days, for instance, rise with the frequency of disputes in general; but they also particularly rise with the occasional big stoppages, which seem more likely to occur when production is low. But big strikes are *also* heavily concentrated in the early months of the year, although output is on the whole no lower then. Two associated factors may help to explain this apparent contradiction. In the first place, it is possible that production *would* be higher in the normal (as opposed to the average) year's first half, because that covers the spring boom but no long holidays. In which case the signal both of imminent recession and for strikes to get bigger may be the failure of the spring boom to materialize or to fulfil expectations: certainly, big official strikes seem to be concentrated about such seasons. In the second place, knowledge that the spring boom may be followed by an autumn recession may make operatives more willing to join strikes which will have the effect of postponing output and work.

But there remain things about the seasonal pattern of disputes which are not altogether easy to explain. In this respect, it is like some other seasonal phenomena, such as death and suicide rates. For suicide and strike frequencies show a very similar seasonal pattern: both rates are at their lowest in the first quarter of the year

[1] There is, of course, a connection between the striker-day peaks of February, April and June shown by Diagram IV/5 and the four very large strikes of the period up to 1962: the strikes at Dagenham in 1952 began in June; that at Austin in 1953 began in February; and that at Standard in 1956 began in April. But even if one omits the effects of these very big stoppages altogether from the diagram, the general level of striker-days remains higher for the first half of the year than for the second.

(drab weather notwithstanding), rise to a peak around May, decline in midsummer, and rise to another secondary peak around October.[1] And explanations for the suicide pattern are only tentative. This is not at all to suggest that strikes reflect suppressed impulses to self-destruction; and 'natural' factors cannot in any case be of major importance to their seasonal pattern, because of the latter's variation between different periods. It is merely to say that, like other human phenomena, strike-frequency and -incidence may be affected by psychological and social rhythms of which we have many hints but few analyses.

In general, however, the relationships between fluctuations in the motor industry's output and in its strike-liability seem both clear, and amenable to consistent and plausible interpretation. As regards the inverse relationship between output and striker-days, there is in any case a historical analogy in the experience of one of the most strike-prone of nineteenth-century industries: the implicit 'conspiracy to strike' by which, it has been suggested, the expanding cotton trade overcame its incapacity to deal with periodic bouts of over-production. Any student of the development of the British car industry might well be struck by the resemblance of the output curve of this most typical of contemporary mass production industries to that of its great historical predecessor. And it would be difficult to deny that when market demand is not pressing, negotiations in the car plants appear to drag unnecessarily, or are often allowed to drift into open stoppages of work.

The connection between the frequency of car manufacturing's strikes and its trade cycle also suggests a broader generalization. Firstly, the 'hire and fire' era in which the industry grew up during the inter-war period, with regular seasonal lay-offs of which many older employees still speak bitterly, saw the beginnings of aggressive wage policy on the part of car workers. A similar development took place in the American industry: hourly earnings had to be high to make up for regular periods of unemployment. Then, the advent of the war began a long spell of full employment and labour shortage. While car-workers' earnings remained both stable and high—and were even boosted higher by that deliberate policy of certain employers which we discuss in a later Chapter—the motor industry was not particularly noted (within the engineering complex, at least) as being strike-prone. The re-appearance of the trade cycle in the 1950s, bringing with it sharp periods of unemployment and redun-

[1] See summary in E. Stengel, *Suicide and Attempted Suicide* (Harmondsworth: Penguin Books, 1964), pp. 31–32. For an exercise, we analysed suicide data for England and Wales for the years 1953 to 1962: the seasonal correlation between suicide and strike frequencies held good.

dancy, seems to have led to heightened insecurity and the return of old fears on the part of car workers, especially from 1956 onwards. And it is precisely from the mid-1950s that the frequency of car workers' strikes began its steep upward slope. The increase is very largely a matter of smallish wage-structure strikes, and it looks somewhat as though car workers have re-adopted and extended their pre-war policy of aggressive militancy on wage-connected issues during good years to compensate for insecurity and short-time working during the bad. Nor is this strategy of 'making hay while the sun shines' inconsistent with the seasonal fluctuations in strike-frequency: rather it is an extension of it.

APPENDIX

WHAT HAPPENED IN 1965?

In 1965 'working days lost' recorded by the Ministry of Labour for the motor vehicle and cycle industries rose sharply to nearly 900,000 —more than double the 1963–64 rate. We have not examined the 1965 records in such detail as previous years, but summary analysis suggests the 1965 total of striker-days in the car firms proper was over 700,000—or about treble the average of the previous three years. This produced a new crisis in motor industrial relations: statements by manufacturers suggested that 10 per cent or more of output was being lost from disputes; in the late summer meetings were held at Downing Street; and in the autumn Mr Scamp was appointed as official chairman of a new Joint Labour Council with certain legal powers of inquiry.

The background to this was a new recession in the car trade. We have noted that in previous recessions—those of 1952–53 and 1956, for instance—the frequency of strikes tended to fall off, but 'working days lost' nevertheless rose abnormally. This happened also in the sharp slump of late 1960. However, production began to recover at the end of 1961: what happened next is shown in the Table IV/A which accompanies this note. (There are very marked seasonal and other short-term fluctuations in all the series involved—for instance, there was an abnormal pre-Budget boom on the home market in 1965, but the normal spring boom failed to materialize: so we have converted them to twelve-month moving averages, presented as quarterly rates to pick out the trends.)

It will be seen that the production trend rose steadily through 1962, but very sharply in 1963—following on a boom in the home market. It then flattened out, falling in late 1964, and continuing down through early 1965. This, too, followed market trends. The export rate began to fall off first, in mid-1964; production was cut and major firms announced short-time working in late summer and autumn, but were persuaded to postpone or curtail this later—partly by union insistence that it would be prejudicial to the improvement of industrial relations.

However, over the winter of 1964–65 the home market (where growth had already slowed down) also began to show a downward trend. Meanwhile, manufacturers' capacity was still increasing—by nearly 10 per cent per year, although since car imports were also running at some 14,000 a quarter in 1963–64, it seems clear that production was already tending to exceed demand by mid-1963. Large-scale excess capacity had thus developed by the end of 1964. (Other evidences of the failure of estimated demand to appear are to be found in falls in total hours worked after mid-1964 and again after mid-1965—*not* at times when 'man-hours lost' from strikes were highest; in a continuing decline of car imports; and in the fact that it was still possible to buy unregistered 1965 models—made before the October Motor Show—from major manufacturers at cut prices in the Spring of 1966.)

Production thus followed the trend of demand. On the other hand, strike-trends obviously followed those of production. The frequency of disputes in the 'motor vehicle' industry rose sharply in the 1963 boom, but the quarterly rate of 'working days lost' stayed fairly steady (for this series) through 1962 and 1963, at around 100,000— which was also about the 1961 rate. The number of stoppages ceased to rise when the production trend flattened, in early 1964. But the quarterly rate of striker-days only showed a marked upwards jump near the end of 1964, some time *after* both production and the frequency of strikes had flattened out.

The 1965 experience thus repeated that of the previous recessions, except that the consequent increase in striker-days was still more accentuated by inhibitions on open lay-offs and short-time. Several of the major 1965 disputes were singularly 'work-time consuming'— the Coventry holiday dispute, the official stoppage at B.M.C. in March, the organized refusals of Friday night-shifts. The average duration of motor strikes rose from under three days in 1963–64 to four-and-a-half days in 1965, and the number of workers involved in each dispute also increased. In effect, excess capacity was partly absorbed, and surplus stocks of unsold cars were reduced, by drawing out such strikes as occurred and thus also extending them. The extraordinary increase in the car firms' strike-incidence during 1965 represented, less a crisis in labour relations, than what was almost a benevolent, if implicit, collective conspiracy.

We can add a note on the way the industry's production trends were reflected in official trade union policy. The Ministry of Labour has since 1960 noted stoppages which it *knew* to have been 'official'. This is not necessarily, of course, a complete indication of the extent of union support for strikes, but for the whole motor industry the picture is set out in Table IV/B. It will be seen (p. 132) that under every index of strike-activity, official support appears to have been at a peak in the depression year of 1960, fell off as car output mounted to the 1963 boom, and then was re-extended as surplus capacity appeared in 1964–65.

Table IV/A—CAR MARKET DEVELOPMENTS, PRODUCTION AND LABOUR STOPPAGES, 1962–65

Quarterly rate* of	1962			1963				1964				1965			
	Spring	Summer	Autumn	Winter	Spring	Summer	Autumn	Winter	Spring	Summer	Autumn	Winter	Spring	Summer	Autumn
Exports (000 cars)	129	135	137	139	143	153	161	167	169	168	162	160	159	157	(154)
New registrations (000 cars)	187	197	207	226	241	253	274	285	294	298	308	299	289	281	278
Production (000 cars)	301	312	326	348	368	402	436	460	463	467	452	445	436	431	431
Strikes in motor vehicles (officially reported)	24	26	26	26	25	29	35	37	39	39	40	41	41	38	41
Striker-days (000s)†	81	101	82	76	73	72	103	105	114	99	154	179	202	206	146

* Seasonal fluctuations eliminated by twelve-month moving average ('Spring'=rate at end March, etc.).
† Excludes one-day general engineering stoppages of February and March 1962.

Table IV/B—STOPPAGES KNOWN TO BE 'WHOLLY OFFICIAL' IN THE MOTOR VEHICLE INDUSTRY

Year	Number	Workers involved (000s)	Working Days lost (000s)
1960	9	8	91
1961	6	4	53
1962	2	3*	15*
1963	3	1	7
1964	9	7	114
1965 (provisional)	9	46	286

* Estimate, excluding general engineering stoppages.

CHAPTER V

WAGES IN THE MOTOR INDUSTRY

(A) WAGE-LEVELS AND TRENDS

Among all the groups of workers distinguished by the Ministry of Labour's periodic inquiries into industrial earnings, those engaged in the manufacture of motor vehicles rank second only to newspaper printers in their wage-level, with average weekly pay-packets for men of £22 9s in April 1964. This figure compared with men's average earnings around £18 a week in the engineering industry proper and a few shillings less than that sum in all industries covered. Moreover, about half the workers in the motor vehicle group are employed in the making of heavy vehicles, buses and so on, where wages are generally less than in the manufacture of cars. In the plants of the car-making firms at this time, men's weekly earnings can be estimated to have averaged rather over £23 10s—which would put the car-assembly operatives about on a par with those old-established aristocrats of labour, the newspaper printers.[1]

The car workers' advantage is still more apparent if one considers what is probably the best available published guide to wage trends and relativities, average hourly earnings. (Implying that the car worker's larger wage-packet was usually earned in a shorter working week than that of the engineering operative.) In April 1964, again, men's earnings per hour in the motor vehicle group averaged 29 per cent above those of adult male workers in the engineering industries, so that the average car-assembler's differential over the general run of engineering operatives must have been at least a third. When one compares earnings by occupational categories—skilled piece-workers

[1] The information on which this Chapter is based was collected from a variety of sources, and represented that available in early 1965. In some cases, more recent information is available at time of going to press, but to attempt to incorporate it could involve considerable calculation to trace other relationships affected. Moreover, where data was obtained from or with the permission of individual firms, no very recent figures are in any case used to avoid the chance of complicating now current negotiations. But such later information as is available to us does not alter the general picture here traced.

in the motor industry with those in engineering, for instance—the differential is to some extent diminished. During 1963, it would appear from a Ministry of Labour inquiry on occupational earnings to have averaged about one-fifth, so that the larger differential for the industry as a whole must to some extent reflect larger proportions of workers in higher-paid categories (like semi-skilled piece-workers) in the motor firms. On the other hand, some car firms often rate a particular type of labour at a higher level than would most engineering firms—so that, particularly, some workers whose qualifications would only classify them as semi-skilled men in engineering plants could be paid as skilled in a car factory. All in all, it would probably not be unreasonable to put the car worker's effective differential above the wages of an engineering operative on similar work at a quarter at least.

The car worker's differential in hourly or weekly earnings is, of course, not necessarily fully reflected in his annual income. Apart from variations in earnings, to which we shall refer later, holiday pay and 'guaranteed week' arrangements in the 'federated' motor firms are usually based on the rates laid down in national engineering agreements, so that their workers' income has been liable to fall relatively more than that of the engineering operative when in receipt of either of these payments. Nor are non-wage or 'fringe' benefits in the car firms generally distinctive as compared with those provided by non-motor firms of comparable size. They mostly offer such welfare services as canteens, and social or sports clubs (though the wide residential dispersal of motor workers in any case means that only a marginal proportion of them actually benefit from the latter facilities). Most of the major car firms have some kind of pension scheme, contributory or non-contributory, and in all the companies it is possible for workers to contribute to a sick-pay scheme—though benefits provided under these arrangements vary widely. But these things are not abnormal in large firms generally.

The 'non-federated' car firms have until recently had a shorter standard work-week than that ruling under engineering industry agreements—the Forty Hour Week (which existed at Ford before the war) had been re-introduced there by 1962, and also applied at Vauxhall. While S.T.I. (which also spent some years in the wilderness of non-federation) had a standard week of 40¾ hours, compared with 42 at federated firms, until standard hours throughout the industry were also reduced to 40 in 1965 under the general engineering 'long-term package deal' of the previous year. Vauxhall also had, at least until very recently, a guaranteed week agreement superior to that for engineering in general. While nearly all car workers have what might be considered the significant chance to buy cars at 15 per cent or so below their pre-tax price: an advantage sometimes said (though not too seriously) to be offered by the car firms as an incentive to good workmanship—if a worker skimps a job, he may get the defective car himself!

However, fringe benefits in general represent a small proportion of labour costs in British industry by international comparison, and to this rule the car firms are not a marked exception. So it remains the car operative's wage-level which is mainly distinctive in his employment status. In this there is nothing particularly new: in 1948, the first year in which a 'motor vehicle and cycle manufacture' group was distinguished in official earnings statistics, its male workers also ranked second only to newspaper and periodical printers despite the then-inclusion of the lower-paid cycle makers in their group, and there is evidence that car workers' earnings were relatively high even in the inter-war period.[1] But they have also been rising faster than the general run for much of their recorded history: between October 1948 and April 1964 men's average hourly earnings in motor vehicle manufacture rose by over 160 per cent, against just on 140 per cent in other engineering trades.[2]

The differential in car workers' wages is, of course, the product of several factors, some of which are not specific to the motor industry itself. Wages in large establishments are in general higher than those in smaller ones, and the average size of factories is certainly greater in motor manufacture than in most other industries. The motor industry originated as a branch of engineering: this point of origin has clearly determined many features, not only of its labour relationships at large, but of its wage-patterns in particular. Thus, engineering operatives in the West Midlands, and especially in Coventry, have for many years enjoyed a wage-advantage over those in other engineering districts (the new Ministry of Labour series of inquiries into earnings by occupation in the metal-using industries showed wages in mid-1964 as being significantly higher, for most categories of labour in the Midlands region, even than in London and the South-East—which for employment in general is the highest-earning area). This advantage, the partial concentration of car plants in the West Midlands has merely emphasized: indeed, one very detailed study of engineering wages has suggested that high earnings in the motor

[1] For instance, even in 1938 earnings per hour at Standard Motors were stated to have been 32 per cent above the then vehicle industry average (by S. Melman, in *Decision-Making and Productivity*, p. 144).

[2] Including cycles in motor vehicle manufacture, and shipbuilding in engineering, up to 1959, when the revised Standard Industrial Classification was introduced. The first inclusion can make little difference to the trend. Neither, probably, can the second; in any case the rise for all manufacturing industries is similar to that estimated for engineering.

industry have owed more to that regional concentration than high earnings in the West Midlands have owed to motors.[1]

The study last referred to, however, was made before wages in the car firms had pulled away from those in general engineering to the extent that they did in the late 1950s. And that the car workers' wage-leadership derived at least very substantially from the prosperity of their industry and its high rate of productivity growth is suggested by the pervasive—if in detail very uneven—effect these things seem to have had on the incomes of other employees in car manufacture than the men on machines and assembly tracks. The hourly earnings differential of its women operatives over those in other industries, for instance, seems even more marked than that of men: so far as one can estimate it, from unofficial sources, it seems to be between 40 per cent and 50 per cent, notwithstanding that women are not employed on shift-work as extensively as men operatives. According to the Ministry of Labour's periodic inquiry into earnings of administrative, clerical and technical employees, the salaries of weekly-paid male white-collar workers in the vehicle industry are the highest in manufacturing, and there is some reason to think motor firms the main contributor to the group's pre-eminence. The earnings of monthly-paid employees are less easy to compare between industries, because of greater differences in the type of work concerned, but for these workers the vehicle group also ranked high in pay terms. Particularly, during the period since the regular official inquiry into these employees' pay began, the 'motor vehicle and cycle' group has shown outstandingly the fastest rate of pay increase for white-collar employees—nearly 37 per cent for men between 1959 and 1964, compared with about 30 per cent for similar workers in engineering, in manufacturing generally, and in all industries covered.[2]

These things do not provide a self-explanatory background to industrial unrest. It is true that in the last few years the wages of the motor industry's male operatives—amongst whom the unrest has been concentrated—have risen slightly less fast than those of its women manual workers, and notably less fast than the pay of its white-collar employees. In the last four years for which data is available, men's wages were rising at 4 or 5 per cent annually (depending on whether weekly or hourly earnings are considered) compared with well over 6 per cent for motor industry salaries.

---

[1] Knowles, with Hill, *Bulletin of the Oxford University Institute of Statistics*, September/October 1954. The strong piece-work tradition of West Midlands metal-working trades is, of course, in several ways a factor in the situation.

[2] The different industrial groupings of vehicle manufacture to which the statistics quoted in this paragraph relate reflect, we are afraid, the ways of official publication in this respect.

However, the closing of the sex differential in the motor plants was too slight—and the employment of women in most plants is too insignificant—for that factor to be considered important. And it seems hardly likely that the salaried employees' recent relative gain has been widely known amongst the manual workers. Moreover, the recency of these trends is in any case such that (even if they did remotely contribute to the maintenance of high levels of unrest in the 1960s) they could not explain the sharp rise in the incidence of motor industry disputes in the 1950s.

The association of the majority of car firms with the Engineering Employers' Federation, and of their operatives with the engineering trade unions, has of course involved the motor plants in general engineering wage-movements. But though some car factories' participation in the general engineering strikes of recent years made a substantial contribution to the rise in their 'loss of working days' from disputes, it does not appear that their operatives or shop stewards have played any very prominent part in agitations around general engineering wage-claims. In basic wage-rates, as in actual earnings, the motor industry has played something of the part of 'wage leader' to the engineering industry, in fact. It seems at one time to have been a not uncommon tactic of the non-federated motor firms to anticipate the development of national wage-negotiations in the engineering trades by waiting until these had reached a point at which some concession by the engineering employers seemed inevitable, and then themselves awarding basic wage-advances rather larger than the federated employers seemed likely to concede—though by the 1960s the American-owned firms' wage-negotiations were no longer so closely related to the national engineering wage-cycle.

But in any case the trend of car operatives' wages has clearly been determined as much, if not more, by events at the plant level as by the effect of engineering national agreements. In the four years to April 1964, again, the latter probably added some 23s or 24s to basic weekly wage-rates in 'federated' firms: but average weekly earnings in the motor vehicle industry rose by 69s.[1] And it *is* perhaps relevant to the increasing dispute-proneness of the car firms during the 1950s that the rise in the actual wages of motor workers seems, so far as it can be traced, to have been rather irregular. Average hourly earnings in motor manufacture largely escaped the post-war Labour government's national 'wage-restraint' of 1948–50, rising by about 5 per cent annually to the end of 1951 (by which time wages in other industries

[1] This is not, of course, by itself a measure of 'wage drift'. In relative terms, for instance, the rise in engineering rates was about 13½ per cent—in motor earnings about 18 per cent.

were closing up to them again). Their movement then began to accelerate, however, to 7 per cent in each of 1952 and 1953, and to over 9 per cent in 1954 and 1955.

After the 1956 recession in the motor trade, however, the pace of advance in its operatives' hourly earnings slowed substantially, averaging about 6½ per cent annually from 1955 to 1960. So it seems quite possible that the failure of wages in the car factories to maintain the rate of increase established in the *early* 1950s provides some contributory explanation of the rise in the frequency of strikes arising (either on the Ministry of Labour's classification or on ours) from straight wage-demands during the *late* 1950s. While the maintenance of a high level of disputes on this score since 1960 (see Table I of Chapter II) might equally well have been encouraged by a further slowing in the advance of motor industry earnings since that date. Following the 1960 recession, and the adoption of a stronger policy in labour relations by the car firms, hourly earnings rose by only 5 per cent a year. During the four years to 1964, indeed, hourly wages in outside industries generally (though not in engineering) were rising perceptibly faster than those in motors.

(B) INTER-FIRM AND INTER-PLANT DIFFERENTIALS

However—and as our preliminary general analysis of Chapter II has already indicated—it is in the structure of wages in the car-manufacturing industry rather than their absolute level that the main source of the industry's wage-discontents apparently lies. And in one respect at least this can be linked with the general post-war movement of car industry pay which has been traced above. Taking average hourly earnings as again the best guide to relative wages, there is clearly a substantial difference between wage-levels in the various firms. In 1962, for instance, average hourly earnings of manual workers at the American-owned firms were apparently about 9s. At the main Oxford and Birmingham plants they were 10s or so. But at firms whose main plants were at Coventry they were over 10s 6d an hour. This represents a difference of more than 15 per cent in average earnings per hour between the lower- and higher-paying firms. Moreover, hourly pay in some plants lay outside this range, and, as we shall again indicate later, the range of hourly earnings between firms is often much greater for particular occupations and jobs. This does not, of course, mean that actual average wage-packets differed quite so widely between plants. *Weekly* earnings in the American-owned firms, for instance, have been brought up to those of others (if not, sometimes, ahead of them) by more extensive overtime: from the early 1950s, Ford and Vauxhall operatives appear to have normally

DIAGRAM V/1 CAR FIRMS
Adult male Average Hourly Earnings

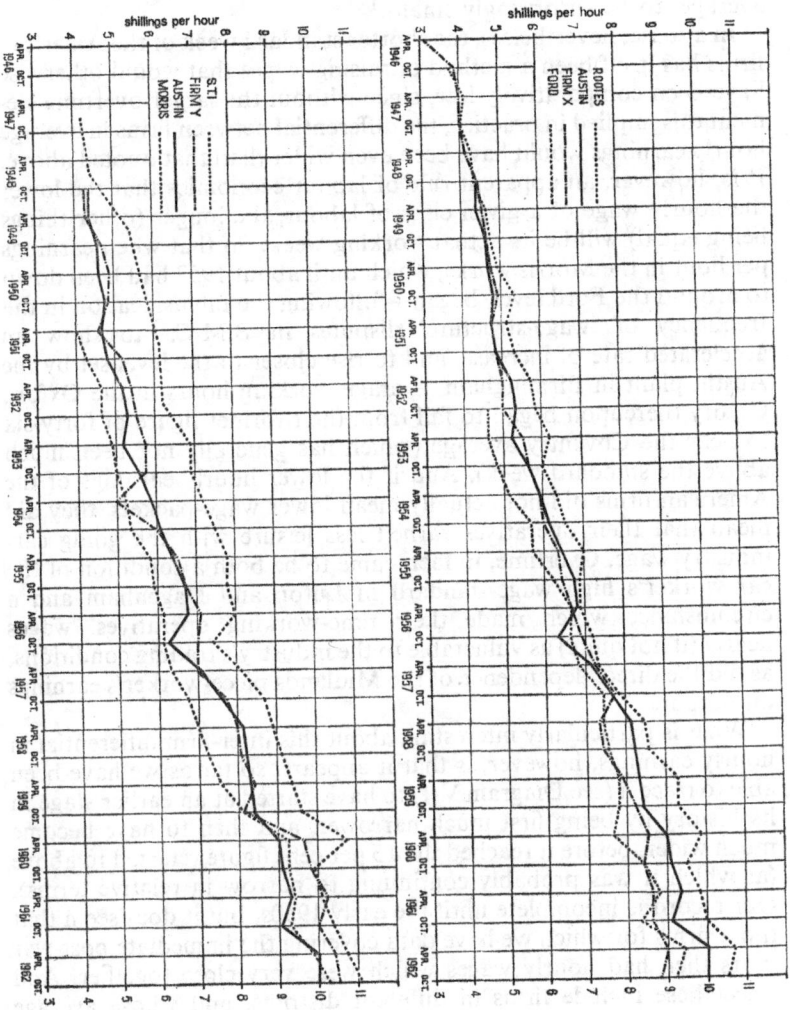

worked three to five hours a week more than those in most of the other firms. And the lower hourly earnings in the American-owned firms may be to some extent attributed to their general use of time-rates: an earnings differential between piece-workers and time-workers is normal in industry (though in motors it turns out, on average, to be surprisingly small).[1]

In a sense, nevertheless, the shorter standard week of the American firms has itself been a method of raising wages that would otherwise have been comparatively low, since without the larger overtime element this implied in practice, the differential between firms in average hourly earnings would have been even wider than that quoted above. It is, however, an apparent rule of labour economics that the lower the hourly wage of a given class of labour, the longer (other things being equal) will be its actual working week. So that when earnings per hour in the Morris works, which until about 1957 had been down to around the Ford level, began—following the intensification in the frequency of 'wage-structure' disputes in B.M.C.—to show an accelerated rate of increase, and to rise closer to the level set by the Austin plant in Birmingham, average working hours in the Oxford factory thereupon began to fall from their former figure of forty-six to near the Coventry average (which has generally not been much above the standard week). And if the lower hourly earnings of the American firms did not actually mean lower wage-packets, they did mean that their operatives earned less leisure with the going car-industry wage. Overtime, in fact, came to be both a condition of the car worker's high wage-standard in Luton and Dagenham and a circumstance which made their time-working operatives' wages nearly (if not quite) as vulnerable to the industry's trading conditions, as did the direct dependence of the Midlands piece-worker's earnings on output.

What is particularly interesting about this inter-firm differential in hourly earnings, however, is that it appears, so far as we have been able to trace it (see Diagram V/1) to have started at an earlier stage in its history by being first much narrower, and then to have become much wider, before it reached the 15 per cent figure referred to above (at which it was probably continuing to narrow in relative terms). Our record is incomplete until the early 1950s, but it does seem that those firms for which we have data covering the immediate post-war years then had hourly wages which were very close together. And since these include firms in different districts, and whose average hourly earnings later diverged considerably, it is reasonable to suppose that until the late 1940s this was broadly true of all the car firms. About this time, however, pressure for output was mounting

[1] See pp. 158/9.

as the car firms completed their post-war reconversion programmes, new models began to come off the assembly lines, and an apparently insatiable export market revealed itself. Competition for labour became intense, particularly in the booming Coventry district (where a precedent of particularly high piece-work earnings for high output had been already established during wartime aircraft production); and the restraints on wages imposed by the employers' sense of caution and mutual solidarity began to give way.

In one way, the break may have already come. In 1945 Standard Motors withdrew from the local engineering employers' association because (what was then) the Engineering & Allied Employers' National Federation wished to limit the firm's right to pursue its own wage-policy, and particularly to base piece-rates and output bonuses on 100 per cent margins above engineering basic rates (as against the $27\frac{1}{2}$ per cent then authorized by engineering agreements). This decision—which, apart from its effect on the car industry, may well have contributed to the commercially unfortunate later history of the firm itself—was openly inspired by a desire to allow no barriers in the way of expanding the firm's output and labour force. We have no detailed earnings figures that go back as far as this date, but it does appear quite likely that the decision was responsible for an early post-war jump in motor industry wages: the differential of car firm hourly earnings over those in other vehicle concerns was by 1947 almost certainly wider than before the war, and such figures as we have for 1946 and 1947 suggest that the car operative's hourly wage was then rising sharply. But by 1947 earnings in the different car plants seem to have been back in line, other firms having presumably caught up with Standard.

At the end of 1948, however, Standard Motors made a new, and this time much more radical, resort to the same tactic. It signed an independent agreement with the district engineering unions which, apart from introducing the new wage-structure and payment system to the Standard plants already referred to (Chapter III), effectively produced there a 20 per cent difference in average hourly pay above that ruling in other motor firms. This time the other firms—whether 'federated' or otherwise—were slower to respond, and for some time Standard Motors operated at a level of hourly wages quite distinctively higher than that of other car manufacturers.[1] But by the early 1950s other Coventry plants—especially Rootes, as our Diagram shows[2]—had already begun to pull away from the generality of car firms in terms of wages paid per hour.

[1] Detailed figures for Standard Motors up to 1953 are cited in S. Melman, *Decision-making and Productivity*, Table 6.
[2] Incidentally, in Diagram V/1 firms have been arbitrarily separated into two

The subsequent course of events is traced by the Diagram. In 1953 Standard earnings per hour were still about 50 per cent above those in the lowest-paying major concerns (then, Ford and Morris Cowley). From that time on, at least, wages in S.T.I. (so far as one can trace their path through the fluctuations to which even *hourly* earnings in individual firms in the motor industry are liable) do not seem to have risen at a pace which was abnormal by comparison with outside industry. But the general pace of wage-advance in the car factories was being pushed up as the other Coventry car plants—first Rootes and then others—were driven to raise their hourly pay to near the S.T.I. level (which they finally approximated to by the early 1960s), and the plants outside the Coventry district were then pressed to close the relative gap between their hourly wages and those of the Coventry firms.

Still more steam was put into this movement after the B.M.C. merger, when the pressure to raise Morris Cowley pay to Austin levels got under way. So that this narrowing of the range between the highest- and the lowest-paying firm from (probably) more than 50 per cent in hourly pay in 1950 to (almost certainly) less than 15 per cent at the present time, was mainly achieved by a generally accelerated upward wage-movement in the car firms during the early and middle 1950s. Indeed, had not the rate of rise in Ford pay, which apparently steepened over 1956–57, thereafter flattened off as the Briggs plant was assimilated into the Ford wage-system, this accelerated general movement might well have been maintained into the late 1950s as well.

What is mainly at work here, of course, is the force of the 'compulsive comparison'—in this case, the effect of information about earnings at other firms and plants transmitted through the unions and joint shop stewards' organizations. Competition for labour between the car plants cannot be a substantial part of the explanation, since several of the firms involved are not in fact competing with each other in this sense (at least, to any significant extent), and the effect of their participation in the movement must have been to raise the differential of their wages over non-car firms in their own local labour markets. Moreover, different degrees of union organization or inadequate

groups to make the picture comprehensible. However, the Austin line has been repeated in both diagrams so that trends for other firms can be compared between the diagrams in relation to it. The Diagram does not by any means indicate the full range of average hourly earnings between individual plants or firms which might be found at any one time, particularly at the lower end of the cash scale. The averages have, however, been selected as themselves covering the great majority of the car industry's workers, and at the same time indicating the limits within which plant hourly average wages for an even greater (if not overwhelming) majority of operatives lay.

communications have sometimes permitted marked differences in wages even between contiguous car plants. Thus, Pressed Steel at Cowley was quite well organized by the unions in the 1930s, and—like Standard—seems also to have followed a 'high wage' policy (though without formal agreement, or break with the employers' association): indeed, by the 1960s earnings there probably approached Coventry levels. But this apparently had little influence on the Morris plant (which is linked to Pressed Steel by conveyor) which was not well organized until the late 1950s, and whose stewards have few associations with those at Pressed Steel.

But it is also interesting that if the inter-firm differential in hourly wages has narrowed during and since the 1950s in *relative* terms, it has also remained pretty constant in cash terms. There seems, in fact, to have been a dual process at work. Once the higher wage-level was established, first for Standard's and then for other Coventry plants, shop stewards in the lower-paid plants attempted to catch up. But in plants where workers benefited from the new differential, there was a struggle to maintain it (Standard Motors itself ultimately rejoined the engineering employers' association, having discovered that neither its high effective rate of pay nor its divorce from the association—nor even a specific clause in its 1948 agreement with the unions to the effect that general and local engineering agreements did not automatically apply to the Company—exempted it from demands that the general wage-increases conceded by 'federated' engineering firms should also be paid to its workers). The net result of these two pressures was to keep the inter-firm differential in hourly pay set up by Standard's 1948 decision (or rather, the resulting range between the higher- and lower-paying firms) fairly constant in terms of cash, but narrowing in relative terms.

This is a situation not unfamiliar in kind to students of pay-differentials in general: it is one, however, of which a necessary condition is a rapid rise in average wages. In effect, the especially rapid increase in car industry wages during the early 1950s provided a partial outlet for the opposing pressures to reduce and to maintain the inter-firm differentials. But as, from the mid-1950s on, the resistance of firms to rising wage-costs was strengthened by repeated recessions and intensified foreign competition (as well, perhaps, as by the development of a government anti-inflation policy which increasingly emphasized 'incomes-restraint') this outlet for the tensions concerned became more and more restricted. They expressed themselves instead in a rising frequency of 'wage-structure' disputes.

One element in the sharp increase in wage-connected disputes in the motor firms during the 1950s was thus the contradictory pressures generated by new inter-firm and inter-plant differentials. (The merger of Austin and Morris into B.M.C. converted what was formerly an inter-firm differential into an inter-plant one within the same firm, and thus sharpened the frictions it implied.) And if one wished for further evidence of the force of 'compulsive comparisons' between wages at related plants as a factor in motor industry unrest, it is surely supplied by the experience of the car firms' extension into the new areas of Scotland and the Merseyside in recent years. The firms that established plants in these districts were persuaded to do so by government pressure rather than the hope of escaping the dispute-proneness of the older producing regions: but clearly, the strikes that began to occur in the new plants were unexpected.

Certainly, however, one factor in the car firms' agreement to set up these plants rather than expand their existing establishments was the ample local availability of labour, with which was not unassociated the considerably lower general level of wages prevailing in the 'development districts' compared with the Midlands and South-East. And the wage-scales initially set up in the new plants commonly provided a distinctly lower pay-level than in the older factories of the same firm (in the federated firms, at least, average hourly earnings in the new districts seem to have been about three-quarters those in their main works—though the figure is influenced by their much greater use of time-rate systems in the new plants). While *all* the firms argued such a differential to be justified by lower productivity in the venture's early experience. Nevertheless, and despite the persistence of significant local unemployment in the new areas, the firms concerned were very soon put under pressure to raise earnings in their new plants to the levels established in their existing factories. Of the disputes in the new plants which we have traced from 1961 through to 1963 inclusive, over half arose from 'wage-structure' and related issues. And to this pressure they all seem to have been obliged to make some concession.[1] B.M.C., for instance, adopted a programme to raise earnings at its Scottish plant by yearly instalments—though hoping that the approach to Midlands levels would be supported by a relatively faster productivity growth.

---

[1] In some instances—for example, the demand supported by a one-day stoppage of Ford workers in 1960 for the firm to pay the same rates at its new Halewood plant as in Dagenham—this pressure seems to have been backed by the stewards at the 'home' factories, not just from solidarity, but also from a fear that lower labour costs in the new plants might lead to a transfer of work to them. And in case this seems to contradict the suggestion—as in the Standard case previously referred to—that stewards in the higher-paying firms also try to maintain their differential, one can only say: 'So it does'! But to expect that shop stewards at all times and in all places will pursue completely consistent policies would be as unperceptive as to demand the same thing of politicians.

Wages in the Motor Industry

(c) plant wage-structures, and 'anomalies'

Not that the elimination of the differences in *average* hourly wages between plants and firms would by any means also eliminate—or even substantially reduce—the potential for unrest in the motor industry's wage structure. During early 1963 we were able to compile from trade union sources a fairly detailed picture of earnings by job or occupational category in most of the major car plants. The picture had gaps, but could be supplemented by information from some individual firms (and in one area by pay-slips collected with shop stewards' assistance); and its results appeared consistent with the data for plant earnings averages and distributions the firms authorized us to use, and with the more general official surveys. At any one time, of course, particular earnings—even when measured on an hourly basis—are liable to be affected by such things as exceptional overtime or 'waiting time'. But we also gather our general picture of pay-relativities in car firms to be not inconsistent with detailed surveys firms have made at other times. Our analysis shows that for *specified jobs* in the car plants the range of average hourly earnings between different firms was often in the ratio of 2 to 1, and seldom less than $1\frac{1}{2}$ to 1—in other words, a range of difference in payment for particular jobs of 50 to 100 per cent, compared with the range of only 15 per cent between firms when the earnings for particular jobs were averaged together.

Now this disparity between the two ranges did not arise because the firms which were, *on the average*, lower-paying were prevented from being lower-paying still by having larger proportions of their operatives in the higher grades. In fact, the reverse was true—Ford and Vauxhall, for instance, apparently have rather low proportions of highly-rated workers by contrast with several Coventry plants (which is by no means the same thing as saying that they also have lower proportions of skilled workers). Nor did the disparity between the job-earnings range and the plant-earnings range arise because, again, the firms which paid less on the average were prevented from being still lower in the scale of relative hourly earnings by having larger proportions of piece-workers. The lower-paying concerns were—as one would expect—those which pay their workers by time-rates alone. The disparity appears rather to be the consequence of an extreme lack of correspondence between the hierarchical orders in which different jobs rank themselves, in terms of hourly pay, as between one firm and another—or even as between the various plants of the same firm (in the case of some 'federated' concerns). So that a job which may in one plant be highly-rated in terms of the plant's internal pay hierarchy may in another plant be lowly-rated, and *vice versa*.

This situation seems largely unintended—in the sense that the apparent anomalies it involves do not reflect, on the whole, different views on the part of the firms concerned as to the most appropriate structure of job-relativities for a car plant. Broadly speaking, the car firms' operatives appear to fall into three bands from the point of view of average hourly pay. Uppermost, with job-earnings averaging, at the time of our survey, roughly from 10s to 11s 6d an hour, are the production workers proper—machinists, engine and car assemblers, press operators, welders and paint sprayers, and so on—on 'payment by results'. In the same band—though at its lower edge—come a number of skilled men whose work is closely connected with production or preparatory to it, like toolmakers or metal- and woodworkers on prototypes. The middle band, with average job earnings per hour spread at this time between 7s 6d and 9s, includes a number of workers ancillary to production itself—internal transport drivers, storemen and so on—as well as, on the one hand, the production inspectors and, on the other, the plant's skilled maintenance men. And the lowest band—with job earnings then averaging 6s to 6s 6d an hour—embraces both such male workers as are graded unskilled (labourers, janitors, etc.) *and* the women operatives in car plants.

These are, however, merely average statements. And the rather curious structure of job-relativities they depict is far from being that which obtains in the few plants where a systematic hierarchy of job-rates has been set up in a co-ordinated way, by agreement at the company level. Nor is it a structure to which the actual hierarchy ruling in any other plant necessarily corresponds. It represents, rather, the total effect of a multitude of separate decisions and pressures on individual job-rates. Thus, the hourly pay of production workers at Vauxhall and Ford fell into the middle band of earnings rather than the upper, but at both these firms skilled workers, whether for maintenance or production, had higher hourly pay than the assembly operatives. On the other hand, the Pressed Steel Company—which at this period had what were, even for car firms, rather high hourly earnings for most grades of production operatives (at least in its main Oxford plant)—yielded at the same time to its skilled workers hourly wages which just reached middling by comparison with the industry average, although the earnings of its maintenance craftsmen were raised somewhat higher by overtime. But in another body-building plant, the B.M.C. factory of Fisher & Ludlow, skilled workers connected with production were earning as much per hour as the production operatives proper, and the maintenance men were not much behind them.

One could extend the list of seeming anomalies at length. For instance, another firm with relatively high hourly pay for production workers was Jaguar: yet its maintenance men and ancillary workers were not then particularly well-paid by industry standards. Rover (where average hourly earnings in general were definitely not of the highest) at this time paid skilled workers auxiliary or preparatory to production better than machine-operators and assembly men, but its skilled maintenance men worse. In S.T.I., the hourly earnings of women operatives (sewing machinists and the like) were as high as those of several categories of maintenance tradesmen in its own plant, and higher than the pay of the same men in a neighbouring firm. But its few janitors (to take another 'fringe' group) were amongst the lowest-paid in all the car firms. Again, generally speaking the occupational group with the highest hourly earnings in the industry appears to be the 'dingmen'—sheet metalworkers whose job is to straighten out dents in the panels of car bodies caused by the accidents of the assembly process: but in the Austin plant dingmen's pay per hour was at this time apparently lower, not merely than production operatives', but also than that of most ancillary skilled workers.

The position of the inspectors in the motor firms is of some special interest, since these are both responsible for the maintenance of the quality of the assembly lines' output, and working in close association with the production operatives. The firms with systematic pay structures have recognized the inspectors' special position by putting them, according to their class of work, close to or above the production men in their pay relativity; but among the car firms as a whole their hourly pay is quite substantially below that of the production worker. So that even in the 'quality' firms, inspectors' average hourly earnings were between two-thirds and three-quarters those of assemblers, machinists and so on. Or again, in most plants maintenance fitters were considerably better paid than other maintenance men, and sometimes notably so; but in a minority of firms they appear to be on the same pay level. And so on. Even the firms with systematic rate-structures apparently have different views about the relative positions major job-groups should occupy—Ford apparently putting internal transport men and storemen on the same level as production workers while Vauxhall grades them lower, for instance.

It is perhaps important that disparities of this kind appear to occur between plants in the same district—or between the different plants of the same concern. However, it is even more important that, if such anomalies appear in the *average* pay for particular jobs or groups of jobs as between plants, they are also likely to appear (in those firms where detailed rates are settled separately for different—often small—groups of workers) *within* a plant for workers at about the same occupational level. And it is perhaps also important that if workers in the car firms generally are well paid by comparison with

PERCENTAGES OF ADULT MALE OPERATIVES AT DIFFERENT PAY LEVELS

DIAGRAM V/2a
Distribution of men's weekly earnings 1960

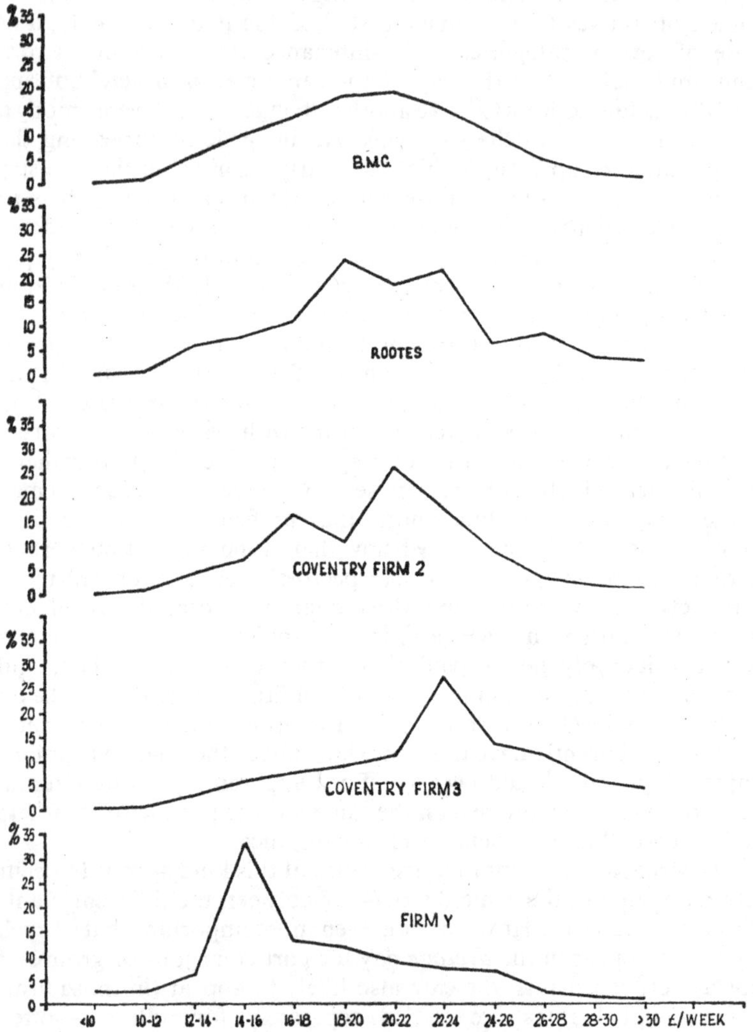

PERCENTAGES OF ADULT MALE OPERATIVES AT DIFFERENT PAY LEVELS

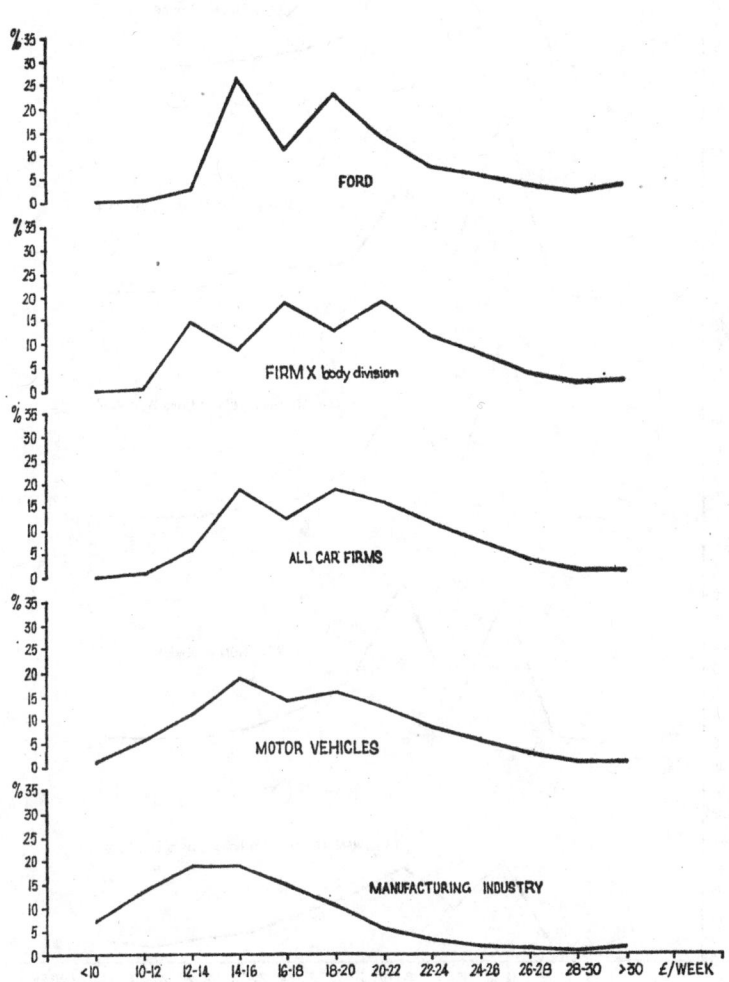

DIAGRAM V/2b
Distribution of men's weekly earnings 1960

PERCENTAGES OF ADULT MALE OPERATIVES AT DIFFERENT PAY LEVELS

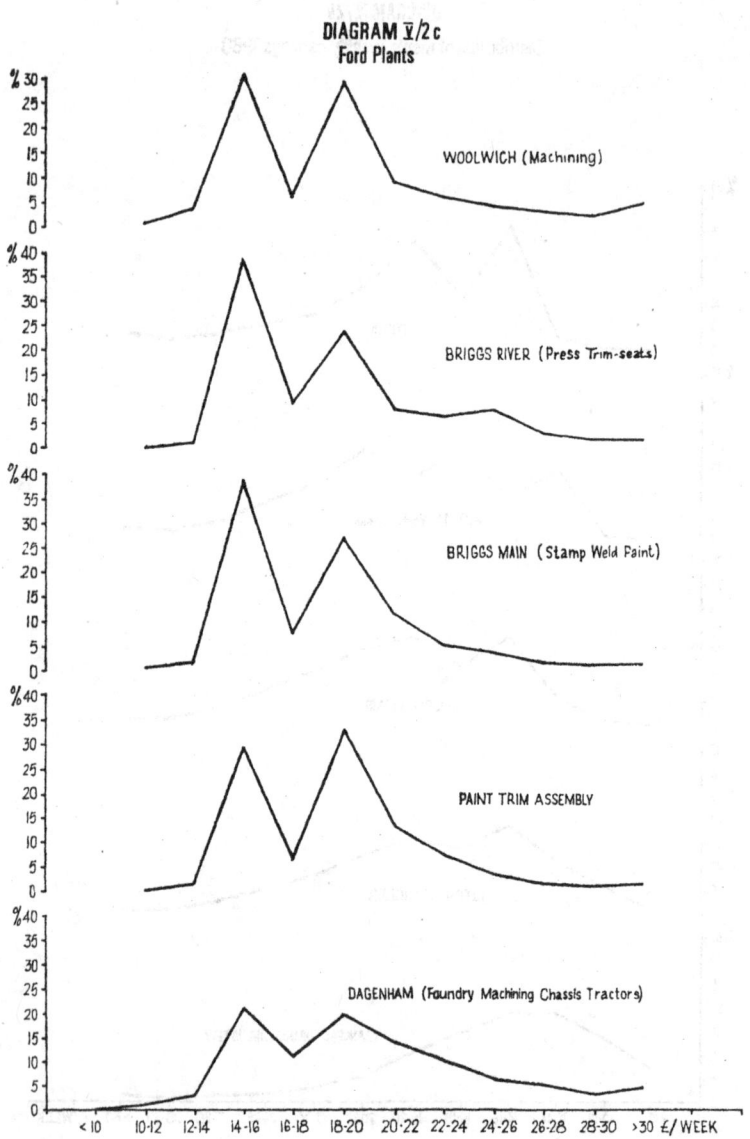

DIAGRAM V/2c
Ford Plants

PERCENTAGES OF ADULT MALE OPERATIVES AT DIFFERENT PAY LEVELS

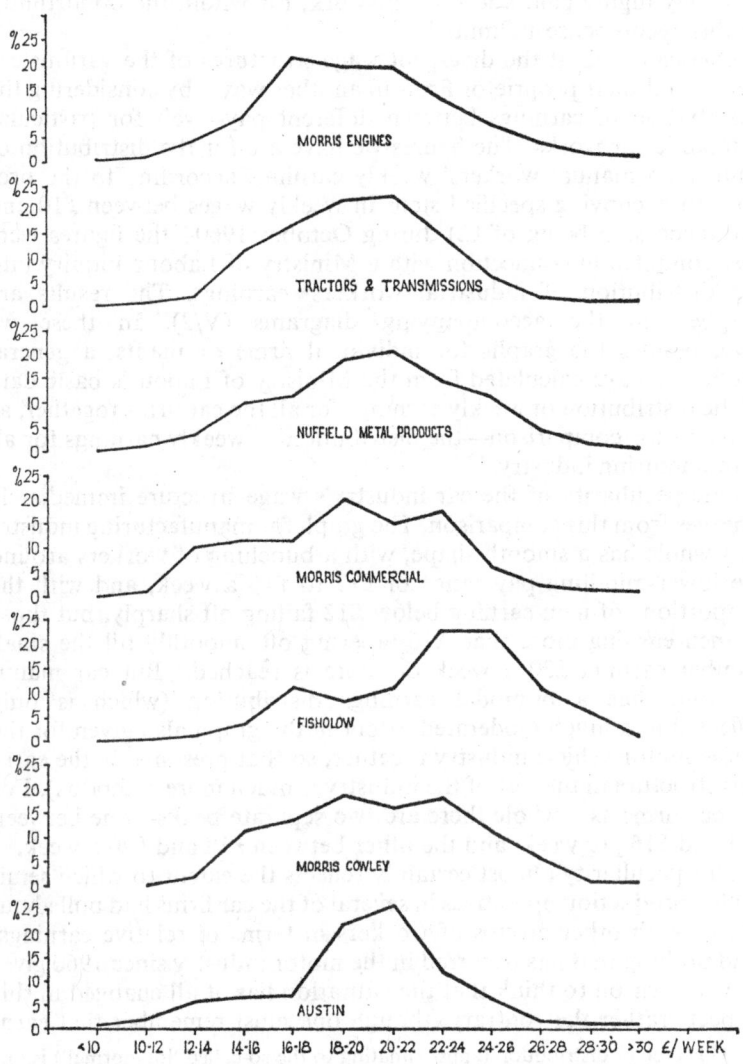

DIAGRAM V/2d
B.M.C. Plants

those in other industries, there are many groups of car industry operatives whose pay is by no means remarkable by outside comparison. Some of these—as in the case of maintenance men, by and large—may be able to make up for relatively low hourly earnings by extensive overtime; but there are others, like inspectors and internal transport workers in plants where the production operatives are both relatively highly-paid and on shift-work, for whom the opportunity of this recompense is limited.

One can look at the divergent wage-structures of the various car plants and their proprietor firms in another way—by considering the distribution of earnings between different pay-levels for particular companies or works. The figures we have are for the distribution of adult men manual workers' weekly earnings according to the proportion occupying specified steps in weekly wages between £10 and £30 (each step being of £2) during October 1960—the figures were first compiled in connection with a Ministry of Labour inquiry into the distribution of industrial workers' earnings. The results are graphed in the accompanying diagrams (V/2). In these we give, besides the graphs for individual firms or plants, a general profile we have calculated from the Ministry of Labour's basic data of the distribution of weekly earnings for all the car firms together, as well as—for comparison—the distribution of weekly earnings for all manufacturing industry.

One peculiarity of the car industry's wage-structure immediately emerges from this comparison. The graph for manufacturing industry as a whole has a smooth shape, with a bunching of workers around the lower-middling pay range of £12 to £16 a week, and with the proportions of men earning below £12 falling off sharply, but those of men earning more than £16 tapering off smoothly till the small number earning £30 a week or more is reached.[1] But car manufacturing has a bi-modal earnings distribution (which is only reflected to a much moderated extent in the graph also given for the whole motor vehicle industry together, so that presumably the earnings structure in the rest of the industry is much more orthodox). For the car firms as a whole there are two separate peaks—one between £14 and £16 per week, and the other between £18 and £20 a week.

This peculiarity almost certainly reflects the extent to which semi-skilled production operatives in several of the car firms had pulled out of line with other groups of workers in terms of relative earnings. And nothing that has occurred in the motor industry since 1960 gives one any reason to think that the situation has at all changed in this respect: rather the contrary (though one must remember that earn-

[1] This type of distribution (approximating to the so-called 'log-normal') is one commonly found in earnings and income differentials in general.

ings in general have, at the time of writing, risen by at least a quarter since the figures were collected, so that all the graphs derived from them could probably be moved to the right to that extent). However, the graph again represents an average statement, and one to which the earnings 'profile' for no particular car firm or plant corresponds at all closely. The profile for Ford, for instance, also shows a bi-modal distribution: but that its two peaks represent, like those of the graph for the car firms as a whole, clusters of operatives earning around £15 and £19 a week is an accident which is quite overwhelmed, in the general picture, by the divergent patterns of other plants. We doubt very much, for instance, whether a profile for Vauxhall—despite the fact that, like Ford, it has a co-ordinated wage-structure—would show the same pattern; although it, too, has a large proportion of workers rated around the basic operative categories, its more refined 'grouping and grading' system would produce more extended brackets of earnings above that level.[1]

But it becomes in any case immediately obvious that despite the close similarity of their technologies, and thus of the types of jobs they provide and of worker they employ, no one of the car firms has an earnings structure which is at all like that of any other one for which we have data. Nor, in spite of the size of the firms concerned, is any one of their different wage-structures 'normal' in the usual statistical sense for earnings distributions: true, the profile for B.M.C. shows a smooth progression, but even that is pushed to the right by comparison with the earnings distribution for manufacturing at large, while its shape is in any case the accidental product of the averaging out of its separate plants' various earnings relativities. But if one takes the three firms whose major establishments are in the Coventry district, it is clear how much the wage-structures even of neighbouring plants can diverge in pattern. Both Rootes and 'Coventry Firm 2' have what is effectively a twin-peaked distribution, but the latter's two peaks are both at lower levels of pay than Rootes'; on the other hand the peak which is higher up the pay scale in the case of 'Coventry Firm 2' contains much the larger proportion of workers, and the percentages of workers earning above this level fall off much less sharply as successively higher steps in earnings are reached. 'Coventry Firm 3', however, has a quite different earnings distribution again, with a very pronounced single peak between £22 and £24 a week, and a long trail of workers earning below that level.

[1] The weekly earnings graphed in these charts incidentally include overtime payments, so that the diagrams for Ford may also give some indication, when compared with that for the car firms as a whole, of the extent to which relatively low *hourly* wages in the American-owned firms—which were still at this time probably some 20–25 per cent below Coventry car plant averages in this respect—were compensated by more extensive overtime.

Labour Relations in the Motor Industry

The importance of these things, of course, is that they imply that any particular job-category of operatives may in one plant be on the same earnings level as other groups related to it in the production process, and in another plant be at a higher or lower earnings level than those groups (as well, incidentally, as having different normal earnings to workers doing the same job in other factories). One can see the same thing if one compares the profiles for plants which do in fact have very comparable processes. The body plant of 'Firm X', and the B.M.C. body-building subsidiary Fisher & Ludlow both have very peculiar earnings profiles; but they are also very different to each other's in shape—the former's distribution having three distinct peaks, including one at a relatively modest level of earnings, while Fisholow's distribution shows a very pronounced 'plateau' in the upper earnings ranges—indicating a concentration of operatives then earning within a pound or two of £24 a week. Again, 'Firm Y' is in some respects comparable with at least one of the Coventry concerns. Yet its earnings distribution profile is almost an exact mirror-reversal of that for 'Coventry Firm 3'.

However, perhaps most revealing in this series is the collection of profiles for the separate plants of B.M.C. itself. Those for the former Nuffield plants—Morris Cowley, Morris Engines, Nuffield Metal Products, and so on—do differ somewhat between themselves, but not so much as to suggest, given their specialization between different processes, that anomalies in their respective earnings structures are important on this evidence alone. Though Morris Commercial is a probable exception, and the parallel series of profiles for individual Ford plants which we also give indicates that where a company has a co-ordinated wage-structure, partial specialization between its various plants will not prevent this structure imposing a high degree of uniformity on their separate earnings patterns. However, the Fisher & Ludlow earnings structure is, as already noted, quite deviant: and particularly, the profile for the distribution of Austin workers' earnings contrasts sharply with the Morris plants. This divergence provides some background explanation to the uprush of 'wage-structure' disputes in B.M.C. since the latter's formation.

To repeat, these profiles are derived from data collected in 1960; but though the earnings distributions of individual plants may have changed, there is no reason to think that their general state of disparity with each other has substantially altered in any other respect than that it now occurs at a higher average level of earnings. And to repeat again, the situation is also quite unintended—in the sense that the wage-structures of most car plants do not represent those which either the firms or (were they able to act together in this respect) the unions concerned would have considered rational, had they been able to examine and guide the development of relative earnings in a co-ordinated way. To a large extent, the situation is due to the various systems of payment that now obtain in the car plants, and particularly to the consequences of disparate attempts to adapt, over the course of time, the wage-system of general engineering to the needs and circumstances of car production.

(D) THE INSTABILITY OF EARNINGS

In principle, the engineering wage-system provides for two types of payment: a straight time-rate which varies according to skill-level (district variations, once numerous, having been progressively eliminated); and a piece-work wage which is compounded of two elements—a basic rate that varies with skill, and a bonus percentage (which particular piece-rates are supposed to yield to a worker of normal ability). In practice, however, a considerable variety of payment systems is to be found in the 'federated' car firms. Many production operatives—machinists, for instance, quite widely—are in fact paid on piece-rates which are individually determined according to the job on which they are engaged. But individual piece-rates are not suitable for operatives—like workers on assembly tracks—whose work is so inter-related that they constitute a single unit for production purposes, and in this case piece-rates or output bonuses have to be determined on a group basis, and the collective earnings shared out amongst the group's members. Though the payment scales that result are by no means necessarily 'straight line' in relation to output: one method, for instance, is to set a target output for the standard week, paying a specified wage if the target is reached *or* exceeded, but partially compensating for any shortfall on that figure by the payment of 'waiting time' for the hours of output thus presumed to be lost.

One problem which arises we have already referred to in Chapter III. This is that, although the earnings of production workers on payment-by-results rise with output, they may do so at different rates for the various individuals and groups who are separated, in any plant, for rate or task determination. And this may occur, not because of any differences in the efforts of the workers concerned but because relative bargaining strengths, skills, or determination vary at the time prices or work-loads are negotiated—*or* because productivity naturally increases at different speeds in the plant's various processes. Where piece-rates are fixed for the smallest practicable unit of labour—the individual or small group—(as may be done on the ground that an incentive is the more effective the more closely it relates earnings to individual effort) this differential effect can only be offset by *ad hoc* adjustment to particular rates so as to raise their earnings yield, either at the time when they have to be revised for other reasons or when dissatisfaction with an existing rate becomes so pronounced that something has to be done about it. But the task of keeping the earnings of production workers in line by this method, in an industry where fairly frequent changes in rates are in any case imposed by frequent changes in products—new models and modifications to existing ones—and a quite high pace of technological innovation, is too formidable to permit of more than partial success. This is why some firms have attempted to reduce the difficulty by grouping production workers into large gangs or teams for output bonus purposes.

A still more difficult problem, however, is that of the 'indirect' workers' pay determination. The tendency for the earnings of operatives whose work is not directly related to production processes—toolmakers, skilled workers in experimental shops or on maintenance, transport workers and storemen, etc.—to fall behind has imposed on the federated car firms a variety of attempts at compensation. One or two firms simply pay some of their skilled men a straight time-rate which is openly much above the local engineering rate for their grade. But more generally, the time-rate for indirect workers has been supplemented in diverse ways: engineering agreements provide that operatives who might normally expect to be paid on a piece-work basis, but are not able to be so employed because of difficulty in devising piece-rates for the jobs they are engaged on, may be paid a 'lieu' rate additional to their basic rate of pay. But this has generally proved an insufficient compensator, and some firms pay a variable 'supplementary bonus' as well.

Alternatively, an incentive element may be introduced into the earnings of indirect workers by paying them bonuses based on the output of the plant as a whole or of a department with which they are connected, or by devising special group or individual incentive schemes for them in which the earnings yield is supposed to reflect as directly as possible their own efforts. The system may incorporate further variables—like a *dis*incentive to undue overtime work. In at least one plant, certain key skilled men receive the average of the production piece-workers' earnings per hour. Different systems of payment for indirect workers of different types may rule within the same firm—or, for a particular class of operatives, as between the same firm's different plants (often because the company has taken over the wage-system of another concern in acquiring the concern itself). Any discussion of wage-systems in a federated firm is thus liable to start with the preliminary explanation: 'Well, it's rather complicated'—or even the confession (from a group of shop stewards): 'We're afraid we don't fully understand all of it ourselves.'

However, a widespread attempt to apply production or performance bonuses to indirect workers is probably responsible for the relatively high proportion of 'payment-by-results' workers in federated car firms. In the motor industry as a whole, the proportion of men manual workers who are so classed is about the same as in engineering at large—47.5 per cent in mid-1964, against 48.5 per cent for engineering. But the two big non-federated car firms pay time-rates only, so the proportion must be higher for other car plants. Data on this is unsatisfactory, but from those plants for which we have it—though there is again a considerable variation amongst these—it seems that the proportion of 'payment-by-results' operatives in federated car firms must be somewhere between two-thirds and three-quarters.[1] Moreover, and though there again seem to have been differences in the trend in different plants in this respect, the proportion appears on the whole to have been rising since the early 1950s.

There is, however (and apart from the inevitability that efforts to modify indirect workers' payment systems in response to expediency have produced anomalies in earnings among the different groups of indirect workers themselves), one general difficulty in this attempt to spread the rewards of rising output. This is that the earnings of piece-working production operatives show other effects than that of *generally* rising productivity. Whenever a product or process is changed, piece-rates (or the output tasks set for bonus payment) have to be adjusted accordingly: though the adjustment may in the first instance be made by a rate-fixer or time-study man, this is effectively a bargaining process, and bargaining under contemporary circumstances tends to start from the assumption that the new task must give at least the same earnings yield as that with which the old task ended. So there is an upwards 'ratchet effect'. Moreover, workers' productivity tends to rise particularly fast in the first few weeks or months after a new task is undertaken, so that by the time this 'running in' phase is completed earnings on the new job are significantly higher than the normal growth of productivity would explain. Thus, the more frequently job-rates have to be changed, the faster earnings of production workers rise. This perhaps explains why machinists and engine-assemblers in the federated car firms on the whole earn rather less than press-operators, car assemblers and other workers on car bodies. Engine designs are changed much less frequently than those for the rest of the car.

[1] Returns from establishments actually show odd fluctuations which probably reflect the classificatory difficulties of the present situation. It is not unusual to find operatives referred to as day-workers even though a large element in their pay derives from a production bonus of some kind.

This tendency of production operatives' earnings to pull away from those of other workers, despite the attempts of individual firms to compensate the latter (B.M.C. and Pressed Steel, for instance, have an annual review of time-workers' earnings in their English plants) also probably explains one marked general peculiarity of the motor industry's wage-structure: that it has virtually abolished the differential for skill. This can be partly shown by the Table V/1.

Table V/1—PERCENTAGE RATIO OF AVERAGE HOURLY EARNINGS (INCLUDING OVERTIME), AVERAGE OF JANUARY AND JUNE, 1963

	Time-workers			Payment-by-results workers		
	Skilled to Labourer	Semi-skilled to Labourer	Skilled to Semi-skilled	Skilled to Labourer	Semi-skilled to Labourer	Skilled to Semi-skilled
All Engineering:	142	126	113	143	132	108
Motor Vehicles:	142	130	109	153	150	102

The table, of course, includes earnings in other motor vehicle concerns than the car firms, but it is almost certainly the latter that dominate the picture. It will be seen that whereas for time-workers the skilled-to-labourer differential in motors during 1963 was the same as in engineering, the semi-skilled operatives were much closer to the skilled man's hourly wage and proportionately more distant from the labourer's. But it is the payment-by-results workers whose position is the more revealing: in their case, the differential of skilled workers over semi-skilled had been reduced to 2 per cent, by comparison with 8 per cent in engineering: but the differential of both skilled and semi-skilled motor workers over labourers was markedly wider than in the rest of the engineering industry.

What has happened in the motor firms is that the tendency for production operatives' earnings on payment-by-results systems to rise autonomously has pushed their wage so close to that of skilled workers that the difference is negligible, even if the latter are also on P.B.R. But attempts to prevent the differential being quite reversed have also pushed up the *skilled* P.B.R. worker's earnings, so that his differential over labourers has actually widened. In the car firms proper, however, very few workers are classed as labourers, anyway. And the normal difference between the hourly earnings of time-workers and P.B.R. workers—though this is smaller in motors

Wages in the Motor Industry

(averaging 6 per cent in 1963, against 9 per cent in engineering as a whole)—has meant that the semi-skilled P.B.R. operative's hourly wage had actually risen above that of the skilled time-worker: by some 4 per cent at this time. Moreover, the process of eliminating or reversing the skill differential appears to be a continuing one; by mid-1964 semi-skilled P.B.R. workers' average hourly earnings in motors were within 1 per cent of the skilled P.B.R. workers', and 7 per cent above those of skilled time-workers.

The virtual disappearance of the skill differential in the motor industry as a whole is symptomatic of a general tendency of its payment methods to erase systematic differences in wages. The problems created by the car firms' wage-systems are, of course, not unfamiliar to the engineering industry in general. But in the motor plants they are enormously aggravated by their faster rate of productivity growth and technological change. We have already referred (in Chapter III) to the specific problems that automation, in particular, has created for payment systems and wage-structures in the motor industry, and to the several attempts that firms have made to overcome these difficulties. The problem of constructing an appropriate payment system for car production in the British industry's particular circumstances is one of enormous difficulty: and any system is likely to have substantial disadvantages. What *is* perhaps desirable—at least in the light of the high dispute-liability of B.M.C. and certain Coventry plants on the score of wage-structure matters—is that there should be a common system within a firm and a district, and especially that some order and uniformity of occupational earnings should rule at these levels. Though it may be hard to achieve this without a measure of agreement amongst the firms as a whole.

One other feature of wages in the car firms seems likely to have made a major contribution to unrest. Our chart of the trend of average hourly earnings in various major car firms over a period has already shown that the general upward movement of the car worker's pay is liable to be interrupted by occasional sharp falls—even in the American-owned firms which pay by time-rates alone. And this instability is still more characteristic of weekly earnings, of earnings generally in the payment-by-results plants, and of the earnings of small groups of operatives or individuals. This is partly a consequence, given the motor industry's payment methods, of the general fluctuations in production to which it has become liable in recent years. It is also a consequence of such more minor disturbances to output as the effects of technical hold-ups, of breakdowns, sometimes of changes in models or equipment, and of strikes in other departments or plants. Occasionally, it results from methods of bonus calculation themselves.

Labour Relations in the Motor Industry

One general source of this instability is variation in hours worked, and particularly in overtime working—which remains an important element in the car operative's wage-packet (especially, as has been noted, in the American-owned firms). The extent to which car industry wages are especially liable to variation on this account may be to some extent illustrated by comparison with other engineering trades —which are themselves not notable for stability in this respect. The Ministry of Labour's indices of total and average hours worked by operatives in manufacturing industry (which are now published monthly) show that over the period 1956 to 1964 inclusive, and taking 1962 as 100, total operative-hours in the engineering, electrical and metal goods group of industries varied between a peak of 105.8 and a low of 94.7—a range of 11.1 points. In the same group average hours worked per head varied within a range of 4.9 points. But in the vehicles group total working hours varied within a range of 14.4 points, and average working hours within a range of 8.2 points— nearly twice as much as in engineering.[1]

Since, again, the group includes sections like heavy commercial vehicles, the output of which has been much more stable than that of cars, one can assume the fluctuation in hours worked to have been considerably greater in the car plants. For the vehicles group as a whole, however, it can be traced in some detail, as in Diagram V/3; it then becomes evident that hours worked there are not merely more liable to general recession than in engineering, but have in the last few years assumed a distinct seasonal swing as well. Again, this may be mainly attributed to the car section. And since overtime in the car firms is generally paid at time-and-a-third on basic rates for the first two hours and time-and-a-half thereafter, these fluctuations in average hours worked may involve disproportionate variations in earnings—especially for the various classes of lower-paid operative, whose pay-packets usually depend more on overtime. Moreover, the average overtime element in pay has on the whole tended to increase with reductions in the standard week, making earnings in car plants more liable to fluctuation on this account.

The second major source of instability in car industry wages is, of course, the method of payment-by-results. In one car plant, for

---

[1] The difference between these two figures—of 6.2 points—incidentally gives some indication of the extent to which the vehicle industries have adjusted to variation in output by dismissals or running down the labour force, as opposed to reduced working hours. Though the fact that this difference is almost exactly the same as for the engineering industries by no means implies that the problem of redundancy has been no greater in vehicles. On two occasions during the period covered—in 1956-57 and again in 1960-61—total working hours in vehicles have fallen by some 10 points within a year: no such sharp falls in labour demand occurred in the engineering group.

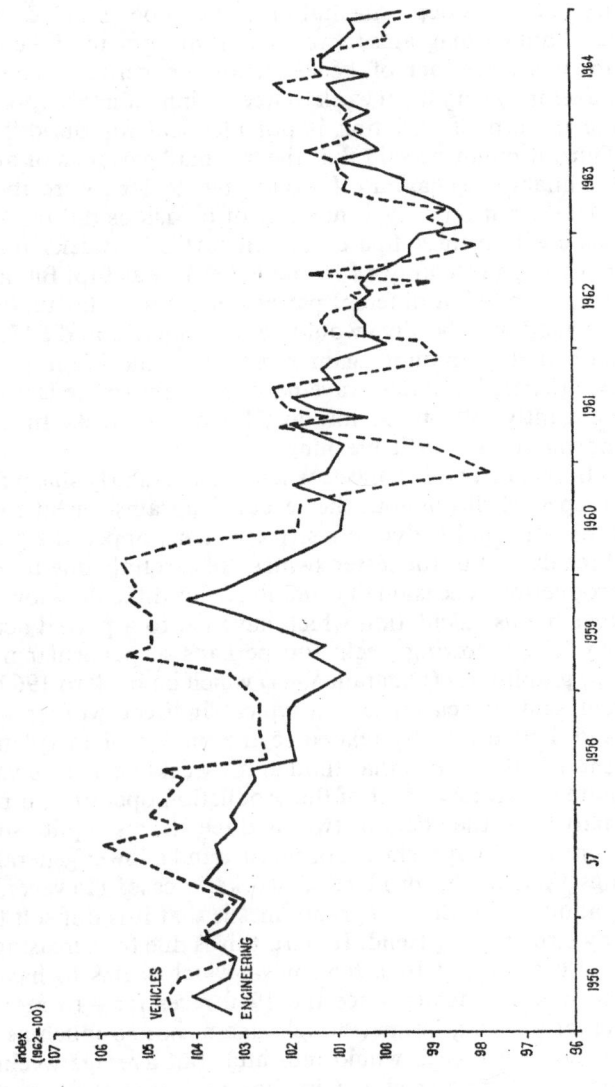

DIAGRAM V 3
Average hours per head worked by full-time operatives

instance, we have been able to trace weekly earnings in several different sections over varying periods up to October, 1963—in two departments, back to the beginning of 1960. Since in this firm bonuses are paid on a departmental basis it can be assumed that each of the resultant six diagrams represents the movement of the weekly wage of any worker in each of the six sections concerned. The extent to which wages may vary from week to week is immediately apparent, although the pattern of variation is not identical for the different sections. Thus, it might be said that the 'normal' earnings of an operative on the final line (Diagram V/4b) during 1962–63 were about £23 or £24 a week: but on only a minority of occasions did his actual earnings come within these figures, and in particular weeks in that period his gross wage rose above £31 and fell as low as £13. But a worker in the trim shop had a different pattern of earnings fluctuation: for him, a 'normal' weekly wage would be between £25 and £27; however, and though this amount again represented the lesser part of his total experience, his actual wage never rose above the last figure but very frequently fell—to as low as £11 in one week. In such a context 'normality' has little meaning.

In one or two instances, where a particularly sharp fall in earnings is repeated throughout the several diagrams—as at the end of May 1963—this fall is due to a strike which stopped the plant for two or three days. But the lesser swings are certainly due to the vagaries of production, occasionally amplified by difficulties or disagreements over bonus calculation which have led to a partial accumulation of pay to a following week. But perhaps of particular interest are the two graph-lines (Diagram V/4a) which go back to 1960. One of these represents the earnings of a typical 'indirect' worker—in this firm—paid a bonus partly related to the output of the plant as a whole. And it will be seen that though his weekly earnings variation is not quite so erratic as that of the production operative, it remains—even apart from the effect of two or three strikes—quite substantial: the more so, perhaps, since it occurs around a lower general level of earnings than in the production worker's case. However, what is also notable about the two graph-lines is that it is difficult to see in them any strong rising trend. In part, this is due to increasing hourly earnings being offset by a tendency—which seems to have appeared in the motor industry since the 1960 recession—to reduce or restrict actual working hours (though, again, not so much as reductions in the standard week would indicate). But average weekly earnings in the plant concerned *did* in fact rise over these years: what has happened in these two cases is that any rising tendency is largely concealed by week-to-week variations in pay received. One supposes that it may well be hard for the operatives concerned to convince them-

VARIATIONS IN
WEEKLY EARNINGS IN PARTICULAR SECTIONS OF A CAR PLANT

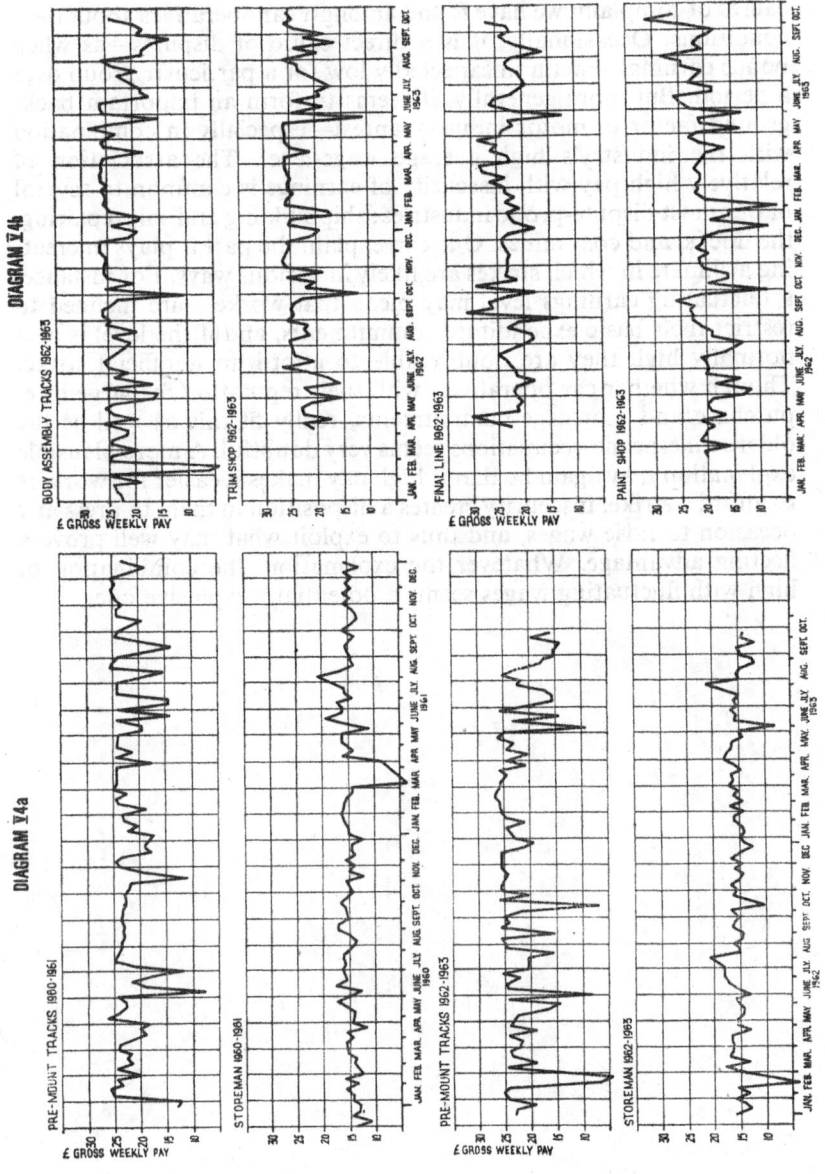

selves of its existence under these circumstances.

This fluctuation in earnings is certainly one of the most common causes of complaint we have found amongst car operatives about their conditions. Occasionally, it is a direct cause of disputes—as when bonus earnings remain unexpectedly low for a particular group over a period. But more generally, it seems to form an important background factor in motor industry unrest—especially in combination with the industry's high average wage-level. The association of relatively high pay with insecurity of earnings is common to several of our most dispute-prone industries: shipbuilding and shiprepairing, the docks, and coal mines. One can explain the part it plays in creating a climate in which strikes are likely in various ways. For instance, a fluctuating earnings level may mean that workers are inclined to restrict their basic expenditure commitments, and if the level is also normally high they are doubly able to afford an unofficial strike. Though whether car operatives, with their reputation for large hire-purchase and mortgage commitments, really fit this as well as the older strike-prone occupations seems very doubtful. A more plausible explanation may again be that if high pay makes it easier for workers to afford a strike, insecurity creates a disposition in them to press any occasion to raise wages, and thus to exploit what may well prove a fleeting advantage. Whatever the explanation, the combination of high with fluctuating wages seems a potentially explosive one.

CHAPTER VI

THE WORK, WORKERS AND WORK SITUATION

(A) SOME 'THEORIES OF STRIKE-PRONENESS'; THE WORK, WORK ORGANIZATION AND WORK SITUATION

Strikes are sometimes explained by relating them firstly to one or more general characteristics of jobs, workplaces, or work communities. For example, an international comparison of strike statistics[1]—distributing 'strike-propensities' by industry—suggests a broad environmental factor: the tendency for some industries to isolate their workers from the wider society, or conversely, to integrate individual workers closely into the general community. Thus (it concludes) miners, dockers, lumbermen, and textile operatives may be strike-prone because their industrial locale creates relatively homogeneous groups of workers which are geographically—or at least socially—isolated from the world roundabout. These groups could be expected to develop identifiably separate interests, traditions, values and standards of behaviour: they become socially cohesive. On the other hand there are the relatively strike-free railway and farm workers, white-collar and commercial employees, whose jobs isolate them spatially and socially from the mass of their fellow workers—or at least throw them less often into each other's company. Here, common interests may be more difficult both to recognize and to foster, and they are blurred by more diverse social involvements.

But this is a relatively crude explanation of strike-liability. More refined, though less neat, explanations look first at jobs rather than communities or places. The same study suggested that the characteristics of some jobs determine, by selection and conditioning, the kinds of workers who are found at those jobs. In its most general form, this

[1] Clark Kerr and Abraham Siegel, 'The Inter-industry Propensity to Strike—an International Comparison', in Kornhauser, Dubin and Ross, eds., *Industrial Conflict* (New York: McGraw-Hill, 1954).

hypothesis classifies jobs as either pleasant or unpleasant. Thus jobs which are physically exacting, rough, or dirty, unskilled, casual or seasonal, may attract or cultivate tough, unsettled, combative and virile workers who are independent of spirit and inclined towards direct action. Conversely, jobs which are physically easy and performed in pleasant surroundings, which require skill and responsibility, are steady and subject to set rules or close supervision, may attract women or a more submissive kind of man. Contrast the jobs of the miner or building worker with those of the bank clerk or shop assistant. But the hypothesis has less general application than that of isolated work communities: farmhands, steel workers, and truck drivers—who don't often strike—are not usually delicate men doing light work; nor are printers, textile workers, and draughtsmen—who do strike—necessarily robust workers.

Other explanations which relate strike-propensity to the character of the work people do or the way in which it is organized include, of course, the presumed effects of monotony and similar inevitable 'disutilities' in repetitive production, which have already been touched on in our Chapter II. But another explanation of this broad type relates industrial discontent and technology in a much more systematic way. Differences in methods of production are held to be the most important factor in determining organizational structures and thus in setting the tone of human relationships at work. One study[1] distinguished between three kinds of technology: unit or batch production, mass or line production, and process production. These differ in the extent to which control is exercised over the physical limitations of production. In unit production the limits are difficult to control, few attempts are made to do so, and the pressure on people at all levels in a firm is relatively light. Mass production can be viewed as an onslaught on the limitations referred to, and the pressures on people become heavy. In process production, the controls become more automatic or mechanical, and the pressure drops again; moreover, workers may resent authority less when it is exercised as much by the process (provided this does not involve mechanical 'pacing' of effort) as by other people. Process production also entails smaller working groups, an increased ratio of supervision to operators, and a lesser need for labour economy—all considered conducive to peaceful industrial relations. In unit and process production firms, industrial relations were found by this study to be on the whole more peaceful than in mass production firms. In short, the production methods seemed to be the most important factor in determining the quality of industrial relations.

The last study referred to found no significant accompanying

[1] Joan Woodward, *Management and Technology* (H.M.S.O., 1958).

relationship between the *size* of the firm and the system of production. But the size of the production unit—in terms of numbers employed—is itself another suggested explanation for variations in strike-liability. A coal mining study[1] suggested that disputes and strikes increased more than proportionately at the bigger pits, and that, within mines of any particular size group, those which had the smaller 'working cells' tended to have fewer and smaller strikes. A similar direct relationship to that between strike-liability and size of pit was found to hold good also for absenteeism and accident rates, and it was suggested that the reasons for this 'size effect' were the disproportionately greater problems of administration and supervision at larger pits. The supervision ratio was held to be crucial: where the tasks of foremen are reduced and their supervisory spans are shortened—the argument goes—they are better able to provide the men under them with what they need to do their work. In the larger units, however, any apparent arbitrariness of management policy and any overt failure of the operational plans tend to be magnified. In summary, strikes in large units are considered to be associated with what may appear to workers as remote, inflexible, and unsympathetic managements.

This supposed 'size effect' also raises—at least in the interpretation of the last study referred to—a question about the relationship between various criteria of industrial discontent. Strikes, unambiguously, are collective and conscious expressions of discontent, but even where there is little social cohesion or no tradition of collective action, discontent may still be manifested in more individual ways, from measurable phenomena such as labour turnover, absenteeism, and accident rates, through sabotage and 'soldiering', to such activity as resentful pilfering. Possible expressions of discontent thus range from the open battle of the strike to that vague borderland of action or events where the intentions of the participants become inseparable from the interpretations of observers. Some connection between these different indicators of discontent seems likely, but there is a difficulty in their composite interpretation: this is whether, and if so to what extent, they are to be considered as *linked* phenomena—so that if an industry's or firm's strike-liability is abnormal, would one also expect its accident or absentee rate to be so too—or as *alternative* forms of expression, so that if dissatisfaction existed but strikes were prohibited, absenteeism would be abnormally high.

This is a point to which we return later. But of these various 'background' (or sometimes, allegedly 'fundamental') explanations

[1] R. W. Revans, 'Industrial Morale and Size of Unit', *Political Quarterly*, XXVII, 3, July-September 1956.

of dispute-propensity, currently the most widely-held appears to be some variant of that which relates it to the character, conditions or organization of the work in car making; and this may be looked at first. In the physical environment of car assembly plants, there is little which might be thought to predispose them to labour unrest. While there are few of the gimmicks of pop industrial psychology in evidence—such as pastel-shaded walls, or the aural bombardment of 'music while you work'—the car plants are on the whole modern, clean, and well-kept. Nor are they cramped. That the standards of lighting, ventilation and heating are generally adequate is suggested by the comparatively occasional character of disputes where, say, fumes in the paint shop, or lack of heating, may be associated with exceptional operating or climatic conditions. There *is* dust in polishing shops, water splashing about in sections of the paint shops, noise and welding sparks in some body shops; but generally, car plants bear few traces of the dark, dirty mills of days past. References to areas known as 'the jungle' or 'the snake-pit' are not to be taken too seriously.

Physical surroundings are not unpleasant, but what of the work itself? Making cars requires neither the brute force of blacksmiths not the intricate patience of watchmakers. Heavy manual labour is exceptional, and some of the bulkiest and most imposing-looking machinery—like heavy presses—may be operated by women. The work is not hard in the sense that people need sweat. Nor are the jobs dirty—trackmen seldom wear protective clothing. But there are other qualities: the monotonous, pervasive 'supervision' of moving conveyors, and their stringent limitations over self-pacing. There have been numerous studies of the effects of mass production methods on workers' attitudes and sense of job satisfaction.[1] Car assembly work is held to require more mental attention than is usual in assembly-line work, and to require relatively more physical effort. Some American studies have found that workers dislike the mechanical pacing and repetitive character of the work, and that their absence and turnover rates were high. Most of the workers surveyed

---

[1] Amongst the many studies, the following have looked specifically at car workers: C R. Walker and R. H. Guest, *Man on the Assembly Line* (Cambridge, Mass: Harvard University Press, 1952), Ely Chinoy, *Automobile Workers and the American Dream* (New York: Doubleday, 1955), S. Wyatt and K. Marriott, *A Study of Attitudes to Factory Work*, Medical Research Council Special Report, Series 292, (H.M.S.O., 1956), and W. A. Faunce, 'Automation and the Automobile Worker', in *Social Problems* VI, 1, 1958. See Robert Blauner, *Alienation and Freedom* (Chicago: University of Chicago Press, 1964), for a summary of this literature. The most recent British study is J. H. Goldthorpe, 'Attitudes and behaviour of car assembly workers: a deviant case and a theoretical critique', International Sociological Association, Sixth World Congress, September, 1966.

by these studies expressed a desire to be transferred to other jobs —being impelled away from the tracks, rather than attracted to specific alternative work. Leaving aside questions of wider cultural differences in attitudes—to work in general and to assembly-line work in particular—between small samples in different countries decades apart, what can be made of these suggested 'tensions of the track' to explain labour unrest in British car factories?

Applied to the British scene, the argument seems dubious. The relation between attitudes and social action remains imprecise, and complaints from workers about boredom or constant repetition often arise under conditions where they might more appropriately be classified as part of the preparatory ritual of workplace bargaining anyway. Nor should the feedback effect of social research findings on workers' attitudes themselves be ignored: the 'monotony' argument in particular has been widely popularized. Assembly-line work in the car factories is comprehensible and meaningful, and not all without variety. Jobs usually comprise a set of operations which may in some cases take up to half an hour to perform, although from five to fifteen minutes is more usual. There are 'tight' and 'loose' jobs, but not a great deal of ingenuity is required to apportion these unavoidable variations in job requirements equitably between the 'team' operating around one track station; nor can operatives be prevented from introducing individual, 'irregular', and trouble-saving variations of the required methods. There is seldom either overcrowding or social isolation: small groups or cliques— even if superficially based—are at least ubiquitous, having the time, the proximity and sometimes the actual need to interact. If these characteristics of track-work were onerous, fisticuffs might be a common occurrence rather than extremely rare. Track-work is less boring, repetitive, meaningless, and lonely than many other kinds of factory work—textile spinning and 'machine minding', for example.

Then there are the demands of continuous attention and constant pacing. It is significant that when car workers complain about their jobs, it is often of 'speed-up'—i.e. of changes in the pacing of work because of a greater load, non-standard parts, fewer men, more inconvenient working conditions, or the breaking-up of experienced working gangs or teams. A sense of 'speed-up', real or imaginary, is inseparable from repeated adjustment required by the many—indeed, almost weekly—changes and modifications of jobs and components which are suffered by most popular models throughout their production lives. And its conversion to a complaint is again a normal part of the workplace 'effort bargaining' ritual. It is the *changes* which produce grounds for argument and negotiation, rather than the normal pace of track-work itself. Stresses may sometimes be produced by occasional demands for peak production from management, or managerial 'quality drives'; but these things are often again regarded as a unilateral change in the terms of the 'effort bargain'. As for mental attention, many of the operations are neither intricate nor complex enough to prevent daydreaming. Some jobs—with the connivance of supply departments—allow trackmen to build up 'banks' of particular sub-assemblies, thus freeing a period for uninterrupted fantasy, a brief spell with a newspaper in the 'works library', or more gregarious activity.[1]

These considerations should not be over-emphasized: track-work as such is not so much positively enjoyable as reasonably tolerable. Car workers in some British plants express a desire to move to track-work from other jobs in the factory—Standard workers are said to have at one time negotiated a 'seniority' agreement with the management to regulate movements of this kind. But the earnings differentials between track and non-track work are here clearly crucial; these serve to override 'tensions of the track' (to the extent that these exist), and reduce their value as explanations for a high strike-liability. However, these explanations are in any case not well supported by such hard evidence as is available. While trackmen are necessarily involved in stoppages to a disproportionate extent (indeed, fill the unwilling role of 'shock absorbers' in many disputes), they do not dominate the initiation of strikes. Analysis of the recorded occupations of those *directly* involved in three hundred strikes in the car factories during the 1960s shows no significant tendency for 'flashpoints' to occur about the tracks disproportionately to their large contribution to the labour force. The quite common view of senior managers, that trackmen are more strike-prone, may reflect an impact on themselves: stoppages on the assembly line proper are more immediately disruptive than those in most other sections. But most of the main occupational groups in car plants have taken strike action at one time or another, apart from such obvious ones as machinists; stoppages of internal transport drivers, storemen, maintenance workers, inspectors, and even clerks have all been fairly frequent.

Assembly-line workers proper are a minority of the car industry's employees, and one would have to postulate their tensions to be quite exceptionally contagious to explain such a wide occupational participation in strikes by reference to them. There *is* an apparent

---

[1] We have received two well-supported reports from foreign car plants of cases where the speeds of machines or conveyors were adjusted, with the connivance of shop-floor management, to allow the workers to reach their desired 'target earnings' in a set number of hours, and then slowed for the rest of the day; so all processes cannot be quite inflexible.

tendency for strikes in some firms to be concentrated for a period in particular plants or sections—for example, amongst paint shop workers at the Cowley works of Morris Motors during the early 1960s. Office workers at Standard were fairly active in this regard during the same years. Much of the overt unrest at Dagenham was once concentrated, for some time, in the 'P.T.A.' or assembly building; and Rover's more recent labour troubles were also concentrated in a new building where its '2000' model is assembled—but where, to the casual observer, the working conditions would seem to be very much more convenient than in that firm's older premises where Landrovers are made.[1] Rootes' on the whole modest strike-experience was, in the late 1950s, heavily concentrated in one of its pressings plants. However, such concentrations of discontent are interpreted, they do not well support the assertion that it is assembly-line work as such which contributes significantly to strike-causation in the motor industry. While if the general technique of car production were of major importance in determining the industry's high strike-liability, it would also be difficult to explain the very unequal distribution of stoppages between plants with almost identical methods of production, *or* the fact that the automobile industry is not relatively strike-prone in most other countries where it is important—*or* the comparative recency of the British industry's own high strike-propensity.

(B) THE WORKERS AND WORKING HOURS; 'AGEING' AND 'GREEN LABOUR'

As an extension of the general argument that the technology of the industry is in some way mainly responsible for its record of labour unrest, the ageing of car workers is sometimes raised by personnel officers and others. (Age, low labour turnover, and length of service are directly related characteristics, but here it is convenient to consider age separately.) It is suggested that track-work becomes more onerous to men who have reached their early forties, that their general irritability and sense of insecurity tends to increase thereafter, and that this predisposes them to greater unrest. The rising strike-liability of the car firms is thus held to be associated with the young workers—who entered the industry at the end of the War—moving into this discontented age group. Those who raise this kind of argument present no supporting data, but it seems worth looking briefly at such analyses of the age composition of the labour force as are readily available. Table IV/1 is based on statistics pub-

[1] Both the Rover and Morris Cowley cases have since this was drafted been the subject of 'fact finding' inquiries by the industry's own joint commission.

lished in the *Ministry of Labour Gazette* (which are derived from samples of National Insurance cards).

Table VI/1—PERCENTAGE OF MALE EMPLOYEES IN EACH AGE GROUP, MOTOR VEHICLES AND OTHER INDUSTRIES, 1950 AND 1964

	Under 20	20–34	35–49	50+
1950:				
Motor vehicle manufacturing	8	36	35	21
Engineering, shipbuilding and electrical industries	8	37	32	23
All employment	8	33	34	25
1964:				
Motor vehicle manufacturing	5	32	37	26
Engineering, shipbuilding, and electrical industries	9	32	32	27
All employment	10	30	30	30

The table reflects both a general ageing of the British labour force and the effects of the entry of the post-war population 'bulge' into employment. In 1964 there were, among all employees, considerably higher proportions of male workers in the age groups both under twenty and over fifty than there had been fourteen years earlier. But in the intervening years, the motor industry's age-structure had developed some specific peculiarities. The proportion of older workers—the over-fifties—in the motor vehicle manufacturing category had increased by about the same as the general increase, though rather more than in other metal-working trades: however, its proportion of such workers remained less than in the engineering groups and very much less than in employment generally. But there had also been a pronounced shift from the younger adult age groups to the groups in their late thirties and forties, which though similar to that in engineering was not paralleled in employment at large. And particularly, there was a very sharp fall in the proportion of juvenile workers. However, this certainly did not happen because young people are unwilling to enter the motor industry, but because high wages give motor firms at least some choice of men. The car firms, in particular, now do very little of their labour force's initiatory training for employment but recruit men who have already been 'broken in' to work routines by other trades—not necessarily factory ones. And it may be relevant to their recent labour relations experience that workers come to them already part-formed by a variety of other occupations, and with high expectations of material improvement.

The Work, Workers and Work Situation

Be that as it may, the table does show that while for the bulk of the post-war period the motor industry has had relatively few older workers, the general ageing of the labour force has, on the whole, affected the motor industry rather more than most other trades. This is probably a combined effect of its rapid early post-war build-up, a relatively low rate of withdrawal from the industry since then, and thus a low rate of replacement of its labour force by younger workers. However, a demonstration of slightly faster-than-average ageing does not prove a greater liability to labour unrest. Somewhat comparable details of the labour force age-distribution are available for two firms in Table VI/2: the figures are for recent years only, and include women.

Table VI/2—PERCENTAGE OF EMPLOYEES BY AGE GROUP IN TWO CAR FIRMS

	Under 20	20–34	35–49	50+
Firm A:				
Staff	6	41	31	22
Works	3	31	41	25
TOTAL	3	33	39	25
Firm B:				
Staff	14	30	29	27
Works	6	31	40	23
TOTAL	8	31	37	24

Not quite comparable figures made available by Rover indicate that this firm had more than a third of its male employees over the age of fifty: and it also seems to have had an at least average strike-liability. However, the figures in Table VI/2 fit fairly well with the 'Ministry of Labour' distribution. It appears that Firm B's manual employees have a rather lower average age than do Firm A's: but the former are very much the more strike-prone.

It may clearly be that as car workers grow older they find assembly-line work harder to bear. But whether a shift in average age of the order indicated by Table VI/1 would make so much difference as to provide a general, or even important, explanation of the car firms' sharply increased labour unrest is another question. Other considerations—and the nature of the imponderables—would seem to outweigh the evidence to this effect. For example, simple observation does not reveal any apparent differences between the age distribution of men on the tracks as against that of other car workers, and nor are there established policies of transferring men from track to other work as they become older—although this may be done in individual cases. One might, in any event, think that strain due to increasing age would be more likely to lead to accelerated labour turnover than strikes; but there is no study of the ages at which men quit the car plants, or even the reasons why they do so. The effect of aching joints on industrial discontent must remain conjectural, and little is known about the effects of decreasing financial commitments as housing becomes wholly-owned and children self-sufficient. How much 'irritation', in any case, is required to offset the realization that there are severe limitations on employment opportunities for older workers—particularly for car workers, who seem to be fairly widely stereotyped as aggressive and spoilt by high wages? In short, the 'ageing effect' does not seem a very useful explanatory contention.

Indeed, an almost opposite theory is also current in the industry—which one might describe as the 'green labour hypothesis'. This is that the rapid growth of car manufacturing involved a disproportionate recruitment of workers who were accustomed neither to labour of the type it demands nor to the procedures of industrial conciliation long-established in the engineering and allied trades: in its extreme form this view attributes the strike-propensity of the car factories to the alleged selfishness and irresponsibility of modern youth. This last variant of the theory is certainly not consistent with the evidence of Tables VI/1 and VI/2, which suggests the average age of car workers not merely to have been rising faster than that of the labour force at large, but to be already higher than the latter's.

The presumed effects of a rapid employment expansion, however, are superficially more persuasive. But in fact, the growth of the motor industry's labour force—as opposed to its production and productivity—has been no faster than that of several other industrial sectors. For the whole period 1948-64 it approximated to $2\frac{1}{2}$ per cent per year, which was not much above that for other engineering industries, and distinctly below that of employment (for instance) in the garage and motor repair sector. Moreover, the employment of manual workers, as we shall show, certainly grew more slowly than that of white-collar employees—who, even in the motor industry, would have diluted its average strike-propensity.

Of course, actual operative employment on car production almost certainly expanded faster than that for the whole motor industry: in the three big firms referred to in Chapter III, by some 4 per cent a year.[1] But two qualifications must be made to this picture of a recruitment which was still only moderately fast, by comparative standards. In the first place, the car plants' employment growth has occurred in three post-war phases: beginning with a rapid initial expansion (mostly at established centres of vehicle production) from

[1] See Table III/1.

The Work, Workers and Work Situation

about 1947 to the 1952–53 recession—and in this period the car firms were not particularly strike-prone. Then there was a phase of only very slow growth in the labour force to the end of the 1950s: and it was in this period that the car firms' strike-incidence suddenly accelerated. And another phase of fast growth came as new plants came into operation in non-traditional areas in the early 1960s: and in this phase the incidence of strikes remained high, but did not increase.[1] There is no coincidence, therefore, between the respective timings of labour force expansion and increased strike-propensity.

In the second place, this growth of motor employment has almost certainly occurred with much less recruitment of new labour than would be the case in several other sectors with comparable employment growth rates. This is because (and we will come back to this point again) labour turnover is distinctly lower in the motor industry —despite its frequent bouts of redundancy—than in male employment at large, so that fewer new workers are required to replace those who leave the industry. Indeed, much of the labour turnover actually recorded by the car firms represents what is to some extent a stage army, of workers discharged in various major and minor redundancies who were later re-engaged, usually by the firm that dismissed them. It is quite normal to meet workers who have had several experiences of this kind. Moreover, many of the new workers themselves—especially in the Midlands and Scotland—have possessed, not merely (as we noted) previous industrial but also trade union experience, and entered the car plants as a calculated choice. The problem, in fact, may well often be, not that the labour is 'green' but that it is far from it. Which is not to say that the opening of new plants may not have involved particular difficulties, especially where a quite raw union workplace organization was involved; but they also provided opportunities: and the new plants have not been *more* strike-prone, on the average, than established ones.

All that emerges from these two contrary hypotheses—which, by way of supposed age or experience patterns, connect the characters of car-making work and workers—is thus a suggestion that the way in which the industry's operatives are recruited or self-selected may be an influence on the quality of its labour relations. Though it is not clear how far its recruitment sources have changed, over time, in a fashion which might be associated with its increased strike-liability—except in so far as Table VI/1 may suggest that the ratio of apprentices is lower than it was in the immediate post-war years. However, an aspect of work in the car firms which seems seldom referred to as a factor in their troubled situation is their working hours. Nevertheless these display several peculiarities, by comparison

[1] Cf., for instance, Table I/1.

with other industries, which have been a not infrequent direct cause of disputes—quite apart from such influence as their arrangement or disarrangement may have had on strike-propensity in general.

For instance, statistical inference might certainly suggest some connection between the increasing incidence of shift working in the motor industry over the past ten or twelve years and the rising strike-liability—even if shift-work arrangements had not themselves become a more common overt issue of contention. Table VI/3 summarizes the evidence obtained on the extent of shift working by the Ministry of Labour through two surveys (the first of which did not, unfortunately, separate motor manufacture within the vehicle group):

Table VI/3—PERCENTAGE OF WORKERS ON SHIFT SYSTEMS, VEHICLES AND OTHER INDUSTRIES

One week of:	April 1954	October 1954
Vehicles	13	33
Engineering and electrical	7	11
All manufacturing	12	20

The increasing extent of shift working generally, but in vehicles in particular, is immediately apparent. In 1964, only metal manufacture (mainly iron and steel) had a higher proportion of shift workers than vehicles, although another continuous process industry, chemicals, followed fairly closely. Some detail is available for motor vehicle manufacturing itself in 1964, when the proportion of workers on shift systems was shown to be as high as 42 per cent—so that motors were clearly mainly responsible both for the large incidence of shift-work in the vehicles group and its increase. And these facts for motor vehicle manufacture as a whole do not seem out of line with what is known of shift working in the car firms themselves. Because of the latter's high capitalization, one might expect the proportion of their workers subject to shift systems to be on average even higher, but there are differences between firms. For example, Ford states that, at any one time, about two-thirds of its workers are on shift systems and that this proportion remains fairly constant over the year. Austin's proportion is similar, but some plants—like Jaguar—have very few workers on shift systems of any kind. At Pressed Steel factories, shift-work affects only about one in eight of this firm's operatives—but these work a permanent night-shift. On the other hand, alternating shifts are normal for production operatives in the bigger West Midlands concerns.

Surveys of the attitudes of employees to shift working have shown the majority of shift-workers to be opposed to the dislocation of their social life implicit in these systems, while studies of the psychological and medical consequences of shift-work—although more diversified in their findings—leave no doubt but that there are some deleterious consequences on individuals who work shifts.[1] There is, however, no suggestion (to the writers' knowledge) of a connection between shift-work and strike-proneness—else why is chemicals processing relatively strike-free? But what is peculiar about the car firms is the *arrangement* of their shifts. Of all the shift-workers in motor manufacture in 1964, only about one in seven worked a double day-shift, and only some one in fifteen a three-shift system (of one kind or another). An eighth were on permanent night-shifts. But as many as two-thirds worked an alternate day and night-shift. This system is unusual in other British industries, and seems so in automobile manufacture in several other car-producing countries (indeed, in one it would be illegal). It involves, normally, operatives working five day-shifts of between eight and nine hours in one fortnight, and four or five night-shifts of eight to ten hours each in the next. The arrangement seems at least an important justification for high earnings in car plants. By it, day and night shifts are thus usually separated by several hours; and a major reason for its adoption by British firms seems to be that it permits them unusual flexibility in the length of the actual working day or night, to meet the fluctuations in production to which the British industry now seems more liable than some abroad.

The arrangement of shift-work in the car firms is thus connected with another feature of their working conditions—the considerable variation in actual hours worked which we commented on in Chapter V. Table VI/4 is derived from the returns of overtime and short-time working collected by the Ministry of Labour, for one week in each month, from manufacturing industries. The number of workers on either overtime or short-time has been taken as the most significant index of the impact of variations in either experience on the operatives. Under both heads, it is apparent that variations in actual hours worked have been much more marked for motor workers than for operatives in the nearest comparable large industrial group, or in manufacturing generally. These variations are especially wide in the numbers on short-time—thus again demonstrating the exceptional liability of motor workers to lay-offs (and the peaks in this series do not seem to coincide with the dates of very big strikes, so they cannot be attributed to the latters' secondary consequences). The variations would be still more pronounced were the average time lost by each worker on short-time taken into account. Average

[1] See, for instance, *Shift Work: The Social, Psychological and Physical Consequences*, by Mott, Mann, McLoughlin and Warwick (Michigan U.P., 1965).

overtime per worker actually doing it remains fairly steady (at about seven to eight hours weekly) but the length of short-time spells rises as lay-offs spread.

Table VI/4—SHORT-TIME AND OVERTIME VARIATIONS, MOTOR INDUSTRY AND OTHERS

(a) ESTIMATED PERCENTAGE† OF ALL OPERATIVES ON SHORT-TIME

During:	Motor Manufacturing		Engineering and Electrical Goods		All Manufacturing	
	Highest	Lowest	Highest	Lowest	Highest	Lowest
1961*	7.8	0.2	0.3	—	2.3	0.5
1962	9.5	0.1	1.0	0.2	2.3	1.2
1963	4.7	0.2	1.2	0.1	2.7	0.4
1964	4.9	0.2	0.2	—	0.6	0.2
1965	8.8	1.1	0.2	—	0.9	0.3

(b) ESTIMATED PERCENTAGE† OF ALL OPERATIVES‡ ON OVERTIME

During:	Motor Manufacturing		Engineering and Electrical Goods		All Manufacturing	
	Highest	Lowest	Highest	Lowest	Highest	Lowest
1961*	42.9	23.0	43.3	38.0	31.9	21.1
1962	42.0	22.9	40.7	31.7	29.6	24.9
1963	44.3	31.5	41.7	31.3	33.1	26.0
1964	47.3	33.4	51.7	55.1	34.9	28.5
1965	50.3	34.9	52.4	38.7	36.5	30.1

* May to December only.
† From figures for one week in each month.
‡ Excluding maintenance workers.

All this, however, bears most obviously on that insecurity of earnings and employment which we have already suggested to have strong associations of various kinds with the car firms' high strike-liability since the mid-1950s. Whether the increasing variation in hours worked which has been demanded of operatives has also had less direct effects on their attitudes—for instance, in making them feel it no very serious matter to interrupt or curtail production since their employers did it so often themselves—we cannot say.

(c) 'SOLIDARITY', 'SIZE' AND 'SUPERVISION'

Car workers are concentrated in certain areas, particularly around Luton, Dagenham, Birmingham, Coventry, Oxford and now Merseyside. Do they form cohesive communities which could respond quickly and collectively to situations affecting their interests? The centres which come the closest to forming 'company towns' are

The Work, Workers and Work Situation

Luton, Dagenham, and Oxford—in that order. But company influence is clearly limited. Firstly, there is the obvious point that the car firms are not the sole, although they may be the largest single, employers in these areas. Dagenham—of bellicose repute—is situated within easy commuting distance of the Greater London employment market. Nor is it unreasonable to assume that car workers are amongst the most geographically mobile of labour sellers. Their high earnings and privileged purchasing facilities permit a relatively high degree of vehicle ownership: space for parking workers' cars has for some time been a problem at the main plants. At any rate, car workers seem to be drawn from considerable catchment areas around the factories—a daily journey to work of over twenty miles being not at all uncommon. These factors serve to dilute the presumed effects of closed communities, even in the company towns. And in the Coventry-Birmingham complex the mixture of industries and influences must make those effects quite negligible. The 'company town' effect is itself open to different interpretations, in any case. Employers who dominate a local labour market are in many ways favourably placed *vis-à-vis* their workers, while the concentration of workers within an area could equally be held to facilitate and encourage collective action—as at Dagenham, for example. Thus to hold that Vauxhall's influence on the Luton labour market makes for docility only implies that it is the traditions of the area which are really important. Which begs the question of how the traditions are formed.

What of social—as against spatial—isolation? There are no obvious characteristics of car workers which might indicate that they are regarded or treated any differently from others in the wider communities in which they live, or that they themselves feel in any way different as car workers. Nor do the shift arrangements throw them into each others' company when away from work. There is no evidence that car workers form indigestible social lumps, or 'reference groups', in the communities in which they live. Inter-firm meetings of large numbers of car workers are almost unknown, even in such centres of tight labour organization as Coventry, although the workers in contiguous plants of the same firm may very occasionally meet in large numbers on common issues. Briefly, car workers show neither that mass solidarity which is often associated with working groups such as miners and dockers, nor the craft solidarity of, say, the London printers.

Collective action requires 'solidarity' of some kind, however. Solidarity is of different varieties. The word may be used for the temporary like-mindedness of a crowd as well as for the common determinations of a small and more permanent group. Within a factory, the degree or kind of solidarity to be found obviously varies with such things as the sort of issue in relation to which it functions, the numbers affected by such issues, the degree of trade union membership and the intensity of workplace union organization. Disputes over issues such as large-scale redundancy, or general union principles, for example, may induce all or most of the workers in a plant to strike, whereas similar support for action on issues of more sectional concern would necessarily require a strong organization to channel information and stimulate and synchronize the movement.

In fact, in the car plants, most strikes 'directly involve' relatively few workers. For example, more than half the strikes publicly reported in the car plants during a four-year period 1960–63 each involved less than 200 actual strikers. The following table summarizes the distribution:

Table VI/5—STRIKES IN CAR FIRMS 1960–63 ACCORDING TO THE NUMBER OF WORKERS DIRECTLY INVOLVED

Number of strikers	Number of strikes
Below 10	4
10–49	61
50–99	43
100–199	47
200–499	60
500–999	40
Over 1,000	44
TOTAL	299

Analysis of these strikes according to the issues involved shows what might be expected on general grounds: most issues of wage-structure involved fewer than 200 strikers, while most strikes about redundancy and dismissals involved more than 200 strikers. Strikes about trade union matters were more evenly spread by size group, but 40 per cent of them were undertaken by between 200 and 500 strikers. Four out of the 24 strikes about union matters involved less than fifty workers, while only five involved more than a thousand. This spread is not as surprising as it might at first appear: single-union issues would account for some limitation of 'solidarity', and some of the wrangles would be over localized issues of workshop representation. Nevertheless, out of some four million striker-days in car firms since the War, less than 15,000 were attributable to 'sympathy' stoppages.

Even within individual plants, the sense of solidarity becomes more diffuse in relation to issues which lie outside rather narrowly circumscribed areas—which may be departmental in scope or even smaller. Strongly cohesive working groups seem relatively few and are very localized—to more skilled occupational categories like the sheet metalworkers, and to isolated sections which have achieved a 'one union shop' and some control over transfers in, mainly: which is not to say that strong feelings may not be whipped up amongst large numbers, given adequate stimulation. But it is almost a truism to say that the larger the group, the smaller the area of common interest: the reasons may be readily suggested—they lie in the extended division of labour itself, and in the administrative problems of organizing large numbers. Most issues start with a specific location within the plant and remain departmental or sectional in scope, and are of little concern to the men even in contiguous departments. There can actually be conflicts of interest between departments or wider groups of workers, quite apart from the organizational difficulties which different union policies and personalities may introduce. For example, in one plant the time-workers were very resentful of the high earnings of piece-workers, and of the presumed unwillingness of the latter to assist them to raise their wages. They resented being laid-off from work for what they saw as frivolous demands, or at least as claims from which they stood to make no gains. While they would not blackleg, solidarity could be of a rather reluctant or grudging kind.

Consideration of solidarity serves to introduce some of the difficulties in the idea of a 'size effect' mentioned earlier in the chapter. This 'size effect' may be translated into a number of dimensions. First there is the large firm, like B.M.C., where there are financial, administrative, and organizational problems in integrating the activities of many plants. Then there are clusters of separate factory buildings on one site, as at Austin or Dagenham. One factory building may form another 'unit'. Lastly, there are the departmental, or even more localized, productive 'units', where the quality of supervision or servicing facilities is of most direct relevance—and is partly the end-product of the size effect of the other dimensions. But taking the largest dimension first, there is little correlation between the size of the car firms and their relative strike-liability. While B.M.C. is the biggest and also the most strike-prone larger firm, the correlation does not hold for other companies. Vauxhall has few strikes, while Jaguar and Rover—with only a quarter and a third respectively of the number of Vauxhall workers—have both many strikes and a high strike-incidence. Rootes—now about half the size of Vauxhall—has had more strikes than Vauxhall, but a lower general strike-liability than Jaguar and Rover. Or if one considers the site complex as a unit, Luton is not much smaller than Longbridge and bigger than Cowley.

Again, at the level of the individual productive establishment the relationship between size and strike-liability is also very doubtful: assembly plants of around four to five thousand men are fairly typical of the industry—and have widely differing strike records. At the departmental or sectional level—that is, at the points of impact of 'arbitrary, remote, or unsympathetic managements'—the problems of establishing correlations become intractable. What units are to be compared? To the man on the shop floor, the managers in adjacent departments are as remote as the board members—whom he can at least sometimes read about in the newspapers: and the number and quality of supervisors needed to minimize or reduce feelings of frustration at what are felt to be management shortcomings must clearly vary according to the product process and the technology, as well as with the more institutional arrangements of company hierarchies and conciliation systems. At this level it is impossible to attempt to test for a size effect without a series of detailed situational studies in any case involving rather arbitrary unit demarcations. There are, however, big differences in the numbers of workers organized into associated productive teams at different stages of manufacture and assembly—according to degrees of mechanization and so on. And our failure to find systematic evidence of special occupational concentrations of strike-proneness is not promising of results for such an inquiry.

One aspect of such hypotheses—the remoteness of management and supervision which is presumed to be associated with size—stands in its own right, however. And here it may be worth attempting some related assessment with the aid of figures of the proportions of white-collar employees. We referred rather inconclusively in Chapter III to the possibility that the proportion of administrative, technical, and clerical employees (A.T.C.) may bear some relation to the adequacy with which production workers are serviced and informed. Inter-industry comparisons of the proportion of A.T.C. employees are possible from officially published records. There are pitfalls in the use of these figures, and the proportion of A.T.C. employees in any case is no index of the efficiency with which their work itself is organized: white-collar employment is probably much more liable than manual work to Parkinson's Law. But for what the ratios are worth, they indicate that the percentage of white-collar employees in motor vehicle manufacturing is lower than in the whole vehicles group of industries, which, again, has a lower percentage than the engineering and electrical group. Since this ranking is in inverse order to strike-incidences, it appears to offer some support for those who hold that higher supervision ratios are likely to be associated with lower strike liabilities.

However, some inter-firm comparisons of the A.T.C. ratio and its movement are also possible. And these leave no such definitive impression:

Table VI/6—PERCENTAGE OF ADMINISTRATIVE, TECHNICAL AND CLERICAL EMPLOYEES IN SOME CAR PLANTS AND FIRMS, 1955 AND 1961

	1955	1961
Austin	13.6	17.9
Morris (Oxford)	16.1	22.1
Fisher and Ludlow (B'ham)	10.9	14.5
Morris (Trac. and Trans.)	12.7	13.3
Morris Commercial Cars	18.6	21.1
Morris's Coventry plants	11.0	12.1
Nuffield Metal Products	6.5	10.8
B.M.C. (*nine plants*):	13.2	17.0
Ford (Dagenham only)	17.8	18.9
Rover (six plants)	19.7	24.4
Firm A	22.5	21.2
Firm B	20.8	18.7
Overall average:	18.8	20.2

The range of these figures leads one to suspect their strict comparability,[1] but the overall pattern is clear enough. The proportions of white-collar employees rose fairly rapidly during the years from 1955—at least for those B.M.C. plants which had previously had a relatively low proportion. And these were years in which this firm's strike-liability also rose rapidly. And among the B.M.C. plants, Morris (Oxford) had both the highest ratio and the highest increase in it—and this was the time when the high Austin strike-incidence was spreading to Morris's. The firm in which the A.T.C. percentage, although relatively high, actually fell, had very few strikes during this particular period. In the case of Rover, the A.T.C. percentage rose the most, and to the highest level of any of the firms (or plants) in the table. And Rover, of course, has been a fairly prominent strike performer over the past decade. So for these firms, it rather looks as though more supervision—in a broad sense—has gone hand-in-hand with more strikes! But the A.T.C. percentage also fell at Firm B, and to a lower level than for any firm except B.M.C.: and this firm was quite strike-prone over these years. The connexion between super-

[1] For instance, the job content of A.T.C. employments in different firms may not be the same. The proportions would also be seriously affected by any redundancy of manual workers during the month (October) for which the figures are collected. Also, although the numbers involved are not large, the sales office staffs are included in the proportion of A.T.C. workers for some firms.

visory ratios and strike-liability is—if one exists—clearly too complex to infer from existing statistical data. And if this material is to be reconciled with the suggestions reported in our Chapter III, it can only be by supposing that it is not so much the numbers of managers and supervisors that is important, as their quality, training and functional organization.

(D) WITHDRAWALS FROM THE WORK SITUATION: ABSENTEEISM, ACCIDENTS, LABOUR TURNOVER AND STRIKES

Strikes, absenteeism, accidents and labour turnover all involve withdrawal from particular workplace situations. Voluntary absence is an individual expression of relative discontent; and changing employers is a similar, but less reversible, action. As we have noted, these and other different ways of expressing industrial discontent may occur together in a particular workplace, or they may to some extent be alternative or substitutable forms of expression. There seems no general rule: in some cases evidence has been produced that strikes, absence and turnover rise and fall together; while in other cases they do not move in unison, and sometimes even show an inverse relationship. This may be inconvenient but is scarcely surprising: if it were not so then the social sciences would be in a more orderly and useful state. Moreover, even to obtain facts on the measurable indicators of discontent is itself not easy. Relatively adequate strike records are available or collectable, but records of absenteeism and labour turnover are not so easy to come by. For example, in the absence of governmental requirements for the reporting of absence from work, some of the car firms just do not keep consolidated records, or have started to do so only in the past year or two. Other firms would not disclose their data. Of the remainder, systematic comparison is made difficult because of the different periods for which figures have been kept, and because of the different methods of compilation.

However, some reasonably accurate assessment of absenteeism is possible. The annual average absence from work for all hourly-paid employees in the car firms is probably about 5 per cent (meaning that the hours not worked by workers absent for all reasons other than strikes or lay-offs is roughly 5 per cent of the total possible hours which would have been worked by those on the payroll in a normal or standard period, excluding overtime). Absence figures are not collected regularly or systematically for other industries, except coal mining, which has of course a very much higher rate.[1] However, for *all* employment the normal percentage of people absent

[1] See *Absence from Work* (British Institute of Management, 1961), for some notes on the general information available.

from work because of sickness or industrial injury for which a National Insurance claim has been made is also just about 5 per cent. And since this 'compensatable involuntary absence' is only a part of total absenteeism, it seems reasonable to suppose that the car firms' absence rate is comparatively low.

As regards the individual firms, some produce an absence rate on a weekly basis, some for each month, and some consolidate the records into an annual average. But the percentage—or rate—is fairly consistent. In the case of one firm, the annual percentage has varied from 3.7 to 4.6 in the years from 1955 to 1963. For the main B.M.C. plants over a twelve-month period in 1962–63 the annual figures were between 3.7 and 6.2 per cent. There is no annual figure for Ford, but the monthly rates for all workers concerned with assembly, body, and machining operations lie mostly between 4 and 6 per cent (although the range for the 'hot metals' group is from 6 to 10 per cent—which would raise the firm's average slightly if it was included with the other departments). In another firm which keeps no systematic figures, the 'floater' contingent to cover absenteeism on the tracks fluctuates between about 4 and 6 per cent again. It would not be very wrong to say that the *average* car worker spent about two hours every week classified as absent (a figure, incidentally, which is at least six times as high as the average 'idleness' due to disputes).

Absence should—and does—vary between plants and divisions of the same firm, if for no other reason than that working conditions differ. It also varies over the years, and over different months of the year, mainly, it seems, for climatic reasons. But our information on the extent of these variations is fragmentary. For example, in the first firm referred to above the annual average has risen slightly but persistently over recent years, from 3.7 per cent in 1956 to 4.6 per cent in 1963. This steady increase has been largely in the amount of 'unauthorized' absence, but the rise itself is only very slight. And variations in the annual rates between different plants within particular companies are relatively large. For example, in 1962–63, the rate at Austin was 3.7 per cent, at Morris Bodies it was 5.3 per cent and at Fisher & Ludlow 6.2 per cent. Comparable figures are not available for Ford, though we have noted that the rate in the foundry and hot metals division is considerably higher than in the other divisions. The rate in the Ford stamping and body division is also relatively high.

The production processes would seem to be the main influence affecting the variation in rates between plants, in that the dirtier and heavier work of foundries and body shops could be held to require more 'rest' periods and there may be more risk of injury. However this may be, a consistent direct connection between strike-liability and rates of absenteeism would be difficult to suggest. For example, Austin has had a lower absence rate than some comparatively strike-free plants, and the Ford Dagenham assembly plant had the lowest of the Ford absence rates but the highest strike-liability of the Ford divisions. But nor does the overall pattern of the figures we have point firmly to an *inverse* connection between the two phenomena. The nature of the data at present available deters one from more elaborate comment on the relations between absenteeism and strikes in the car firms.

Some apparently precise statistical data is available for accidents, at least for some firms and some recent years. Accidents are associated with the kinds of jobs people do, and evidence has been produced that in coal mines accident rates vary directly with strike-liability.[1] Accidents are clearly more than just random events: there is the influence of physical conditions and hazards, but also of anxieties and tensions affecting nimbleness and foresight. Is there perhaps an observable connection between accidents and strikes in the motor industry? Taking a series of industrial accident frequency rates compiled by the Royal Society for the Prevention of Accidents for the years 1960–62, for example, the rates were lower in the Vehicles group than in the remaining twenty-one industry groups listed—with the single exception of 'Professional and Scientific Services' in 1960. This general ranking is suggestive, and it seemed worthwhile to look more closely at accident rates in the car plants themselves. The figures which were made available to us are presented in Table VI/7.

The rate for the Vehicles group as a whole varies between 0.9 and 1.0 for the years 1960–62, and the average for the car plants cited is only very slightly above this group rate. What is clear from the table is that if the considerable variation between plant rates can be related to anything, it is (not surprisingly) to the production processes involved rather than to strike-liability—directly *or* inversely. Foundries naturally suggest a high accident rate, whereas the casting and assembly of carburettors suggest a rather low one. And a higher rate could be expected at the Rootes machining plant at Stoke than at the associated assembly plant at Ryton. Thus, excluding the Morris Foundry—with its particularly high risk—the rates fall into two bands, one of plants or concerns with an average accident frequency between 0.5 and 0.8, and the other with rates averaging 1.2 or 1.3. And the first band seems to correspond largely to sites where flow-assembly tracks dominate—the second band being of those occupied by, or with a large representation of, other processes.

[1] Cf. Revans, *loc. cit.*

Table VI/7—ANNUAL ACCIDENT FREQUENCY RATES FOR VARIOUS CAR FACTORIES, 1958 TO 1962

	1958	1959	1960	1961	1962	Average
Austin	n.a.	0.8	0.9	0.7	0.9	0.8
Morris (Cowley)	0.5	0.7	n.a.	0.6	0.7	0.6
Morris Radiators	1.3	1.7	1.2	0.9	1.1	1.2
Morris Foundry	2.4	2.4	n.a.	3.1	3.7	2.9
Morris Commercial Cars	n.a.	1.2	n.a.	1.1	1.2	1.2
S.U. Carburettor	0.3	0.4	0.8	0.5	0.5	0.5
Ford (Dagenham Estate)	1.4	1.6	1.1	1.2	1.1	1.3
Firm A	0.7	0.6	0.5	0.4	0.4	0.5
Firm C, engine plant	n.a.	1.1	1.4	1.1	1.2	1.2
Rootes (Stoke)	1.2	1.2	1.4	1.3	1.3	1.3
Rootes (Ryton)	0.7	0.9	0.7	0.9	0.9	0.8

Note: These accident frequency rates are calculated by taking the number of 'lost-time accidents', multiplying by 100,000, and dividing by the number of man-hours worked. Overtime is included, and the calculation only relates to hourly-paid workers. A lost-time accident prevents the injured person from continuing his normal employment beyond the day or shift on which the accident occurred.

For concerns for which there is a consecutive run of figures over the table's period, there is perhaps a very slight tendency for accident rates to fall; but they also reach a modest peak in 1960—a year for which the car firms' strike-liability (both in terms of frequency and incidence) also achieved a summit. However, firms for which longer runs of data were available—e.g. Austin—showed declining rates since the War, and some plants apparently had substantially higher rates in the immediate post-war years; and this is suggestive of an *inverse* connection between accident and strike-proneness, rather than a positive one. The Ford rates, falling sharply as the conflicts which led up to the 1962 'October Revolution' at Dagenham[1] mounted, also suggest a similar relationship, as does some Ford data for other years. But the Morris Cowley rate is fairly stable, although the plant's strike-proneness was rising during the period; and we gather that Rootes and Standard experienced fairly steady rates throughout the post-war years. While the firm with the lowest average accident rate—and one which was declining—was also one with a very low strike-incidence for these years. Clearly, much more detailed analyses would be required to establish definitively the relationships between industrial unrest and accidents than

[1] See Chapter IX for some account.

is permitted by the data now available—or by its character; but again the evidence is hardly such as to indicate that these relationships are likely to prove either firm or simple.

In any case the figures themselves should not be taken too seriously. The rates are based on voluntary returns, and the standard of record-keeping varies between plants and over time. In particular, their run is likely to be affected by such things as 'works safety campaigns'. Whatever their real effect, these often seem to produce an increase in recorded accidents! So that just as in the case of minor 'dispute-incidents' in labour relations, apparent frequencies are very much affected by current managerial concern about such things—which heavily influences reportage from shop level.[1] Moreover, such apparent connections between strike- and accident-proneness as particular series display may themselves be the product of third factors which influence both—like changes in the employment situation or earnings. The series may also be affected by such factors as technical change, and changing social insurance regulations. Both exposure to accidents, and the motivations to take care and to report minor accidents may have altered over the years. New plants and new machines may be safer or more dangerous than those they displace, and stoicism in the face of minor accidents is now less necessary than in earlier years. But for what the figures are worth, they at least do not suggest there is a dangerous working environment in car plants, of a kind which (as perhaps in mining) might itself produce a high strike-liability.

Of the indicators of industrial discontent which offered prospects of being compared with strike-liability, labour turnover proved also in practice not very satisfactory. This is not only because of the mere difficulty of obtaining figures—for there are statutory records of a kind—but also because, like measures of absenteeism, there is as yet no satisfactory method in general use for distinguishing between voluntary and compulsory elements in their make-up. 'Quit rates' are seldom used—and even if they were, the measure could be mis-

[1] In an attempt to secure 'hard' data, and on the presumption that the most serious accidents are more consistently reported, we looked at the record of *fatal* accidents (published by the Factory Inspectorate) for the years from 1950 to 1964. Accident rates were not given, nor was there a separate category for motor vehicle manufacture until 1959. And the frequency of such accidents was too rare to permit any reliable association with strike-liability. But a rough comparison with employment figures shows that fatal accident rates for the vehicles group generally would be relatively low—much lower than chemicals, iron and steel, shipbuilding, general woodwork and furniture, for instance, What is more, there is a downward trend to the absolute number of fatal accidents both in vehicles and for all industries covered by the Factories Act. Which gives rise to some dubiety about the reality of the large increase in *all* accidents officially reported over 1963 and 1964. On the 'reportage effect' in strike-data, see our Appendix IIA.

leading in situations where workers warned of prospective redundancy may take other jobs before notices come into effect. Thus variations in the rates of 'discharges' or 'separations' published by the Ministry of Labour—which can be very considerable for particular car firms owing to sharp changes in market conditions—are not a measure of workers' 'voting with their feet' alone (or even predominantly).

Table VI/8—ESTIMATED* ANNUAL LABOUR TURNOVER FOR ALL MALE EMPLOYEES, MOTOR VEHICLES AND OTHER INDUSTRIES, 1960 TO 1965

	1960	1961	1962	1963	1964	1965
Motor vehicle manufacturing	22.8	12.7	16.6	14.6	17.2	20.8
Engineering and Electrical	27.3	26.0	24.4	25.7	27.6	29.3
ALL MANUFACTURING	28.3	27.0	26.3	25.4	29.3	31.9

* The 'discharge' rates for all male employees during four-week periods published four times a year in the *Gazette* have been summed and multiplied by three and a quarter to produce an 'annual' separation figure. The turnover is understated to the extent to which particular persons are engaged by and leave the reporting firms *within* each of the four-week periods.

Nevertheless, Table VI/8 shows that motor vehicle manufacturing —despite its exceptional liability to redundancies—has had much lower rates of labour turnover than manufacturing generally, or than the neighbouring engineering and electrical group of industries. Nor are these years special in this regard (earlier figures are not included in the table because of changes in industrial classification) except that they suggest, if anything, that the rate of labour turnover in motor vehicles has been declining in the longer term—since the early 1950s. However, what stand out particularly sharply are the big fluctuations in turnover in the motor industry, as against general engineering and all manufacturing (notwithstanding the broad sixteen-week base from which the annual figures have been estimated). The big redundancies of 1960 and the lesser lay-offs of 1965 are clearly reflected.

Figures of labour turnover provided by individual firms should not be compared too closely with these general rates—being based on actual rather than estimated separations, and are for hourly-paid workers rather than for all employees. It is not possible to say what effect (except that it is probably only slight) this exclusion of staff turnover would have in general—in some firms the latter is certainly at a higher rate than for the hourly-paid, if only because staff employees include higher proportions of women. The available figures are too fragmentary to warrent a table, but are sufficient to show that collectively the car firms probably have an annual male 'separation rate' lower even than that of the motor vehicle manufacturing industry at large—probably around 10 per cent for the 1960s—but the fluctuations are again wide. For example, in one large firm which had a quite steady strike-incidence and -frequency over the years concerned, the turnover rate varied from over 23 per cent in 1960 to only 7 per cent in 1962. And an attempt we made to use a sample of the firms' returns to the Ministry of Labour resulted in fluctuations so great and apparently arbitrary that we were forced to desist. Thus, both the official and the private records, because they include the involuntary element of labour turnover, allow no meaningful assessment of the way in which voluntary withdrawals might be related to fluctuations in strike-liability. All we can say is that we have no evidence of consistent differences in turnover between firms despite their varying strike-proneness, nor have we heard any suggestion that such differences exist.

But otherwise—and certainly—the very low normal turnover for the car firms as a group, particularly in combination with their low accident and absentee rates, provides no evidence of fundamental and intolerable labour dissatisfactions. Car workers have their grievances, evidently: but these are also clearly not of such a nature that they feel individually obliged to seek relief from them in either industrial truancy or a search for other jobs—much less in a self-injuring carelessness at work. And if accident, absence and turnover rates have been low *because* the car firms' strike-incidence was high, perhaps the industry was getting the best of the exchange.

One further note may also be added to this discussion. Although no general and continuing connections, direct or inverse, appear between collective demonstrations of grievance and the other measureable forms of 'withdrawal from the work situation' in the car industry, there *does* seem evidence that if the collective expressions of specific discontent are suppressed or inhibited in some forceful way, they may find an outlet in a more dispersed and individual fashion. We have been shown figures for one of the big car firms which, in the 1961–62 recession, took the 'firm line' against unofficial action (which was then officially recommended by industry leaders and the government) by dismissing, and thus making an example of, operatives whom it considered ringleaders in such disputes. In the result, its strike-liability fell off quite sharply—for about two years, at least. But during these two years its accident frequency rate rose by over 40 per cent, and its 'work-hours lost' from accidents by nearly 60 per cent. In the plant particularly affected by the preceding events, absenteeism apart from that on account of injury also appears to have risen significantly, notwithstanding a 'tightening up of supervision' (although the figures here may be affected by classificatory

The Work, Workers and Work Situation

factors). And in the same plant labour turnover, comparing the same months in the three successive years involved, seems to have about doubled—although this was now a period of boom in the car trade, when firms were taking on workers, and in the industry generally 'separations' were low. Moreover, at the same time the firm had difficulty in getting its operatives to work overtime to meet production contingencies. Whatever one makes of the trend of different indicators of relative individual dissatisfaction when considered separately, when all apparently point the same way in such circumstances, it presumably means something.

CHAPTER VII

TRADE UNIONS AND SHOP STEWARDS

(A) THE PATTERN OF UNION ORGANIZATION

This chapter will conclude that in the motor industry at least (though a similar development seems evident in several other sectors) there are now in effect two separate forms of workers' organization which, while they are not necessarily in conflict—indeed, interact in many ways which involve co-operation rather than friction—must nevertheless be sharply distinguished. But to discuss the pattern of union organization in the car firms it is necessary first to outline something of that pattern's development. The major influences on the present shape of trade unions in the car industry have been technical change and union organizational strategies. During the 1920s and 1930s the development of mass production involved semi-skilled operators taking over the jobs formerly performed by a variety of skilled tradesmen. And the rate of change was such that even the early cars produced for the mass market were made almost entirely by semi-skilled labour. The skilled men were only retained on production in the quality car factories, where fine workmanship was required. Otherwise they moved over to prototype-making, preparatory and ancillary jobs of various kinds, and to maintenance and repair work.

Many—but by no means all—of the skilled workers were members of the several craft unions appropriate to their various trades (like the sheet metalworkers' organizations) or of the theoretically broader-based ex-craft unions, the Amalgamated Engineering Union and the National Union of Vehicle Builders. But for many years the men who took over their former role in production were very little organized. The craft unions proper did not want to recruit them, the general unions outside the new motor industry took some time to awaken to the possibilities these workers presented, and the skilled members of the A.E.U. and N.U.V.B. were often hostile to dilutions of their ranks. However the Workers' Union, which had a certain membership amongst unskilled and semi-skilled Midlands engineering operatives, amalgamated in the T. & G.W.U. in 1928, and the latter union began to organize car production workers more extensively during the 1930s. Some indication of its success can be gathered from the decisions of the A.E.U. and N.U.V.B. to recruit these operatives more systematically.[1] At first, however, they mainly enlisted the workers who were replacing their skilled members in production jobs. Thus the A.E.U. concentrated on machinists and engine assemblers, and the N.U.V.B. paid most attention to the body-building and trim shops, leaving the assembly lines proper an open field.

By the end of the 1930s, however, the future pattern of trade union organization was becoming clearer. The A.E.U. and N.U.V.B. were now trying to strike out from their respective strongholds in the machine and body shops and were coming almost everywhere into competition with the T. & G.W.U. Partly because of the varying enthusiasm of A.E.U. and N.U.V.B. shop stewards and local committees—still then consisting almost entirely of craftsmen—towards this development, considerable variations were emerging in the strength and distribution of the three unions at plant level. With the spread of inter-union competition, the other big general union, the National Union of General and Municipal Workers, also appeared on the scene, but lagged far behind the other three unions that recruit less-skilled operatives, and only established itself in two Midlands plants at this time (such strength as it now has coming mainly with the recognition of trade unions by Ford). The craft unions, of course, continued to operate for skilled workers.

However, perhaps the most striking feature of car industry trade unionism before the war was the low degree of penetration it achieved. It appears, indeed, that seldom more than a fifth, and often only a fiftieth, of the mass production operatives were union members—who were sometimes in the minority even amongst skilled groups. The major obstacles to trade unionism's extension were the seasonal fluctuations of employment and the hostile attitude of most employers. Several of the great personalities in the new industry were strongly anti-union. Morris, and the American-controlled firms Vauxhall and Ford (following the policies of their parent companies), refused to allow the unions into their plants. Austin and other British firms recognized trade unions but did not encourage their workers to become members; several firms acquired a reputation for

[1] Both the A.E.U. and the N.U.V.B. had, of course, amended their rules to permit the recruitment of less-skilled workers some time before—the A.E.U. as far back as 1901. But these openings were little exploited before the 1930s.

dismissing active union supporters in the off-season.

Wartime changes thus enabled the unions to make great headway in the car plants. Legal orders in any case made it difficult for firms to refuse trade unionists employment, obliged them to apply collective agreements and put them under some pressure to deal with the union workplace organization. And the latter was also encouraged by the employers' desire for mutual co-operation in solving wartime production problems, and by government pressure for joint consultation at the workplace level. The British firms became very much more tolerant of union workplace activities, and by the end of the War both Ford and Vauxhall had recognized trade unions and collective bargaining—but with characteristic differences. Vauxhall signed a district negotiating agreement with the A.E.U. and N.U.V.B. in 1942, at the same time formalizing its existing joint consultative arrangements as an elected Management Advisory Committee and announcing a managerial 'open door' to workers and union representatives. Ford signed its first collective agreement with the unions in 1944, at arm's length through the T.U.C., and a more comprehensive procedure agreement only in 1946. In parenthesis, it may perhaps be noted that, while changes in the policies of the parent firm in the United States and government and T.U.C. pressure in Britain were possibly as much or more responsible for securing Ford's change of front as workplace agitation, the firm's grants of negotiating and grievance procedures came only after strikes. Since then, rank-and-file leaders at Ford have frequently argued that their direct action forced the firm to recognize the unions and have often returned to this point in justification of unofficial and 'unconstitutional' action.

The dramatic intensification of union recruiting activity during the 1940s had two principal consequences: the extension of union membership to the majority of workers in most (but still not all) car plants; and the emergence of two leading unions, the A.E.U. and the T. & G.W.U.—pursued at some distance by the N.U.V.B., which had the disadvantage of fewer local organizers and a more restricted appeal to the workers who entered the factories for wartime aircraft production. It is not easy to form an exact picture of the present distribution of membership between the car workers' unions. The unions' own information depends on returns by voluntary officers in the branch and workplace, and a large proportion of them are not too regular in the performance of such mundane duties. Moreover, a union's membership in a particular sector or plant is an index of its entitlement to representation on such inter-union bodies as Works Committees, and so is liable to optimistic reporting by its representatives. Following a recent suggestion that voting on the union side of the Ford National Joint Negotiating Committee should be in proportion to each union's membership in the company (instead of one vote per union), every union made a census of its strength: but when added together, the results showed 10 per cent more union members than workers 'on the clock'! Nevertheless, by comparing the memberships claimed by district officers and shop stewards for individual plants with each other and with company payroll figures, it is possible to arrive at estimates which are then accepted as reasonable by local union people themselves, and these are summarized in Table VII/1.

Table VII/1—ESTIMATED TRADE UNION STRENGTHS IN THE CAR FIRMS, 1965–66

Firm	Per cent organized (manual workers)	Per cent of trade unionists by union				
		AEU	T & GWU	NUVB	NUGMW	OTHER
B.M.C.	100	37	28	20	3	12
FORD	99	24	41	10	15	10
VAUXHALL	85	66	—	29	—	5
P. STEEL	100	21	47	27	—	5
ROOTES	100	50	33	9	—	8
S.T.I.	100	36	43	15	—	6
ROVER	100	27	15	48	5	5
JAGUAR	100	32	32	25	—	11
Overall	98	35	31	20	5	9

On this basis, the A.E.U. and the T. & G.W.U. probably have between 60,000 and 70,000 members apiece in the car firms, the N.U.V.B. having nearly 40,000 and the N.U.G.M.W. some 10,000 or so. About 15,000 to 20,000 union members are shared between a variety of manual workers' associations—mainly for craftsmen on repair and maintenance work, but including also unions of foundrymen and steelworkers; while in the Midlands a small but sometimes important membership of production workers is held in certain B.M.C. and Jaguar plants by the Birmingham and Midland and the National Sheet Metal Workers' unions (which commonly act as one body in the workplace) and by the National Society of Metal Mechanics, a union which came into the car plants from a traditional local base in the light metal trades. (We have attempted no estimate of non-manual unions' membership). The figure '100' under 'per cent organized' does not mean there are no non-unionists, but that such as there may be are individuals who have slipped through the union net temporarily, or long-standing 'nonners'—abstainers from union membership on grounds of principle or conscience, whose presence is treated indulgently by their workmates. All the 'federated' car firms now accept the principle of the 'union shop' for manual workers subject to this indulgence. Ford's stated position 'encourages' trade union membership whilst formally maintaining that it is not a condition of employment. Vauxhall's expressed attitude is one of goodwill to the unions but of insistence that membership is a question for the individual.

The initial pattern of mass union development in which each major union tended to confine itself to a particular part of the plant has given way over the years to a much more variable distribution. In a few plants special local factors have permitted a major union to become dominant. The A.E.U. district organization's refusal to concern itself with unskilled workers at Oxford, and the early lack of an N.U.V.B. district organization, gave the T. & G.W.U. an initial open field at the Morris Cowley and Pressed Steel Works. The A.E.U., however, early acquired a predominant membership at the B.M.C. plant of Tractors and Transmissions and its exclusive possession (until 1956) of a district official at Luton gave it an advantage over its partner in the first Vauxhall 'bargaining rights' agreement, the N.U.V.B.

But generally, at the plant level, membership is much more dispersed between the different unions. Two factors seem to have been responsible for this development. First, in their eagerness to recruit new members the major unions carried out organizing drives in whatever sections opportunity presented itself. And second, as the techniques of production developed, jobs became more interchangeable, and workers were more often moved around the plant to suit production schedules—carrying their union membership with them. Under current organizational patterns, each major union tends to have a concentration of members in its traditional location—which it may have to share with several other unions—but the bulk of its members are spread over the plant. In rather few cases—notably at Pressed Steel's Swindon plant after a strike which was associated with a period of 'membership swopping' by the operatives, and at Vauxhall's Merseyside plant—have 'spheres of influence' within the plant been agreed between the major organizing unions.

The dispersal of membership which is more usual is an important factor in the character of union workplace organization, and is worth illustrating—as in Table VII/2. This represents that three-quarters of the production division concerned's operatives whose exact union membership could be established (the main A.E.U. strength was in another division, which included the machine-shops). The Woodcutting Machinists' Society's presence in the body shop is

Table VII/2—DISTRIBUTION OF TRADE UNION MEMBERSHIP IN THE ASSEMBLY DIVISION OF A CAR PLANT

Department	T.&G.W.U.	N.U.V.B.	A.E.U.	S.M.W.[1]	N.S.M.M.[2]	A.S.W.C.M.[3]	Other[4]	Total
Body shops	61	5	20	82	140	23	3	334
Body assembly	82	67	12	134	1	—	1	297
Paint Shop	173	12	—	—	—	—	1	186
Saw mill	75	45	15	—	—	88	14	237
Trim Shop	19	377	2	—	—	—	7	405
Trim Track	9	185	2	—	—	—	4	200
Engine test and mount	76	—	71	—	4	—	2	153
Pre-mount and mount	65	397	168	—	1	—	5	636
Final line	99	13	4	—	—	—	—	116
Test and Rectification	111	24	47	3	3	—	—	188
Experimental	—	26	67	1	—	4	1	99
Maintenance	150	5	21	2	1	2	7	188
Service and Despatch	58	13	49	7	—	—	—	127
Stores	161	13	10	—	—	—	1	185
Internal and external transport	37	—	—	—	1	—	1	39
Total	1,176	1,182	488	229	151	117	47	3,390

[1] Sheet metal workers' unions: National Union of Sheet Metal Workers and Coppersmiths; Birmingham and Midland Sheet Metal Workers' Society.
[2] National Society of Metal Mechanics.
[3] Amalgamated Society of Woodcutting Machinists.
[4] Including: N.U.G.M.W., E.T.U., United Patternmakers' Association—and National Union of Mineworkers, National Union of Furniture Trade Operatives, National Union of Dyers, Bleachers and Textile Workers, National Union of Hosiery Workers, Union of Shop Distributive and Allied Workers, Fire Brigades Union, Union of Post Office Workers.

an illustrative by-product of the car plants' historical pattern of union development: a survival of a past attempt by this union to organize metalworkers.

(B) MULTIPLE UNIONISM, AND INTERNAL STRUCTURES

One outstanding characteristic of labour organization in the motor industry is thus multiple unionism. But this has not in itself been very important as a *direct* cause of strikes. The development of the car firms' pattern of union organization—a pattern which is, of course, not unique to them, but finds its parallels in several other sectors of manufacturing industry—was accompanied by quite intense rivalry between the competing unions. But the major unions have thought in terms of plant-wide recruiting fields, and in face of the interchangeability of jobs and workers the A.E.U. and the T. & G.W.U., at least, have not tried to establish specific jurisdictional claims, to particular areas within the plant or to particular classes of mass production workers. So that in general, competition between these unions has taken the form of rivalry in the recruitment of non-unionists or of workers new to the industry. But the case of the N.U.V.B. has been rather different. Inter-union competition for recruits not infrequently shades off into alleged 'poaching' of members from another organization, particularly in plants outside the traditional Midlands centres (where union patterns are by now pretty settled). And perhaps because its weaker position has made it more aggressive than the bigger unions, the N.U.V.B. is more often accused of such tactics. On the other hand, inter-union understandings on the allocation of new recruits at particular plants have sometimes been made between the A.E.U. and the T. & G.W.U. which exclude the N.U.V.B.

Such things, however, have very rarely led to stoppages. A more important cause of strikes has been the 'exclusive jurisdiction' or (still stronger) 'closed shop' tactics applied by certain of the smaller unions in an attempt to maintain their position in relation to the mass organizations. Several craft or ex-craft organizations (including, in some contexts, the A.E.U.) of course maintain an exclusive claim to certain types of skilled work, in the traditional way. But the N.U.V.B. has particularly developed this approach—partly in an attempted preservation of its original craft interests, partly to offset its under-representation in key offices in the shop steward organization (a result of the Big Two unions' superior membership) by establishing sectional strongholds within the plant. Its maintenance of craft claims, despite its ambition (which is still held), to become an industrial union for the vehicle industries, has on several occasions brought it into open conflict with the sheet metalworkers' societies—

the half-dozen minor strikes on demarcation disputes reported by the Ministry of Labour from the motor industry during the 1950s mainly arose from this friction in the body shops. But during the 1960s the N.U.V.B.'s 'closed shop' policy produced some wider disturbance.

These disputes were particularly concentrated at Fisher & Ludlow and Nuffield Metal Products—then B.M.C.'s major body-building establishments—which are in the N.U.V.B.'s militant Birmingham district, and where that union is stronger than in most other car plants. Throughout the 1950s transfers of men between departments had led to shop-floor opposition in both these works, and in 1961 B.M.C. had reached an understanding designed to improve labour mobility with the production workers' various unions, which included the N.U.V.B. This agreement followed the joint national talks held at the Minister of Labour's invitation early in 1961, at which the trade unions agreed to 'give further consideration to the difficulties caused by the arrangements whereby, in some companies, workpeople in different parts of the establishment where similar work is carried out are members of different unions, thus making transfers of workpeople difficult'. In B.M.C.'s case, the understanding that union membership should not interfere with the movement of workers between departments was to be applied in detail by agreed arrangements between plant managements and shop stewards. But the Vehicle Builders' members refused to countenance the transfer of men holding other union cards into departments where they were in the majority unless they joined the N.U.V.B. Several stoppages in B.M.C. establishments followed, including some substantial strikes in 1964.

However, B.M.C. was not the only firm involved in disputes in 1964 over the transfer of labour—there were two substantial stoppages in Coventry. And other factors than inter-union relationships were involved. The resistance to mobility seems also partly a reflection of a certain tendency for solidly-organized workplace groups to develop and claim 'job rights' to working or occupational areas which are for one reason or another thought desirable. Indeed, it began for a while to look as if some members of such traditionally 'open' unions as the T. & G.W.U. were beginning to attempt—unofficially, of course—to control job entry in the same way as the sheet metalworkers' societies. Disputes of this kind—over 'job rights'—are not entirely a consequence of multiple unionism, though they are complicated by its presence: it is not impossible for them to occur *within* a union.

Nevertheless, stoppages involving direct inter-union frictions, though they tended to increase during the early 1960s, still appear to have been responsible only for some 5 per cent of car firm striker-days during that period. During the post-war years as a whole, the more important contribution of inter-union competition to strike-proneness has probably been by way of the stimulus it has given to the general militancy of unions and their representatives at the workplace level during the phase, at particular plants, when union membership was not yet complete, or still not firmly attached to individual organizations. Apart from being especially liable to be marked by strikes against the employment of 'nonners' in one section or another, these periods commonly show a higher frequency of disputes in general, as rival unions seek to demonstrate their effectiveness to potential recruits. This tendency probably contributed to the sharp increase in the strike-proneness of the Morris Cowley works—where the production operatives had previously not been very well-organized—in the late 1950s, as well as to the spread of a high dispute-liability from the established centres of car manufacture to the new areas of production in the early 1960s. It seems not impossible that the occurrence of occasional disputes at Vauxhall's in very recent years is connected with a similar phenomenon, and that they may become more common there as the margin of recruitable non-unionists diminishes.

However, such situations of intense inter-union competition are generally passing ones. Continuing rivalries between unions have in some plants made it difficult to secure firm management-labour agreements, but this is a point to which we return later. It has, however, been quite commonly said that the mere *number* of unions operating in the car firms is a major obstacle to the operation of adequate bargaining and conciliation procedures, and thus to the settlement of disputes—either in detail or through the formulation of general policies to solve the issues they involve. In theory, the federated car firms might be required to negotiate with any one of the Confederation of Shipbuilding and Engineering Unions' thirty-one affiliates, and Ford's agreement now requires the equal representation of twenty-one unions on its central negotiating body—a situation in clear contrast to that of Vauxhall, which (even after its recent recognition of the Electrical Trades Union's negotiating rights for maintenance electricians) still deals with only three organizations.

But even in the conferences of the C.S.E.U. itself, the votes of the A.E.U. and one or two other major organizations in combination could carry any policy decision. While at the company or plant level, the Ford arrangement is quite exceptional—a product of the peculiar circumstances under which that firm accepted collective bargaining in the first place, and of the T.U.C.'s involvement as intermediary. In practice, the management of the normal federated car plant rarely has to deal with more than half-a-dozen unions—and representation on what have become key instruments of workplace labour relations, the Works Committees of senior shop stewards, is heavily concentrated in the hands of the major unions. In twenty-nine such committees whose membership we were able to examine, two-thirds of the 170 or so representatives came from the A.E.U., T. & G.W.U. and N.U.V.B. (in that order of precedence) and only nine other unions were represented in the remainder. While leading offices were even more heavily distributed in the major unions' favour: five-sixths of the key posts of chairman or secretary were held by the A.E.U. or T. & G.W.U. And even in the Ford works committees, in no case were more than three unions involved.

The impact of multi-unionism on the motor industry's labour relations arises not so much from the mere *number* of unions involved as from the fact that the mass of production workers *are* divided between a few organizations, and from the character and organization of the major unions concerned. Their structure is keyed to the generality of their interests—the A.E.U.'s and T. & G.W.U.'s membership of car workers represents only some 6 per cent of their total combined strength of over two million members—and so far as their formal organization relates to those workers' specific problems, it does so mainly through the pattern of national negotiations with the E.E.F. (Engineering Employers' Federation). The T. & G.W.U. has a 'trade group' for the engineering industry, but otherwise has only held occasional regional and national advisory conferences of representatives from its branches with motor industry members. The A.E.U. has, at time of writing, national advisory committees for such odd groups as Army Department employees and wagon repairers, but none for the car workers. Of the other unions, most have only a small minority of their members in the motor industry. Even the N.U.V.B. has a substantial membership (probably nearly half) outside the car plants, including some in railway workshops. The C.S.E.U. has only recently acquired a formal mechanism to channel car workers' interests through the nomination of some national union leaders to the government-promoted Motor Industry Joint Labour Council.

Even more important, perhaps, is the unions' district and local structure. The A.E.U. and the T. & G.W.U., of course, are very different kinds of organization—the A.E.U. having a strong system of elected District Committees, with all local and national full-time officials (which include its small Executive Council) subject to regular re-election by the membership—but also in practice largely drawn from the skilled minority of the latter. While the T. & G.W.U. has a more elaborate system of trade group and regional committees, with a large lay Executive combining that dual representation, and with all officials appointed—except the General Secretary (who is elected for life).[1] Differences in the power structure of the two unions have not been without their impact on workplace affairs— nor have their differences of policy: for instance, on the treatment of redundancy, to take an issue of specific workplace concern—and otherwise in top leadership attitudes (which were reflected in responses to workplace pressures). Up to the mid-1950s the A.E.U. was more on the 'left' in labour movement terms, and the T. & G.W.U. on the 'right'; but with Frank Cousins' accession to the T. & G.W.U.'s General Secretaryship, and changes among the A.E.U.'s leading officeholders, they somewhat exchanged positions.

At levels between the union branch and the top leadership the two biggest unions have formally had neither specialized standing committees nor specialist officials to cater for the interests of motor workers. A.E.U. District Committees in several areas—like Birmingham East—are substantially representative of members from car plants, but the T. & G.W.U.'s area trade group and regional committees are much more broadly based. Again, in several centres— like Oxford and Luton—full-time local officials of these two unions are largely preoccupied with the problems of a car industry membership; but this is an accident of local industrial concentration, and local officials often have much wider responsibilities. So that even where—as in most cases in the car centres—these officials are ex-motor workers—the time they can devote to car plant problems may often be limited. And it is only in rather recent years that the N.U.V.B. has acquired full-time local officers in several car-making centres outside its traditional focus of strength in Birmingham and Coventry.

Connected with this lack of formal specialization, and perhaps more important in its effects, is the fact that the number of local officials has not grown in relation to the increase in union activity at the plant level, and to the problems consequently thrust into the unions' machines. This seems rather more so in the A.E.U.: the T. & G.W.U. appears to have a higher ratio of officers to members in the key districts, and this permits it somewhat to compensate for its lack (except in Coventry) of District Committees by maintaining —what may be as helpful—closer informal contacts between local officials and car plant representatives. But Marsh and Coker noted in a study of 1963 that although the frequency of references from the federated engineering firms to the E.E.F.'s conciliation procedure

[1] For a detailed description of the A.E.U. and T. & G.W.U., structures, see B. C. Roberts's *Trade Union Government and Administration in Great Britain* (Bell, 1956). V. L. Allen's *Power in Trade Unions* (Longmans, 1954) also includes the N.U.V.B. in its valuable analytical tables and detailed references.

had doubled since 1957, there had been no change in the (already comparatively low) ratio of A.E.U. officers to members.[1] Our own study of A.E.U. references of disputes from federated car firms to this procedure in 1964-65—which is detailed in Chapter VIII—found the average delay in cases between this procedure's Works and Local Conference stages was six weeks, against the seven working days the procedure itself lays down as a proper normal interval. It also found that of the many disputes referred from car firms which ended, after full and lengthy procedural treatment, in a 'failure to agree' only some one in ten appeared to have been then taken by the union to a 'constitutional' strike. It seems very possible that had the unions been able to be more active in their use of these procedures, unofficial and 'unconstitutional' strikes would have been much less frequent.

Another feature of the unions' internal structure which seems important is the formal divorce of the union branch—the basic unit of union governmental organization and the constitutional source of union policy—from the union workplace representative system. The A.E.U. has a large number of small geographical branches, with a mixed membership from different industries: in its Birmingham and Coventry Districts, for instance, there are over 180 branches for some 100,000 members, less than a third of whom come from car plants. The T. & G.W.U. has branches which for car workers are usually based on plants or local groups of plants within a company, and which are rather bigger—averaging over 1,000 members apiece in the major English centres. The N.U.V.B.'s branches—which come between the other two unions in size—are geographical in the traditional West Midlands centres, but it has set up plant branches in other areas. And it is often said that plant or factory branches are likely to have higher levels of membership participation than local ones. But we have found no particular evidence that this is so: even plant branches usually meet away from the works, and very low attendances were reported from branches of both kinds—except that factory branches were liable to experience large turnouts when redundancy was threatened at the plant. Otherwise, 'the branch committee and a few other members' seemed typical of attendance.

Partly to offset the inadequacy of the branch as a vehicle for the communication of either membership interests to the leadership or union policy to the workplace, the bigger unions have all devised some machinery for direct representation of shop stewards' viewpoints. The A.E.U.'s District Committees have a formal inclusion—

[1] 'Shop Steward Organization in the Engineering Industry', *British Journal of Industrial Relations*, June 1963.

about one member in six in practice—of stewards' representatives, as well as quarterly district meetings of stewards and (sometimes) of senior stewards alone; but these devices provide no distinct representation of particular industries. The T. & G.W.U.'s (*ad hoc* and occasional) Motor Advisory Committees in London and the Midlands are drawn partly from its senior stewards in the car plants. The N.U.V.B., which has a simple formal structure based on area representation, has both quarterly district shop stewards' meetings and an annual (advisory) national shop stewards' conference.

Nevertheless, attendance at the unions' various shop steward assemblies (though much higher than at branch meetings) is variable —about 25 per cent of ordinary stewards seems normal for the A.E.U., the N.U.V.B.'s appearing rather higher. And these arrangements have been, so to speak, 'clipped on' to the formal structure of union power. Communication of workplace interests to the union leadership proceeds as much by way of the informal relations between local officials and stewards; and the extent of their impact on top leadership policy depends partly on the diversity of that leadership's other concerns, and partly on the relationship between it and the local officers. It seems notable that the N.U.V.B.—very much the smallest of the major unions organizing car workers in total size (some 75,000 members), with the least diversified membership, simplest formal structure and (because of its weaker competitive position) strong concern for its representation in the workplace—has been most forward in formulating policy programmes for motor industry labour.[1]

In sum, the division of the mass production workers who form the car plants' characteristic population between a few major unions, with differing policies, leadership attitudes and internal structures, and involving also differing alliances of labour interests external to the motor industry, has itself made some direct contribution to that industry's recent strike-proneness. But it has particularly created obstacles to the formation of coherent union policies to deal with the issues on which the industry's labour unrest has focused. And these obstacles seem also to have been reinforced by inadequacies—again, partly arising from the unions' structure—in the communication of specific membership interests to the leaderships. A recent incident which perhaps illustrates this failure of communication with some vividness was the protracted 'four-night week' disputes in the Midlands plants during 1965—which were less a strike than a mass abstention from Friday night-shifts. These followed the engineering 'package deal' of December 1964, which provided for a forty-hour

[1] For instance the N.U.V.B. formulated quite detailed proposals on industrial relations policy in the motor industry for its 1966 conferences.

week to be worked in five days or nights; and of all the operatives affected, the car workers were those most employed on shift work. The union leaders had apparently signed the agreement in neglect of those workers' desire—which ought to have been conveyed, if by no other means, by several previous unofficial strikes and at least one major plant agreement on the same issue—to concentrate their night-shifts into four spells. The affair became almost a conflict between the unions' members and those leaders who were, it was reported, alarmed at this demand's supposed rejection of that historic union platform, 'The Eight Hour Day'!

(c) shop stewards: the new 'establishment'

Next to multiple unionism—and to some very large extent connected with it—the most prominent feature of union organization in the car firms is clearly the importance of the shop stewards' role. It is, of course, this aspect of the motor companies' labour affairs on which press and public comment has often concentrated. So that the problems of the British automobile industry's labour relations are sometimes depicted as produced by a struggle for power over the industry's labour force, between the official union leaders at national and district levels on the one hand and the shop stewards at the workplace level on the other. However, the background to the recent development of the shop steward system, and to the shop stewards' increased status in relation to the union officials proper, is the immense growth in domestic, workplace bargaining under the conditions of the past generation. In the presence of a generally continued high employment sometimes amounting to labour shortage, of rising productivity and rapid detailed change (both of technological and other kinds), and of a system of engineering collective agreements which has substantially failed to adapt itself to the recent growth and specialization of the engineering industries, the national agreements negotiated by official union leaders have come to serve only as a framework, a basis of minimum standards common to nearly all the metalworking industries, on which an elaborate structure of detailed wage-rates and employment conditions has been negotiated at the workplace level itself. This development is perhaps partially illustrated in our Chapter on wages: suffice it to instance it here by the fact that (except for Ford and Vauxhall which have their own agreements with the trade unions proper) there are no nationally-agreed rates at all for the semi-skilled operatives who make up the bulk of the car firms' labour force.

Many of the industry's conflicts may be said to arise because this development of workplace bargaining has not yet been fully absorbed by any of the parties to the process—firms and employers' associations, unions *and* shop stewards. And co-ordination on the union side is one respect in which this is so. For the conclusion of national agreements, a loose co-operation between the unions was sufficient: indeed, co-ordination between them was to some extent imposed by the insistence of employers' associations on standard terms of employment. When workplace bargaining became the key determinant of employment terms and conditions, however, this loose co-operation no longer sufficed to provide the intricate and detailed co-ordination now required between different unions' members and officers—for instance, on the many matters which arose not covered at all by national agreements, like the treatment of redundant operatives. The national unions have so far been unable—indeed, have made small attempt—to develop an organization to give the detailed guidance that co-ordination at the workplace level would require (especially since on some of the questions involved they have been at variance with each other). They have mainly confined themselves to briefing their own stewards on such policies as they had as were relevant to workplace negotiations. At that level, the job of co-ordination had thus to be largely done by the stewards themselves.

To be fully effective—in the light particularly of the dispersals of union membership already outlined—shop stewards of different unions have to be brought together to compare wages and conditions in their respective constituencies within the plant, to formulate joint policies on workshop issues, and to make common agreements with their employers. It is this combination of stewards from different unions that gives the workplace representative system such a large degree of autonomy from the unions proper. Such a situation could, of course, arise *within* a union: 'unofficial movements' based on workplace opposition to official union policies are not an abnormal feature of many British union histories. And this has been particularly likely to arise in the A.E.U., with its effective dispersal of power between different elected bodies and officials, and the T. & G.W.U., with its multiplicity of internal sectional interests. But multiple unionism at the workplace, when combined with the other constitutional features of the car workers' unions, makes such an autonomy almost certain. And the probability of its arising was strengthened by the development and elaboration of the stewards' organization itself.

The current complexity—almost formality—of shop steward organization seems little appreciated. In the federated engineering firms the right of workers to be represented by stewards was established by agreements signed during and after the First World War. But in the inter-war period development of this representation was held back by the bargaining weakness of labour, the hostility of many employers, and the reserved attitude of some union leaderships—a reserve which is reflected in the fact that though all the metalworking unions now have stewards, and duly accredit them when appointed, union rule-books other than that of the A.E.U. generally have only sketchy references to their status, rights and duties. The breakthrough came, as with union membership in general, with the War, and the protection and encouragement afforded by war-time circumstances and labour regulations.

Post-war development appears to have been particularly fast from the mid-1950s. At the present time, we would estimate that for the 200,000 or so manual workers in the car firms there are some 5,000 accredited shop stewards. Ratios of stewards to membership appear to vary somewhat between unions: the A.E.U.'s seems to be about 1:40, that of the T. & G.W.U. about 1:60, and the N.U.V.B.'s as high as 1:35. The differences partly reflect these unions' respective concentrations of membership in processes with different-sized working groups: they also reflect variations in historical and current union attitudes to workplace organization. Some of the unions may also have 'shop committeemen'—like the N.U.V.B., again—besides their accredited stewards. On the other hand, about one steward in twelve will also be a 'convener' (or senior steward, or chief steward[1]), elected as the spokesman of a particular union's stewards—or all the stewards—in a department or plant.

This already implies a considerable hierarchy amongst the stewards themselves—although the office of convener is not recognized by the E.E.F. The C.S.E.U.'s rules permit the election by shop stewards of 'Confederation Stewards' (who will also not be recognized by the E.E.F., however) to be accredited by the joint union district committee of the C.S.E.U. itself, but only the Coventry car firm stewards' organizations appear to operate under this system. The federated car firms are permitted by the E.E.F.'s Procedure Agreement to allow Works Committees of seven management and seven elected workers' representatives to play a part in dispute-settlement; but only the leading stewards' committees in Austin, Morris Commercial and Pressed Steel plants conform to this arrangement—and they are elected by the other stewards, not by direct vote of the operatives. Most of the unions' rules require their stewards to form a 'shop committee' which may elect a convener for the union concerned, and in the car plants the most frequent form of joint organization for bargaining purposes appears to be a combination of six or seven of

[1] It will be gathered that there is a considerable confusion of nomenclature, some managements refusing to use the term 'convener' for historical reasons: while 'Works Committee' might mean almost anything, pending further inquiry.

the major unions' conveners as the Works Committee (or Joint Executive, or Negotiating Committee). Some Joint Executives leave it at that: but most go on to elect a chairman and secretary (or again, convener and deputy convener) if not both.

The chief posts in the workplace organization are thus already detached from the formal union machines, since the officers represent no one union but all the trade unionists in the plant. But the majority of car plants have variants of the above system, in which this is even more so. Thus, all the plant's stewards together (who may number up to 600—in the Austin case) form a Joint Shop Stewards' Committee, and this itself may elect the chairman and secretary, or the whole of the Works Committee; and the latter may then in turn appoint its own chief officers. Of course, voting in these affairs usually goes by union, which ensures that the top positions in the steward heirarchy are held by members of the major unions: but leading offices have sometimes been held by members of small unions on grounds of sheer ability. And in one major case—that of Ford—the representative system has been even more disassociated from the national unions.

Most *ordinary* stewards represent only the members of their own union. But in nearly all the car plants there are sections where individual union memberships are too small, and one steward will be elected to represent members of two or more unions (in the plant in Table VII/2 one in six of the operatives were represented by stewards of other unions). In Ford plants, however this 'geographical' constituency is the norm; the company having—again because of the way it accepted collective bargaining in the first instance—saddled itself with twenty-one unions, recoiled from the idea of having up to twenty-one different unions' stewards in every section. And these 'generally representative' shop stewards in turn elect the conveners and Works Committees. In the upshot, however, the arrangement is said to have allowed militant A.E.U. members (many of them taken over with Briggs Bodies) to gain a disproportionate influence in the Ford stewards' organization during the 1950s. But Ford, as usual, is an exception: Vauxhall Works Committees and their 'Negotiating Sub-Committees' are each composed of direct representatives from the stewards of the three unions now involved. One or two federated car plants have an unusually direct system in which committees consist simply of three unions' conveners in each plant. But in general a more elaborate hierarchy, involving a large measure of 'general representation', is the rule.

This is by no means the whole structure of shop steward organization. But it is perhaps sufficient to show that the workplace representative system is now an elaborate institution in its own right. As to its functioning, one can perhaps illustrate by reference to two well established Works Committees operating under rather different circumstances. Since the end of the War the strength of the Austin shop stewards' organization has been well-known in the industry. Until 1953 it was an unofficial committee composed of twenty shop stewards from the fourteen major unions which operate in the Birmingham plant. Following the 'monster' official N.U.V.B. strike of that year a reconstruction took place at the instigation of the C.S.E.U.'s local officials. They hoped that the new committee would become the workers' side of a Joint Works Committee (under engineering procedure) covering the whole Longbridge site, and it accordingly consisted of seven stewards elected annually by the whole body of stewards, with a non-voting minutes secretary.[1] But Austin refused to recognize the committee until after the major official redundancy strike in 1956, when the management began to meet the committee on an informal basis. Shortly afterwards they agreed to form a Joint Works Committee for the Longbridge Site and to recognize the workers' side of it as a Works Committee.

In practice, under the Austin arrangement the seven senior stewards act as part-time negotiators responsible for handling the grievances of 26,000 men. The latest edition (1965) of the handbook given to all Austin workers contains a detailed account of the part that the Works Committee plays at Austin. The management helps the committee to function in a number of ways. It allows it to hold its monthly general meetings in works time and pays wages for the three hours or so that the meetings last. At these meetings, 'held in the Boxing Room at the West Works Canteen', the committee's printed standing orders operate, and at each meeting the members deal with an average of fifty points raised by the chief shop steward (who in this case is the secretary) and forty letters. Conferences on urgent matters are held when required 'under the toilets in the Trentham building'.

Until 1964, the secretary (*and* chief shop steward—*or* convener, as he is generally known, even though the company itself refuses to use the term) used to work about ten hours a week at his machine, but now almost all his time, and to a lesser extent that of the other committee members, is spent in negotiations. While they are thus occupied the firm pays them the factory average earnings, and, where necessary, this is made up to the average of the section of workers with whom the man (nominally) works by shop collections.[2] The

---

[1] Currently there are two members each from the T. & G.W.U., A.E.U. and N.U.V.B., and two sheet metalworkers, one of whom is the minutes secretary.

[2] Some years ago when the convener was not paid for time spent off his job, the plant manager asked him to go over to one of the factories and persuade some

convener can be reached through the telephone by his machine; if he is too busy to handle the problem he will pass it on to one of the other committeemen, but most requests for assistance are made directly to him. Although most of the calls are from shop stewards, many are from managers and foremen who want the convener, or one of the committeemen, to come along to iron out a problem. In effect, the Works Committee—and particularly the convener, the apex of several stages of internal grievance procedure before the local union and employers' association officials are called in—are skilled, and near-professional negotiators.

Jaguar has officially recognized Shop Stewards' Committees for many years. Since it took over Daimler in 1960, the company has had two main Coventry plants, each with a separate J.S.S.C. The firm's 120 or so stewards are elected annually (in theory, at any rate) on a geographical basis and each is automatically a member of one of the J.S.S.C.s. There are six unions in each plant, and the stewards of each union elect their own senior stewards. These senior stewards—as they are in fact called—form the central 'Negotiating Committee' at each plant which meets (frequently) with higher management. Both of the full J.S.S.C.s meet in the firm's time for an hour-and-a-half each month. Report-back meetings on negotiations are held when occasion demands—in the lunch-break, or even during working time: the management's permission must be requested, but is seldom withheld. The company, at time of writing, paid the stewards 5s 10d. per hour during the time they were involved in negotiations and money collected by the shop stewards provided a further 7s per hour to bring the payment up to the assembly-worker's normal earnings. Although all the senior stewards have jobs, in practice about half do not in fact work at them at all, spending all their time on grievance and dispute-settlement; while the others seldom work a normal week—'at the bench', at any rate. People who want to contact them may do so by the factory telephones or call them over the public address system, but stewards can get permission to leave their departments and approach senior stewards personally. The firm also gives other facilities—for example—by allowing use of any internal or external telephone and providing clerical assistance. Its management is also prepared to hear the senior stewards' views on many subjects outside the range of normal collective bargaining—like

---

strikers to return to work. He suggested that the shop steward concerned should be asked to do this; the manager replied that this had been done and had failed. The convener said that he would go over three days later after he had ensured a decent week's wages, and that he could not afford to go sooner. After this incident the convener was paid 2s. 6d. per hour by the company when engaged in negotiations.

production schedules—and to meet the combined Negotiating Committees of both works if necessary. So that although its organization and nomenclature (and one wishes the unions would sort at least that out) differ from those of Austin, the Jaguar stewards' hierarchy fills a very similar negotiating and consultative role.

There are many other Works Committees in the industry as solidly-established as these, and some leading officers of long experience indeed. The T. & G.W.U.'s convener at Pressed Steel's Oxford plant is particularly notable in this respect (though in a very different personal style to Austin's chief steward). And it is some indication of these leading stewards' frequent quality that we have encountered, or heard of, fifteen former car-plant conveners who are now full-time union officials and five who now hold senior labour relations posts with companies. And the picture commonly drawn of conflict between the workplace organization and formal union structure neglects their very real degree of mutual dependence. The unions proper in any case rely largely on the stewards for their finance: they are usually also subscription collectors. And, on the other hand, some Works Committees (for instance, those at Luton, to date) are heavily dependent on the local District Committees and, particularly, union officers: at this level, notwithstanding the difficulties created by the official's plenitude of commitments and scarcity of time, working relations are often close. While most of the unions' lower administrative echelon is in turn managed by people who are also stewards: these appear to supply most of the officers and committeemen for the T. & G.W.U.'s car plant branches and a very large proportion of A.E.U. Branch and District Committee members. In that union's structure, of course, this has sometimes led, in car plant disputes, to friction between the District (which is theoretically responsible for co-ordinating local industrial activity) and the national leadership; and this has been especially complicated where there were (as in the Dagenham case and the Rootes Acton strike in 1961) political incompatibilities between the District Committee or district officials and the Executive Council. But the *potentiality* of such conflict appears to derive, not from the existence of the workplace organization as such, but from a failure to reconcile the system of national bargaining and conciliation (with which the top union leadership is largely concerned) to the development of intensive bargaining at the workplace level.

(D) STEWARDS, STRIKES AND MANAGEMENTS

How far has the shop steward system itself been a cause of strikes? Since the war, about 3 per cent of all reported strikes in car firms, and well over 10 per cent of striker-days, have involved the status of shop stewards directly—in disputes over their recognition by management, the provision of facilities to them, or—particularly—their dismissal. Strikes against the dismissal of stewards, especially, have been a major source of lost working time, accounting for nearly 400,000 'days lost' in the period of our analysis. But stoppages of this kind have also been declining, not merely in relative terms, but in absolute importance. The major concentration of them came during the 1950s, so that in general relations between managements and stewards appear to have settled down in recent years. No strikes of any size over the recognition of stewards, or the refusal of facilities for them to function, have been reported from car plants during the 1960s. The stewards are already an 'establishment'.

The question of how far shop stewards have provoked strikes on questions other than their own rights and status can only be answered in a rough comparative way. If the provocation of disputes were a major part of the stewards' ambition, then one would expect greater strike-liabilities in firms where the stewards' committees were strongest or where they were known for a politically-militant disposition, and fewer strikes where they had a reputation for adherence to due procedure. But it seems difficult in fact to establish such relationships. We discuss the differing strike-proneness of individual firms briefly in our next chapter, but we may perhaps anticipate that somewhat to consider some evidence. For instance, at Rover's main Solihull plant each of the eight unions with memberships there has its own steward organization, and the chief stewards of the major unions form a loose Works Committee. But, partly because of disagreements between the N.U.V.B.—which has there the biggest membership—and other unions, the committee has not functioned very effectively in the past, and each unions' stewards have generally preferred to operate separately. There are rather similar situations in Rover's other plants around Birmingham.[1] But the weakness of the joint steward organization has not prevented Rover contributing significantly more than its proportionate share of strikes and striker-days to the car firms' strike-liability of recent years. There are analagous divisions within the stewards' organization at the B.M.C. body-building plants of Fisher & Ludlow and Nuffield Metal Products, which have already been referred to. And these plants seem to be quite strike-prone. A *very* weak steward organization (though there are now no such organizations, to our knowledge, in

---

[1] This situation has now been somewhat explored by a commission of the Motor Industry Joint Study Group ('Report of an Inquiry into the State of Industrial Relations at the Rover Co. Assembly Works, Solihull', November 2 and 3, 1965), which recommended the unions should work more closely together.

the car firms) may, of course, be associated with comparative peace. But this is not necessarily so of a divided one (Vauxhall's experience of the 1950s notwithstanding).

Or again, each of the main Coventry firms—Rootes, Standard and Jaguar—has a steward organization in its main plant rather like that already described for the last of these companies, and these seem about equally strong. But these firms have also differed substantially in their respective strike-liabilities. From the end of the War up to the mid-1950s, indeed, the Standard stewards—partly because of the semi-managerial role that the firm had conceded them—were then undoubtedly the most tightly-organized in the motor industry: but this was a period of comparative industrial peace for the firm. Or again, the disturbed state of labour relations at Ford's Dagenham estate during the late 1950s was associated with the prominence of Communists amongst leading stewards. But none of the Jaguar stewards' negotiating team are—to the best of our knowledge—currently of this persuasion, and one of its plants' J.S.S.C.s included, at least until very recently, one active Conservative (there are Tory stewards in several car plants, and these are not invariably conservative in industrial attitude). Yet Jaguar seems in fact to have had at least as high a strike-incidence as Ford. And one of the most strike-free federated plants in the motor industry had for some years a convener who is said to have been a militant. Or yet again, both the Jaguar and Austin Works Committees—despite, in the latter case, the very prominent Communism of the convener during the early 1960s—appear to have a certain reputation for insistence on 'the observation of procedure'. And though Austin has somewhat receded, in recent years, from its mid-1950s prominence as a strike-performer, its dispute-incidence does not appear to have by any means positively fallen during the 1960s.

At the least, this confirms that strike-proneness is not susceptible of over-simple explanations. The character of a plant's steward organization—its varying solidarity, structure and militancy—does not seem important as a primary and continuing source of high strike-liabilities. And these conclusions seem confirmed by the experience of one of the writers as a working car factory operative, in a period when several strikes occurred, and he had some opportunity for close observation of the workings of the stewards' organization. The experience is also interesting as illustrating the confused fashion in which real (if in this case, mostly minor) crises in industrial relations develop, as contrasted with the assumed stereotype ritual of institutional conciliation and conflict—and may help to explain some difficulties one has in assessing available reportage of more major and involved events. It is therefore summarized in this

Chapter's Appendix. But this series of stoppages, at any rate, hardly makes the shop stewards, and particularly the senior stewards' committee, appear as stimulating and provoking disputes. Rather, they are attempting to control a number of pressures to which they are subject, including those from the management and outside union officials, but especially including pressures from particular groups and sections of workpeople themselves. Which is not to say that leading stewards (or, for that matter, local union officers) may not sometimes indicate that a 'spontaneous' demonstration will help to secure or expedite a settlement. Although on the whole, the stewards here appear as attempting to minimize trouble; but when trouble seems inevitable, they attempt to assert their leadership, in order to maintain their authority over the operatives.

This in any case suggests that certain factors act as regulators of the leading stewards' activity and policy. One is a comparative flexibility to membership pressures—at least, in the long run (we were told of an instance where a convener had simply ruled a vote of 'no confidence in the Works Committee' from the whole J.S.S.C. out of order and held the position). But if there is often difficulty in filling ordinary stewards' offices (men may still exchange earnings for worry by accepting them), while on the other hand works chairman's or secretary's posts (or the equivalent) are usually held for a run of years and filled in practice by succession, there is also often strong competition—personal, inter-union, or political—for 'second line' positions, like senior stewards' posts.

And another major pressure is the stewards' very real—if again, long run—dependence on the management itself. In a sense, the leading stewards are performing a managerial function, of grievance settlement, welfare arrangement and human adjustment, and the steward system's acceptance by managements (and thus in turn, the facility with which the stewards themselves can satisfy their members' demands and needs) has developed partly because of the increasing effectiveness—and certainly economy—with which this role is fulfilled. And it may be significant here that Ford, which for many years had the least amiable relations with the workplace organization, also appears to have the most extensive personnel and industrial relations staff. At any rate, steward leaderships which have persistently failed to find managerial acceptance have usually ended by being thrown out of the plant. The chief stewards in car factories are often the skilled survivors of a long experience of balancing and accommodating these contrary pressures—even if they demonstrate a variety of both personal techniques and collective relationships with the formal union organization in the process.

But since we have referred to the Ford situation of the late 1950s—

and since public impressions of the realities of workplace representation seems still considerably influenced by the comments of two Courts of Inquiry (the 'Cameron' and 'Jack' reports[1]) on the shop steward system at Briggs and Ford—we may perhaps add a further note on that system's special history. We have noted how the circumstances of Ford's recognition of the unions led, not merely to the involvement of an unusually large number of national trade unions in its negotiating procedure, but to the introduction of a shop steward system which was unusually dissociated from them. The Ford negotiating system, however, provided no such role for stewards or local union officers in workplace bargaining as does the wage-system of the federated car firms: wage-rates are fixed in direct negotiation with the trade unions—who are usually represented by their national officers—for all the Ford plants as a group.

On the other hand, for a time-work plant the only possible equivalent to the federated firm's piece-rate bargaining is the negotiation of the efforts to be returned for the fixed hourly wage-rates; and in this area, at least, Ford made no concessions to collective bargaining, regarding work-loads as exclusively a matter for managerial determination. Formally, the function of shop stewards in Ford was thus limited to a participation (for most of them, indirect) in the firm's Joint Works Committees, which are essentially a procedure for dealing with individual and small group grievances in each department. And that Ford itself regarded shop stewards as possessing a much more limited role than did the federated firms is shown by the more restricted facilities it has so far provided to them. In effect, the steward organization in Ford was thus involved in an attempt to establish standards for the use of labour informally, on a 'custom and practice' basis, and in face of the disapproval of top management—even if it met with frequent concession from lower-level supervision. The result was necessarily a situation of immanent conflict, combined with a general frustration of the steward organization which provided a basis for militants to assume the leadership. And this frustration was particularly aggravated when Briggs was absorbed in the Ford organization, because Briggs—though also a

---

[1] *Command* 131, 30/3/57 and *Command* 1999, 3/4/63. Some further account of the major disputes concerned is given in Ch. IX, and this is based substantially on these reports. But at the time, such comments as Lord Cameron's on the 'private union within a union, enjoying immediate and continuous touch with the men in the shop, answerable to no superiors and in no way officially or constitutionally linked with the union hierarchy', or Professor Jack's—'There is no doubt that over a number of years the company had been frustrated and put to unreasonable inconvenience by a militant element among their employees'—were undoubtedly taken as having a wide application to shop steward organization in general.

non-federated concern at the time of the take-over—had a quite opposite system to that of Ford, in which each plant's steward committee had itself been accustomed to negotiate wage-rates and working arrangements separately. These things seem a sufficient background to the development of that 'endemic conflict' situation in certain Ford plants, to which we refer later in this study, but which ended only with the 'October Revolution' at Dagenham in 1962.

(E) THE 'COMBINES', WEAKNESSES OF THE STEWARD ORGANIZATION—AND 'PARALLEL UNIONISM'

But to return to the less deviant cases. The development of the shop steward system in recent years should not mislead one into overlooking its limitations. Apart from the divisions within certain plant organizations to which we have referred, there are, fairly generally, limitations on the leading stewards' administrative resources. Despite the increasing provision of facilities by managements, conveners and senior stewards still commonly have to work from a base beside their nominal post by a machine or an assembly line, and carry their files about with them. Vauxhall—characteristically, again—has provided its Luton Works Committee with an office and clerk, but this is currently quite exceptional. Managements generally have the advantage in recording and secretarial facilities. The stewards' finance is usually limited—some unions allow a 'shop levy' or the retention of part of their subscription, but Works Committees are often reliant on the proceeds of raffles or draws to meet their expenses, and sometimes to make up losses of earnings.[1] But a particular limitation of the workplace organization is its circumscribed horizons.

This leads into another elaboration of the steward system. All the major firms now have several plants apiece, and these are also sometimes widely scattered—there are B.M.C. plants in England, Scotland and Wales. Within Ford and Vauxhall, there is at least co-ordination so far as wage-rates and basic conditions are concerned through their direct agreements with the unions. But there is no such co-ordination —although in view of the extent to which anomalies in relative wages have contributed to the industry's labour disputes this would appear to be a matter of some importance—for the other firms,

---

[1] The large financial resources of the Briggs and Ford stewards—reported as £3,000 monthly in the former case during 1956—and which permitted them to maintain their own office and staff outside the plant and to publish a newssheet, seem to have come mainly from unusually efficient draw-organizers. The Austin Works Committee's current income averages below £150 a month.

since their wages and working arrangements are largely determined by workplace negotiation. The employers' federation is also organized on a local basis, and its conciliation procedure in any case formally prohibits external comparison in plant references. The national unions have, at time of writing, no arrangement for co-ordinating bargaining in different plants of the same firm; in theory, the district union organization is—in the A.E.U., at least—responsible for co-ordination between plants in the same locality, but it is often difficult for a District Committee to spend much time, in a concentrated and diverse industrial region like the West Midlands, on the affairs of a single company's workers. And there is, in that case, still the problem of co-ordination between unions. The C.S.E.U. has 'Confed'. District Committees for some purposes of inter-union co-operation, but this machinery is rarely enlisted or effective in relation to specific workplace negotiations.

Such co-ordination as there currently is, on the operatives' side, between bargaining in the separate plants of a federated car firm has thus been largely developed by the shop stewards themselves. There are 'Combine Committees' of representatives from the stewards' joint bodies in all the car firms except Rover—where the inter-union difficulties already noted have prevented the formation of one—and Pressed Steel, where the policy of the T. & G.W.U.'s leading stewards at the main Oxford plant has been opposed to such associations (though not unfavourable to assisting Works Committees to establish themselves in others of the firm's factories).[1] Combine Committees may operate at several levels, and the leading stewards' organization in any plant may thus be associated with several such bodies. In a sense, the Austin Works Committee was a Combine Committee before it was recognized by the management, because it linked the different stewards' groups of several factories on a single site; and this was also the position for the Ford stewards' Combine Committee on that company's main Dagenham estate. However, the association is usually wider.

Clearly, Combine Committees may otherwise be of four kinds. Committees linking up the shop stewards at a firm which has several plants in the same district are now particularly well established in the Coventry area. The 'Negotiating Committees' at Rootes's Stoke and Ryton factories co-operate closely, and there have been joint references from the two plants to engineering disputes procedure. Morris Engines (part of B.M.C.) has five plants in Coventry, which are organized under only two Works Committees, and these in turn send representatives to a local Combine Committee which

[1] Since B.M.C.'s acquisition of Pressed Steel, Oxford T. & G.W.U. stewards have also refused to send representatives to the B.M.C. Combine Committee.

meets regularly to exchange information and discuss current workplace negotiations—and also has occasional joint meetings with representatives of the Works Committee at the unit's foundry at Wellingborough, which is well outside the district. Since Jaguar took over the Daimler works, the two stewards' committees have had a 'Joint Executive'—a title in this case suggested by the firm itself. One of the strongest local Combine Committees is that for S.T.I., representing five plants in the Coventry district, which meets monthly in the firm's time, and has for some time been recognized by its management.

Such local committees, particularly, have achieved a degree of formality approaching that of the basic workplace representative organizations themselves. They may have their own officers, and key posts at the plant and local combine levels may even be 'traded' between different unions' stewards—for instance, so that each of the unions with substantial membership in the plants involved holds the chair of either an important Works Committee or the local combine association. It is notable, however, that what might be the second type of combine—a local committee from plants of different car firms—has not developed. Even where two such neighbouring works are largely organized by the same union, as in Oxford, no such association has appeared. And when one moves on to the third type of combine—a national association between the stewards of one firm's plants in different districts—it is also interesting to find, in the one car-making group which is also associated with large-scale heavy vehicle production, S.T.I., that only one of the several Leyland plants has been represented at its national combine stewards' meetings. If spontaneous workers' organization follows a line of traceable economic interest, it appears to be orientated towards the product market, rather than towards the labour market.

However, to the extent that each major company specializes in car and light vehicle production, national inner-firm Combine Committees are also well-established. Thus, the Rootes Stewards' National Committee has been operating for over a decade, and is now composed of three delegates from each of the firm's plant Works Committees, who meet monthly in London. Standard's national combine represents the stewards of eight plants (only excluding, to avoid giving the firm occasion to fear a breach of commercial secrecy, one works where prototype and experimental work is carried on); it is also noteworthy for including representatives of the white-collar unions—of draughtsmen, technicians, clerks and supervisors—who are unusually strong in S.T.I. But the most extensive is, of course, that for B.M.C. itself.

The B.M.C. Combine Committee was formed at the time the

Austin/Morris merger was announced at the end of 1951—it was, indeed, first called 'the Merger Committee'. The Austin stewards' committee first approached the Morris stewards to form a joint body covering the new corporation, but eventually, agreed to join an existing Morris Combine Committee which had been operating for some years. Under its current constitution, the national committee consists of two delegates from each of thirteen former Nuffield plants plus an equivalent number from the Austin site (though in practice, delegations' size and voting rights are not restricted). It holds regular bi-monthly meetings, and elects a chairman, secretary and treasurer annually. Each B.M.C. plant also nominates a delegate to a standing committee of the combine, which meets when the officers determine a matter is urgent. The major function of this association, however, is to provide information on changes in output, earnings and working arrangements in each of B.M.C.'s plants. About forty delegates attend each bi-monthly meeting and a formal record is kept of proceedings, which consist mainly of reports from individual factories.

In practice, however, these national Combine Committees do not seem to have been particularly effective. Thus, although the B.M.C. committee has received delegates from each of B.M.C.'s manufacturing units, one of its weaknesses is that the support it receives from different plants varies considerably—least coming from those works where rivalries between the main unions are acute. Another is the lack of systematic collection and analysis of information from which voluntary bodies without full-time officers are prone to suffer. And it is chronically short of cash: its attempt to maintain a newssheet for B.M.C. workers, for instance, failed for this reason. In brief, the committee has served as a somewhat imperfect forum for the exchange of data: which is perhaps unfortunate, since of all the car firms B.M.C. has been most affected by wage-structure disputes—arising from anomalies in payment within and between the company's many plants—which are themselves largely a product of unco-ordinated workplace bargaining.

All the major Combine Committees have suffered from the same weaknesses, although to different degrees. The Rootes national committee seems to have had an unusual continuity of representation. But the Ford committee, for example, benefited from the high concentration of Ford workers in the South-East of England, from the efficiency of the Dagenham stewards' fund-raising efforts and from the help (after 1956) of an informal group of local union officials. Even though the majority of delegates had much less travelling to do than their B.M.C. counterparts, however, there have still been difficulties in maintaining regular attendance, and this (together with the habitual vagaries in the flow of factual material) made it difficult for the committee to build up a systematic dossier of changes in working arrangements and conditions in the firm. The Jaguar Combine Committee has also benefited from concentration of the firm's employees in Coventry and from unusually good facilities provided by the firm itself: even so, its resources of staff have been inadequate to enable it to organize, maintain and check the information potentially at its disposal.

No industry-wide Combine Committee has been able to maintain itself. During the middle 1950s an 'unofficial' attempt was made to link up the various federal committees in the car firms through a forum for the interchange of views and information at industry level. A body called 'The Big Six' (so named because it consisted of representatives from stewards' committees in B.M.C., Standard, Ford, Vauxhall, Rootes and Rover) arranged to meet quarterly, and in fact organized three large conferences—at Birmingham, Coventry and Oxford. These conferences were substantial weekend affairs, arranged by a special steering committee and attended by around three hundred shop stewards apiece. Just how 'The Big Six' was formed has not transpired, but it seems to have developed partly from the desire of the Combine Committees then operating within B.M.C. and Standard to see a common stand taken on certain issues —at this time there was widespread concern about the possible effects of automation, and one conference was devoted to that subject.[1] Not surprisingly, the trade unions proper saw in these activities an attempt by left-wing militants to organize the motor industry's stewards behind an alternative leadership. Their officials felt that the development was largely inspired by the Communist Party; and indeed, many both of the leading shop stewards and of the outsiders who addressed the meetings were either Party members or sympathizers. And the movement was apparently not unconnected with certain attempts by the World Federation of Trade Unions (which is, of course, Communist-dominated) to promote a permanent international liaison committee of automobile workers. But the meetings were apparently well supported as these things go, and so presumably filled a need for a contact with colleagues in other firms and a joint approach to the car industry's problems which the unions themselves were not fulfilling.

[1] For an account of the meeting which dealt mainly with automation, see 'Report of 2nd Conference of Motor Car Shop Stewards, Oxford, September 25, 1955' (*All In Favour Say Aye*, Reliance Printing Works, Halesowen). Shirley W. Lerner and John Bescoby, in 'Shop Steward Combine Committees in the British Engineering Industry' (*British Journal of Industrial Relations*, IV, 2, July 1966) also refer to this movement—as well as to 'combines' outside the motor sector.

Trade Unions and Shop Stewards

Whether the official unions' hostility made much contribution to the inability of an authentic industry-wide stewards' organization to develop seems doubtful. The effectiveness of the stewards' associations seems roughly in inverse proportion to their distance from the workplace. The national firm-wide Combine Committees, for instance—though the organization of mutual support in strikes may well have been one of the original motives for their formation—appear to have played no very significant role in relation to disputes at particular plants unless these involved very general issues (like '100 per cent trade unionism' or the 'four-night week'). But these committees were attempting to provide at least an information service and some consequent measure of co-ordination in bargaining between the separate establishments of a company—of a kind which our chapter on wages, perhaps, may indicate to have been desirable. And they were certainly hampered in this by the hostility of firms and official union leaderships, to say nothing of the absence of the administrative expertise and financial support which the unions proper could have provided.

In this respect, things seem in process of change. We have noted that local Combine Committees have been recognized for some time by certain firms. The conversion of the informal committee of local union officers which occasionally met the Dagenham stewards before 1962 into a formal visiting panel involved an implied acceptance of the combine system at the main Ford site. Rootes' directors have on certain occasions met the firm's national Combine Committee in the past. And at time of writing, both Vauxhall and B.M.C. have had exploratory discussions with a view to regularizing national combine arrangements with union and workplace representatives. In a sense, a new formal system of labour relationships is emerging from an informal one. But in the process, a certain conflict with established national negotiating and conciliatory institutions seems inevitable.

The shop steward organization, then, has developed mainly to fill in the inadequacies of current union structure when confronted with a situation in which national bargaining largely deals with certain minimum wage-rates and related questions, together with occasional general wage-advances for the whole range of metalworking industries as a group—while the effective level of operatives' wages and many other aspects of their working conditions are overwhelmingly determined at the plant level, or in direct negotiation with individual companies. At the same time, the shop steward system is itself inadequate to meet all the requirements of the situation. It does not always provide full co-ordination between the different working groups in bargaining activities and grievance settlement at the workplace level. It is particularly weak in achieving co-ordination in this respect between the different plants of the same firm. And it is almost totally ineffective in achieving co-ordination at the level of the motor industry as a whole. While at these levels the unions' official machinery has also so far provided for no effective co-operation, and sometimes actively discouraged the efforts of stewards to fill the gaps.

This situation seems a very large factor in the car firms' apparent inability to allay demonstrated discontents on their operatives' part in recent years. But it has also had certain further consequences. There is a state of what might be called 'parallel unionism'. For the car workers, in effect, the unions proper have become mainly a society for obtaining occasional general wage-increases and for demonstrating class and occupational solidarity by means of membership. So much so, that what union a man is actually a member of has, for many operatives at least, become largely irrelevant so long as he is a subscriber. While unofficial strikes are not generally 'strikes against the unions': they are simply conflicts to which the unions' existence has become, again, largely irrelevant. Though there is a—more or less—close interaction between the unions proper and the workplace representative system at local level, the national unions have (and the same may well be true of the engineering industries at large) little impact on the detailed determination of car industry employment conditions and labour relations.

In this respect the shop stewards' organization has become the real union—and one with an almost similar degree of elaboration and complexity. And because this organization is now the main agency for the bargaining of actual working conditions—with what amounts to its own full-time negotiators—it has assumed, in relation to managements on the one hand and the rank-and-file of operatives on the other, many of the characteristics that the official unions once displayed under the earlier development of national or industry-wide collective bargaining. The senior stewards, like the full-time union officials before them, are forced to assume something of the role of buffer between the employer and the operatives. Differences in the attitude of individual stewards may have some effect, just as the differing attitudes of national union officials before them affected industrial relations in some measure. But, in general, the stewards' organization is under pressures that compel it towards certain responsible patterns of institutional behaviour—'responsible' at least in the sense that its leaders are obliged to balance a variety of group interests against the particular sectional claims with which they are confronted, and to bear in mind the long-term desirability of maintaining good negotiating relations with managements. So (as our Appendix perhaps suggests in detail) a new phenomenon has appeared: the 'unofficial-unofficial' strike—the strike, that is, which has not merely the normal quality that it is not approved by the official union hierarchy, but is particularly not first approved by the shop stewards' leaders. In the motor industry, at any rate, this type of dispute appears to be becoming the norm.

APPENDIX

SOME SMALLER STRIKES: FROM THE INSIDE[1]

During the observer's employment (with the agreement of management, union officers and stewards) in a working and 'participant' role there were three stoppages big enough to be recorded by the Ministry of Labour at the plant concerned. All three brought the whole factory to a halt and in total involved over 20,000 striker-days. On a tight definition of work stoppage, however—i.e. including such events as dinner-break meetings which significantly over-ran time, and protest marches round the office-block during working hours—there were at least thirty such separate events. It is impossible to give a complete catalogue of them—neither the personnel manager nor anyone else in the factory had up to shortly before this time attempted to keep a complete account of even their number, let alone the issues, personalities, or times involved. But some departments had records of a kind, and it is a consolidation of these accounts which are referred to above. Such disputes were sufficiently frequent to be normal: so much a part of normal working life in fact as, when they involved one department only, to be without interest to the rest of the factory, unless large-scale lay-offs and reduced bonus-earnings resulted. The situation also appeared self-perpetuating in the sense that there was a common belief on the workshop floor, which seemed to the operatives to sum up their everyday experience, that 'if you do nothing you get nothing'; while supervisors on the other hand also often expressed (and sometimes acted on) the belief that all claims, protests, demands, had to be opposed on principle or 'the situation would soon get out of hand'.

The disputes experienced directly by our observer appeared to involve real issues: and while some members of the Conveners' Committee felt that many of the situations they were heir to arose more out of the personal foibles of particular stewards at the departmental level, it is perhaps no less significant that stewards themselves apparently had often to be goaded into reluctant action by their electorates. A series of stoppages in one particular stores will serve to illustrate this. These arose because a production bonus scheme, whereby all of the dayworkers in the factory shared equally from a bonus pool the contents of which varied with the number of

[1] To avoid personal identification, certain titles in this note are synthetic.

cars completed and man-hours worked, was felt by the spares storemen (and other stores departments) to be insufficiently related to their own efforts. A major complaint they made, which was borne out by the observer's experience, was that stoppages or short-time working which affected production (and hence their bonus) were accompanied by unaltered and sometimes increased effort on their part. In short, the bonus was no incentive to them—although its average level was a substantial proportion of their earnings. Its fluctuations were felt to be inequitable.

An agreement had been reached with the management which, according to the storemen, stated in effect that within a period of eighteen months each department would—after appropriate time-study—be put on to an 'individual incentive scheme' whereby the workers' earnings would be related to their own efforts as a department. Some of the other stores had been put on to the new bonus scheme, and the resultant increase in their bonus was well known and envied. In at least one case, their success was believed to have been achieved by a series of stoppages. Fourteen of the eighteen months had elapsed, and the delay was causing comment. The department's two stewards had been approached to press emphatically for action, and they had apparently taken the matter up with the supervisor on several occasions but without visible result. Direct action by the storemen was finally set off by three weeks' consecutive and substantial drops in bonus level.

The suggestion to 'do a downer' arose amongst a group of men preparing to go home at the end of the day. Their idea was to express their protest at the delay in introducing the new scheme and at the drop in bonus, and to get assurances that the matter would receive quick attention—particularly as there were rumours that two of the three time-study estimators employed by the firm were leaving at the end of the week ('because', it was said, 'they were underpaid'). In the morning this group approached the department's stewards for an immediate meeting with the Convener, and decided to put their coats on but gather outside in the yard when the starting hooter sounded. They did so in a body, calling out to the others in the department to join them. There had been no meeting of the shop to 'authorize' this action: it was itself both a protest and a request for a meeting. Within five minutes, the sixty workers in the department had gathered outside, one of the stewards had gone to find the Convener and the other addressed the gathering to the effect that they had now expressed their protest and should decide to start work 'and come out again in two hours' (when there was an official tea break, although he did not specifically mention this), by which time it was hoped the Convener would have been found. The steward said he had heard that other day-workers were holding similar meetings and this was the explanation for the Convener's absence. He stressed that his suggestion would be the 'correct' procedure to adopt (though in terms of the engineering disputes procedure this was hardly so), but two of the original group opposed him on the grounds that they had to show that they meant business. There was no formal vote on this, but by general assent the department decided to stay out.

When the Convener arrived he informed the men that other disputes on the same issue were taking place, and that a meeting between the shop stewards' central committee (of which he was also chairman) and the management had been arranged for that afternoon. He recommended a return to work. Discussion became heated and acrimonious, and it became fairly clear that there was little sympathy between the Convener and his members in the stores—there was talk by the storemen of piece-workers (who apparently included all the senior stewards) having little time for the troubles of day-workers. It also seemed that the meeting which had, fourteen months ago, accepted the agreement to introduce a new bonus scheme was considered by many of the storemen to have been unrepresentative. However, while the 'downer' was a protest, there was little general agreement on just what it was against or on the best action to demand. Some wanted to press for an immediate increase in their bonus pending the new scheme's introduction, but this was side-stepped by the Convener, who promised to take up instead the matter of the alleged delay. His recommendation to return to work was then adopted unanimously, somewhat surprisingly after a half-hour of wide-ranging discussion, during which very diverse views had been aired.

This 'downer' had throughout its course involved sixty persons and lasted just two-and-a-half hours. It was typical of the series which the same issue involved over the course of the next three months. And it indicated that action of this kind did seem to produce results which had not been obtained by mere requests. Moreover, in these cases at least, the stewards were not the focus of discontent; rather, the stewards tried ineffectively to control the general discontent of their members. However, the strike meetings were cathartic in the sense that many issues and grievances were ventilated at them, and problems became dissolved into the lowest common denominator. This was more apparent the larger the scale of the meeting; and the practical upshot was that, having been raised first on the floor, matters were left to the formal leaders—i.e. the Conveners or the departmental stewards—to sort out as best they could.

There was similarly a number of small stoppages by groups of trackmen, which were largely protests against erratic short-time working with its effect on earnings. They were comparable with the day-workers' disputes in that pressure for action was being put on the stewards by their members, and the departmental stewards in turn were pressing the Conveners' Committee for results. There was, however, a widely-held view—extending to most of the local trade union officials—that the main reason for the short-time working was not the technical difficulties which the firm cited, but a shortage of orders: it was held that technical troubles would soon be put right if the cars were wanted. In these circumstances the Conveners were in an invidious position: they were being pressed by their members for militant action while at the same time believing that such action would play into the hands of the management. It certainly seemed that a small stoppage in one section of the tracks would lead to a disproportionate number of men being laid off for a disproportionate time, so the efforts of the committeemen were concentrated on containing the issue, under a policy of keeping as many men at work as possible. Their efforts were not always successful. Their control over general stewards' meetings deteriorated, and there were several motions of 'no confidence in the Committee'.

In the case of one such stoppage the erosion of the senior stewards' control was the main factor in an almost complete walkout of the factory—day-workers included. The issue in dispute concerned an alteration in the amount of 'waiting time' payment due to a gang in the body shop. The men concerned later admitted that an excessive amount had been claimed under a wrong assumption, but the point at issue was whether there had been any consultation about the alteration. The facts were never finally clarified; but in any case the gang stopped work in mid-morning in protest, and could not be induced by their Conveners—members of two unions were involved —to return. Immediately the stoppage had taken place, all tracks except the final line (which had a backlog of uncompleted work) were given one hour's notice of lay-off by the management; but neither this fact, nor the refusal of the management to convene a meeting on the issue while a refusal to work continued, carried weight with the gang. However, the notice of lay-off was then extended for a further hour by the management, under the impression that further attempts were to be made by the Conveners to get a return; whereas in fact the stewards from all the tracks met to consider their position.

It was at this meeting that several track stewards, in exasperation at the firm's policy—as they saw it—of laying-off the tracks in reprisal for the body-gang's stoppage, carried a motion to bring the whole factory to a halt. The trackmen who had already been laid off, but who were standing about awaiting the report-back of their stewards, were told to consider themselves on strike in sympathy with the body-shop gang. It was only the fact of having to act under pressure of time that prevented some of the stores and supply departments from joining the stoppage, as their stewards had not all been advised of the 'unauthorized' meeting which carried this 'one out, all out' resolution. Members of the Conveners' Committee subsequently admitted privately that they were opposed to the 'one out, all out' policy, and that though they had not spoken in favour of it neither had they opposed it sufficiently forcibly. They had, in short, bowed to pressure from the floor against their better judgment, and they justified this by stating that their grip on the situation had been weakening steadily for several months.

In the largest stoppage of the period, the course of events was in fact complicated by what was later admitted to be a strong mutual animosity between the main personalities involved: the industrial relations manager and the recently-elected Convener of a union of metalworkers and mechanics which in this plant had only a minority membership. The immediate point at issue, however, was the metal fitters' claim to control labour recruitment: the firm wished to engage four additional metal fitters against their workplace representatives' wishes, and in the event took the matter out of the Convener's hands by contacting the union office directly. The Convener then requested a meeting with the industrial relations manager over this 'breach of procedure'. The issue then became primarily one about the constitution of this meeting, and at which stage of 'procedure' it would take place. There followed a period of wrangling involving the local official of the union who had been brought in by the firm, and also involving extended meetings and overtime bans by the metal fitters. This went on for several days, and ended in a full-scale walkout on the metal fitters' part—and consequential lay-offs of other operatives—when their Convener refused to accept the presence of the personnel manager at the meeting 'in an informal capacity'. The firm argued that he had been a party to the preceding wrangling, but the steward held that a hearing by him was the last stage in domestic procedure and his presence at this meeting would bias him if matters proceeded to that resort. All this while the stewards' central committee was on something of a limb, because it was a metal fitter's dispute only at this stage.

When this had been sorted out, however, and a full-scale return to work had taken place, the firm felt it necessary to post a notice about the factory, just before another meeting over the issue, because of what it considered 'the considerable confusion in the minds of employees as to the truth of the affair . . . and (the belief) that management had been made to climb down because of the strike'. At this point the stewards' central committee asserted its position by stating the notice to be 'provocative and ill-timed'; it did in fact lead to further walk-outs by the metal fitters, and further lay-offs by the firm. Negotiations between the firm and the Conveners' Committee on the subject of the notice, its replacement, or the posting of a further notice alongside it, lasted for two more days, during which time production was effectively at a standstill. Eventually, a return to work took place on the recommendation of the local union officials, 'to allow negotiations on the notice to proceed' (in the aftermath, the notice remained in some places for several months, and the negotiations faded out inconclusively).

The last stoppage especially illustrates both the way in which the issues at stake may change in the course of a dispute, and the muddled fashion in which real industrial events—as opposed to the formal stages of 'procedure'—often proceed! But the series also indicates some of the specific pressures—disadvantageous wage-comparisons, earnings fluctuations and so on—which have contributed to the car industry's recent dispute-record.

CHAPTER VIII

THE FIRMS COMPARED: AND THE EMPLOYERS' ORGANIZATION

(A) BIG FIRMS AND SMALLER ONES

One of the most notable features of the development of the wave of industrial unrest in the British car plants from the 1950s has been its apparent discrimination between firms. In public comment, for instance, a contrast commonly drawn was between the alleged strike-proneness of Ford and the seeming exemption of Vauxhall from labour disputes. But in fact neither of these firms is quite so exceptional in these respects as is widely supposed. Relative to their employment, other companies have been even more dispute-liable than Ford: and some other plants have been quite as dispute-free as Vauxhall. It would thus be quite unrealistic to analyse the motor industry's recent high dispute-propensity in terms solely of such general factors as those discussed in earlier chapters. Because of the very small number of large firms involved, and the extent to which two concerns in particular dominate car manufacturing, this would beg the question of whether the whole pattern was not in fact largely determined by abnormal relationships in one or two firms alone.

In Chapter IV we have already noted the greater sensitivity of labour relations in the minor or Independent firms as a group to the state of trade: here the separate strike-liabilities of the major and minor firms is first discussed more fully. Comparisons spread over forty years and more inevitably strain any basis of grouping. For each firm in the two groups, we have included the experience of all concerns which have merged in it, and the categories therefore necessarily mix the experience of firms such as Jaguar and Daimler, for example, which merged only recently. But the major firms—or the Big Five of the years from 1953 onwards—are basically the Big Six of the pre-war period, and it is changes in relative market shares in recent years which makes the grouping here less appropriate. Two of the Big Five have for some years produced around 70 per cent of

The Firms Compared: and the Employers' Organization

British cars, while Standard's relative position has seriously declined —although this firm still produces considerably more vehicles than Jaguar or Rover, if the difference in the *value* of its output is less marked. The basis of distinction between major and minor firms has become not so much size of firm as type of output: the Big Five produce mainly popular models, while the Independents are a now much diminished group of 'specialist' producers. This is one justification for placing Pressed Steel amongst the minor firms, although in employment terms this firm's rapid growth finally made it larger than Rootes and put it on a par with Vauxhall.[1] However, in spite of the unavoidable untidiness in the division of what is now such a small number of firms, the distinction between the groups remains meaningful for our purpose.

It has been suggested that size of firm is itself a major factor in industrial unrest, big ones being more liable to strikes than small ones. We discussed some aspects of this suggestion in Chapter VI, and the statistics here certainly offer no evidence to support it, even though the very biggest strikes are necessarily confined to the major firms. For taking the inter-war and War years together, the Independents actually had rather more strikes than the major firms, and were responsible for nearly half of the industry's total striker-days— a figure which must, even then, have been very disproportionate to their share of the car firms' total employment. Again, a third of all the strikes we have traced (as well as a third of the post-war ones alone) have occurred in Independent plants—including all the smaller firms, like Jowett, which have ceased car production. The more substantial Independents—Jaguar, Rover, and Pressed Steel— each seem to have had at least as many stoppages as Standard, which was once thought one of the more strike-prone larger firms. The grouped figures are summarized in Table VIII/1—where the effects of the national engineering stoppages have been, as usual, excluded: their inclusion would substantially raise the minor firms' share of striker-days, since nearly all of them are 'federated'.

Changes in the strike-liability of the minor firms in the post-war period would seem to confirm the conclusions we drew in Chapter IV as to the effects of market pressures on the more marginally competitive concerns. In the late 1940s, and particularly in the slump and 'take-over' period of the early 1950s, the strike-liability of the minor firms fell off from its level in the early post-war years—in sharp contrast with that of the major firms. But in the late 1950s, the Independents' strike performance recovered: they accounted again for about a third of the strikes, and for about a sixth of the striker-

[1] As elsewhere in this study, our analysis was largely completed before Pressed Steel's merger into B.M.C., the tables including it terminating at the end of 1964.

Table VIII/1—STRIKE-LIABILITY OF THE CAR FIRMS: BY GROUPS

	MAJOR FIRMS		MINOR FIRMS	
	Number of strikes	Striker-days (000s)	Number of strikes	Striker-days (000s)
1921–30	16	72.6	11	11.5
1931–39	20	104.6	17	121.1
1940–44	52	120.2	69	161.4
1945–49	45	239.5	33	63.0
1950–54	43	626.7	16	56.8
1955–59	131	667.6	66	153.0
1960–64	296	970.3	105	369.6
1921–64	603	2801.5	317	936.4

days—this last figure being just about proportionate to their current share in car workers' employment. Despite the sharp slump of 1960 and 1961, the strike-liability of the minor firms has continued to rise: their proportion of both strike-frequency and striker-days is now more than a quarter of the totals for all the firms together. This suggests that workers in minor firms more than make up in booms for their unaggressive posture in slumps.

There is nothing outstandingly different about the pattern of dispute-causation in the Independent firms as a group which could satisfactorily explain their generally disproportionate strike-liability.

Table VIII/2—PERCENTAGE OF STRIKES BY CAUSE AND GROUPS OF FIRMS

Period	Cause:	Wages, wage-structure and work-loads	Redundancy, dismissals, etc.	Managerial arrangements, working conditions, etc.	Trade union relationships, etc.
1946–52	Major firms	40	22	16	22
	Minor firms	38	31	11	20
1953–59	Major firms	51	21	9	19
	Minor firms	55	18	10	17
1960–64	Major firms	49	21	21	9
	Minor firms	69	17	11	3

The Firms Compared: and the Employers' Organization

Taking the post-war years (for which we have the fullest information), the distribution of the Independents' strikes by causes approximates to that for all firms together (compare Table VIII/2 above with Table 3 in Chapter II: in both tables strikes are grouped by our own causal classification, not that of the Ministry of Labour). Only in the 1960s has the Independents' share of wage-structure and work-load disputes been exceptional (at the expense of their share of stoppages on trade union and managerial issues), although it was slightly higher than the proportionate share of such issues in the major firms' disputes during the 1950s, as well. This can be only partially due to the fact that the Independents still all use 'payments by results' wage-systems (unlike the American-owned members of the Big Five), since this was also true during the early post-war period, when their proportion of wage-disputes was lower than in the major concerns.

Table VIII/3—PERCENTAGE OF STRIKER-DAYS BY CAUSE AND GROUPS OF FIRMS

Period	Cause:	Wages, wage structure and work-loads	Redundancy, dismissals, etc.	Managerial arrangements, working conditions, etc.	Trade union relationships, etc.
1946–52	Major firms	67	24	3	6
	Minor firms	17	26	2	55
1953–59	Major firms	18	36	4	42
	Minor firms	71	9	6	14
1960–64	Major firms	48	23	15	14
	Minor firms	64	21	12	3

When one considers the distribution of striker-days between the various causes of dispute—as in Table VIII/3—the position of the minor firms is rather different. Even without the general engineering stoppages over wage-demands (which, proportionately speaking, must again have affected them rather more than the Big Five), almost three-fifths of all their post-war striker-days have been due to wage-disputes, as against two-fifths in the major concerns. This implies that wage strikes tend to be relatively bigger and more stubborn in the smaller firms. It rather looks as if a major source of the Independents' special strike-liability has been the resentment of their on the whole more-skilled workers against high earnings by the 'popular quality' operatives of the big firms. Jaguar, for instance, is in the same district as Standard, where earnings were for a long period considerably higher than in other firms. The more recent strike-efforts, at least, of workers in the minor firms seem to be directed at keeping up in the earnings league rather than at defending (or promoting) issues of principle, such as those which surround union recognition and organization. And these efforts are, of course, concentrated in boom periods—the strikes being nevertheless fairly longish because management in the smaller firms is more mindful of profit-margins, perhaps. And the relative unimportance of wage-disputes in the minor firms in the immediate post-war years arises at least partly because Standard had yet to set the new slope to the rate of increase of car workers' earnings—and thereby to raise the tension of 'coercive comparisons', especially in the Midlands.

Three other points are noteworthy in the two last tables. First, the decline, over the whole post-war period, in the relative importance of employment issues as a source of the minor firms' strike-liability. This is clearly so in terms of the frequency of disputes on 'labour surplus' problems, and was markedly so in terms of their striker-days attributable to such issues during the late 1950s. With the thinning-out of their ranks, and the consolidation of their survivors into companies that in most other industries would be considered very respectable units, their workers have again become rather more obdurate in defence of their employment rights. Even so, it is clearly the big firms' operatives—who, paradoxically enough, have on the average been in the more secure position—who have made most of the running in the post-war movement for more job security.

Secondly, there is the very marked decline in the comparative importance of trade union relationships as a cause of dispute after the 1950s. And this is so whether these involve (and in practice these theoretically distinct issues are often difficult to separate from one another) questions of 'union security' or membership, inter-union problems, or relations between shop stewards and managements. It reflects that apparent settling-down of the new system of workplace union representation, and its acceptance by management, to which—despite the superficial evidence of conflict which is conveyed by strikes on *other* issues—we referred in our last chapter. But to judge by the severity of particular stoppages on trade union relationships (of which the column of relative striker-days gives, in the context, some indication), this movement does seem to have occurred in two waves. In the immediate post-war years, there was a run of biggish stoppages on such questions in the minor firms; but in the late 1950s the pressure moved on to the bigger companies. This probably

THE FIRMS COMPARED: AND THE EMPLOYERS' ORGANIZATION

reflects some priority for the smaller firms—with their higher proportions of skilled men and (thus) convinced trade unionists—in the post-war consolidation of the shop steward organization.

And the third—and perhaps most significant—point is the jump, during the 1960s, in the relative importance of disputed 'managerial functions' as a source of conflict. In the *frequency* of stoppages about managerial arrangements this is only evident in the bigger companies; but in terms of 'working days lost' it is very noticeable for both groups of concerns—so that even in the smaller firms, strikes on such issues have become much more stubborn. It looks very much as if, having largely consolidated itself by this time, the workplace union organization was moving on to widen its bargaining scope beyond the area of wages and earnings.

(B) STRIKE-EXPERIENCE OF INDIVIDUAL COMPANIES

In analysing the position of individual firms, we cannot appeal to official strike records. But even were not such very extensive Press references available (at least for much of the post-war period), a little knowledge of the motor industry suffices to identify most of the plants *Gazetted* as suffering from 'principal stoppages', and the latter seem responsible for some four-fifths or more of all days reported as 'lost' from car industry strikes. Practically all the other stoppages of which some record exists can be similarly traced to individual firms by Press or geographical evidence. And so far as *numbers* of strikes are concerned, those publicly recorded, whether by official agencies or the Press, represent only a sample of all 'dispute-incidents' (as we showed in Chapter II) and can be treated as such. At any rate, the post-war strike-experience of the industry can, we think, be not too

Table VIII/4—STRIKE-LIABILITY OF THE INDIVIDUAL FIRMS: 1946–64

	Of all strikes	Percentage: Of striker-days	Of 1963 employment
B.M.C.	44	41	32
Ford	11	25	24
Rootes	8	5	5
S.T.I.	6	9	4
Pressed Steel	7	6	11
Rover	8	5	4
Jaguar	9	6	3
Others	7	3	17
	100	100	100

unfairly apportioned between the firms as in Table VIII/4 (bearing in mind that Vauxhall and Rolls-Royce have had only isolated and very minor stoppages throughout the period, and are, therefore, grouped with 'others').

Not too much should be inferred from a comparison with the third column in Table VIII/4, as the firms' rates of employment growth have differed. For example, Rootes has not expanded its labour force to the same extent as Ford and B.M.C., and Standard's labour force declined sharply in the late 1950s.[1] But the table does give some indication of the relative contribution of the individual firms to the industry's strike-liability. B.M.C., Rover and Jaguar contributed significantly more than their share per employee, whether measured in terms of strikes or striker-days, while Ford—despite the public fuss—apparently accounted for no more than the average proportion of striker-days.

However, Table VIII/4 excludes the effect of two things of which some account must be taken in comparing the strike-liability of individual firms. In the first place, the 'striker-days' column makes no allowance for the effect of general engineering stoppages. In most of the tables in this study, these have been excluded, as originating outside the motor industry, even if they affected most of its member firms. But in this case, their effect must be reckoned with: all the major engineering strikes since the War have been in support of straightforward wage-demands; similar demands have also been presented to firms not affiliated to the Engineering Employers' Federation, and where these have led to stoppages it would be improper to set the resultant 'man-days of idleness' to the account of the non-federated firms concerned without making some allowance for the parallel experience of the federated plants. But secondly, none of the detailed estimates in this study so far have made any allowance for the 'secondary idleness' caused by strikes to plants *other* than those where the disputes themselves occurred.

This last exclusion follows the canons of the Ministry of Labour's own strike-statistics, where reported 'working days lost' are confined to those experienced by the plants directly involved in disputes. In any case, no systematic record has been kept of such 'secondary idleness' as may have resulted at other establishments, and hitherto in this study there has been no point in attempting to estimate it, because it

[1] Complete employment series for all the firms which have merged in the present manufacturing groups were not available, so no exact estimate of each group's average share of post-war payrolls was possible for the whole period. However, the 1963 proportions are probably not too far off the mark, subject to the *relative* declines in the Standard and Rootes shares, since so far as the other firms are concerned these declines seem largely offset by Vauxhall's relative growth.

would make little significant difference to such things as the distribution of striker-days between different causes of dispute or between major and minor car firms *as groups*. When one is dealing with individual firms, however, the position is rather different. This is largely because of the wide variation between companies in the degrees to which they integrate their manufacturing facilities at a particular site, or specialize between sites. Thus, Ford's plant was until recently heavily concentrated at Dagenham, where the effect of its labour stoppages has been overwhelmingly registered—so that in one year for which a comparison is possible, some 90 per cent of Ford's 'man-days of idleness' due to disputes appear to have been publicly recorded in some way. At the other extreme, the great dispersal and specialization of B.M.C. plants means that a very large part of B.M.C.'s 'man-days of idleness' due to disputes takes the form of a 'secondary loss'—at plants not themselves on strike—which is not usually reported. Again, for one recent year less than half of all B.M.C.'s striker-days seem to have been publicly registered. This may have been an extreme instance, but even so, if one wished to take this 'secondary loss' into account, it would possibly be conservative to regard reported striker-days for B.M.C. since the group's formation as being a one-third under-estimate (so that the actual figure was at least 50 per cent greater than that used in Table VIII/4). The other firms have been much less dispersed in their organization than B.M.C., so that for them, the *average* degree of under-statement on account of the unreported 'secondary loss' (at least from internal disputes) is almost certainly very much nearer the Ford than the B.M.C. position.

We have already estimated the striker-days at federated firms caused by general engineering stoppages during the post-war period to total some 800,000. The 'secondary loss' caused to each car firm by its own disputes cannot, of course, be reckoned with any precision; but from the data published by the Ministry of Labour for certain years[1] and from such records as have been made available to us by individual firms we think it may well have been about one million working days for the same period. And if allowance for these two things were to be made in the individual firm's share of total striker-days, the position shown by Table VIII/4 would be in certain cases very much altered.

---

[1] See Chapter II, pp. 55–6. It should be noted, however, that our own rough estimate of 'secondary loss' here does not include such further idleness as may have been caused to particular firms by stoppages at *other* concerns, including component suppliers. For very recent years estimates are also now possible from certain figures collected and published by the car manufacturers, and one application of these is considered in the present Chapter's Appendix.

Thus for Ford—a non-federated firm, nearly all of whose striker-days have been already accounted—the share would fall to 18 per cent, a figure very much lower than its recent share of car firm employment. So that, although by the standards of most outside industries Ford would still remain a comparatively strike-prone concern, in car manufacturing terms its average post-war strike-liability has, apparently, been rather low—only Vauxhall, Rolls-Royce and Pressed Steel having experienced a lower strike-incidence measured in terms of striker-days to employment. The relative position of the smaller firms is not very much changed by the above, except that S.T.I.'s share of total car industry striker-days falls and Pressed Steel's rises—in each case to between 7 and 8 per cent. But B.M.C.'s share jumps considerably—on the rather conservative assumption stated above, to about 48 per cent. Relative to their employment, in fact, the B.M.C. and Jaguar plants as groups have probably each had about twice the strike-incidence of Ford since the War, and Rover has not been far behind; while B.M.C. plants have been responsible for about half of all 'working days lost' from disputes by car plants during that time. Indeed, B.M.C. might very well claim to be the most strike-prone of all major British enterprises—manufacturing, mines, docks and shipyards included.

Even unamended, however, Table VIII/4 does reveal what is probably the main reason for Ford's somewhat over-stated post-war reputation for dispute-liability. The percentage of recorded *strikes* attributable to individual concerns is not, of course, changed by the previous calculations. And it immediately appears that if the Ford share of striker-days has been low, its share of strikes has been even lower. Ford, in other words, apart from being itself very big, has also had a disproportionate share of big stoppages—which are the ones which attract most public notice. Those in Rootes, Rover, and Jaguar, however, have been smaller than the norm. The relative peace at Pressed Steel is also apparent from Table VIII/4, while the small contribution of 'others' to strike-liability is, of course, due mainly to Vauxhall's record.

But Table VIII/4 also disguises important changes which have occurred in some of the firms' strike-proneness since the war: Table VIII/5 shows the annual average strike-liability for three successive post-war periods. And B.M.C.'s particular contribution to the industry's increasing strike-liability can now be also assessed more narrowly. In the 1950s after the B.M.C. merger, this concern accounted for more than half the increase in the number of strikes for the car firms as a whole, and in the 1960s for almost two-thirds of the same increase. Again, in terms of striker-days incurred by individual establishments involved in disputes (that is, even ignoring

The Firms Compared: and the Employers' Organization

the effect of general engineering stoppages and B.M.C.'s disproportionate 'secondary loss'), the whole of the increase in the 1950s could be attributed to B.M.C.—if self-cancelling shifts between the other firms were disregarded. (Indeed, if the effect of the very large Austin strike of 1953 were also omitted, B.M.C. would still account for more than half this increase.) In the 1960s, however, in spite of a rocketing strike-frequency, the firm contributed only about a fifth of the further increase in striker-days. This is subject to the same calculating omissions as the previous table, but it does imply both significant changes in the pattern of strikes in B.M.C. itself and a rather more important role for other firms.[1]

Table VIII/5—ANNUAL AVERAGE STRIKE-LIABILITY OF INDIVIDUAL FIRMS

	1946–52		1953–59		1960–64	
	No. of strikes	striker days (000s)	No. of strikes	Striker days (000s)	No. of strikes	Striker days (000s)
B.M.C.	3	18	12	84	39	106
Ford	3	51	3	21	8	52
Rootes	1	4	3	4	6	19
S.T.I.	—	—	3	27	5	17
Pressed Steel	*	*	3	9	6	21
Rover	1	4	2	2	7	24
Jaguar	2	10	3	6	5	18

* Means less than 1.

If one allocates the B.M.C. dispute-experience to the firm's constituent parts, Austin immediately appears as a fairly regular strike-performer since the 1920s, and—except for the war years when *all* strikes tended to be small—strikes there have generally been large. Moreover, in only three years since the War has Austin been strike-free, yet in no year has the number of strikes reported there exceeded four. The strike-free years were 1949 (after a larger-than-usual strike

[1] Apart from the definitional limitations already referred to, Table VIII/5 is subject to the reservation that it has been partly compiled from Press reports, and where this produced a total differing materially from the total for the 'car assembly industry' we derived from official records, we have adjusted all the figures proportionately so that the former total corresponded to the latter. However, such discrepancies—particularly for striker-days—were not great, since they only involve some rather small disputes which were either not identifiable in the official summaries, or though in the summaries, could not be attributed to firms from Press reports or geographical evidence. (We are, of course—as in other tables in this study—only concerned with stoppages which were big enough to be 'recordable' in the sense of the Ministry of Labour's statistical definitions.)

in 1948) and the two years following the very large stoppage of 1953. We return both to these strikes and the ensuing calm spells later. On the other hand, whereas the Morris plants in the Midlands have been normally strike-prone, the main Morris works at Cowley had only one reported stoppage in all the years to 1955 (and this includes the war period). It was not until 1959 that strikes at Cowley exceeded two in any year. But from 1960 on, these works have had an average of more than a dozen reported each year: and in 1964 just a quarter of all B.M.C. strikes were at Cowley. However, most of these strikes were small.

What has happened since the merger of Austin and Morris into B.M.C., in effect, is that Austin, while remaining fairly strike-prone, has not contributed much to the motor industry's general increase in strike-liability; but the high Austin dispute-proneness has affected the other B.M.C. plants and, particularly, a rash of small strikes has appeared at Morris's main assembly works. Hence especially the increase in the strike-frequency for B.M.C. We have yet to discuss strike-causation at individual firms: here it is sufficient to note that the Morris disputes have occurred not only over wage questions but over a wide range of other issues. With earnings initially considerably lower at Morris than at Austin, and with comparatively high earnings also in the adjacent Pressed Steel plant at Cowley, dissatisfaction with wage relativities readily accounts for the appearance of wage strikes. Reasons for the diversity of other issues involved are less obvious. But the unpublished report of a joint inquiry during 1964 into the unrest at the Morris plant is said to have pointed to unsatisfactory working conditions—in an old paint shop in particular; while the appointment of an industrial relations manager shortly after the inquiry is suggestive of a previously unfilled need.

The last table also shows that if Ford's relative strike-liability has been exaggerated by popular reports, it has at least been fairly continuous. The pattern of strikes at the other major firms—Rootes and Standard—has special features. Despite Standard's one-time reputation for strike-proneness, it appears to have had no disputes worthy of report before 1954 (although there was one very minor stoppage in 1936, and another four small ones during the War). In 1954, however, Standard had a biggish strike against the dismissal of several shop stewards, followed in 1956 by a very large strike arising out of redundancy. These two stoppages—which followed changes in managerial policy[1]—account for almost all of Standard's striker-days in the 1950s, since which time the firm's strike-incidence has been relatively modest (and often involving white-collar workers). However, in plants now part of Rootes—which until the late 1950s

[1] See Chapters III and V.

THE FIRMS COMPARED: AND THE EMPLOYERS' ORGANIZATION

had a peaceable repute—there have in fact been a pretty steady two to three strikes per year in most of the peace-time years from the mid-1930s, while during the War Rootes strikes numbered four or five annually. The frequency rose during the 1960s (due largely to disputes in the group's new Scottish plant) but the Rootes strikes have remained smallish. This does not fully emerge from Table VIII/4 because the firm has had one or two largish strikes over redundancy —outstandingly at Acton in 1961—so that Rootes's strike-incidence, too, is highly concentrated in time. Both Standard and, particularly, Rootes (see Table VIII/6) have had a large share of redundancy disputes, perhaps because they have each produced mostly for a middling price-range which may be specially sensitive to car trade fluctuations.

(C) THE 'CYCLE' THEORY: AND DISPUTE-CAUSATION AT THE PLANT LEVEL

During the 1960s, Jaguar and Rover have clearly been contributing more to the industry's strike-liability than their share of employment would indicate. But discussion of this is more meaningfully conducted in relation to the firms' different patterns of strike-causation. Here we turn for the moment to a phenomenon suggested by Table VIII/5 and the previous paragraphs: the alternation of strike-waves with periods of industrial peace. Analysis of strike data has convinced some observers of the existence of what are rather misleadingly termed 'cycles of strikes'—that is, several consecutive years of belligerent activity on an industry-wide scale.[1] Firms, as well as industries, may show something of this kind. For example, Pressed Steel has apparently had a marked 'cyclical' strike record—as follows:

1929–31	Four very small strikes, each 100 striker-days or less.
1932–33	Nil
1934–38	Six largish strikes, averaging 6,000 striker-days
1939–41	Nil
1942–45	Five small strikes, none of more than 300 days
1946–52	Nil

Followed by a sequence of medium-sized stoppages (see Table VIII/5) from 1953 to 1964. Again, we have already referred to the virtual absence of 'recordable' strikes at Standard and Morris (Oxford)— even during the War—until the 1950s. Taking such phenomena in

[1] A. M. Ross, 'The Prospects for Industrial Conflict', *Industrial Relations*, I, October 1, 1961.

association with the persistent strike-proneness of some firms and the continuing freedom from disputes of others, in fact, one can reasonably interpret the whole pattern as representing the normal operation of statistical chance. In short, 'cycles' of this kind seem to us neither particularly interesting nor very meaningful as such: they are mentioned merely to emphasize the importance of particular circumstances in explaining particular strike situations. Some strikes have a train of successors: others do not.

Periods of relative peace interspersed in otherwise chronically strike-prone situations do, however, seem to be more interesting. The Austin case has been mentioned: after a regular one or two stoppages annually at Austin since the War, the largest single-firm strike in the history of the motor industry occurred there in 1953. For two years after this there were no stoppages reported at Longbridge, and none of any size until 1957. Again, after a series of stoppages at Dagenham in 1951 and 1952—including the very big ones of the latter year—there were none reported in 1953; nor was it until 1956 that Dagenham had another large strike. More recent examples occur in the case of Rootes following the three-month-long confrontation of 1961 at the Acton plant, and at Dagenham again after 1962. Logically, these 'peace pauses' *might* seem to be as much a reflection of exhaustion as of the success or effectiveness of the policies which preceded them; though here again, particular circumstances are all-important.

Table VIII/6—CAUSES OF POST-WAR STRIKES, BY FIRM

Percentage attributable to:	Wages, wage-structure and work-loads	Redundancy, dismissals, etc.	Managerial arrangements, working conditions, etc.	Trade union relationships etc.
B.M.C.	50	18	16	16
Ford	32	25	29	14
Rootes	52	40	8	—
S.T.I.	54	16	14	16
Pressed Steel	68	20	6	6
Rover	75	8	10	7
Jaguar	55	24	9	12
Other firms	35	28	19	18
All firms	52	21	15	12

However, to return to the individual firm's pattern of dispute-causation. Table VIII/6 expresses the number of strikes due to each main category of causes as a percentage of each firm's total strikes.

The Firms Compared: and the Employers' Organization

B.M.C.'s distribution thus closely approximates to that of the average (not surprisingly, perhaps, since it was responsible for nearly half the disputes recorded): the mere number of dispersed establishments which make up the group, and the virtual plant autonomy over labour relations matters which has existed in it for most of the period, would in any case tend to inhibit any oddity in the distribution. And we have already discussed the records of B.M.C.'s two main assembly plants separately. Suffice it to add that not only is there a clear association in timing between the post-war acceleration in the motor industry's strike-frequency and the merger that produced B.M.C., but that disputes specifically on questions of wage-structure have played a disproportionate part in the rise in the group's strike-liability. Some years ago, one of the writers commented on B.M.C.'s labour relations that ' . . . the rapid technical integration that followed the merger was not matched in handling the labour problems it created'.[1] Despite the changes which have occurred in the group's top management since that was written, it looks as if these problems remain unsolved. Now that B.M.C. has taken in Pressed Steel—so that it becomes the employer of over two-fifths of the car industry's workers—these difficulties seem likely to aggravate themselves: unless the new grouping makes a fairly radical approach to the question of its wage-structure in particular.

However, the picture and circumstances of Ford are quite different from those of B.M.C. Ford's very simple national wage-structure based on time-rates is reflected in the low proportion of wage-disputes—although it only partly explains it, and is perhaps not the most important single influence. For the wage-system does not prevent disagreement over work-loads, while being 'non-federated', Ford's is more liable to direct wage-demands. More important is the outstanding proportion of disagreements about management questions, which together with unusually frequent strikes over individual dismissals and the arrangement of working hours, etc., make up over half of the Ford strikes we have traced. This adds up to a Ford image (or, perhaps, only partly-Anglicized projection)—of a thrustful, competition-minded management which, while it now negotiates freely on wage-rates and other basic terms of employment with national trade union officials, has resisted the implications of workplace labour organization.

The picture which has already been emerging of the leading Independent firms is confirmed in the table. Wage issues are the predominant cause of their strikes, while management and trade union questions are of much less importance—except that Jaguar

[1] In 'An Analysis of Post-War Labour Disputes in the British Car Manufacturing Firms' (Turner, with John Bescoby), *Manchester School*, May 1961.

has apparently had the normal proportion of strikes on union relations. And this is possibly a reflection of the firm's substantial arrangement around a single remarkable and independent personality —a structure perhaps liable to have produced, besides its real virtues, intermittent friction with the collective restraints of workplace labour organization. Security of employment also appears as an important issue in disputes at Jaguar—probably because, unlike Rover, it has until recently had no stake in commercial vehicles equivalent to the Landrover, which would cushion the fluctuations of private car markets. The very high proportion of wage disputes at Rover may again be associated to some extent with a lagging wage-level during the 1950s, when hourly earnings in the firm seem to have fallen noticeably behind other major Midland plants, although it has a relatively large proportion of skilled men: and this in turn may have reflected some isolation from the wage pressures of Birmingham and Coventry. But Rover's more recent crop of wage disputes seems particularly identified with wage-structure problems in a new plant.[1] However, the fact that Pressed Steel has the second highest proportion of wage disputes is probably not so much due to its having more stoppages on wage questions than other firms as to its having fewer disputes than they on other issues. In particular, it resembles Rootes in having an unusually small number of conflicts on managerial arrangements or trade union matters, so that its general state of labour relations would appear rather good.

There are, however, difficulties in comparing the strike-liabilities of different firms in terms of their respective *proportions* of disputes due to various causes. As in the case of Pressed Steel above, a concern's share of stoppages on a particular issue may appear abnormally high mainly because it has experienced relatively few disputes on other questions. Furthermore, the method does not reveal the effect on a firm's actual *incidence* of strikes—in terms of striker-days to total work-time—because it may have many small disputes, which are nevertheless not very important because they are characteristically small and quickly settled. On the other hand, it may be equally misleading to compare individual firms' strike-liabilities in terms of the striker-days attributable to different main heads of dispute, because in this case the pattern for particular firms is likely to be disproportionately affected by the events of one or two big stoppages—which are

[1] The difficulties of this establishment were of course held largely responsible for Rover's high strike-liability by the Motor Industry Joint Study Group's only published report as such, of November 1965. Its fact-finding commission into Rover commented that 'The simple truth is that neither side has quite matched up to the formidable challenge of the P.6 line innovation.' However—as our Table VIII/5 perhaps indicates—Rover's dispute record is of rather longer standing than that event, if it was not previously abnormal for the industry.

The Firms Compared: and the Employers' Organization

not necessarily representative of the total experience of the firms concerned. Thus, nearly a third of the post-war striker-days for Standard and Rootes is traceable to two big strikes on redundancy. Moreover, the analysis is, of course, not very refined in its treatment of dispute-causation at the company level—the table, for instance, grouping strikes about individual dismissals and redundancy together, although these may, in particular firms, reflect very different types of management-labour friction. These broad groupings were adopted because of problems of classification and significance in one or two instances where very small numbers of reported disputes are involved.

We have made some attempt to overcome these difficulties of analysis and presentation in this Chapter's Appendix. The effort is very tentative, but the picture is fairly consistent with the general evidence available, and the results do appear to convey something more of the factors which have led to such marked variations both in the total strike-liability of individual firms and in its particular causation, as well as some further general factors. For instance, the federated car firms as a group seem to display certain common patterns of dispute-causation in respect of what might be broadly termed 'wage-related' issues, though differing markedly between each other in their liability to disputes on other questions. And this 'federated firm pattern' is almost the opposite to that displayed by Ford. But the analysis is perhaps particularly interesting as including a group 'strike-profile' for the very small car-making firms, which have not previously between distinguished in this study (being classed with Vauxhall and Rolls-Royce as 'other firms' in the last table).

Thus, while the total strike-incidence of the very small concerns appear to have been about average for the industry, under most heads of dispute their strike-frequency has been relatively low— almost certainly because of the weak bargaining position of workers in firms whose market position has been especially marginal. Just for the latter reason, however, these firms have also had a disproportionately high frequency of stoppages on redundancy and 'work-sharing' questions. And they have also shown a relatively high dispute-liability on the score of both trade union relations and management issues. This is probably accounted for by the high proportion of craftsmen they employ, which has led to disputes about such matters as demarcations and dilution, work-allocation and labour transfers or substitution. Moreover, when very small, big, and very big firms are compared, it is again interesting that no particular connection between a firm's size and its dispute-liability appears under any single head of dissension. One might, for instance (on the 'size and morale' hypothesis referred to in Chapter VI) have expected disputes about management questions to be more frequent in the larger concerns: but this does not seem to be the case. While the fact that the very small firms as a whole appear to have had about the same strike-liability as the mass production concerns despite their difference in technology again throws doubt on the latter's explanatory significance.

We can add one further note as to the possible effect of the policies of individual managements on the motor industry's strike-incidence. We remarked earlier that of the workers involved in car plant disputes, just over half were, on the average, reported as laid-off on account of stoppages though not themselves on strike. Though in earlier years the records do not always seem very reliable on this point, more recently they have become more precise and detailed, and it was possible to analyse the reports attributable to car firms year-by-year through the early 1960s. In the result, it immediately appears that this average figure of 'indirect involvement' is significantly inflated by the particular trend of certain firms. Some variations in this ratio between companies are readily understandable: one would expect, for instance, that Ford, which has been notable on the whole for rather big strikes committing a high proportion of its labour force, would have a lower than average ratio despite its high degree of concentration and technical integration. But there are few such differences between other companies which could substantially affect the figure (which, of course, relates only to the plants actually involved in disputes, not those 'secondarily' affected). Nevertheless, over a run of years very large divergences in the ratio emerge between firms. And these differences cannot be connected with, for instance, such things as the intractability of particular shop stewards' committees (which might, by prolonging disputes, produce a higher 'indirect' involvement of operatives) because they show no parallelism with the average length of stoppages at particular firms—which is also calculable, and which reveals no such wide variation.

Thus, no workers were reported to be indirectly involved in the very few stoppages traceable to Vauxhall during the period. And in Rootes, the suggestion of a generally conciliatory attitude already conveyed by its low proportion of disputes on trade union relations is reinforced by the apparent fact that only one worker was, on the average, laid-off for every three who actually struck.[1] But in some companies the ratio of workers indirectly involved in stoppages

---

[1] The figure, of course—as in the case of other companies—relates only to plants actually involved in strikes, and thus does not include those laid-off at the firm's Coventry plants on account of its major stoppage at Acton in 1961; but such evidence as is available for Rootes does not suggest such 'secondary involvements' from disputes to have been in any way abnormal either.

appeared comparatively high—being in one case just the reverse of Rootes, with three workers laid-off in disputes on the average for every one directly involved. One explanation for these divergencies may be, of course, that some firms are not as good at improvising to maintain production as others. Alternative explanations, however, may be that certain plants have made particular use of disputes as an occasion to regulate output to market conditions (a possibility also indicated by our Chapter IV) *or* that their managements have developed a habit of laying-off other workers—if not in deliberate reprisal then in sheer irritation—whenever a serious dispute occurs in one section or department.

(D) INSTITUTIONAL FACTORS:
THE EMPLOYERS' FEDERATION, AND 'PROCEDURE'

However, it must by now be fairly clear that though, because of the size of car industry firms and their small number, events in particular companies—and especially the biggest—have contributed much more heavily to the car industry's record of labour conflict than they would in most other industries, those events alone can only provide a very partial explanation of the car firms' general high strike-liability. As we have now shown, the pattern of strike-causation varies widely from company to company, as well as within companies from time to time—so that the motor industry's own 'fact-finding commissions' could legitimately pick out paint shop conditions in the main Morris works and inadequate human organization of a new model's debut at Rover as the key sources of dispute at those plants in 1964 and 1965. But the general post-war strike-proneness of the industry remains. As does the mystery of why one or two firms should have been largely exempt from it.

The last problem, we leave to our concluding chapter. But as regards the more general problem, we have already—in Chapters IV and V—remarked on one broad circumstance that would, in any industry, be likely to be associated with a high dispute-liability: the widespread insecurity of employment and earnings which seem to have been characteristic of the car operatives' condition since the early 1950s. And this and an earlier chapter have picked out a number of specific causes of dispute as contributing unduly heavily to the car firms' strike-incidence—redundancy and labour surplus itself, wage relativities and systems outstandingly, and the exercise of managerial authority in relation to such things as task assessment and assignment or the disciplining and discharge of individuals. These things would have been revealed by a statistical analysis even more rough and ready than our own, and from already-available data: indeed, analyses which picked out several of these sources of labour unrest amongst the car workers were published early in 1961, and achieved some publicity at the time.[1] The question also remains, therefore, of why no attempt was made to settle these problems in a general way, by action between the industry's collective organizations—as (see our Chapter X) had occurred in several foreign automobile industries? Alternatively, why did no solution to them gradually emerge from the detailed settlement of individual disputes, arising at the plant or firm level, so that policies were evolved to dispose of these irritants?

To the first question, the answer must in some large measure lie in the union organization, as we have already suggested. There was, for instance, the apparent incapacity of the many unions loosely federated in the Confederation of Shipbuilding and Engineering Unions, none of them with a majority interest in the car firms and hardly any with a majority of its membership in that employment, to press demands designed to meet the specific grievances of car industry operatives—or even to formulate those grievances in a generalized way. To the second question the answer must lie, in some measure again, with managerial inadequacies. There are such things as the industry's own joint fact-finding commissions drew attention to (in their inquiry into the specific cases reported above), as failures to define grievance procedures within the plant systematically and precisely, to maintain regular joint consultation at that level, or to ensure that workers are adequately informed on the plant's employment terms, practice and intentions. It seems significant of an attitude that on several aspects of labour conditions some firms appear only to maintain such summary statistics as are required for the Ministry of Labour's published national series—and are not even able, for instance, to distinguish between dismissals and voluntary withdrawals from their employ: and that while recently firms have begun to collect (and even publicize) figures on disputes in undiscriminatory detail, they are not always able to analyse them according to the grievances involved. The question of attitudes sometimes reaches beyond a mere paucity of sophistication or specialists in dealing with such problems into, for instance, an apparent belief that labour unrest is not the product of specific circumstances to be analysed, and if possible changed, but an irrational or recalcitrant movement to be alternately bought off or put down: or further still, into the viewpoint noted in our report on some workplace labour relations from the inside, that it is the role of 'supervision' to oppose all claims from the shop floor on principle.

Nevertheless, the moves by most firms—in reaction to the particular

[1] In the two papers by Mr John Bescoby and one of the present writers previously quoted.

The Firms Compared: and the Employers' Organization

strike-surge of 1959–60—to give personnel management and internal labour relations a status indicative of closer attention by appointing specialists at or near directoral level appear to have had disappointing results. And if in part this was because firms then considered these problems sufficiently catered for by their nomination as a director's province, there seems also one other major factor on the management side which is relevant to the situation. This is the collective organization of the employers, and the traditional system of industrial conciliation (known throughout the metal-working industries as 'Procedure') which is associated with it. It was remarked above that the 'federated' firms appear to have certain patterns of dispute-causation in common. And it can be noted here that their strike-incidence, in terms of striker-days per employee again, has been very much higher as a group than that of the non-federated concerns: at least two-and-a-half times as high, in fact, over the whole post-war period. Nor would that relationship have been radically altered had Vauxhall had the same strike-liability as Ford.

The Engineering Employers' Federation is an organization of some 4,500 firms employing more than one-and-a-half million workers in the British metalworking industries other than shipbuilding and shiprepairing. (There is a separate association of shipbuilding employers, though because many firms belong to both organizations through their marine engineering interests, and because they employ several important skills in common and deal with the same unions, movements in the two groups have always been closely linked). Firms affiliate to the E.E.F. through some forty district associations: small concerns predominate in the Federation's membership—about a third of its affiliates have less than fifty workers apiece. Though special agreements apply to one or two sections of the trades covered (such as those for steel erection, or typewriter servicing) these are mostly of long standing, and the Federation's constitution does not provide for the formal representation of particular industrial interests. Such interests are recognized by the establishment of committees to, for instance, negotiate the sectional agreements referred to, and by the co-option of individuals to various boards. But even some of the big integrated firms which now provide a large proportion of the Federation's affiliation have no formal existence from its viewpoint: B.M.C., as such, is not federated—its association is through the affiliation of its subsidiaries to district employers' organizations. Like that of the unions, on the whole, the E.E.F. structure remains fundamentally general, or 'horizontal', in character.

Formal relations with the unions proceed via two channels. On the one hand, *ad hoc* national negotiations between the C.S.E.U. and the Federation from time to time lay down such things as minimum time-rates for the main classes of skilled workers, labourers, women and juveniles; basic rates, and standard 'piece-work supplements' (which actual piece-work prices or bonuses are supposed to be fixed so as to yield to the various classes of payment-by-results workers); payment for holidays; the standard normal week and overtime rates; and a minimum guaranteed weekly wage. Differentials for one or two groups of craftsmen are negotiated separately with the unions concerned, but negotiations on a district (as opposed to a national) basis are now actually exceedingly rare—the differentials that once existed between local engineering rates being in course of elimination under national agreements.

On the other hand, a 'Procedure' for dealing with disagreements arising at the workplace level exists in the current form of the 'Provisions for Avoiding Disputes', which date in essence from 1898. Workers are required to raise a grievance first with their foremen. Failing satisfaction, the matter may be taken, either by 'deputation' or through a shop steward if one has been appointed' to the head shop-foreman or departmental manager.[1] Through their union, operatives may then ask for a Works Conference, which will be attended by officials of the union or unions concerned and the local employers' association. Appeal from the Works Conference is to a Local Conference away from the factory, where union officials present the men's case to a panel of local employer representatives. Cases still unresolved may be referred to a monthly meeting of national union and employer representatives held at York, and called 'Central Conference'. However, any case at Local or Central Conference may be referred back to a further Works Conference—when suggestions of a more or less definite character as to subsequent negotiation may also be attached—and a dispute may similarly be referred back from a Works Conference to further negotiation between the management and stewards concerned. There is no provision for independent arbitration at any stage of the 'York Procedure', as it is sometimes called. Nor does it provide for regular joint meetings (except, by convenience, at York itself), nor for meetings on any other issue than specific grievances arising.

'Procedure' thus derives pretty directly from the nineteenth-century arrangement whereby 'deputations' of workers were admitted by employers to present their claims or grievances—partly for which

[1] Actual internal procedures vary somewhat from firm to firm, and in practice further stages of reference to a shop stewards' convener or chairman of conveners with the factory management commonly intervene. However, such arrangements have no formal place in 'Procedure' proper, except to the extent that it permits reference to 'Works Committees' of a prescribed form; and subsequent stages are more rigid.

reason two recent students have described it as a system of 'employer conciliation' to distinguish it from the arrangements of other industries.[1] It has, nevertheless, been subject to an increasing use in recent years: for 1964 the E.E.F. reported that over 4,000 disputes had been taken to Works Conference stage, or nearly three times the number of a decade before. True, the frequency of strikes for the metalworking industries at large has also—as we noted in our introductory chapter—been rising pretty fast over that period. And though Marsh and Jones, in the study already referred to, estimated that some 80 per cent of cases at Works Conferences were 'disposed of' at that level, and only some 3 per cent or 4 per cent remained ultimately unsettled, these figures seem subject to some qualifications.

Firstly, a proportion of Works Conferences—some 5 or 6 per cent on our estimates—is held on cases which have already been right up to Local or even Central Conference level and then referred back. Secondly, another proportion of cases—which is rather hard to estimate but is probably of at least the same order—does not result in agreement at Works Conference but is nevertheless not taken further in Procedure (for instance, because the union considers a renewed informal approach to the management likely to be more fruitful, or because the issue itself has lapsed for one reason or another). And thirdly, 'disposal rates' at successive stages of Procedure seem to be declining as references to it increase—the E.E.F. figure for manual workers' Works Conferences in 1964, for instance, comes out at 76 per cent against Marsh and Jones's 80 per cent for 1958–63, also from E.E.F. data.[2] And in any case the frequency of 'constitutional' strikes—held after all the stages of Procedure have been exhausted—has sharply risen: in the 1950s only about one a year was recorded, but in 1964 there were 44.

(E) THE RESULTS OF 'PROCEDURE'

However, we are less concerned with the efficacy of Procedure in general than with its particular application to the federated car firms.

[1] A. I. Marsh and R. S. Jones: 'Engineering Procedure and Central Conference at York in 1959: A Factual Analysis', *British Journal of Industrial Relations*, II, 2, March 1964.

[2] The increase in references to Procedure at Works and higher Conference level may thus to some large extent reflect a declining 'disposal rate' at the level of direct negotiations between managements and stewards. No general data exists for grievances dealt with without either official intervention or recordable withholding of labour, but the private joint inquiry into Morris (Cowley) was told that less than 5 per cent of disputes brought to the works superintendent were taken to Works Conferences. If the rate a year before was 4 per cent, references to external Procedure would thus have risen by a quarter.

And in this sector, at least, Procedure does seem to have been notably less effective as an instrument of conciliation. We have analysed some 160 cases from the engineering trades in general which were handled at various levels of Procedure by the A.E.U.'s Divisional Organizers or its Executive Council in 1964–65, and compared them with a similar number of cases from federated car plants dealt with by the same union. Each sample (which was randomly selected for the general engineering cases, and approximated to a year's continuous run of cases from car firms) includes some thirty Local and a similar group of Central Conference references. In the recent past, the A.E.U. has been involved in some four-fifths of all manual workers' references to Procedure, itself initiating nearly two-thirds of them.[1] The disproportion arises partly because the general unions in engineering have on the whole been less solidly organized and less well-equipped with shop stewards to initiate cases, while some strong craft unions have been reluctant to refer disputes to Procedure, regarding it as biased (one highly respected craft union leader, indeed, operated on the principle that no case should be taken up officially unless the men concerned had first struck of their own accord). But it does mean that the samples can be taken as representative. For the car firms, from which some 150 to 200 cases a year seem currently referred to Works Conferences, it is particularly complete. The comparison's first result may be presented as follows:

Table VIII/7—RESULTS OF CONFERENCES UNDER FEDERATION CONCILIATION PROCEDURE, CAR FIRMS AND ALL ENGINEERING, 1964–65

	Percentage:	Agreement recorded	Referred back or* equivalent	Adjourned	Failure to agree recorded
All Engineering	Works	64	2	19	15
	Local	30	9	26	35
	Central†	11	33	—	55
Car Firms	Works	32	5	21	42
	Local	10	14	10	66
	Central†	3	45	6	45

* Includes for Central Conferences some cases 'retained in the hands of the Central Authorities', usually implying a difference in the tentativeness of the suggestions which may be attached to a remit.

† Including South Wales Regional Conference, to which no preliminary reference to Local Conference is involved.

[1] According to Marsh and Jones, *loc. cit.*, Table 8.

The Firms Compared: and the Employers' Organization

It is at once evident that the chance of reaching a definite settlement at any level of Procedure is considerably lower for cases referred from the car firms. The percentage of agreements recorded, for instance, is at Works Conference level only half that in all engineering. Fairly clearly, if a case has not been settled at this level its prospect of securing an agreed recommendation from higher stages of Procedure is not high anyway, but even so is only one-third the engineering average in car firm references.[1] The A.E.U.'s 'General Office Reports' do not permit one to trace the result of adjourned Conferences in many cases, but one can reckon at least the proportion of these which result in a definite failure to agree and are remitted to a higher procedural level. And since in our samples three out of four cases 'referred back' to Works level in engineering at large resulted in final agreement, against only five out of eight cases so treated in the car firms, one can complete the picture by tracing the current likely result of Procedure for any hundred grievances passed to it in the two groups—as in Table VIII/8 on the next page.

It is again evident that reference to the higher stages of Procedure adds little to the incidence of definite agreement, either in the engineering trades generally or in the car firms alone. But whereas passage through the successive levels of conciliation away from the plant at least increases the proportion of agreements recorded to over 70 per cent in the engineering instance, in car firm cases it still results in only 38 per cent of agreements. Moreover, to achieve that result half the car firm references will have to go to a stage beyond the Works Conference, and a third of them to the further stage of Central Conference, against about a quarter and a tenth respectively in the general group. While about half the cases so processed will in any event only be ultimately referred back to the factory level without definite settlement—nearly four times as many as in general engineering cases.

The proportion of cases labelled 'outcome uncertain'—of which, to repeat, some will be dropped or otherwise taken out of Procedure —is probably normally much the same between the two groups (the two Central hearings for cars in this category representing adjournments pending the outcome of national negotiations). And if one supposes, probably not unreasonably, that one way and another agreement is reached in about the same proportion of such cases as in those 'referred back', some 11 per cent of issues referred to Procedure

---

[1] The only respect in which the above data seems significantly out-of-line with Marsh and Jones's results (*loc. cit.*) is that its proportion of cases referred back from Central Conference for all engineering is on the low side: and this is possibly accounted for by the inclusion of Welsh Regional cases. It does not in any case significantly affect the results of the next calculation (Table VIII/8).

in engineering at large would remain unsettled—which seems consistent with Marsh and Jones' estimates (granted the qualifications to the latter already cited). A third of car firm cases, however, would still have no definite settlement. And one can perhaps add that, on our samples again, out of any hundred cases referred to Procedure at the levels of official participation, one appears currently likely to end in a 'constitutional' strike in engineering at large, against three from the federated car firms.

Table VIII/8—TYPICAL OUTCOMES OF REFERENCES TO FEDERATION CONCILIATION PROCEDURE, CAR FIRMS AND ALL ENGINEERING, 1964–65

		Agreement	Referred back	Outcome uncertain	Failure to agree
100 cases in: *All Engineering*	Works hearings (100):	64	2	11	23
	Local hearings (22):	6	2	4	10
	Central and Welsh hearings (11):	1	4	—	6
	Referred back to Works or internal level (8):	6	—	—	2
	Final outcomes:	77	—	15	8
100 cases in: *Car Firms*	Works hearings (100):	32	5	13	50
	Local hearings (48):	5	7	3	33
	Central and Welsh hearings (35):	1	16	2	16
	Referred back to Works or internal level (28):	18	—	—	10
	Final outcomes:	56	—	18	26

But since criticism of the E.E.F.'s conciliation process has largely concentrated on the delays involved, it is perhaps worth looking also at the time factor. Marsh and Jones calculated that some thirteen weeks elapsed between the first formal Works Conference and Central Conference in cases referred to the latter in 1959, of which

The Firms Compared: and the Employers' Organization

six weeks represented the average delay between Works and Local level. Our own data yields a similar result to the last, but suggests a much longer mean delay than the residual seven weeks between Local and Central hearings—over eleven weeks for car firm cases. We do not know whether this represents a general result of the greatly increased flow of references to Central Conference, or is a peculiarity of our car firm cases (we assume the latter in the following calculation, but the alternative adjustment can readily be made). In cases referred back to Works level a further six weeks average lag appeared to have ensued before conclusion—and it must be remembered that before a grievance gets into formal Procedure it will often have already spent several weeks in negotiation within the plant: under current circumstances, it would probably not be immoderate to reckon at least a month on average from the first opening of an issue to the convening of a Works Conference on it.[1]

On this basis the average time between the first raising of an issue submitted to formal Procedure and its disposal (or recording of failure to agree) is over seven weeks for all engineering cases and more than thirteen weeks for car firm references. A case which proves difficult, however—involving, say, one adjournment at Works or Local level and final reference back from Central Conference[2]—would average seven months in general and eight months in a car plant issue. And the likelihood of such an upshot would be three times as great in the car factory instance as in general engineering. (It is perhaps significant, indeed, that this probability seems in each group about the same as that of the process ending in a 'constitutional' strike.) It is commonly argued that the value of Procedure lies not in the number of definite settlements produced by its stages, but in the help these convey to the ultimate attainment of agreement at the workplace level itself. However, very many issues—such as those arising from dismissals—involve matters which will almost automatically arrange themselves on the management's terms unless they are quickly settled otherwise. Moreover, in industries subject to rapid technical and other changes, the context of a particular dispute is itself likely to alter materially in a quite short period: the run of a job

---

[1] No data on this point has been systematically gathered by any of the collective organizations—to our knowledge—but in a run of twenty consecutive cases referred to Procedure from one car plant, the average period was over eight weeks. If this is typical the estimates that follow should be adjusted accordingly—at least, for car firm cases.

[2] This is not the extreme case: one reference in our car samples, having gone through this process, was again sent back to Central Conference, and another was held at Works Conference level by repeated adjournments over more than four months. While in several cases, the lag between Local and Central Conferences appeared three or four weeks longer than our eleven weeks average.

for which rates are disputed, for instance, may itself last only a few weeks or months. And it is part of the E.E.F.'s view of 'managerial functions' that Procedure requires, if a management decision is challenged, work to continue on the employer's conditions unless and until a reference to Procedure produces a different result.[1]

Under the circumstances, it seems understandable, not merely that many trade unionists should feel themselves better advised to insist on continued direct negotiations by managements than to have disputed issues removed from the factory, but that they should also regard the effect of Procedure as being partly to deprive them of the benefit even of such favourable settlements as result from it. This is one factor in the growing use of informal conferences at Local level in preference to formal Procedure; though failure to agree in such meetings conveys no sanction to a strike. An issue's passage through Procedure can, of course, be expedited somewhat—though possibly, given the present staffing of the unions and employers' associations, only at the cost of delaying settlement on other cases. And it is again significant that procedural delays appear to be materially shortened in cases where an 'unconstitutional' strike has occurred. Our own sample of such cases is too small to provide a reliable indication of this effect—only one in a hundred references involved a stoppage before Procedure was completed—but in Marsh and Jones's study the average time between Works and Central Conference was cut by two weeks—and the median time by four!

But the E.E.F.'s insistence on the sanctity of 'managerial functions', when combined with the foregoing, helps to explain another peculiarity of the cases referred to its conciliation. If one judges the relative importance of the different issues on which disputes may arise by the relative frequency of strikes about them, then issues other than those involving wages and work-hours are very much under-represented in the cases referred to Procedure. In our sample of hearings from engineering as a whole, only 18 per cent of Works and Local Conferences were held on issues such as redundancy, dismissals and discipline, the allocation of work and other managerial decisions, or relations with stewards—which is probably (though we have not attempted the formidable task of classifying all engineering disputes in the same way) only about half the general frequency of stoppages on these matters in the whole complex of metalworking trades. The discrepancy is particularly marked for the car firms, where in 1964

---

[1] The referability of both dismissals and piece-price disputes to Procedure is formally uncertain or variable, though such references are usually accepted: for detail, see Marsh (*Industrial Relations in Engineering*)—as also for certain temperings of the 'managerial functions' rule in some specific types of dispute.

over 40 per cent of all recorded strikes occurred on such matters. But only 20 per cent of references to Works and Local Conferences from car firms dealt with such questions. In other words, a particularly large proportion of just the categories of dispute which have bulked so largely in our increased strike-liability since the 1950s are not in any case referred to the conciliation procedure of the great industrial sector overwhelmingly concerned.

Historically, the E.E.F. has always insisted that, though it would negotiate with the unions on wages, working hours and closely related questions, matters other than these constituted 'managerial functions', in the exercise of which employers might (nowadays, at least) consult with workers' representatives, but where final decision must rest in the management's hands. This is not an attitude which can be generally maintained in practice at the workplace itself, where managements these days frequently adopt informal agreements or understandings which compromise the principle. But it is one on which the Federation certainly stands in relation to proposals for more formal or general arrangements on such questions: and knowledge of this position is fairly clearly a factor in the reluctance of many trade unionists to submit disputes on the matters affected to Procedure. And one could perhaps add that even on wages—with which references to Procedure are overwhelmingly concerned—the Federation's agreements do not, for the car firms, at least, provide a useful guiding reference for the settlement of individual disputes.

In general, of course, engineering earnings are much above the rates prescribed by national agreements, and this is particularly so (as we showed in Chapter V) in the motor industry. The current three-year agreement provides for minimum weekly earnings to be raised by six-monthly additions to levels at which they will, by January 1968, replace the co-existing minimum time-rates and provide new minimum P.B.R. standards. In essence, this repeats an earlier 'levelling-up' exercise attempted by a 1948 agreement: it seems no more likely than the latter to produce a greater uniformity in metalworking wages in general, since a major factor in the present dispersal of engineering earnings for comparable skills—the process of workplace bargaining over piece-work prices and for the rectification of the anomalies in actual wages which largely result from it—will continue unregulated. Average men operatives' earnings for a standard week were in the car plants in 1965 well over twice the new engineering minima established in that year, and there seems no reason to think that the discrepancy will be significantly altered by the three-year agreement's final act. Meanwhile, moves for a general revision of engineering wage-structure—recommended many years ago by Court of Inquiry—have apparently ground to a halt before the difficulty of devising a realistic universal wage-pattern for the diversity of industries and firms embraced by the Federation. The Federation thus has no systematic standards or principle which it can apply to the settlement of the many wage-disputes referred to its Procedure—beyond an expressed objection to competition for labour between its members which, to the extent that it is at all effective, is again likely to be more so in car workers' cases as coming from the most highly-paid group.

One reason for the high strike-proneness of the car firms, and of the federated firms in particular, seems thus to be that the present organization, attitude, agreements and conciliation procedure of their employers' association provide no effective basis for the settlement of the major issues in dispute between the firms and their workers. While on the other hand, affiliation to the E.E.F. may well have to a significant extent inhibited the development of positive policies to deal with these matters by individual firms. Of the larger federated companies each has separate plants in different localities —sometimes in several. And the E.E.F. is organized on a federal, district basis. In any dispute, therefore, Procedure requires that formal reference from the plant management concerned should be, not to the company's head office but to the local engineering employers' association, and thence to the E.E.F. itself. In the past, this enabled the firms' directors to neglect their labour relations because it was assumed that the E.E.F.'s local services met their needs. Even in some big recent stoppages, it has been unclear whether the company concerned or the employers' association was handling the matter at issue. And the appointment of Industrial Relations Directors by several federated firms does not seem to have led to any radical alteration in the pattern, which leaves the responsibility of the firm itself in some degree uncertain.

APPENDIX

THE STRIKE-LIABILITY OF INDIVIDUAL FIRMS

Diagram X attempts a combined comparison of both the incidence *and* frequency of disputes at individual firms with the car industry norm. In this Diagram the rectangle at the top represents in area the average post-war *incidence* of strikes for all the car firms together, in terms of striker-days to any given number of employees. At the same time the rectangle is divided into segments according to the average *frequency* of disputes due to particular issues.

The profiles for individual firms which follow are arranged so that under each division of the main 'industry' block, the height of the firm's segment shows the *frequency* of stoppages on that issue compared with other causes of dispute at the same firm—and at the same time how far this frequency exceeds or falls short of the industry average. So that, for instance, it is at once evident that strikes in B.M.C. plants about 'wage-structure, work-loads, etc.' have been relatively much more important even than is normal for the industry, while those on the same cause at Ford have been less important than the average; or again, that S.T.I. has had a disproportionately large dispute-liability on the score of 'trade union relations, etc.' while Rover has had an unusually fortunate history on this account.

On the other hand, the total *area* of each firm's profile indicates—very approximately—its overall strike-incidence by comparison with the industry norm—so that one can again see, for example, to what extent B.M.C.'s experience in this respect appears to have exceeded the industry average, while Ford's is significantly below it. In this Diagram, we have attempted to make allowance for the effect of general engineering strikes on the overall strike-incidence of each 'federated' firm. And to put integrated and decentralized firms on the same footing, we have also included some estimate for each company of the 'secondary loss' of working days, caused by disputes at particular establishments to other plants *in the same firm*.

This involves the major dubiety of the Diagram: it may include a substantial under-estimate of this 'secondary loss' in the case of B.M.C.; and since the B.M.C. group has—even on 'Ministry of Labour' criteria (which exclude such 'secondary' losses)—experienced at least two-fifths of all post-war striker-days in car firms, there would then be a similar underestimate of the car firms' total strike-incidence in the top, 'industry' block. *We have therefore marked, by*

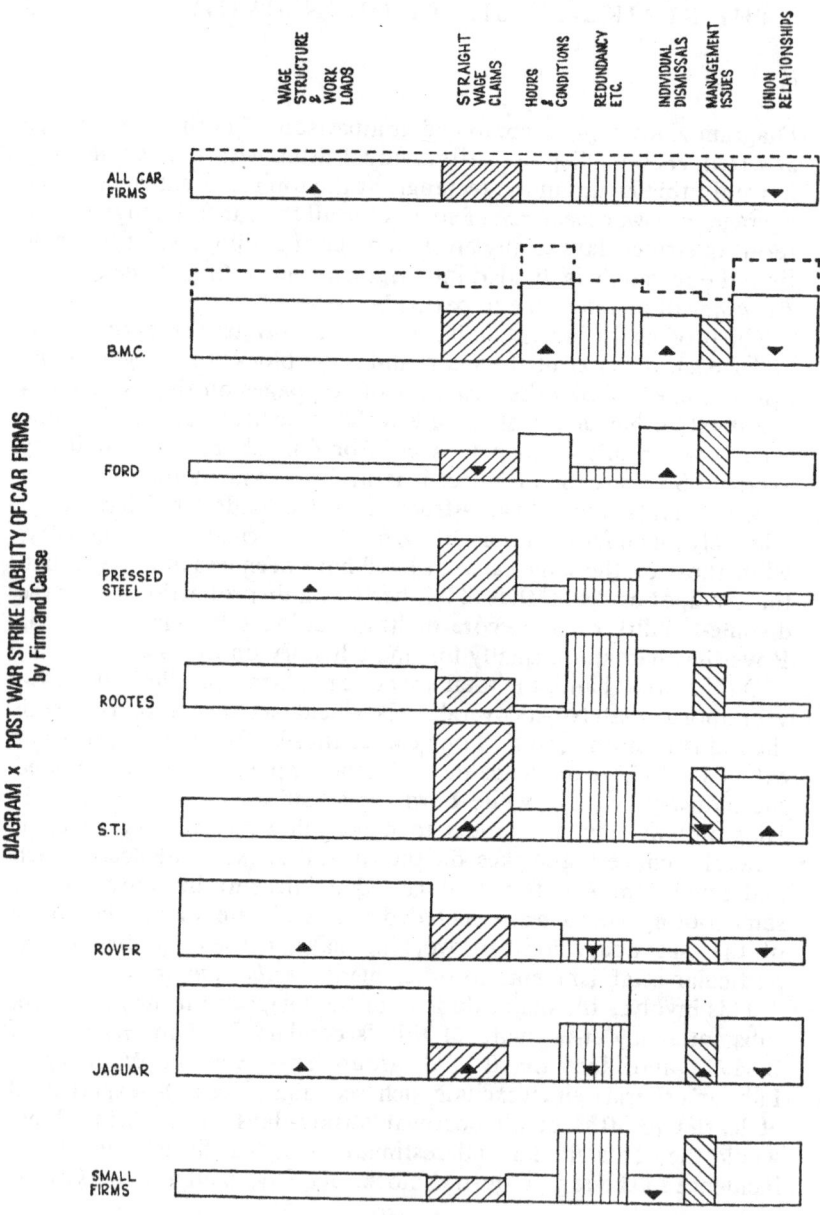

The Firms Compared: and the Employers' Organization

hatched lines in the Diagram, what the area of the main 'industry' block, and the height of the B.M.C. profile, would be on an alternative estimate of the 'secondary loss' referred to. This would be on the assumption that the *ratio* of 'secondary loss' for B.M.C. for 1962–64, which is deducible from the figures of 'working hours lost from strikes within the company' presented by the manufacturers to the Royal Commission on Trade Unions (see Appendix IIA), was also typical of the corporation's experience *from its formation*. The strike-incidence of the other firms is not, as the Diagram indicates it, significantly affected by this problem—though some of them (especially Pressed Steel) may have experienced disproportionate loss of working time from stoppages at *other* firms. This type of 'secondary loss' is not reckoned in the Diagram's estimates.

In the Diagram, firms are arranged in descending order of size as measured roughly by their average employment over the post-war period so far as we can reckon it. Thus, we have included a profile for the very small firms (as a group) which have not previously been separately distinguished in this study. This last estimate presents special difficulties, since it includes some concerns which no longer exist, but the resultant picture appears of some interest. However, Vauxhall and Rolls-Royce do not appear in the Diagram because their strike-incidence has been too small to show.

On the other hand, again, in this chart the causes of dispute are arranged starting from the biggest ('wage-structure, etc.') and otherwise roughly in accordance with their likely degree of overlap—so that 'hours, etc.' follows 'straight wage-claims', and 'redundancy' follows 'hours'. A reason for this is that the Diagram is more detailed than Table VIII/6. The average block refers to about 100 strikes, and reported strikes are themselves only a small sample of all disputes. Nevertheless, where the number of strikes in a particular segment is small, it may be unduly influenced by marginal classificatory decisions, and the arrangement to some extent offsets this effect.

The chart covers the whole post-war period: the problem in selecting a shorter period is just the seeming 'cycles' of disputation and relative peace at particular firms referred to in Chapter VIII, which make picking another appropriate year from which to start invidious. However, nearly five-sixths of all car industry strikes recorded also occurred in the decade to 1964, when our analysis ended. And where, in any firm, a particular cause of dispute has shown a persistent tendency to become more important relatively to other issues over the period, or to decline in relative significance, this has been indicated in the segments concerned by *arrow signs* (so that, for example, it seems that friction on the score of 'trade union relations' has been in both B.M.C. and Jaguar declining in relative importance).

It emerges, for instance, that the 'federated' firms as a group seem to display certain common patterns of dispute-causation, with a relatively high strike-liability on account of 'wage-structure' questions, and a rather lower one from straight wage-claims and from issues of working hours and conditions. This relationship is exhibited typically by the Rootes, Rover and Jaguar distributions, and is precisely the opposite pattern under these three heads of dispute to that displayed by Ford. B.M.C.'s departure from it—by a particularly high relative frequency of strikes about working hours and conditions—is probably due to the special concentration of the 'four night week' disputes involving shift workers in the 1960s in B.M.C. plants, and to the troubles in the Morris Cowley paint shop already referred to. Standard's variation, with a disproportionately high strike-liability arising from straight wage-claims, is partly due to its period of dissociation from the Engineering Employers' Federation and partly to the several stoppages of white-collar workers which have affected this firm. The similar variation by Pressed Steel may be possibly merely a classificatory effect: because the newspapers did not bestow as much interest on this company as on those which are more obviously producers of cars until quite recent years, accounts of stoppages there have been sketchier, and a larger number of wage-disputes have had to be left as due to 'straight' wage-claims for want of clear information to the contrary. (Thus one biggish stoppage in its collection arose from a wage-claim at the Swindon plant: but this may itself have been provoked by higher rates in Oxford.)

The common pattern of 'wage-related' disputes (as they might be broadly called) in the federated car firms seems again fairly easily traceable to the rather chaotic wage-structure which their adherence to the traditional engineering wage-system has produced; while straightforward wage-demands or claims for reductions of working hours are relatively few because these are substantially met by the periodic general improvements conceded by the engineering employers. Ford's opposite pattern arises partly from its simple wage-structure (so that stoppages under this head have mainly concerned questions of work-loading) and partly from its fairly determined efforts to extend shift working: more frequent disputes over working conditions have possibly also been a consequence of that generally tougher management line which is reflected too in its particularly high score of disputes on its exercise of managerial functions.

For the rest, the comparative pattern of disputes on other issues than the 'wage-related' ones in the federated firms appears to have been very much a matter of each concern's particular market or union

The Firms Compared: and the Employers' Organization

circumstances and managerial policies. Thus Rootes and Standard both show the relatively substantial record of redundancy disputes which has already been remarked as one result of their insecure commercial history, and which contrasts sharply with the low strike-liability under this head of Ford, Pressed Steel and Rover—with their firmer market positions. But Rootes has also had a relatively high frequency of stoppages on individual discharges—which is perhaps, in view of its very low score of disputes on account of union relations, associated mainly with its experience of fairly frequent labour surplus, possibly making it more willing to discharge its less-wanted workers. In Standard's case, however, strikes against individual dismissals (apart from those of shop stewards) have been very few—not so much, probably, because these are not objected to by the operatives as because the unusually strong union control over engagements there makes them a rare occurrence.

There seems some similarity, in fact, between the Standard dispute-pattern and that for the very small firms as a group. In Standard, the early post-war concessions to the union workplace organization put the latter in a position somewhat analogous to that of the strong craft groups in smaller concerns, and this contributed to a high proportion of conflicts on management questions and union relations when the firm's direction changed. The only respect in which its pattern differs substantially from that of the very small firms is in its relatively higher proportion of wage-disputes—which presumably reflects the fact that its market position has not, on the average, been quite so uncertain as the lesser group's—and particularly, again, of straight wage conflicts: but this partly arises because its white-collar workers set out to emulate its operatives' tight organization.

In Ford, on the other hand—and unlike the Standard case—a high frequency of stoppages over management questions goes with a disproportionate strike-liability on account of the dismissal or disciplining of individuals; which perhaps confirms that some of the 'aggression' in this case was reciprocal. While B.M.C.'s strike-profile (apart from such things as have been previously mentioned) is unique in that under every single head of potential contention its dispute-liability has, as the Diagram measures it, been greater than the industry norm—and this despite the extent to which B.M.C. dominates the latter.

Another contrast is between the Rover and Jaguar profiles—for two firms now very similar in size and speciality, and not far separated geographically. For both these concerns, the Diagram shows not merely the expected abnormal frequency of 'wage-structure and work-load' disputes, but that this has in each case been increasing relative to other sources of labour conflict. For Rover this seems readily explicable in terms of the firm's one-time lagging average wage-level and the particular difficulties which attended the introduction of its '2000' model in a new plant during the early 1960s. No such ready explanation presents itself for the Jaguar phenomenon —since in this firm production earnings have in recent years been up in the front rank, and no parallel major innovation to the Rover venture was involved. However, while Rover's strike-liability on issues unrelated to wages is unusually low, Jaguar's appearance of a rather extensive dispute-proneness on such matters (particularly individual dismissals) is partly a reflection of some biggish disputes in the *immediate* post-war years (see Table VIII/5)—one or two in Daimler, which is included in the profile (as in the cases of other firms which have merged into the present manufacturing groups).

CHAPTER IX

THE BIGGEST STRIKES: AND THE ROLE OF INDIVIDUALS

(A) 'SIZEABLE STRIKES': AN ANALYSIS

Another way of looking at the record and situation of individual car firms in respect of industrial unrest is to follow through some of the bigger disputes in detail. But before we do that, it may be as well to say something about the bigger car industry strikes in general. Like personal incomes and trade union membership, strike-liability is heavily concentrated in a few examples of the statistical population: most of the total of striker-days is due to a few sizeable stoppages. More precise measurements depend on definitions. If 'sizeable' strikes are arbitrarily taken to be those which involve 20,000 striker-days or more, then these strikes together account for almost three-fifths of the car firms' total of such 'days lost' for the whole period from 1921 to 1964, even excluding general engineering stoppages. Despite logical expectations that all car firm strikes would tend to become big strikes—because of the highly integrated production processes, the large scale of activity concentrated in few plants, and a consequently higher incidence of workers 'indirectly involved'—of the total of 920 recorded by us since 1921 only forty-two have been sizeable. These forty-two, however, together account for well over two million out of a total getting on for four million striker-days in the car firms during that time—apart, again, from those 'days lost' attributable to engineering strikes or to the 'secondary loss' from disputes.

But 'sizeable' covers perhaps too broad a range. Within the category there are what might be called 'moderate' strikes involving up to 50,000 striker-days apiece, 'middling' strikes of from 50,000 to 100,000 days, and 'monster' strikes each of more than 100,000 days. Of the total number of sizeable strikes, twenty-nine have been moderate, nine have been middling, and there have been four monsters. As in the case of strikes generally, the incidence of striker-

Table IX/1—SIZEABLE STRIKES

Period	No. of strikes	By size*			Workers involved (000s)		Striker-days (000s)	
		Moderate	Middling	Monster	Total	Average per strike	Total	Average per strike
1921–39	4	3	1	—	26.7	6.7	158.5	39.6
1940–45	3	2	1	—	29.5	9.8	153.7	51.2
1946–51	5	4	1	—	37.7	7.5	209.5	41.9
1952–57	8	3	1	4	94.5	11.8	788.4	98.6
1958–64	22	17	5	—	168.1	7.6	824.6	37.5
1921–64	42	29	9	4	356.5	8.5	2,134.7	50.8

* Moderate=20,000–49,999 striker-days; middling=50,000–99,999 striker-days; monster=100,000 or more striker-days.

days is 'log-normally' distributed: the four monsters together are responsible for over 600,000 'man-days of idleness'. But refinements of this kind reveal the statistical hazards. Although size seems most meaningfully measured in terms of total striker-days, there are the problems of discriminating between, say, the one-day protest stoppage of 37,000 workers in all Ford plants, and a series of stoppages by 4,000 men over particular night-shift arrangements at various B.M.C. plants, which lasted six months and was also, in total, a moderate strike. And both these strikes were in 1960: in what sense is grouping by size meaningful in a series extending over forty years?

However, the statistical analysis does draw out some salient points, as the table opposite demonstrates. Perhaps of greater significance than mere concentration of striker-days is that the sizeable strikes are becoming more frequent: and that their causes have been changing. Of the total, twenty-two—or more than half—have occurred since 1958. Up to 1945 there had been only seven—three of them during the War years, and all seven about wage matters. All four of the 'monsters' occurred in the five years from 1952. And in the post-war period the big strikes have come to be more about questions which are identifiably ones of principle—like, for example, such trade union and job-security issues as the dismissal of shop stewards, the transfer of workers and redundancies—rather than about wages. But the period of the monster strikes seems also to have closed at a turning point in the till-then declining concern about wages. In the seven years since 1958, wage issues—mainly structural questions rather than straightforward claims for increases—have been the stated issues in just half of the twenty-two sizeable strikes. Assuming that big strikes are more likely to be motivated by matters of basic principle, what the changing issues in such disputes substantiate is certainly a growing concern with job-security rather than living standards—not an illogical change when living standards have for long been rising. But the re-introduction of wage matters as major issues possibly reflects sharp changes in the rate at which this rise has continued, at least for the car workers or particular groups among them.

However, the frequency of big stoppages has not increased in proportion to the total number of disputes in recent years. Up to 1957, and excluding the War, about 7 per cent of strikes turned into sizeable ones in any period. Since 1958 only 4 per cent have done so. This is in accordance with the general rule that an increase in the number of strikes produces a disproportionate rise in the frequency of small stoppages. But if the ratio of big to small strikes is also taken as some index of the efficiency of industrial conciliation—one function of which is presumably to stop small strikes becoming big ones—then this is notably less effective than in the War period, when only 2 per cent became sizeable.

It is interesting that the increasing size and integration of car plants has, over the whole period, again had little apparent effect on the dimensions of stoppages. The average number of workers involved in each 'sizeable strike' was 6.7 thousand before the war, and some 7.5 thousand for most of the post-war years. There was an average of 12 thousand men in each of the big strikes between 1952 and 1957, but this was the age of 'monsters', and the figure is also related to the exceptionally high concentration of workers at two of the main plant complexes concerned. The duration of the average sizeable strike cannot be derived from the statistics.[1] The men involved are rarely all on strike for the whole period, anyway, and there are complications due to partial returns to work and to the length of time it may take for a strike to spread, as well as over night-shift involvement. But the number of calendar days which a strike is officially considered to have lasted is available. Big strikes have, of course, varied greatly in length, but only seven of the forty-two lasted less than seven calendar days. Sixteen lasted from one to two weeks; eleven from a fortnight to a month; and eight lasted more than a month. Big strikes, on the whole, are also long ones.

There is no clear-cut association between the length of the strikes and the stated issues in dispute, beyond an unexceptionable tendency for strikes about matters other than wages to last longer. These are, in effect, employment and trade union issues, as only three of the sizeable strikes have not been about these or wage questions. And it is interesting also to note that five of the seven big strikes over trade union relationships have occurred in the most recent period—which perhaps fits in with what we have said in an earlier chapter about the effect of an increase in trade union support as a contribution to the higher frequency of bigger stoppages: though the big pre-war strikes probably also had more union backing than was usual in the immediate post-war years. The seasonal distribution of sizeable strikes also supports a previous suggestion: they have begun in all months except November, but most often in February—and the inverse connexion with production requirements seems clear. They are nearly four times as frequent in the first quarter of the year—when demand is generally at a low level—than in the last.

But the most significant feature of the big strikes is their distribution by firm, and more particularly by individual plant. B.M.C. has had about the number that could be expected on the basis of its share

[1] Except in the sense—which has been used in one or two other contexts in this study—of 'average days struck per striker'. In this sense, the average 'sizeable strike' has lasted three times as long as smaller stoppages.

The Biggest Strikes: and the Role of Individuals

of output—that is, eighteen in all up to the end of 1964. But eight of these have been at the Austin works at Longbridge. Big strikes there have been recurrent: they have happened more or less regularly over the years for which we have records, and together they account for over half a million of B.M.C.'s 850,000 striker-days incurred in big stoppages. B.M.C.'s merely proportionate share of big strikes can be thus attributed to the relative absence of such disputes on the Morris side. No strike at any Morris plant has ever exceeded 50,000 striker-days, and even the 'moderate' kind did not start appearing until 1959 (although some Morris plants were involved in the 'middling' redundancy strike at various plants in 1956). And Morris's modest entry into the big-time league has been at least a statistical substitute for Austin's exit from it: after the 'monster' of 1953, Austin's next appearance was in 1962 only.

Eighteen of the sizeable strikes, involving almost a third of the striker-days attributable to all car industry strikes of whatever size, have occurred at two places: Longbridge and Dagenham. But big Ford strikes have been a purely post-War phenomenon, the first being a middling stoppage in 1946 over wage and trade union issues.[1] The Briggs and Ford 'monsters' of 1952 together accounted for almost a quarter of a million striker-days. These were followed by two middling Briggs stoppages in 1956 and 1957, and a third series which began in 1959. Also in contrast with the Austin experience, big strikes at Ford are becoming more frequent (or were, until 1963). From 1959 there was a sizeable stoppage at Dagenham each year until 1962, when there were two. This later series mainly involved trade union relationships.

After the Ford and B.M.C. allocations, only fourteen big strikes remain, and these are spread fairly evenly over the other firms. Standard has had three, the same as Jaguar and Daimler together. Pressed Steel, Rootes, Rolls-Royce, and Rover have each had two. The Rolls-Royce strikes should perhaps be set apart: they occurred long ago—1937 and 1943—amongst workers then engaged on armaments production. Others of these 'residual' stoppages are widely dispersed in time and place. For example, the first big Rootes strike was at Coventry in 1945, the other at Acton in 1961. The two big stoppages at the Daimler works were in 1946 and 1964, whereas the Rover stoppages are both affairs of the 1960s. There is little that can be said collectively about these fourteen strikes, although two of them are considered separately later in this Chapter, as being of some special significance in themselves.

---

[1] Though, apart from the stoppages in 1944, one against a wage-cut in 1933 nearly came into this category.

LABOUR RELATIONS IN THE MOTOR INDUSTRY

A sizeable strike, if examined closely, could scarcely be said to be typical of anything but itself. Yet it seems worthwhile to survey a few of the very big stoppages of recent years, one of which we followed on the spot whilst it was in progress, and others being covered not only by extensive press reportage but by the reports of Courts of Inquiry. It might be objected that to single out the Austin and Ford strikes for this purpose is misleading, in that, for many years, the industry's output of finished cars has been similarly concentrated at the two centres. The mere size of the works at Longbridge and Dagenham pre-supposes that many of the large strikes would tend to occur there anyway. But near half of the sizeable strikes have been conducted by what has probably always been less than one-third of the total number of car workers (as we define them), and the proportion of striker-days attributable to the Ford and Austin workers in sizeable strikes alone is higher than their proportionate contribution to the car firms' labour force. Nor have the Ford and Austin workers been free of the smaller and more typical stoppages. Again, merely on the matter of size, for the past few years the Vauxhall complex at Luton has had a labour force equivalent to that at Longbridge, no large strikes apart from a one-day closure in 1965, and only very occasional small ones.

Moreover, and as we have just noted, big strikes are usually long strikes. The number of workers involved is almost always large if a strike lasts more than a few days: the sizeable strikes are less those which spread than those which are not settled quickly. Whether settlement of a strike is speedy or not depends on several interrelated and variable factors, including the kind of issues involved, the heritage of mutual attitudes and traditions, the existence of expedient machinery or 'procedures', the pressure of economic forces, and not least of all, human fallibility. Very big strikes often involve important principles, a climate of mutual ill-feeling and mistrust, and sluggish, ineffective procedures. Confrontations often occur when the pressures for production are least compulsive, but soon develop complications and misunderstandings. Again, in an industry like car making, changes in jobs and working methods take place almost daily, and this continually creates potential sources of friction. The bigger strikes are partly a measure of the sophistication of the individual plant's personnel in dealing with these unavoidable (as well as some avoidable) hazards. Many of the big strikes did not begin 'sizeably', nor did they develop quickly from their small beginnings. They often seem to mark a situation where issues arising first on a merely departmental scale have not been resolved without intense and prolonged struggles, ultimately involving economic confrontation from entrenched positions on either side.

THE BIGGEST STRIKES: AND THE ROLE OF INDIVIDUALS

It is these positions which make such big stoppages especially revealing.

(B) AUSTIN, 1953

Austin workers—to start with them—struck in some strength in 1921 over an employment issue, but the history of sizeable strikes at Longbridge really begins in 1929, when there were two—both in protest against wage-reductions. One of these early stoppages involved 11,000 men. The next big strike occurred in 1938, when workers there were recorded as being engaged in aircraft manufacture. Both this one, and another in 1944, were over wages. During the post-war years, the intervals between the big strikes at Austin became shorter: there was one in 1948 over the fixing of piece-rates; another in 1951 over redundancies which included a shop steward; and a 'monster' in 1953 over a very similar issue. Austin was the focal point in the middling stoppage of 1956, over large-scale redundancy, which involved several of the Midlands plants. Six years then elapsed before another of the big Austin strikes occurred: in 1962, when 16,500 men were out for a week in pursuit of increased bonus rates. But the outstanding strike in the series was the monster of 1953. It is also the one on which most information is readily available, as it was the subject of an official Court of Inquiry under the Industrial Courts Act of 1919.[1]

At the time of the 'McHugh' strike (so-called after the affair's most prominent actor), at the beginning of 1953, Austin employed about 17,500 hourly-paid workers, of whom about 2,200 were members of the N.U.V.B.—the third largest union at the works after the A.E.U. and the T. & G.W.U. These N.U.V.B. members were the men who were directly involved in the stoppage. The dispute had a clearly-identifiable genesis in a redundancy in August 1952. There were no special redundancy agreements, although the issue was a very live one and had been the subject of both Works and Local Conferences under the engineering conciliation procedure during the previous year. The local employers argued that the problem was a national one, and that therefore, agreement must be reached at national level and not imposed upon individual firms. The engineering employers' national federation, however—while recognizing certain moral obligations towards redundant workpeople—had consistently held that the 'hiring and firing' of labour were 'managerial functions', and not within the area of negotiation with the unions. The practice at Austin was to give redundant workers the customary week's notice but to try, as far as possible, to transfer them to other

[1] *Cmd.* 8839, of 7/5/53.

employment at the works. Recruitment was also stopped during the lay-offs, and in general, when labour was taken on again, the firm tried to re-employ ex-Austin workers.

The procedural conferences on redundancy in 1951 had resulted in an undertaking by the firm to tell the Confederation of Shipbuilding and Engineering Unions' officials in advance about any large-scale redundancy, and August, 1952 was the first time when this undertaking was put into effect. The Confederation's district officials were informed—on the day before the notices of redundancy were issued—that production of a particular model (the A90) was being discontinued, and that this would mean discharging some 700 hourly-paid men and about 100 staff. The company also affirmed its intention to apply the principle of 'last in, first out' within each section involved; but one misunderstanding which arose out of the meeting with union officials was whether this rule was to apply to the section actually engaged on the discontinued model.

This misunderstanding encouraged a suspicion on the N.U.V.B.'s part that one of its members was being victimized for his trade union activities. John McHugh had worked at Austin for over twelve years, although not continuously: he had been discharged five times due to trade circumstances since 1928, and had once left of his own accord. His last period of employment had begun early in 1948, shortly after which he had become a shop steward. By 1952 he was regarded by the union as their chief shop steward at the works (though this was then not an office recognized by the management). He was president of his union branch, secretary of the Austin Motor Joint Shop Stewards' Committee, and chairman of the Austin-Morris stewards' 'Merger Committee', amongst other union offices; and management could scarcely have been unaware of his activities and importance to the firm's labour organizations. But despite his many offices, the strike throughout its course was a single-union affair directed by the local officials of the N.U.V.B. The Joint Shop Stewards' Committee played no formal role, apart from the preparation of some supporting literature.

All employees working on the A90 model were discharged, and McHugh was one of the last batch to receive notice. The possibility of preferential treatment for shop stewards had arisen at departmental level when the lay-offs first began, and almost from this stage the contentions of each party about the intentions of the other had taken shape. The N.U.V.B. claimed that McHugh was being victimized for his union activities, and pointed to his transfer two months earlier to the A90 section as evidence of his being manoeuvred into a 'condemned cell'. It was maintained also that the form of his discharge was unusual—that he was not required to work his notice, was therefore unable to apply at the personnel office for a transfer to other work, and that unlike others he was not invited to apply. On the firm's treatment of shop stewards, reference was made to earlier disputes over their discharge, in 1949 and 1951.

The management held that the N.U.V.B. was using the situation to establish a precedent for preferential treatment of shop stewards—a principle which had been unsuccessfully pursued in the past. The victimization charges were rebutted: transfer to the A90 had been an alternative to an earlier discharge for McHugh; it was held that, in any event, the management had had no knowledge that this model was being discontinued until very shortly before the redundancies were in fact declared. McHugh was still on the firm's payroll during his period of notice, and was, therefore, able to use the transfer facilities. The management held, finally, that McHugh was a good, average shop steward, active but not troublesome, and that its own record in relation to the treatment of shop stewards was good.

After hearings, the Court of Inquiry concluded that the dismissal of McHugh 'was neither selective nor irregular in form, and cannot be attributed to victimization on account of . . . trade union activities'. The dispute, the Court held, 'was not based upon any real grievance as to (McHugh's) dismissal or the form which it had taken, but was designed by (the Area Organizer of the N.U.V.B.) to secure the principle of preferential treatment for shop stewards, a principle which formed no part of the official policy of his own union, nor . . . of any other union with membership in the Company's works'.

The strike had taken a surprisingly long time to develop, as a chronological summary of events demonstrates. On September 5, 1952, McHugh had received notice of discharge, and an abortive meeting between the Area Organizer and the Works Manager to secure his transfer to other work took place. On September 9 the N.U.V.B. members held a meeting during working hours in breach of the 1922 engineering procedure agreement, which induced the Works Manager to order that McHugh was not to be re-employed without specific reference to him—an instruction which did not come to light until the Court's hearings. During September, McHugh applied for re-employment, the union's Area Organizer asked for a Works Conference, this conference reached no agreement, and the matter was referred to a Central Conference (between the national officials of the C.S.E.U. and the employers' association) arranged for October 10th. The Joint Shop Stewards issued a leaflet supporting the N.U.V.B. and the use of procedure, and the union paid victimization benefit to McHugh.

The Central Conference at York adjourned the matter for a month, and at its November meeting issued a statement that although the employers were satisfied that McHugh's dismissal had taken place properly, they intended to honour the undertaking giving preference to redundant workers when engaging new labour. The unions took this statement to imply that McHugh would be re-employed, and on November 17th, he applied again for employment but received no definite offer. At the end of November, the firm notified the local employment exchange of vacancies for body builders, and the union pressed the local employers' association on McHugh's re-employment. The association's reply was that McHugh must take his chance with everybody else. What seemed an opportunity for an obvious solution to the dispute, which could have been taken without prejudice by both parties, had been allowed to pass by.

The Central Conference in January finally 'failed to agree'; the N.U.V.B. local officials wanted action, and were supported by the union's National Executive, who requested the Confederation to press the employers' national federation for a speedy settlement. This was not forthcoming, and on February 7, 1953, after five months of 'procedure', the strike started. Over 2,000 N.U.V.B. men withdrew their labour, and over 7,000 other men were sent home. The union was demanding McHugh's re-employment in terms of the general undertaking to re-engage redundant employees. But the management had given no undertaking to re-engage every one of the redundant workers, and took the union's demand as being aimed at the 'very far-reaching precedent' of preferential treatment for shop stewards.

After the strike had lasted ten days, the Confederation suggested its reference to a Court of Inquiry, but the N.U.V.B. left the strike in the hands of its District Committee for a further three weeks before asking the T.U.C. for assistance in obtaining this governmental intervention. On March 23rd, a mass meeting of the strikers endorsed this action, and on the same day the management issued a notice that strikers who did not resume work by the end of that week (i.e. by the 27th) would be regarded as having left the firm's employ. The N.U.V.B. expressed its willingness to recommend a return to work at a meeting called for the Monday after, but this offer was rejected. The breakdown in relations remained complete.

When the ultimatum had expired, about 1,600 of the strikers had not returned, and were dismissed. On March 30th, the production programme was reorganized, and the guaranteed week applied to members of other unions who had not yet been recalled. The Court of Inquiry was set up early in April, and during its sittings there were inconclusive discussions about the terms on which the now-dismissed strikers would be re-engaged. The Ministry of Labour records the stoppage as having ended on May 5th, by which time the majority of the strikers had in fact resumed work. In all, the dispute had involved 239,000 striker-days. McHugh was not re-engaged.

(c) FORD, 1957–63

Large stoppages at the Dagenham plants have been as chronic as those at Austin, but began later, and continued into the 1960s. Of the total of ten sizeable strikes at Dagenham—which involved altogether 624,000 days—one half have occurred in the years from 1959. The almost complete absence of strikes in the pre-war years reflects the weakness of trade union organization: as in America, Ford neither encouraged nor recognized unions until World War II, and did not establish formal bargaining relations with them until 1944, under pressure from the Ministry of Labour and the T.U.C. A stoppage at the Briggs body-building plants in 1941, over the dismissal of a shop steward, had ended in an official inquiry and the subsequent recognition of a system of plant bargaining without the intervention of national trade union officials.[1] The system had been extended to all Briggs plants by 'company agreement' in 1944, and it was the later contradiction between this 'local autonomy' in collective bargaining at Briggs and the highly centralized Ford system which became a source of considerable difficulty after the merger of the two firms in 1952. For since 1946, when the firm had its first sizeable stoppage—over a wage-increase and trade union recognition—Ford has had a procedure agreement for channelling grievances from the shop-floor to a joint committee of management representatives and national officials of (now twenty-one) trade unions.

The second big Dagenham stoppage was in 1952, over redundancy and the rejection of a wage-claim. This strike involved both Ford and Briggs plants and lasted about a month, accounting for 247,000 striker-days. Then there were two middling stoppages at Briggs in 1956 and 1957, over redundancy and a dismissal, after which Briggs is no longer identified as a separate organization, and production, wages, and working conditions had been 'integrated' into the Ford structure. But the second of these stoppages led to the appointment of a Court of Inquiry whose report provides considerable information about the conduct of industrial relations at Dagenham.[2] From 1959 to 1962 there were the sizeable annual stoppages, in which trade union matters and dismissals featured prominently, and which reached a climax in the winter of 1962. Again there was an official inquiry, and the 1962 events are worth closer consideration.

[1] *Cmd.* 6284, 16/5/41.
[2] *Command* 131, 30/3/57.

But first, the affair of 1957. The celebrated 'bellringer' dispute highlighted difficulties which had been present even at the time of the 1952 strike. It is similar in many ways to the 'McHugh' strike at Austin, in the deep concern with redundancy displayed by operatives and a willingness of the trade unions to formally support members in issues relating to the status of shop stewards. But the Court of Inquiry interpreted its terms of reference more widely than at Austin, and documented in some detail the long tradition of industrial discontent at the Briggs plants, and how this had in no way abated in the years since the plants had come directly under Ford management. The circumstances of the dispute can be briefly stated. In November 1956, as a consequence of the Suez crisis, the firm had discharged 1,700 men. The unofficial 'shop committee' of one department had thereupon passed a resolution calling for an immediate meeting if anyone in the shop was dismissed, suspended, or ordered on night-shift. Two months later, two stewards were suspended for an unauthorized absence from work, this disciplinary action taking place in the presence of one McLoughlin, chairman of the 'shop committee' already referred to. His response was to call an immediate shop meeting—by ringing a handbell—against the specific instruction of his foreman, and thereby causing a stoppage of work. He was suspended immediately after the meeting, and dismissed on the next working day. This started a strike by all members of the Engineering Division, which brought the plants rapidly to a halt. The strike action had been decided upon at a mass meeting attended by the local officials of the A.E.U., of which union McLoughlin and the other suspended stewards were members.

The company appealed to the central Ford National Joint Negotiating Committee to have the dispute handled in accordance with the procedure agreement, which had since 1955 provided for grievances to go through plant Joint Works Committees and union district officials to the N.J.N.C. And the A.E.U. initiated an informal meeting of its Executive Council with the management after the strike had been in progress for four days. At this meeting it was agreed that McLoughlin be suspended pending the outcome of negotiation—which had to be preceded by a full resumption of work. The strikers returned to work—having been 'out' a week—and the company met the A.E.U. Executive Council on the following day but failed to agree with it on the issue of McLoughlin's re-instatement. The matter was referred to the N.J.N.C. five days later, where a union appeal was made for re-instatement not so much on its merits as in an endeavour to clear the way for the unions to improve discipline amongst their members at Briggs. 'Failure to agree' was again recorded and the A.E.U. went ahead with a strike ballot. Of an estimated 2,000

THE BIGGEST STRIKES: AND THE ROLE OF INDIVIDUALS

A.E.U. members at Briggs, the ballot recorded 1,118 in favour and 429 against strike action. The official strike was, however, forestalled by a decision of the Minister of Labour to set up a Court. In all, the dispute had involved 8,300 men and 27,700 striker-days.

The unions held that McLoughlin had been made the scapegoat for a whole series of incidents for which he was in no way responsible, and that in the general setting of unchecked minor stoppages, aggravated to a large extent by the attitude of supervisors, it was unjust to single him out for so severe a punishment—particularly as his area of the plant had been comparatively peaceful. The management argued that its intention to discipline flagrant breaches of procedure had been well advertised for over nine months, that this was the first such breach in which the instigator could be clearly identified, and that to re-instate McLoughlin would make the task of supervision impossible. In the event, the Court found McLoughlin to have been justifiably dismissed. But the conclusions and recommendations covered a much wider compass.

The more general issues lay in the chronic industrial ill-feeling and in the failure of the Ford Procedure Agreement to curb unofficial stoppages despite apparent good will and cordial relationships between the company and the unions at national level. Each side threw the major part of the blame for this situation on the lower ranks of the other. The Court concluded that the greater measure of responsibility for the continued existence of bad relations rested with the workers, and that a section of the stewards' organization was largely identified with the unhappy situation. It was considered that '... Communist influence has made use of the shop stewards' desire to protect their own interests and powers to the further detriment of good industrial relations with consequent damage to production, but that it has not been the prime cause of the trouble on the workers' side'. The continued existence of an uncontrolled shop stewards' organization was held to be undesirable in the interests of the unions, the workers, and the firm.

The management's share of responsibility lay mainly in its hesitations in making the fullest use of the agreed procedure for effective discussion and the resolution of differences. The Report noted 'a certain insensitivity in the mental attitude of the Company towards those whom they employ', 'an attitude of mind (at higher levels) tending towards regimentation', 'a desire to impose, rather than agree by negotiation', and mentioned specifically the firm's unwillingness to make effective use of the Joint Works Committees. There was evidence that the management was more concerned to confront the unions with general criticisms of their members' behaviour than to attempt to identify examples of this. Some substance was attributed to workers' complaints of crowded and inconvenient working conditions and dilatoriness in remedying them, but progress on these matters was acknowledged.

These findings are useful for present purposes because they documented a situation which remained almost unchanged up to the end of 1962. In this year there were two sizeable stoppages at Dagenham, and one which would just miss inclusion in this category by a few hundred striker-days. The first occurred in January, over a change of line speeds in the foundry. Over 1,200 struck work, although the total involved rose to over 12,600 during the week the strike lasted, and altogether there were 24,000 striker-days. The almost-sizeable stoppage occurred in midsummer, and is an identifiable stage in the course of events which led to the appointment of another Court of Inquiry[1] to examine the threat of an official stoppage early in 1963. The '1962 season' at Dagenham is also associated with a firm line of action in regard to unofficial strikes taken by at least two other firms after the government-initiated 'joint talks' in the industry of 1961.

During August 1962 there was a dispute over 'the transfer of certain long-service employees from one section to another' (as it was officially described). During its course, 335 men stopped work, and about 5,700 were sent home. The strike lasted a week and involved 19,300 striker-days. While not quite sizeable, there were several notable features: it began on the first day back at work after the annual fortnight's holiday, when domestic treasuries might be expected to have been under some strain, and during a critical period in the production of a major new model in the Ford range. It clearly demonstrated the new 'firm line' in the company's handling of its labour relations. The subject at issue—the movement of labour—entailed a conflict between custom-and-practice on the shop floor and the terms of the national agreements. It was also inseparable from the question of labour-loading at a point in car production where changing production pressures may readily become acute—final assembly.

Other background features were important. On the management side there was an expectation of more competitive conditions following expansion of the industry's capacity, and the European Common Market negotiations. At Board level, the former Director of Manufacture had been reappointed as Director of Industrial Relations. American Ford had, not long previously, acquired the outstanding minority shares of the British company, and, following this, special attention was given to reorganizing management structure. In May 1962, the planned re-organization was put into effect, causing stresses from sudden change about which both some managers and some

[1] *Cmd.* 1999, 3/4/63.

senior stewards spoke privately in colourful terms. These pressures in management had made themselves felt to the trade unions in the months before the strike. There was also a series of delays by the company in considering a general wage-claim, and eventually a decision by it to withhold consideration of the claim until a conference had been called to re-assess some of the wider issues of labour relations at Dagenham.

On the shop floor, the increased pressures took the form of a new quality drive—visible in posters and banners exhorting better work, and tangible in the form of greater insistence on standards by the inspectors. Stewards spoke of increased tensions between inspectors and supervisors, which were then communicated to the operatives. But there was little change in the tempo of official trade union activity during the months prior to the strike. Concerted union pressure could at best operate sluggishly on matters other than the annual wage-claim. The unions' inability to move quickly or effectively as a group was openly admitted, nor had they attempted to bring the stewards' organization under formal control, nor to appoint a smaller operating committee of union officers to expedite grievance settlement. This is not so say that individual unions did not operate vigorously on matters affecting their own members (for instance, through their local officials) or that the four main unions did not have informal working arrangements for concerted action when the need arose. But on balance, the industrial relations machinery on the labour side was much as it had been in 1957.

At the start of the annual holiday shutdown in July, 1962, an issue about labour-loading in one section of the assembly plant—the repair garage—was left in abeyance. When work recommenced, some men only temporarily allocated to the section due to a backlog of work there were transferred out again, and to this there was no objection from the stewards. But then a further contingent was ordered out of the area, and it was around these transfers that the issue pivoted. For the repair garage involved some variety of tasks and high overtime earnings. In the words of the stewards, these were 'plum jobs', and a departmental arrangement had been established by custom whereby vacancies in the garage were filled by progressive movement of men down the tracks. The men ordered out of the garage were regarded as part of the normal complement of the area, and many of them had had long service there. Nor was the company operating the usual 'last in, first out' principle. Discussions during the day proved abortive, and in the late afternoon all the repair garage workers walked out, the rest of the plant being then sent home.

The discussions had centered on the reasons for the transfers: the management held that because of the quality drive and general tightening of inspection, not as many jobs would be coming to the garage as before, although the actual number of cars going through would increase. The stewards argued that transferring men 'back down the line' would in fact cause a 'speed-up' and hence more work, and pressed for figures on how much the actual work-load was expected to be reduced. In the absence of such figures, they then demanded the preservation of the 'status quo', to allow the issue to be resolved in practice, or failing this, wished to register 'failure to agree'—i.e. a request to refer the matter to the next stage in procedure. Neither course was acceptable to the management, which stood by the right to transfer labour as it thought fit.

The strike spread to the night-shift, and lasted for the rest of the week, during which time the issue was pursued first by the local union officials and the plant management, and then between the national officials and the firm's central labour relations staff. At this latter stage the issue had crystalized: the unions were asking for the 'status quo' pending a review of the work-load, while the management stated unequivocally that they were no longer going to recognize domestic or customary arrangements, and that the transferability clause in the agreements was to be strictly interpreted. Nor would they negotiate further 'under duress'—that is, until the strikers had resumed work. At this stage, conflict between national trade union officials and stewards became apparent: the former advised a return to enable negotiations to proceed, while the stewards held that this would be capitulation over a vital issue. A meeting of strikers on the fourth day of the strike—Thursday, August 2nd—decided to stay out.

The management followed the 'firm line' through: on the Friday, letters were posted to the strikers instructing them to return to work the following Tuesday (Monday being the Bank holiday) or face termination of their employment. Owing to a shift-rotation, the first to have to report were men not directly affected by the transfers, and they started work. By mid-day the strike was over and the tracks were moving again. In post-mortem statements, the management stated that the 'firm line' was taken unilaterally only because the unions had not accepted an invitation earlier in the year to discuss the improvement of labour relations generally—and that, anyway, the strike was breaking before the letters were issued. Some stewards blamed the shift changeover for their defeat; others thought their failure to raise sympathetic action outside the area in which the dispute took place to provide an indication of the small support which the strikers might have expected to receive had they in fact stayed out. Some union officials spoke of the stewards' organization as having been in decline for some time, adducing the refusal of men to follow the stewards' lead on several occasions in the months prior to the strike. The dispute was referred eventually to the full trade union side of the N.J.N.C., but faded out inconclusively. At least in retrospect, however, it was anticipatory of the events which followed.

For two months later, another 'McHugh/McLoughlin' type of dispute occurred, when a strike of 7,200 men for a fortnight involved 70,000 striker-days. A week prior to this strike the delayed wage-increase had been granted, as part of a deal with the unions in which the disputes procedure was also to be improved: a panel of district union officers was to visit Dagenham regularly to conciliate grievances, and the national union officials and senior management people were each to meet shop stewards' representatives at least annually.[1] But the visiting union panel had not yet had time to form, while the joint statement issued by the N.J.N.C. had reaffirmed the company's right to 'discipline' employees who took unofficial action. On October 17th, a steward in the assembly plant—Bill Francis of the A.E.U.—held a meeting (albeit during the dinner-break) without management permission and was dismissed. This led to protest stoppages, and by the end of the day to a complete shutdown of assembly operations.

It was not this dispute in itself which was the subject of the Inquiry, but the threat of an official stoppage in February 1963, arising out of the company's decision not to re-employ certain of the strikers (as well as some of those who had been laid-off in consequence). For the strike had continued while Francis's union had considered the case, had involved officials of the N.J.N.C., who then achieved the strikers' agreement to a return to work, and had become a matter of principle about the method of selecting workers to be made redundant. In short, management used the unofficial stoppage as the occasion to disembarrass the firm of a number of workers whom they considered to be unsatisfactory, disloyal, or disrupters of their business.

There was misunderstanding over the method to be used. The redundancy list became a black list: those who were not to be recalled to work were successively reduced in number from 'several hundred', to seventy, to forty, to thirty-five, and finally to seventeen, over months of negotiation which coincided with a reduction of the purchase tax on cars, and the subsequent spurt in production. At this figure the negotiations stuck; the unions gave notice of official strike action (in spite of unfavourable ballots), and the Ministry of

[1] The revised procedure is set out in a statement of October 12, 1962, which is contained, together with the details of the arrangements which were thus extended, in the September 1965 edition of the Ford Motor Company's 'Agreements and Conditions of Employment'.

Labour intervened to set up a Public Inquiry. During the Court's hearings, the management insisted on the right to dismiss employees whom they found unsuitable. The unions maintained that there had been a breach of faith over the application of redundancy, that the firm was unjustly discriminating against (or victimizing) those it refused to re-employ, and that it had provided no evidence of specific misdemeanours by these men.

The Court recognized the management's right to engage and discharge labour as it thought fit, 'subject always to the proviso that the exercise of this right is seen to be fair and equitable'—but suggested that the cases of each of the seventeen be examined further. The Court was not satisfied that there had been adequate discussion with the unions in this regard. It was held to be generally undesirable that punitive action should be taken after 'misdemeanours' had been allowed to occur unchecked over a number of years, although there were extenuating circumstances in justification of management's policy. The aftermath of the Court was extended but inconclusive discussion, which in fact produced no further reduction in the number dismissed. Two years later there were reports that more than half those thus designated as trouble-makers were still unemployed.

(D) 'THE FIRM LINE': PRESSED STEEL AND ROOTES, 1961

The importance of the big Ford and Austin stoppages, then, seems to be that Longbridge and Dagenham have been to some large extent battlegrounds over which the undecided issues of principle that figure in the relations between the car firms and their workers have been fought—if not, as yet, determined. On the employers' side, there is the insistence on 'managerial functions'—on certain prerogatives the exercise of which employers have traditionally taken the view is not finally subject to negotiation: such as the selection of workers for dismissal or redundancy and, in the Ford case particularly, the right to determine work-loads and the allocation of labour. This attitude has in effect often made appeals to 'procedure' in such disputes ineffective, since it was known in advance that no such appeal was likely to produce an agreed solution.

On the union side, there are again the complications implicit in the unions' present structure. In the Austin 1953 case, the N.U.V.B. attitude played a large part: the union's E.C. is reported to have short-cut the rule book to declare the strike official, and was known to be influenced by a fear that the company's merger into B.M.C. would result in its being squeezed out by the two giants, the A.E.U. and the T. & G.W.U., whose national leaders might deal direct with the new corporation's directors. And the N.U.V.B.'s stand was in any case visibly prejudiced by the absence of direct support from other unions. In the Ford instance, there was the long-continuing inability of the twenty-one unions represented on the national negotiating committee to produce a more effective mechanism for dealing with the company and for channelling workplace grievances to a level where negotiated settlement might be practicable. In both Ford and Austin cases, there is the ambiguous position of the stewards—among whom even the moderates may apparently find themselves exposed to risks in the fulfilment of their union duties, but are neither always effectively directed by the unions in their courtship of those risks nor assured of protection if they materialize. And finally, there is the influence of a sequence of major conflicts in producing attitudes of entrenchment on both sides which made definitive settlements of the issues in dispute difficult if not impossible.

Two major disputes at other firms in the 1960s are worth some discussion, because—in association with the Dagenham affair of 1962–63—they raise a question of some general interest. There is one theory of strikes which we have not directly discussed, but which has had a repeated currency in connexion with motor industry disputes. This is that strikes are caused by agitators. The theory, of course, is as old as strikes themselves, though it has never acquired much support from detached students.[1] And our examination of the effects of the strength or otherwise of shop steward organization on the strike-liabilities of individual firms, and of the detailed course of minor disputes at a particular plant, does not support the view that shop stewards generally play an 'agitational' role in labour relations. Nevertheless, it could still be held that the attitudes and influence, either of particular individuals or of particular groups, have been a significant factor in the car plants' propensity to labour unrest: and these two further stoppages do seem to offer some evidence for that opinion.

The stoppages concerned followed the joint motor industry talks held under the Minister of Labour's aegis early in 1961. The agreed statement issued at the end of the talks (which is summarized in our Chapter I) had been particularly insistent on the 'constitutional' procedures which existed for the settlement of disputes: 'We attach paramount importance to the adherence by all parties both to the letter and spirit of these procedures which provide solid foundations for good relations in our industry. Without the observance of the procedures the other efforts now being made will be largely nullified and unofficial strikes doubtless continue.' The statement was pub-

[1] For instance, Knowles's conclusion: '... the power of political agitators to play on grievances is largely a function of the reality of the grievance and the time elapsing before it is dealt with.' (*op. cit.*, p. 39).

lished in April 1961: its practical effects showed almost immediately in the handling of a dispute which had begun at the Swindon works of Pressed Steel early in the same month. The effects also extended, however, not only to the handling of the Ford stoppage of late 1962, but—perhaps most important in its results—to that of a protracted dispute at the Rootes subsidiary plant at Acton during the last quarter of 1961. In all three cases there was rigid insistence on formal procedures, and identifiable groups of 'troublemakers' amongst the strikers lost their jobs.

The strike at the Swindon plant lasted for six weeks. About 1,200 skilled workers struck when a wage-claim to bring their rates into line with those of similar workers at the firm's main works at Oxford was finally rejected. Over 2,000 other workers at the plant were laid off, and some of these later joined in the strike, which altogether contributed 57,000 striker-days at Swindon alone to the year's total. Members of several unions were involved: the main one, however, was the A.E.U.—and the strike was largely in the control of a group of stewards having a fairly militant history. As at Ford, the strike committee was assured of the support of the A.E.U.'s District Committee, six members of which had early in the proceedings been suspended by the union for this support, given in open defiance of union instructions to the strikers to return to work.

After the strike had lasted a month, the management issued individual notices to the strikers to resume work or consider themselves discharged. This failed to induce a mass resumption of work, but in fact broke the strike, as there was a steady drift back over the next fortnight. Most of the strikers were eventually re-employed— initially as new starters and without their service and other increments. But the hard core of stewards and other workers whom the management had felt to represent the main source of its labour troubles at the plant since production first began there, in 1956, was not re-engaged. The *Guardian* of September 4, 1961, reported the Minister of Labour as having said that '... action taken in regard to the unofficial strike at the Swindon plant of the Pressed Steel Company in April was one direct outcome of the (national joint) talks. There is much other evidence in union journals, works' newspapers and public statements by representatives of the two sides that follow-up action is being taken along the lines agreed.'

The strike at Rootes' subsidiary—British Light Steel Pressings at Acton—took a more dramatic and long-drawn-out form. It began at the end of August 1961, and lasted for three months, virtually halting Rootes' car production from about mid-October, and accounting for a total of 51,000 striker-days at the Acton plant itself (with an additional official estimate of 450,000 striker-days by wor-

The Biggest Strikes: and the Role of Individuals

kers rendered idle at other establishments in the motor vehicle industry). It was particularly interesting as involving a firm still essentially in control of a family—and one, moreover, with a commercial rather than the engineering background more typical of car industry managements, and, on the whole with a conciliatory reputation in labour matters. In this case the issue concerned a possible redundancy. After comparing production schedules for the various Rootes plants, the (unrecognized) Rootes Shop Stewards' Combine Committee concluded that the firm was stockpiling components produced at Acton with a view to declaring a redundancy. The stewards believed that this policy had been previously attempted by the firm at another subsidiary—Thrupp and Maberley—in October 1960, when a two weeks' strike of the group's main English plants had extracted a 'work-sharing' agreement instead. The Acton plant was unusually strongly organized, and a previous stoppage there in the same year had led to a tart exchange between the A.E.U. Executive Council (which protested at the firm's appearing to negotiate with the unofficial Combine Committee) and the firm—which commented on the union officials' own inability to end the strike.

The feared redundancy at Acton was raised with management, who claimed they were not yet ready to discuss the production schedules. A mass meeting was called and a protest stoppage decided on. When this achieved no response, a further mass meeting of the production workers resolved 'to remain on strike until the management declare "no redundancy" and start negotiations on a shorter working week, short-time working or work-sharing' (the men had been working overtime, and claimed there was already a local work-sharing understanding).

The affair's development was accompanied by considerable confusion, especially on the union side. Most of the skilled workers at Acton refused to join the strike (apart from a brief demonstration by E.T.U. members at a late stage in events)—partly, it seems, because of some resentment at the stewards' policy of levelling-up wage-differentials. The Engineering Employers' Federation promptly denounced the stoppage and, on the ground that the local union officials had failed to secure a return, itself directly approached the four national unions involved (the A.E.U., N.U.V.B., Sheet Metal Workers, and Metal Mechanics), which ordered their members to return to work—the A.E.U. threatening expulsion. The A.E.U. District Committee thereupon protested at the Executive Council's intervention, claiming that it had itself the right to 'approve' strikes in the first instance, and that the stoppage was justified by a decision of the A.E.U.'s policy-making body, the National Committee. The

Sheet Metal Workers' district committee accused the A.E.U. leadership of trying to settle the dispute unilaterally, and itself later declared the strike 'official' for its own membership.

The strike continuing, after some weeks national officials of the unions and the E.E.F. agreed on a formula for a return to work, under which no dismissals would take place at Acton for a month and immediate discussions would take place with the stewards. This arrangement, however, was repudiated by the strikers—who themselves drew up an alternative formula in consultation with the local union officials, and which they claimed was acceptable both to the plant management and the local (London) employers' association. To an outsider, the practical differences between the 'official' and 'unofficial' formulae appear subtle: however, the firm's direction denied cognizance of the latter, and the district employers' official declared the matter to be out of local hands. Rootes—whose attitude had clearly hardened—had meanwhile sent each of the 1,000 strikers a letter declaring that if he did not return to work he would be discharged; and this move failing, followed it up—some six weeks after the strike's commencement—by giving notice to some 8,000 other workers in the group until such time as supplies from Acton were restored. So that within a few days the firm had 'ceased to exist as a productive unit'.

A new attempt by the national union officials to arrange a settlement through the E.E.F. met with no success, and the Ministry of Labour's Industrial Commissioner refused to intervene in the affair. While Rootes now announced that in any case some 150 of the strikers would not be re-employed, and that the re-engagement of individuals would be subject to their 'value to the company'. At Acton, a drift back to work started, and the original refusal of the skilled workers to join the strike now permitted some production to be resumed: the transport workers agreed to handle the output, and the Combine Stewards' Committee decided that it could not declare Acton parts 'black' because workers elsewhere, after some weeks of lay-offs, would not apply such a ruling. Further local attempts to arrange agreed terms for a general return to work were repudiated by the company: and after a thirteen weeks' stoppage the Acton stewards were obliged to accept defeat, and recommended the 500 or so remaining strikers to go back in the virtual certainty that this would involve their own inclusion among those not re-engaged. It was left to the hitherto excluded local union and employers' officials to conclude the terms of surrender, and nearly all the twenty-nine original members of the Acton stewards' committee in fact lost their jobs.

The Biggest Strikes: and the Role of Individuals

(e) The 'Agitator Theory'

Rootes had thus 'made a stand against unconstitutional action', though probably at considerable cost to itself (the figure of £3,000,000 circulated persistently, and guaranteed-wage payments to the Coventry plants in the earlier phase must have been of the order of half-a-million pounds)—and although at at least two points in the dispute the difference between the strikers' successively modified demands and the company's position seemed small enough to have permitted a local settlement. And for two or three years no further important dispute was reported from the Acton plant. So that in each of these three 'sizeable strikes' of 1961-62—the Pressed Steel and Rootes stoppages, and the Ford affairs—events ended (and there was fairly clearly a certain process, if not of co-ordination, at least of imitation at work) in the same way. A group of workers whom the firms concerned thought 'troublemakers' or worse were dismissed, and the immediate consequence was a sharp fall in those firms' strike-liability—at least in terms of 'working days lost'. On the face of it, this is formidable evidence for the 'agitator theory'.

Some qualifications must, however, immediately be made to this conclusion. First, there is reason to think that in each of these three cases the group of operatives thus treated had in some measure isolated themselves—or become isolated—from their fellows in the same company. The Ford stewards had been drawn, by that pattern of management-labour relations which we described as in part a consequence of the Briggs takeover, into a sort of minor guerrilla (unpredictably punctuated by large 'flare-ups') which apparently induced a sort of industrial war-weariness in the rank-and-file. The A.E.U. men at Swindon were apparently out of sympathy with the shop steward leadership at Pressed Steel's major plant in Oxford, and did not obviously enjoy the strong support of the semi-skilled workers at Swindon itself. Rootes' Acton plant, though small, had been the scene of a quite disproportionate number of disputes, which caused frequent lay-offs in the remote major plants in Coventry; the Acton stewards had apparently called the strike without getting the preliminary approval of the group stewards' Combine Committee; and even at Acton itself the skilled workers' support was lacking. In each case, therefore, the bonds of sympathy—never particularly strong between car workers, anyway—had been overstrained, and the men concerned were supported by no broad movement for their defence. In other companies, however—and particularly in the case of B.M.C.—it would be difficult either to select such a focus of 'opposition' or to guarantee that its attempted liquidation would not be met by a widespread reaction from other employees.

But secondly, one cannot exclude, as a major explanatory factor in the relative industrial peace which followed these three events, the simple 'exhaustion effect' which we have noted in the case of other big strikes. The impact of the dismissals appears to have been limited, both in distance and in time. At all three firms together, there were twenty-one stoppages big enough to be recorded in 1960, after the events of 1961–62 the number fell to seventeen in 1963; but in 1964 it was up again to twenty-seven. And though their annual total of striker-days was still substantially below the pre-1961 norm, it also appeared to be creeping up. While if the new disputes were also concentrated in the companies' newer plants, in Merseyside and Scotland, there were in 1965–66 reported stoppages at the main Oxford plant of Pressed Steel, in Dagenham, and even at the Rootes Acton plant (one, curiously enough, over the employment of coloured workers). Moreover, it seems pretty clear that the men dismissed in 1961–62 had unusual difficulty, to say the least, in finding other jobs. There was certainly a feeling among the operatives that the employers were determined to 'make an example of somebody'; and an understandable reluctance to present oneself as a candidate for rustication may well have had as much to do with the result as did the removal of alleged disruptionists. If the case (the only one for which we have information) of the firm in which both accident rates and labour turnover increased after the dismissals means anything, it is presumably that managerial surgery inhibited only one expression of discontent, not its motivation.

Nevertheless, the problem remains: if the 1961–62 dismissals did not prove the 'agitator theory', it is still not quite disposed of. And here, we think, one must try to separate two aspects of it: there is the role of organizations (especially, in the context, political ones); and there is the role of individuals. Many shop stewards in the car firms are 'militant' in some political sense or other—most usually, that they are distinctly on the left of the Labour Party. But this is normal for the engineering trade unions, and we have no evidence that the proportion of such militants is exceptional in the motor firms. In the context of permanent and continuous bargaining which workplace labour relations in the 'federated' firms now involve, stewards are naturally likely to be selected for a certain tough-mindedness, for an active, individual or aggressive temperament. And such temperaments are also likely to express themselves in definite political views. There is, in fact, usually little competition for the steward's job (indeed, Rover complained to the joint 'fact-finding commission' which investigated its plants in 1964 of the high rate of withdrawal from and turnover in stewards' offices): those who stick are often necessarily both tenacious and motivated—and the motivation is not uncommonly personal beliefs.

The question, however, is how much difference such political beliefs or associations make to industrial behaviour. And our own judgment is that they make (in the present subject, at least, and on the average) rather little. As we concluded from the 'participant' experience already reported, circumstances themselves tend to press the stewards into courses of action which are as much moderating as inciting. Against, for instance, the broad complaints of 'Communist interference' with their business which firms have sometimes made, one must set the very good opinions, conveyed to us privately by several plant managements, of individual Communists in leading positions among their stewards. One manager described the Communist chairman of his works' stewards' committee as 'an invaluable buffer' (describing, of course, a function, not a personality). Indeed, one reason why opinions of this kind are not more openly expressed is a very reasonable fear that they might bestow a 'kiss of death' on such stewards' standing with their members; and better, in any case, the devil one knows.

There are two possible broad exceptions to the aforesaid judgment. One is that militant political opinions may make—at least, temporarily—for aggressive industrial behaviour when they are held by competitors for union office. But such competition also produces industrial militancy when those involved in it have no special political virtue to demonstrate: Catholic workers making a bid for leading stewardships, for instance, have also often adopted an aggressive stance towards the management affected; and the same phenomenon occurs when the competition is between members of different unions. And—at the level of ordinary stewardships, at least—such competition for office is itself (perhaps unfortunately, from other points of view) more the exception than the rule.

The more important exception is probably in what one might perhaps call the 'endemic conflict situation'—the situation which, though untypical and abnormal, appears to have crystallized in part of Ford's Dagenham site during the mid-1950s, and may well also have been characterized by Rootes's Acton plant in the late 1950s. In such situations disagreement, mistrust and detailed aggression or defence have become acquired attitudes. They may owe their origin to managerial acts or defaults, but habitual disputation may nevertheless thrust people into the operatives' workplace leadership—if only from the unwillingness of others to assume responsibility in tricky and contentious circumstances—who not merely have a formal belief in 'class war' as an instrument of social change, but are temperamentally adapted to recurrent conflict.

In parenthesis, one could perhaps well say that such endemic conflict situations can only be securely resolved by the separation of the leading personalities from them. Though it seems questionable whether in that case the process ought to be confined to the operatives' side of the affair: unless it is both selective *and* complete, the danger is that the perpetuation of acquired supervisory attitudes—if not more positive managerial 'revanchisme'—may finally reproduce the original situation. And it is perhaps worth noting here that practically all the very big strikes considered in this Chapter have both involved the dismissal of stewards and occurred in circumstances where the car trade was generally slack. So that if the car workers have exploited the booms in activity, to impose earnings increases and restrictions on managerial discretion by workplace pressure, managements appear to have not infrequently taken recessions as an opportunity to disembarrass themselves of some of the leaders those movements threw up.

As an agitational organization, the British Communist Party seems in any case of dubious industrial effectiveness. Some evidence of this is perhaps contained both in the failure of its efforts to support a continuing national organization of motor industry shop stewards —an organization for which a strong industrial *raison d'être* in fact existed—and in the almost complete absence of 'sympathy' strikes in the car firms' recent history. The Party's representation amongst full-time union officers has sometimes produced an ambiguous attitude on the part of its members (at official and *lay* levels of trade unionism) towards unofficial strikes or movements. It appears, despite the evident agitational opportunities provided by the car firms in the last decade or so, only to have organized a systematic committee of Party members in the car factories after its 1965 Congress (though the motor industry was presumably covered before by a King Street advisory committee of engineering trade unionists). And for much of the past decade Communist sympathizers at the workplace level were themselves divided: stewards from one plant told us they had seven Communist members—'three Russian, three Chinese, and one Yugoslav'.

This is not to exclude a marginal Communist Party effect in certain major stoppages—though in just what direction this operated has not always been clear. The Rootes Acton affair of 1961, for instance, was apparently complicated by the presence of three Communists amongst the four local full-time union officers concerned: but at one stage the Party fraction in the plant was reported to have urged calling the strike off to avoid embarrassing those officials with their union Executives, while 'Trotskyist' support of the strike was sometimes more evident. And there is again the special case of Dagenham in the late 1950s, where the C.P. group appears to have been particularly strong (reportedly with over 100 members including fifty stewards), and was clearly heavily involved in what had developed into a habitual confrontation of management and labour. But even there the Communist organization seems to have fallen into some disarray during the October, 1962 events. And generally in proportion to its membership (small enough, anyway), the Communist Party now seems much less active as an agitational force than such minor sects as the Anarcho-Syndicalists and Socialist Labourites: and we have been told of only one motor plant where a significant Trotskyist representation among the stewards was also evidenced.

The role of individuals, as opposed to organizations or beliefs, involves, of course, much bigger considerations. This is a problem for history and philosophy, let alone for a minor aspect of industrial relations. Suffice it to say that a strike generally requires certain conditions: a sense of what sociologists call 'relative deprivation'—of grievance which is thought both justifiable on comparative grounds and remediable; a distrust of, or disappointment in, the orthodox channels for expressing it; and a willingness to act in other ways which itself implies a relative absence of fear for the consequences, some degree of preliminary organization, and a minimum of leadership. Individuals can clearly influence these conditions at several points; but, on the workers' side at least, they can hardly create the comparative circumstances which stimulate the initial sense of grievance. They can rarely, in other words, create the situations which may lead to strikes.

Moreover, one factor seems, in the car industry case, to set fairly narrow limits to the potential influence of individual workplace leaders. The car workers' sense of collective interest seems pretty closely restricted—to matters of small group or sectional concern. As we remarked in Chapter VI, the communal solidarity displayed by miners and dockworkers, for instance, appears mainly notable for its absence—indeed, the basis for it in identical working circumstances, social experiences and personal backgrounds hardly exists. It is, therefore, just not possible for individual rank-and-file spokesmen to gain the personal predominance over wide groupings of men which has often been achieved by unofficial dockers' leaders, for example. There is no 'spontaneous mass solidarity' for such leaders to canalize and personify. In many car workers' strikes, it seems hardly possible to detect a leadership at all.

Again, this is not to say that stewards of a particular personality type may not sometimes make small troubles into big ones: but it would probably be equally true that weak stewards, who fail to take up their members' grievances or to press them with appropriate vigour on the management's attention, are a cause of just as much unrest. On the average, individual influence seems to us small and dispersed—except to the extent that leading stewards have been accepted as mediators by managements themselves. The case, however, is rather different on the management side in the car firms, which have often owed their growth and tendency (in human as well as commercial or technical respects) to powerful or remarkable personalities. The views and policies of Henry Ford are still not without their evidences in Dagenham and Halewood. One might ponder how much of the labour relations history of B.M.C. reflects a certain ascendancy of Lord Austin's imprint on the Birmingham partner to the merger over that of Lord Nuffield's influence on the Morris participants. Or how much of Vauxhall's relative equability derived from its twenty-five year management by Sir Charles Bartlett.

CHAPTER X

INDUSTRIAL RELATIONS IN FOREIGN CAR FIRMS

(A) GENERAL CONSIDERATIONS: AND THE U.S. INDUSTRY, UNION AND STRIKE-LIABILITY

There are two good reasons for attempting some international comparison of labour relations in the automobile industries. One is that the limited number of countries concerned makes the exercise a fairly practicable one. The assembly of cars from imported parts is now a widespread economic activity: Belgium, Ireland and Switzerland in Europe; Brazil, Uruguay and the Argentine in Latin America; Israel, South Africa, Egypt, India and other countries—all these have plants for the assembly and finishing of vehicles the parts for which are mostly manufactured abroad. And these assembly plants provide an obvious basis upon which domestic automobile industries will ultimately establish themselves, by way—as has already happened to some large extent in Australia—of increasing the proportion of parts manufactured in the country of assembly. However, the capital requirements for the manufacture of automobile engines, transmission systems and body sections are so considerable, and the advantages of large-scale production so marked in this industry, that only a few countries can be considered mass production car producers proper (the assembly plants of the other countries referred to have sometimes been erected to circumvent tariff or other import barriers, rather than on grounds of initial cost advantage). While the same considerations have ensured that within each of the producing countries proper, output has become overwhelmingly concentrated in the hands of a few enterprises only.

The second reason for attempting an international comparison is that the technology of automobile mass production is remarkably uniform between countries, so that the human structure of production—the arrangement of working groups, the number of workers involved at any one plant, the types of skill required and jobs provided—also differs little from country to country. Thus, although the United States produces nearly half the non-Communist world's current annual output of twenty million motor vehicles, several European motor plants are quite as advanced technologically, and have quite as high a degree of automation, as anything to be found in the U.S.A. itself—and this applies not merely to the major American companies' various European subsidiaries. Moreover, the degree of technological advancement does not differ much between the various large-scale car producers—or does not differ so much in any one process of car production that particular companies can be said to be very much more advanced than others. This relative technological uniformity makes it possible to isolate this factor from other determinants of the state of labour relations. And it at once appears that a similarity of technique with the British motor industry by no means implies a similarity in strike-liabilities, or in industrial relations at large, on the part of foreign automobile industries. Nor do the latter have much resemblance in these respects to each other: so the British industry could not be argued to be merely the exception that proves some technologically-determined rule.

One factor that immediately emerges as of prime importance in the state of labour relations in any national motor industry is the general industrial relations system of the country concerned. This can be illustrated first for the biggest industry of all, that of the U.S.A. Collective bargaining in America takes place mostly on a plant or company rather than an industry-wide basis, between a single employer and, if not a single union, then at least one major union. And this is true of the American automobile firms—though where there is a considered union strategy, and where companies may collaborate in bargaining or emulate each other's agreements, distinctions between industry-wide and company or plant bargaining become largely formal. American collective agreements—or labour contracts—have the force of law and are for a fixed period: they are comprehensive and carefully-worded, usually with provision for arbitration on points of disagreement, and specifying procedures for negotiation over grievances.

Apart from the 'national emergency' strike provisions for enforced mediation and an eighty-day 'cooling off' period, legislation recognizes the freedom of employees to strike against private employers within broad limits. Labour contracts may contain limitations on this right in the form of blanket no-strike clauses, or they may reserve certain matters as 'strikeable issues'. Unions may be sued for damages if they authorize a strike in violation of a contract, but union officers and members are protected against such actions. 'Wildcat' ('unofficial') strikers lose the legal protection they would have if taking part in strikes authorized by their union, and may be dismissed or disciplined by the employer. Such disciplinary cases are then often put through the grievance procedures specified in the labour contract. Violations of contract generally are very seldom referred to the country's courts, and in practice industrial disputes are settled through the established collective bargaining machinery. Within this general industrial relations framework, the American car firms bargain with the United Automobile, Aerospace and Agricultural Implement Workers of America (U.A.W.).

The American motor industry has been characterized by very rapid growth (particularly in its early years), by large-scale fluctuations in output, and by continuing concentration in the hands of a few producers. The rapid and erratic growth are shown, at least for the past three decades, in the accompanying Diagram X/1—and the concentration, by the fact that in 1965, four firms produced over nine million cars: of these General Motors (G.M.) made more than half, Ford made over a quarter, Chrysler made one-sixth, and American Motors made one-twentyfifth. In addition, these firms produced about 90 per cent of the total American output of nearly two million trucks and buses (so that heavy vehicle production is much less separated from car manufacture than in Europe).

Several distinguishing features of the American industry's labour relations have, of course, been imposed by the U.A.W., which has been a major force in the industry since the late 1930s.[1] The U.A.W. is a product of the big breakthrough in labour organization which was associated with the New Deal and its enabling legislation. Before this, union influence was minimal. The change came suddenly and violently: from 1935, the car industry was singled out by the new C.I.O. as an area of potential recruitment for industrial unionism, and organization thereafter was rapid. The success of sit-down strikes at G.M.'s plants at the end of 1936 marked a turning point: a previously struggling organization became a force to be reckoned with. Chrysler was organized soon after G.M., although Ford managed to resist organization until 1941. But by 1942, U.A.W. membership had reached almost half-a-million.

Both the American President and the laws of the land had encouraged labour organization, while discontent had provided the negative impetus to union growth. This arose from irregular employment, limited job security and low annual earnings despite relatively high wage-rates. Unrest was also provoked by specific managerial practices: re-engaging at the flat rate men who had been laid off work at higher rates shortly before; insensitive introduction of

[1] The early years of the U.A.W. are documented in Walter Galenson, *The C.I.O. challenge to the A.F. of L.* (Harvard University Press, 1960)—referring, of course, to the Congress of Industrial Organizations and the American Federation of Labour respectively.

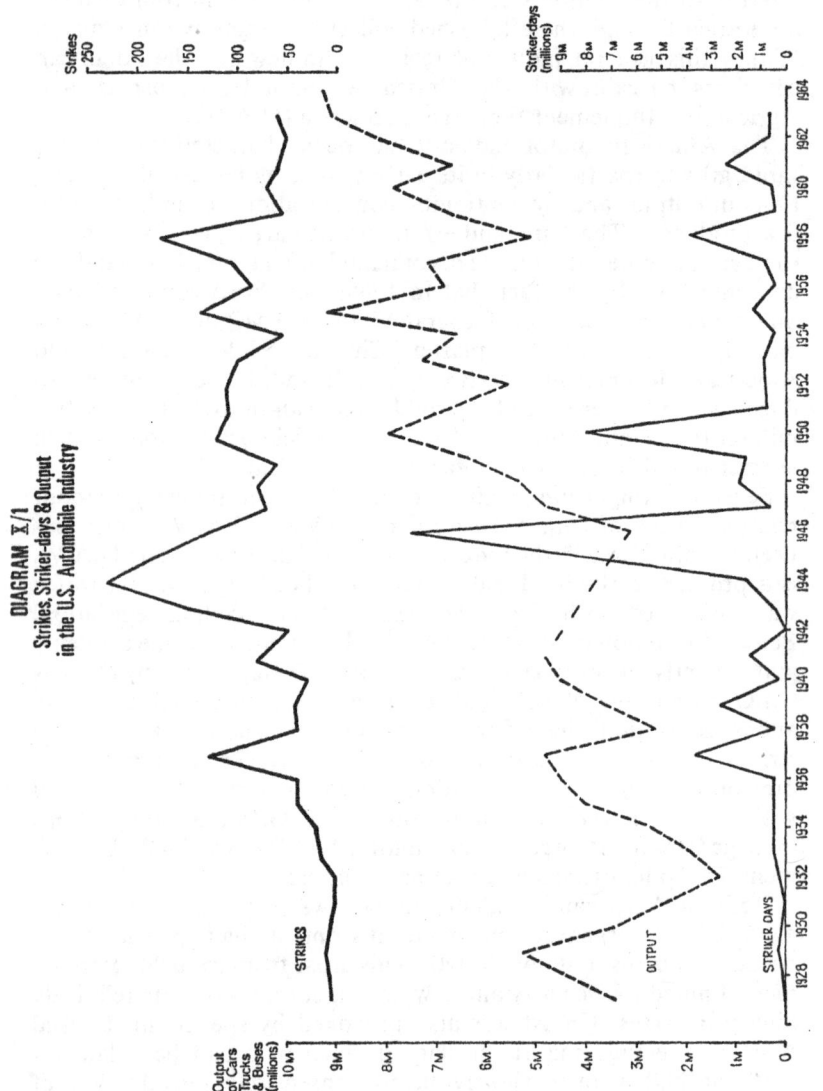

DIAGRAM X/1
Strikes, Striker-days & Output
in the U.S. Automobile Industry

Industrial Relations in Foreign Car Firms

'speed-up'; widespread employment rackets based partly on the considerable responsibility and discretion given to foremen. In particular, the firms' espionage systems of the 1930s gave rise to intense bitterness, and Ford's long drawn-out resistance to trade unionism had been maintained largely on the sheer physical force of its 'Service Department'.

The U.A.W.'s birth was thus spectacular, and many achievements were concentrated within the first few years. For example, production standards—line speeds and labour loading—became negotiable. Changes in these matters which either side might wish to introduce had now to be taken through the grievance procedure, up to but not into arbitration—being reserved as 'strikeable issues' by contract. Application of the 'seniority rule' to job tenure had systematized the burdens of irregular employment, and the arbitrary authority of the foreman had been abolished. There was now a defined grievance procedure, company espionage departments had been disbanded, and wages and conditions were being improved at regular intervals. So that the union's further growth was slower and less exciting only by contrast. After the War, when the leadership of the union had become more settled (its earlier history was marred by bitter factional and personal conflicts) the U.A.W. became for a time the largest American trade union. Over 90 per cent of the eligible workers in the car industry are now members of it, and of the union's total membership of around 1.1 million, about one-half are in the car producers' plants.

Something both of the U.A.W.'s development and of current bargaining patterns in the U.S. motor industry is also reflected in the strike-trends traced by Diagram X/1. By international comparison, work stoppages generally in America are fairly frequent and unusually long. This pattern is related to several features of the growth of U.S. industrial relations. Mass union organization is comparatively recent, and stable collective relations are still in the making, at least in a number of major industries. Inter-union rivalry (like that at one time prominent between A.F. of L. and C.I.O. organizations) has predisposed union leaders to militancy as an organizational weapon—a predisposition exacerbated by strong employer hostility that lasted well into the Second World War. Whereas centralized or industry-wide collective bargaining apparently tends to reduce strikes (perhaps by taking labour costs out of competition), the structure of collective bargaining in America is still relatively decentralized despite the growth of pattern bargaining. There is the traditional 'business unionism' of American labour: union industrial action is not so tempered by political involvement as it often is in Europe, and gains have been much more sought by bargaining than by pressure for social legislation. And there is a public acceptance of trials of economic strength with which can be associated the state's unwillingness to make full use of its not inconsiderable power to intervene in labour disputes.

By comparison with other American industries, however, the motor industry is not now a prominent strike performer. The industry's strike-liability reached one peak in the years when the U.A.W. was fighting for recognition, another at the end of the War, and thereafter only became notable in years when major contracts were being re-negotiated. Apart from these years, the industry's strike performance (at least in the post-war period) has been well below that of steel, construction, and the other metalworking industries. Thus the official strike records for the motor industry—as is shown in our Diagram—allow a rough division into three historical phases. The first phase runs up to the mid-1930s: before the development of mass union organization, stoppages certainly occurred, but there is no consolidated record of them, and in total they do not seem to have been important or numerous. It is not until 1933 that the number of strikes occurring in any one year rose above twenty, and that the total of striker-days rose significantly. But the frequency of stoppages rose steadily in the early 1930s, and the incidence was at a consistently higher level than ever before, reflecting the growing unrest and discontent of that period.

The second phase covers the decade until the end of the War, and is marked by great fluctuations both in the number and size of strikes. Up to the organization of Ford in 1941, the overall incidence of stoppages had been declining again, but these years were marked by numerous 'wildcat' strikes in violation of contracts—due both to the pent-up enthusiasm of the period and to the factional struggles within the automobile workers' union. The number of strikes reached an all-time high of some 230 in 1944, and striker-days reached a similar record peak of fifteen million in 1946. As in the British industry, the War years were notable for a progressive increase in both the number and duration of strikes, which culminated in the wave of labour unrest affecting many industries in 1945-46. Settlements arising out of this early post-war period mark the onset of the third phase.

This third phase is characterized by pattern bargaining and long-term contracts, the fluctuations in the strike-incidence from year to year being attributable to the specific issues arising in particular negotiations. It is during this period that two levels of strike-causation seem to become—at least in principle—distinguishable. Basic contract negotiations by the International Union may be accompanied by full-scale strikes in all of a firms' plants, and it is these full-scale strikes which account for most of the incidence of the peak years of 1950 (Chrysler), 1955 (G.M. and Ford), 1958 (G.M. and Chrysler), and 1961 (G.M. and Ford). These contract bargaining peaks, arising from both national and local negotiations, are in addition to—or seem to be superimposed upon—a basic or 'residual level' of strike activity, which remained fairly constant throughout the 1950s at an annual figure of around a hundred stoppages, involving between one-half and three-quarters of a million striker-days. This 'residual' activity may be attributed both to disputes leading to the clarification of strikeable issues in the contracts and to 'wildcats' not supported by any union authority—but in what proportion is unknown. At any rate, it is clear that the very effective American bargaining machinery, and its accompanying grievance-settlement procedures, have by no means quite eliminated the small unauthorized strike.

While data is not available to allow recent comparison of strike-liability between firms, it is known that there are considerable differences among them. For example, according to company figures, over the five-year period from 1950-54, the total of 'lost time' per man due to stoppages in Ford plants was just under 75 hours. (This figure, incidentally, was higher than the relative strike-incidence of British Ford and Briggs Bodies together during that time, which included this group's biggest post-war stoppages.) However only fourteen of U.S. Ford's 'lost' hours were unauthorized or in violation of contract. And comparable time 'lost' for General Motors was less than three hours, only two of which were unauthorized. This low figure suggests another British analogy: and both U.S. Ford's and G.M.'s figures here must mainly represent the distribution of the 'residual' strike-activity referred to above, since in these years there were no major stoppages over contract re-negotiation at either company. The Chrysler plants are also remembered as being subject to many unauthorized stoppages during the early and mid-1950s, while such strikes have re-appeared at some General Motors plants in recent years. It seems clear that small short stoppages, if they are not such a prominent feature of the post-war labour scene in America as they have been in Britain, are far from unknown there.

Considering the strike-history of the American industry as a whole, two features are worth noting. The first is the tendency for strike-liability and output to rise and fall together. The peaks of strike-frequency, striker days and production coincide (in the War years, of course, output figures are incomplete), with the major exception of the contract negotiation years of 1958 and 1961. Unlike the British experience, however, strike-incidence falls off sharply with the onset of recession: it cannot be said that strikes have been useful to the American industry for filling in slumps—apart from expiry dates of labour contracts not always being accommodating in this regard. The second feature of note is that, despite the establishment of stable collective relations in the industry, its strike-incidence has since 1950 fluctuated around double the pre-1937 level of striker-days. After the wartime peak, the number of strikes increased persistently until at least 1959, when it fell off—but still remains well above the pre-1937 level. In short, contrary to some generalizations, successful organization and stable union politics, combined with employer acceptance, very systematic collective bargaining, and some legal controls, are far from having caused car workers' strikes to 'wither away' altogether.

(B) BARGAINING IN THE U.S. INDUSTRY: SYSTEM AND RESULTS

As dominating the largest of all motor industries, it is perhaps worthwhile to go into some detail on the U.S. autobomile firms' labour arrangements. In 1963, there were about 460,000 production workers engaged on the automotive operations of the five main U.S. producers—a drop of some 75,000 on the comparable figure for 1957. Of these, 5 or 6 per cent were women—much the same proportion as in the British industry.[1] This is one indication that, despite the size of the American vehicle output, the technology of car production remains fairly constant across national frontiers. There are, at any rate, few visible differences between American and British assembly plants, and the British visitor to an American plant is surprised only by the familiarity of his surroundings. Some of the older plants are larger and multi-storied, but the internal layout, processes, and pace of production in both these and the newer, smaller plants do not differ observably from the British pattern. Differences in dress, jargon, and the size or opulence of the product are not basic to the industry's technique.[2]

[1] Data on employment and wages in this section are taken from two wage surveys undertaken by the U.S. Department of Labour's Bureau of Labour Statistics: *B.L.S.Report No. 128* of July 1957; *B.L.S. Bulletin No. 1393* of April 1963. Other information about the wage structure has been taken from R. M. McDonald, *Collective Bargaining in The Automobile Industry*, (Yale, 1963).

[2] A recent study compared labour productivity in the car industries of several countries. Making certain assumptions and statistical adjustments, this concluded that labour productivity (in terms of vehicles produced per employee per annum) in U.S.A. was in 1950 three times as great, and in 1959 twice as great as in the U.K. The main reasons for these contrasts are not to be found in differences in pace of work and work content in the assembly plants. Nor indeed, does there appear to be any simple explanation, though the economies of scale no doubt have much to do with the contrast. See A. Silberston, 'Problems involved in international

Industrial Relations in Foreign Car Firms

Two main features of collective bargaining in the American motor industry distinguish it from the British national negotiations: first, the long-term nature of the resultant agreements—which enables a breathing-space for thought—and second, the formal integration of local or plant agreements into the process. The institution of the long-term 'package deal' agreement for the U.S. car industry was a major innovation pioneered by G.M. and the U.A.W. in a two-year agreement of 1948, and a five-year agreement of 1950—the radical nature of which may have been obscured by later criticism of the 'soft' 'General Motors era', which some American commentators hold the contracts to have initiated or represented. At any rate, too much can be made of the company basis of bargaining. The parts of a contract negotiation 'round' are not unrelated; there is a well-defined system of 'pattern bargaining' over basic economic issues, whereby the key settlement reached with one firm sets the standard for agreement with other firms. This is a logical development in an industry having a few, highly competitive producers, and one main union—which has itself applied a national strategy to its separate negotiations.

'Pattern bargaining' did not become established until after the War, hastened and perhaps encouraged by the wage-settling procedures of the War Labour Board. For more than a decade the union then managed to pick off the companies one at a time, and this success put pattern bargaining under increasing strain. There was a brief 'exchange of information' between Ford and General Motors during bargaining in the boom year of 1955—which did not, however, lead to effective co-ordination between them. But in 1958, company co-operation moved firmly and unambiguously in the direction of 'parallel bargaining'—in which Chrysler now also became involved. The tactic was an open one and it succeeded: there was at that time little chance that the threat of a 'focused' strike against one company would have the same effect as in 1955 because the stoppage would have come at the end of a poor sales season with stocks of unsold cars at a high level. But the continuation of parallel bargaining is by no means assured: apart from the companies' general caution in the face of public anti-trust policy, in 1961 the union outflanked the firms. When presented with more or less identical offers from the Big Three, the union induced the smaller firm of American Motors to set a substantially higher pattern in return for concessions in the 'work-rules' area. And in 1964, with sales booming, there was a return of the familiar pattern settlements, when Chrysler broke under threat of a strike.

comparisons of labour productivity in the automobile industry' in *Labour Productivity*, J. T. Dunlop and V. P. Diatchenko ed. (McGraw-Hill, 1964).

Pattern bargaining is about basic economic issues, but some matters are reserved for local settlement at the plant level—amongst the most important being 'production standards' (work-loads) seniority provisions and union facilities. The fairly extensive strikes of 1964 took place over local issues, but with the International[1] Union's support—after the basic contracts had been negotiated but before they became operatively embodied in local agreements (which led to quips about the U.A.W.'s new 'settle now and strike later' tactics). At the local level, bargaining is a continuing process, which merely reaches a climax in contract re-negotiation periods. However, issues may sometimes be allowed to accumulate, and a certain amount of 'horsetrading' can be conducted when the International Union is called in over a 'strikeable issue'—a process which has brought complaints from the firms about the use of strikeable issues to alter non-strikeable terms of basic agreements.

On the union side, there is separate machinery for dealing with each firm. For example, a General Motor Council, of union delegates from each of that firm's plant locals, co-ordinates demands and formulates policies, assisted by functional sub-councils (for body, foundry, stamping, tool-and-die departments, and so on). These sub-councils also elect the Negotiating Committee which participates with the International Union officials at the bargaining table. The work of the Councils is guided and co-ordinated by a system of parallel International Union departments. In short, the U.A.W. Executive Board formulates the basic economic programmes, which are subject to a ratification procedure; and the function of the Councils is to develop sets of proposals which incorporate both these basic demands and more detailed proposals which originate in the plant locals.

The union's structure thus provides a system of direct communication between the workplace organization and the central leadership, which is in turn organized to deal directly with the individual company (though difficulties with the positions of special groups—skilled trades in particular—within an industrial union have also led to the creation of committees to represent these interests in the formation of union policy). On the firms' side the industrial relations machinery at G.M. is also typical. The Board's Policy Committees are advised by functional policy groups headed by senior executives, and one of these groups handles labour relations. The central labour relations staff are responsible for negotiating and administering the national agreement and handling attendant grievances. While each division and plant has its own

[1] Many American unions call their central organization 'International', since—like the U.A.W.—they also organize in Canada.

specialist staff which negotiates local agreements, although all these are subject to central approval.

As regards the results of this bargaining system, the most marked differences between the American and British industries are perhaps in their wage systems and structure. In America, incentive methods of payment are largely absent (in the 1957 and 1963 official wage surveys, over 98 per cent of the production workers were found to be paid on a time basis). The change from piece- to time-rates took place mainly during the 1930s, and partly as a result of union pressure. The small proportion of workers in the tool-room and skilled maintenance trades are frequently paid by a system of differential pay grades, but most workers are paid, in each plant, according to a single rate set for a wide range of work.

Associated with the broad job-classifications is the relative lack of pay differentials between the main occupational groupings. Most production jobs do not lend themselves to meaningful differentiation; and in an industry where minor job changes occur almost daily, wide classifications of work (e.g. grinder, assembler, checker, etc.) present fewer areas of friction. Rate-fixing and formal job-evaluation processes are thus not a feature of the wage-system. But the establishment of rates for new jobs (or for radically changed jobs) is a 'strikeable issue' in the labour contracts, so that disputes in this area are reserved for bargaining and are not subject to settlement by arbitration. However, the main area of negotiation at the plant level is 'production standards' (now that 'seniority' arrangements are largely settled).

It is another distinctive feature of the pay-structure that individual or personal differentials are highly circumscribed. Union pressure has eliminated 'merit ranges' and sex-differentials on production jobs. Automatic or partially-automatic movement through their pay grades has been established for some skilled workers. However, the gap between general starting and 'final' rates, and the length of probationary periods, have been sharply reduced. These narrow differentials can be illustrated in a general way. The wage survey of 1963, for example, showed that three-fifths of production workers earned between $2.70 and $2.90 an hour—a range of less than 8 per cent. To encompass a comparable proportion of British motor workers, an earnings range of more than 50 per cent would be required. Moreover, in the American case fewer than 1 per cent of operatives earned less than $2.50, and fewer than 2 per cent earned $3.50 or more.

Changes in the U.S. industry's occupational differentials have, however, been taking place. From its earliest days, the U.A.W.'s policy—as an industrial union—was to raise the rates of the lowest-paid categories of worker. And up to 1955, general wage increases in the industry tended progressively to narrow occupational differentials, as all such increases had taken the form of 'across the board', cents-per-hour advances. The quarterly automatic wage-adjustments incorporated in the 'escalator' clauses of long-term agreements to meet cost-of-living increases remain on this basis. But since the 1955 contracts, the annual 'improvement factor' also provided by long-term agreements to adjust wages in line with productivity increases has been changed to a percentage basis with a fixed cents-per-hour minimum. The effect of this has been to slow down or halt the decline in differentials. And following unofficial strikes and 'breakaways' amongst the skilled workers in protest against the deterioration of their wages relative to production workers, the effect of flat-rate increases on their differentials has been more than offset by special increases for skilled men, which have now become a regular feature of contract settlements. In short, wage differentials between production workers and skilled tradesmen in general have been maintained recently, while within each of these groups the differentials have narrowed.

Inter-plant and inter-firm wage differentials have also been reduced since the 1930s. With the notable exception of G.M., geographical differences between the plant wage-levels of each firm have been eliminated; and the 1964 contract between G.M. and the U.A.W. provided for an 'equity fund' to eliminate the geographical differentials between its plants during 1965. However, a possible qualification to the levelling of inter-firm and inter-plant differentials follows from the emergence of a new policy on the U.A.W.'s part, which implies the abandonment of the principle of the standard rate. This new policy was embodied in the union's profit-sharing proposals of 1958, since the union was in effect then sponsoring the idea of gearing 'compensation' levels at least partially to each firm's ability to pay. But it remains to be seen whether this was more than a temporary bargaining gambit on the U.A.W.'s part.

But the levelling of inter-company (and thus inter-plant) wage differences has in any case to be qualified by the effects of differing fringe benefits, which placed American Motors (as well as Studebaker and Kaiser-Willys when they were still producing cars) clearly at the top of the 'employee compensation' league. This feature is clearly in contrast with the tendency in most industries for wages to vary directly with the size and profitability of firms: the explanation is held to lie, on the one hand, in the inability of the smaller companies to absorb a major strike and hence their tendency to bow before union pressure, and on the other hand to variations in the bargaining efficiency with which managements have met their labour counterparts.[1] In any event the rapid growth in supplementary and indirect forms of worker compensation has been one of the most notable developments on the wage front over the past twenty-five years. The system of private benefit programmes (again in contrast with the British industry) today accounts for about one-fifth of total payroll expenditure in the industry. This includes paid holidays and vacations (which, with the exception of Ford, are commutable into extra cash) as well as premium payments for limited overtime and shift working. However, it particularly includes the cost of pension and welfare plans, where the union has been instrumental in the development of private pension, life and health insurance, and supplementary unemployment benefit schemes all designed to supplement basic rate programmes. The 'S.U.B.' is especially notable as the partial embodiment of the union's demand for an 'annual guaranteed wage' in defence against technological or other forms of unemployment.

To sum up, labour relations in the American motor industry seem to be comparatively rational, forthright, and enterprising. A primary factor in their present pattern was the sudden and viable development of a trade union uncluttered by tradition, with a young and vigorous leadership, originally nurtured in protective legislation and public approval, which nevertheless had to fight hard (and on more than one front) to establish itself. These factors seem more important in accounting for the success of the U.A.W. than the mere fact that it is an industrial union, for in many ways the existence of special groups within the organization has been a problem to the leadership. But the U.A.W. has concentrated on the major disabilities of motor workers—unstable earnings and job insecurity—and has enforced a firm centralized control over major policy areas while at the same time allowing scope for the continuance of considerable local autonomy over matters—such as 'seniority' and working arrangements—which are of great importance at the plant level.

As in other countries, differences in labour relations and strike-liability between different firms are present, but these have been minimized by the superimposition of pattern bargaining, and by long-term contracts. Strikes are largely kept under the control of the union throughout the periods when a contract is in force, and are guided to serve the interests of the union as well as its members when large issues are at stake. The arrangement has enabled managements and the union to reflect constructively about the problems of the industry and of ways to handle them—so that several initiatives have come from the biggest firm itself. Bargaining campaigns are conducted on an elaborate scale in full public view, and may extend for a

[1] See R. M. McDonald, *op. cit.*, Chapters 6 and 7.

period of up to a year before a contract is due to expire, with increasingly formal soundings on the rival programmes and intentions. In these circumstances the relatively high strike-liability which, on the average, results is probably less an indication of damaging conflict than a measure of the strength of the system. It is, indeed, openly acclaimed as such. But even considered on their own, and without benefit of international comparison, strike-patterns in the American car firms are clearly less attributable to the industry's technology than to broader features of the country's industrial relations history and arrangements.

(C) GERMANY

Next in size to the American Motor industry, and with an output of some two-and-a-half million cars a year only slightly exceeding the British, is the West German automobile industry. Moreover, the German motor industry, unlike its competitors in North America and Europe, has had a record of almost uninterrupted growth since the Second World War. One substantial firm—Borgward—has gone bankrupt, but this was not due to any general crisis in the markets for German cars, and other firms have not even experienced the marked seasonal swings in demand which have become characteristic of some other motor industries in recent years. In some respects, the German industry resembles that of Britain in its structure, however. The biggest single producer is still Volkswagen (which is remarkable, among other things, for having two-fifths of its shares publicly-owned), but two American subsidiaries also contribute largely to West German output—German Ford and Opel, which is controlled by General Motors but is (unlike Vauxhall's relation to British Ford) rather the bigger producer of the two. Daimler-Benz, which produces Mercedes cars as well as lorries, compares with the Jaguar group as a maker of quality cars, though its output is larger and it also has certain co-operative arrangements with Volkswagen—which in turn now also controls Auto Union. B.M.W. and N.S.U. also have small shares of the market.

The general industrial relations system of the Federal Republic is highly legalistic by comparison with that of Great Britain. Collective agreements are contracts legally enforceable by special Labour Courts, so that a strike during the period for which any collective agreement has been signed is illegal, and actions for damages have been successfully brought against unions which have been alleged to have ignored this proviso. Collective agreements are usually signed on a regional basis for particular industries, and may be extended by law to apply to firms which are not members of employers' associations. All enterprises above a certain size are required by law to have a Works Council elected by the employees, which has specified rights to consultation on matters of labour policy and, to some extent, economic policy: the German law of 'co-determination' precludes employers from determining unilaterally certain matters which in Britain would be reserved as 'managerial functions'. In larger undertakings, a proportion of the Supervisory Board (which, under the West German system of management organization, stands above the full-time Board of Management and appoints the latter) is to consist of workers' nominees; and there is in addition an economic advisory committee of employee representatives. So that both the area which in Britain would be covered by voluntary collective bargaining and that which would be covered, if at all, by joint consultation are in Germany subject to legal procedures.

A general agreement signed in 1954, between the D.G.B. (the West German T.U.C.) and the central employers' federation (the B.D.A.) recommends a standard conciliation procedure to their affiliated organizations, and includes a draft text which has been incorporated in most industrial agreements, including those affecting the motor firms. But some of the questions which would be matters for bargaining or attempted bargaining in England are in any case the subject of actual legal regulation in the West German instance. Thus for most of the post-war period overtime working has been effectively limited by a legal maximum working week of forty-eight hours. (The standard work-week in the metal trades was forty-four until 1962, and will be reduced to forty in 1967.) On the other hand dismissals, whether of individual workers on disciplinary or similar grounds, or of groups of workers on economic grounds, are effectively restricted by a right of appeal to the Labour Courts. In the case of a proposed reduction in the labour force employed, for instance, an employer would be compelled to demonstrate the economic justification of any redundancy involved: a Court might accept that a cut in total hours worked was unavoidable but order short-time working instead of dismissals. And even if it accepted the need for dismissals to occur, the workers' representatives might appeal against the selection of individuals. All in all, the dismissal of workers is a rather difficult matter, and this combined with the restriction on overtime working has given a great deal more security and stability of employment and earnings to German workers, and compelled the German motor firms to plan their expansions very cautiously. On the other hand, the system also acts as a deterrent to unofficial strikes, since the Labour Courts would not support an appeal against the dismissal of unofficial strikers.

Most of the West German motor firms belong to their appropriate regional employers' federation for the engineering industry, although their personnel officers (like their British opposite numbers) meet periodically to exchange informations and views. However their employees are organized by a single giant 'industrial' union for the metalworking trades. This is I.G. Metall (Industrie Gewerkschaft Metall), whose more than two million members make it probably the largest trade union in the non-Communist world. And although I.G. Metall has a well-staffed system of regional offices, it has no special section of membership, or specially appointed officers, for the automobile industry—or for any other industrial group except the steel industry. So that no separate system of collective bargaining exists for the motor industry: the regional engineering agreements apply to the car firms, with the exception of Volkswagen, which has, for historical reasons, a separate agreement of its own. When the Volkswagenwerk at Wolfsburg was re-opened after the War, and under especially difficult conditions, it was virtually the only engineering works functioning in its locality and the new employers' associations made no objection to a separate agreement. I.G. Metall has, however, since attempted to get separate agreements with other motor firms—partly because, as in England though probably not to quite the same extent, these are generally paying wages considerably above the agreed rates for the metal-working industries—but has failed. In the case of German Ford, which was at one time—like British Ford—'non-federated', the union's approach was met by Ford's joining the regional employers' association. In the case of Daimler-Benz, an official strike of the firm in 1963 was retaliated by a general lockout of the metalworking industries in the Baden-Württemberg region—the first lockout of German workers since the 1930s.

The 1963 strike, however, arose from no causes which were specific to the motor industry, but was virtually the result of a strategic decision by I.G. Metall: the union believed that many firms in the engineering and allied industries could afford to pay agreed rates considerably above those provided under the regional agreements, and deliberately selected two major concerns in Stuttgart—Daimler-Benz and the electrical firm of Bosch—which were obviously highly profitable and in which union membership was strong, as targets for a policy of selective pressure in support of a general wage-increase demand. This precipitated a regional lockout of some 300,000 metalworkers for several days and ended in a compromise; it was also the biggest industrial stoppage in West Germany since the War. In fact, of course, strikes are rare events in the Federal Republic, and unofficial strikes are almost unknown; and to these rules the motor industry is no exception. And this has remained true despite the virtual disappearance of unemployment and the emergence of a severe labour shortage (the German car firms are increasingly dependent on foreign labour for any expansion of their labour force, and already have substantial proportions of Italian, Spanish and even Turkish workers).

The very low liability of West German workers to strike may be explained in various ways. Certainly, their relative security and the high rate of growth in their real earnings, and therefore the rapid improvement in their living standards when compared with their previous conditions (immediately after the War, say) are no doubt background factors—though prosperity in other countries has not always automatically led to industrial peace. It is also commonly said that German workers are 'well-disciplined', but this does not appear to be demonstrated (in other respects than their low strike-liability) to quite the same extent as seems widely supposed. In Cologne, for instance, the writers were told that there was a high Monday absentee rate and that workers were reluctant to work overtime, although it was possible that they were more acquisitive in Stuttgart. But in Stuttgart, their information was that absenteeism was quite a large problem (to the extent that there were local jokes—'How many workers work at Mercedes?' 'Nearly all of them') substantially because a large part of the labour force had smallholdings in the surrounding countryside, and took days off to look after the land, particularly at harvest time. There was, in fact a sort of operative called an 'Industriebauer' (i.e. an industrial farmer). However, no doubt—it was said—things were different at Rüsselsheim. But at Rüsselsheim—and so on.

The writers' impression is that some part of the West German freedom from industrial conflict to date must be set down to the system of legal workers' representation. Some West German socialists are disappointed in the general system of 'co-determination', although in heavy industry the provision for workers' representation in management is more extensive than in manufacturing generally (including motors). But this may be because they expected it to effect a total transformation in management-labour relations—indeed, a virtual disappearance of the distinction between the two sides. However, the system of legal Works Councils does seem to have had a not inconsiderable effect. In many works the Councils are clearly an important influence. They provide a formal vehicle for negotiation supplementary to that provided by collective agreements, a formal procedure for dealing with the grievances of individuals or small groups of workers, and a formal mechanism for consultation on management economic policy. Several managements in the motor industry clearly attach considerable importance to them—and to the quarterly general meetings of employees to which they report—as channels of communication with the workers. Equally the trade unions, though they once had fears that the Works Councils might become a rival organization to themselves, now regard them as an established and significant vehicle for representing workers' interests and devote some trouble to training their members on them (the workers' representatives are almost invariably trade unionists), to servicing them, and to maintaining a link between them and the unions' own 'Vertrauensmänner' (who are almost, but not quite, shop stewards).

Beyond such things, there are the usual differences between firms, such as one finds in Britain and the U.S.A. The highest wages appear to be paid by Volkswagen, although according to trade unionists actual working conditions are best at Auto Union (now the former's subsidiary). Ford has a rigid time-wage system, with eight grades and a half-yearly bonus paid on attendance. Opel dominates what is almost a company town at Rüsselsheim, but unlike Vauxhall has kept its production bonus system (though the bonus bears a much smaller relation to basic wage-rates than under most British incentive schemes) because in circumstances under which it is difficult to dismiss workers it thinks some positive incentive worth retaining. Volkswagen also has a bonus system: however, this no longer bears any direct relation to production, but is determined from time to time on the general prosperity of the firm. Mercedes has both time-wage and 'task-wage' systems, the rates under each being reviewed annually in accordance with productivity. And so on.

There seems to be a very considerable difference in the degree of union membership between firms—Ford, for instance, having a low percentage of trade unionists and Opel a high one (again, the reverse situation to that of their allied companies in Britain). But all firms seem much more paternalistic than their British equivalents. It is common, for instance, to provide workers with company housing, to supplement public pensions substantially, to pay bonuses for such occasions as Christmas and for personal eventualities of various kinds, to give holidays for such family occasions as marriages, births and so on, and to organize various social and welfare services—extending down to frequent children's parties. And in general of course, expenditure on 'fringe benefits' is much higher than in the British motor industry. This area, together with that of the special bonuses of different kinds, is one that the companies have tried to keep out of negotiation with the union, though they have not infrequently discussed and determined these questions with the Works Councils. In the union's view it represents as much a part of wages as do basic rates, and ought therefore to be equally negotiable through collective agreements. This is one potential area of future industrial conflict.

(D) FRANCE

The French automobile industry consists essentially of four firms—two big, Renault and Citroën (in which is now incorporated Panhard), and two medium-sized, Simca and Peugeot. Renault is remarkable in being a completely nationalized undertaking—which has nevertheless a co-operative agreement with the family firm of Peugeot. Simca is controlled by the American firm of Chrysler (having already had connections with Fiat of Italy). As in the German case, the pattern of industrial relations in the French motor industry has pronounced national characteristics. Collective bargaining takes place largely through legally-supported, regional 'conventions collectives' (for the metalworking trades in this case) which are extended by law to firms not affiliated to the signatory employer association in the industry concerned (and these firms include Citroën). There is a legal system of 'conseils d'entreprise' (or 'comités d'établissement')—elected works councils which are mandatory in all firms with more than fifty employees—and a supplementary system of elected workers' delegates ('délégués du personnel') which is again required by law in all firms with more than ten workers.

There seems to be a high degree of employer solidarity in France (the affiliated motor firms all belong to a single giant employer association for the private enterprise engineering and metallurgical industries) which is not matched on the workers' side. There is, in fact, a multi-unionism of a very different (and more divisive) form than in Britain—the different metalworkers' unions which cover the automobile industry being split on roughly political and religious lines. While apart from the Communist and Socialist unions, and the union originally associated with the Catholic social movement, there are several so-called 'Independent' unions. These include a would-be industrial union for motor workers, which seems in fact confined largely to Renault, another separatist union based on Simca (which seems to have a somewhat dubious independence), yet another 'confédération des cadres', composed of supervisory or higher-skilled employees, and so on. It is by no means unusual for one group or another—even for one of the major unions—to refuse to sign a particular collective agreement; and it is said that this often occurs because the union concerned knows that the contract will be implemented anyway, once the other unions have signed it, but wants to make capital out of criticizing the agreement. This was apparently a common tactic of the C.G.T. (Communist) union at one time, but has also been adopted occasionally by the Christian union—the Catholic union federation in France[1] seems to have been moving to the left since the mid-1950s—as well as by other groups.

The divisions between the unions—as well, apparently, as some weariness amongst the workers with the strike-waves which affected the metalworking industries in the late 1940s and early 1950s, and which were partly politically inspired—no doubt accounts for the comparatively low percentage of union members among French auto-workers. Estimates vary; and there is a tendency on the part of one or two union groups to claim as members all the workers whom the other unions have not. But it seems fairly clear that only a minority of the French motor workers are dues-paying union members; and in one or two plants the minority may actually be fractional. Which does not mean that the non-members may not follow union leadership, particularly in voting for the plant delegates and works councils, and otherwise on the occasions when the major unions are united. In an economic sense, the French trade union movement still seems in some ways at a relatively primitive level of development, in which the distinction between trade unionist and non-unionist seems less sharp than it is, say, in Britain or the U.S.A. Because of past political conflicts, the number of ex-members is very high.

But in any case, the frequency and incidence of strikes in the French motor industry also seems relatively low. There has, apparently, been a considerable decline in the strike-liability of the automobile workers since the mid-1950s. In fact, the strike-incidence of the French economy in recent years has been concentrated—despite the traditional radicalism of the French metalworkers, especially in the Paris region—not in manufacturing industry, as in Britain on the whole, but in public services. The reason for this seems to be that, whereas wages in manufacturing have risen rapidly with the fast growth of French production and general full employment (a substantial proportion of French motor workers, though less than in the West German industry, are foreigners) the wages of public servants and employees in public services have been held back in the interests of national anti-inflation policy. So that the automobile industry represents an area of comparative industrial peace.

There seem also to be two background factors in this situation, however. Although the French motor industry has been very vulnerable to fluctuations in demand in recent years—there was, for

---

[1] This federation (the former C.F.T.C.) has changed its title from 'Christian' to 'Democratic' (C.F.D.T.) to remove its official link with Catholicism, but the change is currently subject to legal dispute.

instance, quite a sharp recession in the automobile trade over 1963–64—the French car firms mostly seem to pay a considerable attention to the security of their employees. The French automobile operative's pay is probably particularly exposed to such fluctuations because, even more than in the British industry, it depends substantially on regular overtime working: normal working hours were forty-eight per week throughout the French industry at the time of the writers' inquiries (although discussions for a reduction were proceeding, at least in Renault) despite the existence of a 'legal' standard week of forty hours.

But the Renault agreements include provision for a fund financed by the firm for the 'régularization des ressources'—to make up the pay of operatives in whole or in part when working hours are cut back. This proviso was specifically introduced to offset seasonal fluctuations in activity. The same agreements also provide for hourly-paid workers to be transferred to monthly salaried status after periods of service which vary with the grade concerned. Simca has a category of 'ouvriers commissionés' which has a similar degree of security, and to which operatives may be transferred after periods of satisfactory service. And Citroën, at the time of the writers' inquiries, was introducing a similar system. Citroën appears particularly security-conscious (no doubt an effect of its traumatic experience of 1933–34, when the firm was bankrupted and André Citroën himself died suddenly—the company is now owned by Michelin); it seems to have deliberately kept its expansion well within the growth of demand and to have been especially cautious in adventuring into the unstable export market. But Peugeot, while it has had no formal system for regularizing the employment of its operatives, also seems in fact to have maintained a high degree of stability of employment—having, for instance, a very high proportion of long-service operatives.

The second background factor is probably the pace-setting effect of the famous 'accords Renaults' themselves. The first company agreement signed by Renault goes back to 1950, but the critical ones are the two-year agreements signed at intervals since 1955 which, apart from the clauses mentioned above and various other provisions of a progressive character, award an automatic minimum increase in wages of 4 per cent per year to distribute the benefits of technical progress. However, it seems symptomatic of the extent to which initiative in workplace labour relationships lies in the hands of management in France that the agreements contain no detailed wage-rates or joint procedures for determining job-classifications. Another symptom of the relative weakness of the unions at the workplace level appears to be the lower status which the French Works Councils seem to have as compared with those in Germany.

There are, again, substantial differences between companies. The generally progressive policies of Renault probably owe as much to the personalities of the firm's post-nationalization chief executive, M. Lefaucheux, and his successor M. Dreyfus, as to the fact of nationalization itself. Citroën was described by executives of other companies as a 'maison fermée'—*not* a closed shop (the degree of union organization seemed very low indeed) but a house that kept itself to itself. And there seemed to be an emphasis in managerial policy on personal relationships within the firm, despite its size; wage-rates were claimed to be individually determined, there is a merit bonus system, a great deal of attention is paid to selection for promotion from grade to grade, and so on. Peugeot is an old-established family firm, and shows many traces of it: the company's main works is near Belfort, isolated from the main complex of the industry in and around Paris, which has perhaps encouraged local paternalism (although the firm has not been quite strike-free—indeed, in 1955 it was involved in a general stoppage of its workers in support of a demand for a reduced working week). Simca was generally unpopular in union circles, and even officials of other firms described the Simca independent workers' association as a 'company union', while the Christian union had brought a complaint against the company—as well as against Citroën—for exercising 'undue influence' in elections to its Works Council. The firm seemed to show some traces of its former association with Ford (it acquired the latter's plant when Ford withdrew from France): it once had a payment-by-results system but has abandoned this for straight time-rates. And it is fairly clearly influenced by its old relation with Fiat.

(E) ITALY—FIAT

Fiat is perhaps the most interesting of all the major European motor producers—at least from the viewpoint of this study. The general theme of this Chapter has been the importance in automobile labour relationships of particular national systems of industrial relations, and the variations within each national pattern imposed by individual firms. In the Italian case these two characteristics come together. Alfa Romeo merits some attention as being a firm of a special kind: it is wholly owned by the engineering organization Finmeccania which is in turn controlled by the public holding company I.R.I. (the Institute of Industrial Reconstruction, a body formed in Fascist days to revitalize derelict industries—and on which the new British Industrial Reorganization Corporation is partially modelled). All profits of Alfa Romeo are ploughed back into the firm, and it runs

Industrial Relations in Foreign Car Firms

a progressive incentive scheme for its employees. But it and the other minor Italian car producers between them—Lancia and Ferrari—have only one sixth of total Italian motor vehicle output. The rest comes from Fiat, which is very much more than just another big motor firm. It is not only the biggest private enterprise in the Italian economy: it occupies a much more dominant position in Italian industry than does, say, even General Motors in that of the U.S.A.; and while two-thirds of its workers are employed in car production it also produces commercial vehicles, railway equipment, aircraft and marine engines, controls the O.M. engineering company, has associated civil engineering concerns, participates in other enterprises jointly with Finmeccania, and has a wide range of other engineering activities. Fiat, in fact, is an economic empire—thus occupying a key position in the Italian social order from other viewpoints than the strictly economic one.

The general structure of Italian labour relations is that a national central agreement, signed on the one hand by the formidable employers' association Confindustria and on the other hand by various trade union federations, lays down minimum wages by region and periodic 'cost of living' adjustments. Confindustria has also signed sectional agreements for certain industries, including the metal-working trades, which provide special wage-scales for the workers concerned and standard working weeks below the legal maximum. There is also a system of Works Councils in all enterprises with more than forty workers. And although this operates by collective agreement, and not by law, it nevertheless has a considerable importance —not least as an indicator of trends in the Italian labour movement. This is because of the highly political context in which Italian labour relations appear to operate. Though the Italian unions have not been really strong at the workplace level (in the Fiat plants, for instance, union members are certainly a minority, and the unions do not seem to have enough funds to pay strike benefit) the overwhelming majority of workers vote in Works Council elections, in which candidates stand as representative of rival union groups. As in France, there are Communist, Socialist and Catholic union federations, as well as 'Independent' unions: such a union (which has, like that in Simca, been described by officials of other organizations as a 'company' union) is particularly important in Fiat. And the result of works elections is closely watched—not least, by the employers themselves. The distribution of votes in Fiat Works Council polls seemed to be given almost as much attention as the firm's profit-and-loss account.

The history of labour relations in the Italian motor industry actually goes back to well before Fascist times. In 1906 there was a general, and semi-political, strike in Turin. At this time the now-defunct 'Itala' car company signed an agreement with the metal-workers' union F.I.O.M. (now Communist-dominated, but then a general organization) which provided a union shop, engagement of labour through the union only, a company-financed workers' housing and pension scheme, a Works Council and an arbitration procedure, together with a 'no-strike' clause guaranteed by a financial bond on both sides. Dissension in the union led to a later failure to renew the agreement; but the Works Council was preserved and became generally imitated in Italian industry after the First World War. But the present history of industrial relations in Fiat really dates from the events of 1948, when the world-wide conflict between Communist and non-Communist tendencies in the unions came to a head in Italy with a violent split between the factions in the previously-united trade union movement. A succession of events, including the formation of an alliance of then-minority anti-Communist groups in the unions, culminated in the attempted assassination of the Communist leader Togliatti, and was followed by a general strike called by the Communist union leadership. In Turin, a revolutionary 'Committee of Public Safety' was formed, and for several days the great Fiat Mirafiori works were held by sit-down strikers who also seized the firm's principal executives. After the strike's collapse, a succession of splits, alliances and counter-alliances in the unions finally crystallized into the present grouping. But for the management of Fiat, the experience seems to have been critical.

From then on, the firm appears to have evolved a tactic of isolating and weakening the Communist union by making substantial concessions, first to the Socialist and Catholic union representatives, and then, when an Independent union was re-formed at the works after a strike in 1954, also to the Independent union. In this tactic, the Communists effectively acquiesced by refusing to sign collective agreements at the works level; a major agreement for Fiat workers was made in 1956, despite the existence of an elaborate agreement for the metal trades generally, through the non-Communist representatives on the Works Council, and renewed in 1959. In essence, the company's concessions comprised a high-wage policy, a policy of 'committing' workers to the firm by elaborate training schemes and relative job security, and an extension of the firm's already substantial welfare and fringe benefits.

In detail, the Fiat wage-system includes first the basic rates laid down under the metal trades collective agreement and the cost-of-living bonus agreed centrally between the unions and Confindustria. But these only account for about half the normal wage: there is a separate structure of some fourteen detailed pay-rates in each of the separate Fiat plants (but controlled by the firm's head office) and a system of production bonuses negotiated with the Works Councils. This system includes both a small-group bonus and a general bonus for the plant concerned, each bonus being regulated so as to offset the naturally-different rates of productivity growth in various sections of the concern, and to limit the variation of bonuses as far as possible within a range of 5 or 10 per cent. But the total effect has been to produce a level of earnings very substantially above the average for engineering outside the firm. Relative job-security has been secured by giving preference to long-service employees and by transferring workers between the firms' diverse activities to offset a recession in any one branch—though the current dominance of car production has meant that the firm has had to respond to the severe short-term recessions which have affected the Italian car industry from time to time of late by heavy short-time working. The firm's 'fringe benefits' and welfare services are particularly extensive. The Fiat Employees' Mutual Benefit Association, for instance, now operates a very elaborate health service which extends not merely to workers but to their families, and pays grants for a variety of personal needs, including sickness, but also including such occasions as weddings, funerals, etc. Its annual expenditure is some £8,000,000, for about 130,000 employees.

All this seems to have achieved a substantial effect. Apart from an incident in 1962, Fiat's workers have not been affected by any major strike since 1954. The Communist vote in the annual Works Council elections declined from about 75 per cent in 1948 to between 20 and 25 per cent since the mid-1950s, giving way at first to the Socialist and Christian unions. But the vote for the Independent union's representatives has risen since the mid-1950s so that by 1960 it had secured the largest number of Council members. Of late, however, the Socialist union appears to have made some recovery—it and the Christian metalworkers' union have usually collaborated in negotiations and the Christian union has been a fairly consistent advocate of bargaining at the workplace level.

Fiat, however, has also been relatively flexible in its labour policy, as it demonstrated in 1962—the year of Italy's 'opening to the left' in national politics. And it was to some large extent the development of agreements through the Works Councils that produced that year's crisis in Italian industrial relations. The unions had increasingly come to feel that this development was undermining their own national agreements. In the summer of 1962 the metalworkers' unions launched a series of strikes ('token' strikes, they would be called in England—general stoppages of the engineering industry, each lasting a day or two) in support of demands for higher wages, shorter standard hours, and particularly for direct bargaining with the unions at the workplace level—not instead of, but supplementary to the national agreements. Fiat workers began to be drawn into the movement. I.R.I. started to negotiate on these demands for the sector of the metal industries under public control; and almost immediately Fiat followed suit, without waiting for Confindustria's approval. The first Fiat agreement providing union recognition in plant bargaining was signed only by the Socialist and Independent unions; but after further strikes an improved agreement was produced which was signed by all the unions, including the Communist grouping. Fiat's move initiated a virtual landslide of 'agreements on account' by private enterprise engineering firms; and in the end Confindustria was forced to negotiate a new general agreement with the various engineering unions, which provided not only wage and hour concessions but a new system of 'articulated bargaining'— with separate functions laid down for negotiations at the national, industrial and plant levels respectively. Fiat thus demonstrated that it would rather accommodate itself to a movement to the left among its workers than risk its industrial peace.

(F) SWEDEN, JAPAN, SOME OTHERS—AND A COMPARATIVE NOTE

Other non-Communist countries which produce cars in a small way (as opposed to assembling them from imported parts) include Holland and Australia. In each case the motor firms represent no significant variation from the specific national patterns of industrial relations within which they operate, and these patterns are probably so well known that they can be dealt with very briefly indeed. In Australia, where the Holden car is produced by a General Motors subsidiary, the system of national compulsory arbitration lays down a basic minimum wage and 'skill margins' above it, but there is a considerable amount of supplementary collective negotiation within this framework. What is interesting in this case is that the American U.A.W. has sent an official to testify for the Australian union in a hearing of Holden wage-claims. The arrangement was made through the International Metal Workers' Federation, which is also setting up special consultative councils for the workers of 'international' car manufacturers, so that it may forecast some inter-country co-ordination in union activity in such companies.[1] The firm that produces the Dutch 'Daf' car is quite small and makes no departure from the general form of Dutch industrial relations policy, in which collective agreements at the industry level must be approved by a national

[1] At going to press, a bulletin of the first joint meetings of councils for G.M., Ford and Chrysler workers from sixteen unions in fourteen countries, held in June 1966, has been received.

central joint body of employer and union representative operating within a framework of broad government instruction on wage-policy principles, while the yield of piece-rates and incentive bonuses fixed at the plant must be kept within a nationally-determined margin over the industry wage-rates. However, the Swedish and Japanese situations merit some closer attention.

The Swedish firms of Volvo and Saab also have their basic labour contract regulated by a national pattern—in this case of fixed-term agreements (two years has been the most common period) arranged through highly centralized bargaining. So that the periodic agreement on minimum wage-rates and general wage-revisions for the metal-working industries (which covers the motor firms) has usually had its main content determined by previous central negotiations between the powerful national union and employer federations, L.O. and S.A.F. However, the Swedish situation is perhaps particularly interesting because the Swedish system of labour relations and wage-negotiations has in recent years been quite widely put forward as a potential model for the improvement of industrial relations in Britain, and—more specifically—because the Swedish car firms resemble the British 'federated' companies (and are unlike those in most national automobile industries) in having a very large proportion of their workers on piece-rates or 'payment-by-results'. Some 90 per cent of Saab's car-production operatives, for instance, are paid on incentive or bonus systems related to output.

Collective organization is both extensive and highly integrated. There is no formal 'union shop', but union membership seems generally accepted as a behavioural norm, and approximates to 100 per cent for the car firms' manual workers, notwithstanding that these apparently include proportionately more women than in Britain, as well as a large minority of foreigners. All car plant employees belong to a single large union (for the metalworking sector) which has a quite centralized structure based on 'works clubs' —factory branches which are not separated from the workplace representative system: so that the 'club chairman' in each plant is also the chief union negotiator, corresponding to the British chairman of a Works Committee. There is also a high degree of co-ordination within the parallel metalworking employers' association, which includes the car producers as member firms. Moreover, several aspects of labour relations besides general wage-movements are regulated by central agreements between the L.O. and S.A.F.—for instance, provisions for joint consultation through Works Councils elected via the union club, and arrangements to encourage the introduction of time-and-motion study, and to deal with disputes arising from it.

On the other hand, legal regulation is also distinctly more important, in industrial relations than in the British case. For instance, working hours (of men, as well as women and juveniles) are controlled by law—so that the British car firms' system of night-shift working would be at least very difficult to get authority for in Sweden—and there is a legally enforceable 'right to organize'. Notably, of course, collective agreements have legal force, so that a strike or lock-out for their revision (or about their interpretation) is illegal for their stated duration. And there is a special Labour Court to supervise these matters, with power to levy damages on defaulting organizations or individuals (according to whether the stoppage is official or unofficial). However, it seems arguable to what extent the system of legal enforcement alone has contributed to the low frequency and incidence of strikes (the major risk of the Swedish conciliation system is the rare one of a major industry-wide or even— as was threatened in 1966—general stoppage during the periodic central negotiations). Maximum fines on workers, as opposed to unions, are not high—amounting only to the equivalent of three or four days' normal pay; so that the deterrent to unofficial strikes seems much less than to official ones. Action is not always taken against strikers—recently, one of foreign workers in a car firm went unpenalized; and there have also been small strikes of white-collar employees. Go-slows which do not reduce production more than 20 per cent appear to be within the law. And strikes on some potentially explosive issues which are not regulated in detail by collective agreements—for instance, work-loads or certain dismissals—may also be legal. While other means of pressure on managements are in any case, in the Swedish state of labour shortage, not ineffective: dissatisfied workers may threaten to leave the plant as individuals; in one car firm a whole paint shop's staff issued a Press advertisement for other jobs.

So far as the Swedish car firms are concerned, the major tangible contributant to industrial peace appears to be a very close joint control by the union and companies over earnings and efforts. Indeed, the tendency of earnings to 'drift' upwards, unevenly and irregularly, under piece-rate and P.B.R. systems with high productivity growth, seems to have been largely mastered (so that automobile workers' wages are no longer particularly high by comparison with those in engineering plants generally). Both firms have a simple rate-structure (with five steps in each of their plants) into which all tasks are fitted by job-evaluation. Bonus earnings are limited, either directly or by provision for re-study if earnings rise by more than was anticipated; while there are high 'fall-back' rates to guard earnings against output fluctuations. For certain categories of worker, 'merit rates' and quality bonuses operate, but these are related as far as possible to actual production.

Two general factors help the system to work. First, the application of time-and-motion study under national agreement and supervision: work loads are determined by agreed methods (simple 'element' systems, devised by a central bureau, for assembly and similar operations, time-study to the extent that these cannot be applied) in which the union works-club committeemen have been trained. In disputes, the firm's time-study man is enjoined to act primarily as an expert supplier of data required by both parties, and there is provision for appeal to and investigation by a specialist joint council for the metalworking industry—and, in procedural cases, to a joint board of L.O. and S.A.F. And when settled, piece-rates which have been disputed are paid retrospectively to the commencement of the task concerned. The second factor is the system of plant wage-negotiations: apart from the wage-increases arranged under periodic national agreements there is in each car firm an annual joint review of earnings at the plant level, the effective purpose of which is apparently to ensure that average pay keeps its position relative to wages in other metalworking establishments in the district, but at which the earnings and work-loads of groups which have fallen 'out of line' inside the plant are also adjusted, and line speeds are determined for the next year.

In the car firms, at any rate, the famous Swedish 'wage drift' thus appears to have become a highly organized affair. And other areas of potential collective conflict do not seem wide. Redundancy has been a very rare experience for the Swedish car workers, but at the time of the writers' inquiries national negotiations were in train on union proposals for an extension of the rights of Works Councils to information both of proposed lay-offs and on other matters of company policy and economics. However, unions already had the right to demand an investigation of cases of redundancy or dismissal by the Labour Market Board (a national joint body) and it did not seem likely that major disagreement would develop on these questions. On the other hand, a smoothly functioning and comprehensive institutional system seemed far from having solved all the Swedish car firms' labour problems. Absenteeism appeared to be rather higher than is normal in the British firms—about 8 per cent was reported for one of the companies. Refusal of overtime working was said to be common, even where the union had approved it. And the firms appeared particularly concerned about labour turnover: the rate of industrial 'job-quits' in general seems to have been rising in Sweden over the past decade, but one car plant reported 75 per cent of male workers engaged as leaving within a year. One might speculate how far an unusually rational system of collective organization has driven the less articulate forms of discontent into individual modes of expression.

A few words about the Japanese industry may also be in place—for reasons other than those of completeness alone. Although car production is still not on the western scale (currently running at about one-third of the British), in total motor vehicle output Japan is the fourth producer in the non-Communist world, outranking France; and even in cars, it may well possess one of the world's major industries in the very near future. Moreover, Japanese labour relations in general are less well known than those of the other countries referred to. Particularly, although Japanese industry as a whole has a high strike-incidence—notably more so than the British—the motor plants represent one of its least strike-prone sectors.

There are several motor firms (indeed in the view of the government, which is at present putting pressure on them to amalgamate, too many) and labour organization—as in most other Japanese industries—is on an 'employment' basis, through separate plant unions. The plant or firm unions are linked in loose industrial federations, which may in turn be affiliated to one of several rival national union centres. These federations are rather preoccupied with political questions, and particularly with the defence of unions' legal rights. Collective bargaining takes place partly by way of annual or biennial 'struggles'—broad campaigns for wage-increases or reductions in hours which end with modifications to the separate plant agreements to the extent that they succeed. A distinction, however, is drawn between 'permanent' and 'temporary' workers (who make up a significant part of the labour force) and unions do not usually negotiate for the latter.

This distinction is one aspect of the paternalism which characterizes the larger Japanese employers' relations with their workers. 'Permanent' workers become, so to speak, part of the establishment. Thus all such workers are entitled to a minimum annual pay-increment, which varies according to age, service, and other personal factors (often including 'merit'). A typical collective agreement—for the Nissan company, the biggest of the two large-scale car makers (the other being Toyota)—provides not merely for a 5 per cent average annual wage-increment, but for a guaranteed wage of 60 per cent of normal earnings for up to six months to a permanent worker who had to be laid-off. In fact, such workers are very rarely dismissed, and the company provides pensions, as well as housing and medical services, for them. Past Nissan agreements have also provided for a 'study' of wages when prices *or* taxes change, though these changes are now usually covered by the annual union agreements; and in fact, wage increases in the company have averaged 11 per cent annually in recent years.

The paternalism of the motor companies, however, is also reflected in their relations with the unions themselves. In the early 1950s there were unsuccessful strikes against large-scale dismissals, which led to the collapse of the then-leftist All-Japan Automobile Workers' Union and to a subsequent partial revival of the unions under strong company influence. This is not altogether an unusual situation in Japan, but the car workers' unions seem an advanced case of it. The attitude of the workers themselves to their union leaders 'collaborative' philosophy appears to be ambiguous. On the one hand, it is said that the comparative weakness of the unions and their lack of independence has led to informal restrictions of output by the operatives, in an attempt to control change and uncertainty and as a substitute for open strikes. On the other hand, the dependence of permanent workers on the prosperity of their own company, and their fears of being thrown into the much lower-level 'temporary' and small-firm labour market by a failure on their firm's part, would limit even such expressions of discontent.[1] So that if the British car firms are an extreme instance of a national tendency in one direction, the Japanese car plants equally seem an extreme case of a national tendency in another direction.

We see, then, that the similarity in technology between the different national automobile industries has led to no parallel similarity in their labour relations experience. Nor is the motor industry particularly strike-prone, except in Britain and the United States. Generally, labour relations in the car firms appear determined by two things: the specific national patterns within which they operate, and the concentration of car production itself—which means that car firms are both big and few, so that the policies and circumstances of individual companies have a greater than normal influence. The American industry has been to some extent an exception to the first rule—and was also once a focus of industrial conflict—since it has itself been a pattern-setter for national labour relations in general. This is largely because it has represented one of the major areas of American trade union development since the 1930s, while the U.A.W. remains one of the most active and original of United States unions: and the biggest car producer, G.M., has itself taken several initiatives in the field of labour relations. At the same time, the pattern of

[1] At time of going to press, the Prince Company workers' union—the firm having been taken over by Nissan—has seceded from the socialist Metal Workers' Federation, and merged in the Nissan Company union, which suggests the firm's paternalism to be not altogether unmatched by a response on the workers' part.

industrial conflict in the American industry has differed substantially from that in the British, centring rather in the occasional major battle on the basic terms of labour contracts than in the persistent minor guerrilla by which the British industry is characterized.

The Italian motor industry is also something of an exception to the first rule because in this case the major firm concerned is itself so big, so central to the whole national economy, and so conscious of the political and social implications of trends in its labour relationships, that it has itself become something of a pattern-setter for Italian industry as a whole. But the European motor industries are, on the average—as is also the Japanese—less strike-prone than is industry in general. And in this situation there seem certain common factors. In the major Continental and Japanese car producers' plants, the degree of union organization is lower—and in several cases, conspicuously lower—than it is in most British and American motor concerns. In certain countries there are legal restraints on strikes—and particularly on unofficial or 'wildcat' strikes occurring on issues other than the periodic general revision of collective agreements. On the positive side, in most European industries there is the system of Works Councils, operating by law or by general national agreement; moreover, a much larger proportion of labour costs takes the form of 'fringe benefits' than in Britain—and it may be that these are less liable to the conflict-causing 'compulsive comparison' than are direct cash wages; and there is, on the whole, a considerably greater security of employment and earnings than in the British industry.

One can add one further element in the contrast between labour relations in the British and in the Continental European car firms. This is that the differential between the earnings of their workers and those of engineering operatives generally seems significantly lower than in the British case. This is true whether cash wages or total labour receipts be considered—as is shown by Table X/1.

Table X/1—RATIO OF MANUAL WORKERS' AVERAGE HOURLY RECEIPTS
OCTOBER 1961*

Automobile industry to all engineering	France	Germany	Italy
Cash wages	1.16	1.11	1.28
Total labour costs	1.18	1.12	1.23

* Estimated from: 'Le Marché Commun: Salaires et Charges Sociales Comparés,' *Union des Industries Métallurgiques et Minières*, Paris.

Comparable data is not available for Sweden, but there too it appears that the differential of car workers over metalworkers' wages in general is not marked. On the same basis of comparison the hourly earnings of the British car worker were at least one-and-a-quarter times those of all engineering operatives together. So that only in Italy, where the relative wages of motor industry workers were boosted by Fiat's special concessionary strategy, was the automobile operative's differential over other engineering workers as high as in Britain. This perhaps reinforces the suggestion of Chapters IV and V, that relatively high earnings *and* relatively great insecurity are an explosive combination. But at any rate, international comparison seem to demonstrate fairly conclusively that there is nothing in the technology, economic organization, or high rate of growth of the automobile industry that makes for an especial liability to labour conflict.

CHAPTER XI

SUMMARIES AND CONCLUSIONS

(A) THEORIES OF STRIKES AGAIN: BACKGROUND FACTORS, INSECURITY, AND THE FUNCTIONAL ROLE OF STRIKES

We had perhaps best begin by recapitulating this study's purpose. We are interested in the development of labour relations in the car firms—and particularly the latter's history of industrial disputes—primarily as an outstanding case of a more general phenomenon. This is the sharp rise in the incidence of strikes, and especially (for industries other than mining) in the frequency of strikes, in Britain over the decade from the mid-1950s. This rise is remarkable in two ways. First, it followed a generation's comparative industrial peace, which seemed—since it continued over contrasting periods of pre-war mass unemployment, wartime labour shortage and labour controls, and post-war full employment—to be mainly a product of the consolidation and settlement of the system of collective bargaining and industrial relations which emerged from the troubled 1920s (thus also appearing to offer an incidental justification of that system). And secondly, the increased dispute-liability of British industry during the past decade also contrasts with an apparent world tendency for labour unrest to decline. Moreover, there was no very obvious change in British economic circumstances during the 1950s—in the level of unemployment, for instance, or in the trend of living costs—with which this sharply increased strike-liability might be obviously associated.

The economic consequences of this increase were probably insubstantial—at least, for industry as a whole: 'time lost' through disputes still averaged less than two hours per employee each year, even after quite generous allowance for various forms of understatement in the official strike-statistics. The movement's significance is rather for the light it may throw on the appropriateness and adaptation of an established system of industrial relations to contemporary labour expectations and social-economic requirements, and in a more general way, on the sources of industrial unrest. And for such

Summaries and Conclusions

a study, the car firms offer advantages which go beyond the fact that the British motor industry represented one of the sectors in which the increased dispute-liability was particularly concentrated.

In so far as public interest in the car industry was inspired by a concern for the impact of its disputes on its output and competitiveness, that concern was probably very much exaggerated—as we suggest in our introductory chapter. But if public interest in motor industry disputes was disproportionate to their economic significance, it did have the merit—from our viewpoint—that it secured them an unusually full press coverage. The special advantage of the car firms for our purpose, however, is that they represent a distinctive group of large enterprises, so highly specialized as to be readily distinguishable from other industrial undertakings, and relatively homogenous between themselves—being very similar both in their markets and technologies—and yet differing substantially in their labour relations experience. And the same things are true for the foreign car-making industries, which are limited in number and also each consist of a small group of large concerns—with similar market situations and technologies, not merely to each other but also to the British industry. The car firms thus represent an unusually appropriate field for—what has to be a central technique of social science—comparison.

For instance, one thing that the comparative method—or rather, a combination of that method and simple statistical analysis—immediately requires us to do is, if not quite to dismiss, at least to question a number of 'theories of strikes' or of 'strike-proneness'. Thus, a currently-fashionable view among industrial sociologists and some industrial relations specialists links the state or organization of labour relations in particular industries or enterprises with their specific technologies—the argument being that a given technique of production imposes particular social relationships on its human participants, and confines them within determinate 'socio-technical systems' which will produce qualities and phenomena which are not fully under their control. The argument is a useful corrective to the theories of 'plant sociologists' who by apparent implication regarded the social relations existing within the enterprise as, in a sense, 'free'—that is, determined largely independently of objective factors or of circumstances external to the plant, and manipulatable accordingly. But the British car firms, for all their comparative technical uniformity, have displayed a very wide variation in their respective experiences of labour unrest. Nor is the automobile industry particularly strike-prone in other countries. There seems nothing, therefore, in the technology of car production which especially predisposes the motor industry to irascible human relationships.

Similarly, we find little in the proposition that the development of industrial unrest is connected with the consequences of 'automation' or a high rate of technical advance and productivity growth in general. Again, technological change has affected all the bigger British car firms, at least, as well as all the different national automobile industries, in pretty much the same degree; but they have very different liabilities to labour disputes. And in the American case, the industry's rapid post-war advance in productivity coincided with an actual decline in its strike-incidence. In the one major British instance where automation was associated with an important industrial stoppage, it was also—almost accidentally—associated with redundancy. But redundancy has been a major cause of disputes whatever its source: and technological change has rarely induced it. Similarly, technological change has complicated the difficulties which arise from the British industry's singularly involved wage-structure, and may have been in the background to one or two minor 'demarcation' disputes or other stoppages involving craftsmen's status. But these problems arise from the particular impact on the industry's wage and union systems of a high rate of change in general, to which technical innovation makes only a secondary contribution.

Again, there seems nothing in the motor industry's case to support the view that a high strike-proneness is likely to be linked with geographical isolation: if anything, the more isolated plants seem to have been less strike-prone. Particularly, we find no obvious association between the relative size of a firm or plant and its relative dispute-liability. Nor do we find anything that would link a high dispute-liability with 'remote' supervision—at least, to the degree that 'remoteness' can be measured through the ratio of supervisory and managerial staff; the quality and organization of management seems more important than its mere numbers and proximity to the operatives. And again, our material does not very well accord with the theory that industrial unrest runs in autonomous cycles—certainly not for the motor industry, and nor for the individual firm. There *are* cases where a firm has experienced a sequence of strikes followed by a period of relative peace: but there are equally instances of firms which have had only one or two isolated stoppages, and one major case of a firm with a pretty continuous history of frequent disputes extending back over decades. The most that one can say is that a firm which has once experienced a *sizeable* stoppage is quite likely to have another; and that a run of big stoppages is likely to end in a more or less lengthy phase of calm. And these can hardly be regarded as very portentous statements—much less as usefully precise ones.

Yet again, there seems nothing to associate the high strike-liability of the British car firms with the nature, in one respect or another, of

Summaries and Conclusions

the work they offer. Working conditions, on the whole, are superior to those in several industries which are much less strike-prone—like textiles—and disputes specifically concerned with poor working environments have been relatively infrequent. Widespread shift-work is a disadvantage of car manufacture, and the rather unusual shift arrangements of the car firms have themselves been a cause of disputes: but there seems no other direct association between shift working and strike-proneness. And neither the general monotony of mass production work nor the specific 'tensions of the track' provide plausible explanations, because disputes have not been confined to the occupational groups which would appear most exposed to boredom or strain, but seem to have been fairly widespread among workers on all types of job—including some which involve a certain variety or which are exempt from the persistent pressures of the production line.

There have certainly been cases in which production pressures have aggravated the apparent general dispute-propensity of the industry—for instance, when a management has been attempting to force an increased output through a temporary 'bottleneck' in the productive sequence, or workers have been subjected to conflicting demands for higher output and better quality at the same time. But we know of no reason to think that such occurrences have become more widespread or that they have been more likely in particular firms; so they could explain neither the industry's increasing strike-liability nor the latter's unequal distribution between firms. Nor does the particular version of the 'monotony/tension' theory of strike-propensity which we have encountered in the industry itself—that an increasing dispute-proneness represents the reaction of an ageing labour force to the continued demands of assembly work—seem to stand up to inter-firm comparison. Similarly, the 'green labour' theory—attributing strike-proneness to an exceptional influx of workers without experience of industrial work routines or of proper union procedures—does not seem very useful as a general explanation.

Similarly, again, one finds rather little in the car industry experience to support what might be called 'the agitator theory' of strikes. The theory, though recurrently popular, suffers from a certain definitional vagueness. In our context, it could have three alternative meanings. First, that political groups cause industrial conflict. One should certainly not exclude an effect of political associations in two or three cases, though even there they do not seem to have been central. But as an agitational group, the British Communist Party seems on the whole to have been ineffective in the car firms, whether in particular strikes or in its support of 'unofficial' organizations within the unions; and other political factions have certainly been even more marginal in their impact. The second interpretation would ascribe a generally inflammatory role to shop stewards as such. And for this there is clearly no evidence. Strikes have been as common in plants where the stewards' organization is weak or divided as where it is strong: and there is more to suggest that senior stewards attempt to control the development of disputes and are pushed into stoppages from behind than that they lead workers into such crises. And the third meaning could be that particular individuals (who may also be stewards, or/and possessed of emphatic political opinions) incite disputes.

This third proposition is, in the last analysis, beyond assessment—because it involves the much more general (and virtually insoluble) problem of the role of the individual in social events at large. Two comments only are possible: one, that industrial stoppages may be as often caused by weak and ineffective workplace representatives as by strong or irascible ones; and two, that in the particular technical and social environment of the car workers the area of effective individual influence is usually rather limited. In the rather rare workplace situation which might be described as that of 'endemic conflict', individuals of the appropriate personality type may become important—but it seems unlikely that they have the power to create such situations. And some individuals among the senior shop stewards—of very divergent political attitudes—have achieved a much more enduring influence from outstanding social skills, long experience, and established acceptance in the role of mediator and negotiator by managements. Otherwise, the possibility of individual domination seems largely confined to quite small groups. That is to say—on the operatives' side: this could not be said of managements, where the impact of powerful personalities on whole organizations is frequently evident.

Alternatively there is the view that strikes are only one expression of a pervasive industrial dissatisfaction (or 'low morale') which is likely to emerge also in high accident rates, absenteeism and labour turnover. This, our evidence certainly fails to support. Accidents are not frequent in the car firms by comparison with other industries. Absence from work is (so far as one can judge) comparatively modest—except in the special case where it amounts to a collective movement, as with the refusals to work Friday night shifts in the early 1960s or the Coventry car workers' insistence on taking their summer holiday at the customary time in 1965. And, despite not over-rare lay-offs and redundancies, labour turnover seems comparatively low. Nor is there much apparent difference in these things between the more and less strike-prone firms. Labour disputes

Summaries and Conclusions

appear to have been the product of specific discontents rather than a generalized disgruntlement. On the other hand, there *may* be a sense in which strikes, absenteeism or accidents, and labour turnover are interchangeable 'wastages'—at least to the degree that the removal of the direct outlets for grievance provided by strikes may produce an increase in other possible expressions of it.

Moreover, there do seem to be two specific conditions which may well have contributed to the British car firms' high strike-liability— or at least, in which they seem on the whole to differ from most other industries and from many foreign automobile concerns. One (which is implied in the peculiar age-structure of the car firms' labour force) is that they recruit very few workers as juveniles, but take on adult labour from a variety of other occupations. Many of these do not involve the restraints and limitations of mass production work, so it seems reasonable to suppose that car workers accept these things quite consciously as one price for the high wages that draw them into the industry. On the other hand, their previous working experience limits their sense of 'committal' to the industry: they know they can do other jobs, and have some personal familiarity with the market for labour. Car workers, in other words, if they are not altogether 'economic men', are probably more so than most other workers and nearly as much so as their employers.

The second specific circumstance of labour in the British car firms seems even more relevant. This is its combination of a general pay level which seems, in relative terms, unusually high, with both marked anomalies in wage-differentials within the car industry *and* a very considerable instability of earnings. The high average wage-level may in part be regarded as a compensation for the instability: but the association of the two things seems, in some other industries, also to be identified with a high strike-proneness; and it appears readily explicable that it should be so. There is the sense that, since phases of high demand and output are fleeting, opportunities to extract concessions from managements should be exploited while they are available. And the frequency with which managements themselves lay men off, put them on 'fall-back' rates, or vary their overtime, makes it seem nothing abnormal for workers to withhold their labour. While high earnings make it easier for them to do so.

A general connexion between a high strike-liability and irregularity of employment has been noted by other students of labour unrest[1] and this appears to provide at least an important background circumstance to the rapid increase in the car firms' dispute-proneness during the 1950s. In the decade from 1952 their growth was three

[1] See, for instance Knowles (*op. cit.*, p. 180) on building, referring also to an American study, *Waste in Industry*, by Doten, of 1921.

times interrupted by short but severe recessions, and the seasonality which was so marked a feature of the motor industry's pre-war activity pattern also to a large extent returned. The parallelism of the economic and strike trends seems more than coincidence. Particularly, there does seem to be a sense in which strikes in the British motor industry have fulfilled a function which is quite apart from the explicit grievances or issues which are their occasion. Our statistical analysis shows that the *frequency* of disputes—and notably of wage-connected disputes—has varied pretty directly with the output of cars, and this pattern accords with general industrial experience and (except that the peak has been higher during each successive boom) requires no specific explanation. What is unusual in the car firms' recent dispute-record is that, though strikes are fewer in slumps, their size and duration increase so much at such times that the level of striker-days (or 'working days lost') is much higher than in boom periods.

This is not to be explained by an increase in strikes against redundancy, though such stoppages have generally been more severe than those on other issues. The explanation seems to be a combination of the effects of (anticipatedly short-term) recession on workers', unions' and employers' attitudes. Workers, in the more prosperous concerns at least, have during slumps apparently been more willing to strike on questions other than those concerning their own small-group interests: and the consideration that this might postpone dismissals and lay-offs—perhaps till they become unnecessary—may not have been irrelevant to this attitude. Unions, for a variety of reasons, have been more willing to support strikes at such times, which helps to make them bigger. And managements—particularly—have been less keen to settle disputes quickly. In effect, and notwithstanding that these affairs may be accompanied by all the usual aggressive displays and mutual complaints—nor that they may be exploited by one party to them or another to secure some tactical advantage for future use—there is an implicit 'conspiracy to strike'.

A large part of the car firms' high strike-incidence, in other words, has apparently represented the industry's substitute for formally-agreed means of dealing with recurrent labour surplus. And on the workers' side, at least, this functional aspect of strike-proneness may be confirmed by some peculiarities of the industry's seasonal patterns. On the one hand, its strike-liability (here, in terms of both frequency *and* incidence) is concentrated into the earlier part of the year. On the other hand, though one would expect output to be higher in the year's first half (and other car trade indices—like average hours worked when working, or secondhand car prices—are higher then) in fact it doesn't seem to have been. If these two things

(B) CAUSES OF STRIKES: 'FAIR WAGES' AND 'JOB RIGHTS'

In sum, then, we are driven to the conclusion that strikes in the motor industry have been caused mainly by the kind of pressures that strikers themselves give as reasons for striking.[1] Since it is rather unfashionable these days to believe that people do things for the reasons they say—or even think—they do, we had better add one qualification to this statement. It does *not* assert that in every stoppage the grievance that apparently emerges as its justification was in fact the initiating cause—or even that it really expressed the most important resentment of the strikers. Nor does it say that strikes do not sometimes happen by mistake—through defects of 'communication'. What it *does* say is that car firm strikes, at any rate, have had their roots in a pattern or complex of conscious grievances which are 'real' in the sense that one can see that they might very well —applied to oneself, for instance—be an adequate motive for action, and that this pattern of grievance is reflected with a high degree of correspondence in the pattern of stated strike-causes. The only 'background' factor which seems to us of unquestionable relevance to the high dispute-proneness of the car industry is its pervasive irregularity of employment and earnings—and this in any case also emerges amongst the explicit causes of conflict.

The point can perhaps be elaborated by a very summary recapitulation of the contrast between the car firms' strike-liability in the inter-war period with their very much altered post-war incidence and pattern of labour dispute. This is done in Table XI/1 on p. 334. The average manual employment of the car firms in the inter-war period was just about half that of the post-war years (implying that the incidence of strikes rose five-fold meantime.) The striker-day figures, of course, exclude not only the 'secondary loss' of working time caused by stoppages to plants other than those directly involved—which, including the effect of disputes at component manufacturers, may have added 50 or 60 per cent to the total of striker-days. They also

---

[1] This, of course, to some extent echoes the comment made not so long ago by a once-famous Liberal newspaper: 'The average working man does not sacrifice the whole of his pay packet and his union strike pay without feeling—rightly or wrongly—that he has a just grievance' (the *News Chronicle*—now merged in the *Daily Mail*—on a gasworkers' strike in August 1946, quoted by Knowles, *op. cit.*).

Table XI/1—CAR FIRM STRIKER-DAYS BY CAUSE
(For the establishments involved)

000s**	Inter-War*	Post-War†
Straight wage-increase demands or wage-reductions	100	400
Wage-structure and work loads	150	900
Trade union relations, etc.		600
Redundancy, short-time, etc.		600
Individual dismissals, etc.	50	250
Management questions		200
Working hours and conditions		100
TOTALS	300	3,000

** To nearest 50,000; * = 1921–39; † = 1946–64.

exclude the effect of general engineering strikes, which proportionately to the labour force, probably led to a 'loss of working days' which was rather similar in each of the two periods. But these strikes, too, had greatly changed their character between the two eras. The post-war general stoppages were all demonstrations launched, during the course of elaborate negotiations between the C.S.E.U. and the E.E.F., to induce the employers to raise a wage-increase which was either offered or certain: the major pre-war general stoppage was the bitter lockout of 1922, in which the unions' defeat petrified the present formal restriction of workers' bargaining rights to matters outside the area of 'managerial functions'.

But the most notable thing, of course, is that although wage-issues —and particularly questions of wage-structure or work-loading— are responsible for a very large part of the car industry's increased dispute-liability, by far the greater part of the latter is attributable to causes which, before the War, were hardly significant as a cause of conflict. In the two pre-war decades, only one-sixth of all days 'lost' in plant disputes was attributable to non-wage questions: in the post-war period the incidence of such stoppages has risen nearly tenfold, and their frequency—relative to the labour force, again—is up in much the same proportion. While within that period, certain non-wage issues, in particular, have displayed an increasing importance: redundancy to an extent which naturally varies somewhat with the level of production; and most recently, individual dismissals and other questions arising from the exercise of 'managerial functions'.

SUMMARIES AND CONCLUSIONS

However, wage-disputes themselves have also greatly changed in content when compared with the pre-war years. At that time, stoppages under what is still the most important single head of conflict—wage-structure and work-loads—largely concerned resistance to cuts in piece-rates or, occasionally, to 'speed-up'; nowadays they overwhelmingly (apart, that is, from the 'effort bargain' disagreements which have been mainly concentrated in Ford's plants) involve what are in effect anomalies or inequities between the pay of comparable groups of workers, or in the pay of a particular group over a period of time.

In a general way, of course, all this may be regarded as an effect of prolonged general high employment and the concomitant strengthening of trade union organization. But this in itself explains little: granted that the bargaining strength of workers—their ability to press demands and grievances on their employers—has been greatly improved by these things, what explains the *kind* of demands they in fact press? And at this point it seems possible to link up the post-war development of labour unrest in the car industry with that general and national acceleration in strike-frequency during and since the 1950s which is this study's primary focus of interest. This is because, in the economy as a whole also, the increasing strike-liability was associated with a marked change in the pattern of ostensible dispute-causation.

On the one hand the proportion of stoppages attributable to non-wage issues rose remarkably: disputes about what the Ministry of Labour calls 'other working arrangements, rules and discipline' seldom constituted more than 15 per cent of all strikes recorded annually in the whole statistical history up to the 1940s; but their frequency increased rapidly from then on, until they accounted for a third of all stoppages. The general picture is again much affected by the changing relative importance of mining disputes, of which an unusually large proportion seem attributable to such causes, but for which no pre-war breakdown is available. However, in the whole metalworking industrial complex—which we have ourselves separated from the records—less than ten disputes a year were, on the average, due to these issues in the inter-war period, and by the early 1950s still only some twenty-five stoppages annually were thus classified. But in the 1960s more than eighty such strikes have been reported each year. On the other hand, disputes about wages also showed a marked change in character: strikes officially classified as being about wage-questions *other than* wage-increases or decreases again accounted for a much higher proportion of all stoppages in the post-war years, and while this comparison too is affected by specific trends in mining, our evidence for the metalworking group of industries is that such stoppages have there increased in very close relation to the non-wage disputes already referred to.

These things can perhaps best be interpreted as reflecting a major change in manual workers' expectations. In the inter-war period unions—and their workplace organization, to the extent that it was then capable of playing a separate and distinguishable role—were mainly preoccupied with a struggle to maintain wages, and such other labour standards as had been previously established, in the face of persistent mass unemployment. In some cases—as of those of the miners and textile workers—the struggle was effectively to preserve a minimum of subsistence. First signs of an altered pattern of labour demands and expectations emerged during the War itself, in the changing emphasis of discontent which then appeared in unofficial disputes. But in the immediate post-war years, when most workers still had personal experience of an industrial situation characterized by bargaining weakness on the part of labour, and many also remembered the slump that followed the post-war boom of the First World War, there was little confidence that the new state of affairs would continue. It was only after several years that high employment and an almost automatic annual gain in wages and purchasing-power came to be regarded as the normal condition of affairs. However, with these things established by experience—and with memories of the contrasting inter-war period diminished both by distance and the dwindling of that period's survivors—the horizon of labour expectations lifted.

This change in expectations seems best expressed in two ideas or beliefs: the idea that wages should be 'fair' in comparative terms; and the idea that performance of a job establishes property rights in it. The influence of 'fair comparison' as a basis of post-war wage-determination is almost too obvious to need elaboration. At the level of national wage-agreements and of institutional pay-determination it has been arguably the most important single factor in wage and salary movements, dominating not merely the arguments of trade unions but those of professional associations of all kinds, as well as the conclusions of independent pay review bodies and commissions. So much so, indeed, that successive governments have thought it necessary (in their pronouncements on the incomes policy problems of full employment) to caution arbitrators and wage-fixers generally against accepting 'fair wage' comparison as an overriding criterion—while nevertheless asserting at the same time the central validity of just such a standard for the determination of public employees' pay. It is only natural, therefore, to find that the concept reflects something more than an institutional convenience: it clearly embodies a deep popular sentiment. It is an obvious further implication of the

SUMMARIES AND CONCLUSIONS

'fair wages' idea that earnings should be maintained by comparison with their recipients' past experience: and this has a particular reference to many piece-work disputes in industry. But the demand that work-loads, as well as wage-rates, should be negotiable is also a logical extension of it: since it would be meaningless to insist that earnings should be 'fair' in comparative terms without requiring that efforts, too, be regulated by agreeably comparative standards.

The idea of 'property rights in the job' is less familiar to institutional regulators of employment contracts—whose post-war experience has largely obsessed them with the processes of upward pay-adjustment—and is alien to the employer's natural concept of labour as a purchased commodity, to the price of which such things as recognition of long service or of personal considerations are attached as desirable and serviceable humanitarian concessions. It is nevertheless a concept which is already accepted to the extent that it is a virtual right in most public employment—as the term 'established' itself conveys for civil servants—and has a *de facto* or even formal recognition in many salaried and professional occupations; while with the Contracts of Employment Act of 1963 and the Redundancy Payments Act of 1965, with their initial recognition of 'job ownership' and partial provision for employer-financed 'compensation' for job loss, it has received a certain legal embodiment for workers generally.

The concept of 'job property rights' is also, however, an idea with far-reaching implications. In manual workers' terms, it extends not merely to the sense that operatives should not be turned off *en masse* when it is no longer profitable to employ them, or that the individual worker should not be deprived of his property rights established by service without appeal from the decision of a management which now finds his presence undesirable: it also includes the idea of rights to a particular job at a particular place, and may extend to the right to consultation in anything which may affect the future value of his 'property'. Managements, for instance, often find difficulty in understanding resistance to the introduction of additional workers in a section or to transfers of labour from department to department; but this arises from a failure to appreciate that jobs which are similarly paid are nevertheless not necessarily of equal values to their incumbents; they may carry different opportunities of overtime or promotion, different degrees of interest or of independence and freedom from supervision—or simply the special values that come from familiarity and accustomed personal relationships. In a large sense, the idea of 'property in the job' is the employee's compensation for his relative lack of property in the capital that employs him.

In effect, the pursuit of 'fair wages' in detail and the protection and elaboration of 'job property rights' have become—even though these concepts are rarely consciously expressed as principles of its operation—the central business of union workplace organization and the emotional basis of its strength. Which explains the other continuing strand in post-war labour disputes—and particularly those in the motor industry—of conflict over the recognition and rights of the workplace organization itself. What makes these ideas seem reasonable is not just an awareness among manual workers—themselves on the average much better educated and informed than before the war, and with an increasing proportion of white-collar people among their own families and acquaintances—that many of these ideas' implications are already applied to salaried employees, but a knowledge of the willingness of managements (if intermittently and inconsistently) to concede them in detail when pressed.

In essence, these two ideas cannot be said to be without a certain economic rationale. Logically and universally applied, the principle of 'fair comparison' as a basis for wage-fixing would produce exactly the same result as economists would expect to emerge from a perfect labour market—namely that jobs which require similar degrees of skill, involve similar responsibilities or efforts, and are analogous in respect of their intrinsic interest, unpleasantness or other 'net advantages', would be identically paid. Labour markets, of course, are far from perfect in an economic sense: but this only says that where wages for comparable occupations differ, they should do so only in respect of other recognizable and consistent references, such as the local shortage or otherwise of particular skills. And it can hardly be said that variations in earnings and earnings relativities such as those described in our Chapter V conform to such criteria. While it can reasonably be argued that, even in an imperfect labour market, a pattern of equal wages for comparable skills will still achieve the best distribution of economic resources.[1]

Similarly, it can again be reasonably argued that the effect of freedom to 'hire and fire' on the employer's part is to bias his choice between alternative production methods in favour of those which are capital-saving rather than labour-saving. A firm which is presented with a given demand of which the permanence is uncertain—as it always is in some degree—and can meet that demand at identical costs by either of two methods, one of which involves more plant and the other more labour, will (other things being equal) prefer the labour-using method because if demand falls again the workers can be laid-off, whereas the capital costs would continue. Which is not to say that all the elaborations of the 'property in the job' idea can be

[1] This seems to have been the conclusion of the O.E.C.D.'s international group of experts: see *Wages and Labour Mobility* (O.E.C.D., Paris, 1965).

similarly supported. But it at least raises the question, for instance, of how far the high rates of investment which seem largely to explain the distinctively rapid growth of Japan and West Germany since the War are attributable to the restrictions imposed in those countries on the ability of employers to dismiss labour once engaged (or, for that matter, of how far the principle of the British Redundancy Payments Act, which in effect charges the cost of redundancy compensation largely to a form of indirect taxation rather than the individual employer, was soundly based).

However, the point is not so much whether or not these ideas are in principle reasonable, as how far they are negotiable. And in respect of their labour relations the outstanding difference between the British and foreign motor industries, at least, seems to be just the extent to which the principles of 'fair wage comparison' and 'job rights' have, by one method or another, been embodied in their terms of employment. Their wage-structures are quite notably more uniform, both within particular firms and on the whole between them (the Swedish manufacturers even manage to operate a piece-rate payment system without the anomaly and conflict which distinguishes their British counterparts). The principle that efforts, as well as wage-rates, shall be subject to agreed determination is accepted in the American and Swedish industries, as well, implicitly, as in the German. By law, generally-accepted convention or industrial agreement, workers are much more protected against dismissal, and both 'property rights in the job' and rights to workplace representation and consultation are more effectively recognized—by such things as 'seniority provisions' and plant grievance settlement in the American case, or legal works councils in the European. The question, therefore, becomes one of why the same concepts have had so much less influence on formal British agreements and joint arrangements?

(c) OBSOLESCENCE IN INSTITUTIONS

But this last question can also be associated with another general problem: why has the recent British growth in dispute-liability been especially concentrated in the engineering and metalworking industries? Several factors have interacted to produce this concentration. In the first place, the traditional engineering piece-work wage-system—under which piece-prices, and alternative 'incentive' or lieu bonuses with their accompanying work-loads, are all determined at the workplace itself—has involved, in industries where the frequency of change both in products and techniques is naturally high, and where productivity growth is also naturally fast but unevenly distributed between branches and sections, a parallel unevenness in the automatic gains of earnings from rising output, and in the possibilities of improving earnings yields by workplace bargaining. The system thus proliferates anomalies and instabilities in earnings which conflict with the 'fair wage' principle, at the same time as it requires continuous workplace negotiation for its own maintenance. So that this is linked with the second factor, the equally traditional engineering shop steward system.

The shop stewards are the workplace agents of the engineering unions, and the union officers most closely in contact with workshop affairs and with the rank-and-file of operatives. The shop steward system has thus become an automatic vehicle, not merely for the discontents produced by the engineering wage-system, but also for those arising from the insecurities which the metalworking industries' high rate of change provokes. Marsh and Coker, in a previous study of the A.E.U.'s workplace representation and activity,[1] noted that the increase in the number of engineering shop stewards was particularly rapid from the mid-1950s on, and they associated this with the acceleration in frequency of both references to 'procedure' and stoppages from that time—to suggest that these things reflected what we might call a 'maturing' of the shop steward system. And after a quarter-century's high employment and continuous workplace negotiation, the steward organization has, in some major plants, certainly become almost as elaborate, experienced and 'institutionalized' as the unions proper. But as a device, workplace representation is virtually as old as trade unions: it seems equally reasonable to regard all these evidences of increased union workplace activity in the last decade as a response to that lifting of manual workers' expectations which followed several years of post-war high employment and rising wages.

Against this upsurge of workplace expectations and activity, however, there are the formal organizations and procedures of the engineering unions and employers. The extraordinary fact that the engineering unions have continued to allow their major relations with the employers to be regulated by the terms imposed on them after their defeat in the 1922 lockout—despite both their own criticisms of the resultant settlement and a generation's high union strength and bargaining power—becomes comprehensible only when one considers the unions' own structure. The multiplicity of associations concerned in the engineering industries, and their diversity of type—including craft, multi-craft, ex-craft, general and would-be industrial organizations, many of them in real or potential competi-

[1] 'Shop Steward Organization in the Engineering Industry', *British Journal of Industrial Relations*, June 1963.

tion with each other, and several of the biggest with their majority membership interests quite outside the engineering trades—in any case makes any concerted policy beyond a general wage-demand exceedingly difficult of formation. So that the only significant new initiative in wage-policy in recent years—the 1964 three-year 'package deal'—came from the employers' federation; while at the time of writing, major engineering unions are still not agreed whether redundancy should be absolutely opposed or merely adequately compensated. The union's federal organization, the C.S.E.U., is singularly weak in terms both of status and staffing in relation to its affiliated bodies—much more so than was, say, the old Miners' Federation; it has no powers of independent intervention in factory or local affairs, and has in any case no specialized structure to deal with the separate problems of the several distinct industries that now compose the engineering group.

Even were a significant part of the efforts of the unions' full-time officials not wasted in the duplication and other inefficiencies attending multiple unionism, there would be too few of them for the responsibilities thrust upon them. Local officials have been increasingly pressed, in recent years, by the demands of representation in the disputes referred to formal conciliation procedure: and these disputes, as we have shown, do not include a full display of the issues agitating the workshops. The leading national officers have been preoccupied for many years with the repetitive annual ritual of general wage-demands imposed on them by the persistent 'wage-price spiral' of the last quarter century: if the three-year agreement of 1964 releases some of their energy from that process it seems in any case likely to be engrossed in the constantly-ramifying business of union representation in governmental and similar committees. Research staffs—on whom these days a large part of the duty of union policy preparation inevitably falls—are generally minimal, and of comparatively restricted status. They are, to a large extent, preparers of briefs for the national representatives, and are not generally expected to explore and anticipate developing membership demands and interests, or to review the union's own functioning in relation to them.

The internal structure of the major unions is not, in any case, particularly conducive to the rapid flow of new membership concerns to their top leaderships. The expanding diversity of industrial and sectional interests the very big unions now embrace within themselves is not matched by their internal provision of specialist officers and representative bodies. The constitution of what is, in the motor industry case, perhaps the key union, the A.E.U.—though formally elaborately democratic—has hardly proven favourable to coherent and consistent policy. While even its democracy is in one sense limited, since the mass of semi-skilled operatives who now compose the majority of its membership remains substantially under-represented in its officialdom (a situation which seems also true of the N.U.V.B.). The T. & G.W.U.'s trade group structure is still largely adapted to the pattern of formal national negotiations with employers' association, rather than to the actual development of special membership interests. For the elucidation of such interests, the N.U.G.M.W.'s structure is considerably less developed. And among the unions at large, the continued basing of formal union constitutions on the branch—and particularly the local branch—has meant, in face of the transfer of real foci of industrial interest to the workplace itself, not merely a probable decline in membership participation in constitutional union management, but an inadequate communication of actual membership expectations and emergent special concerns to the unions' top leadership.

On the other hand, there is the Engineering Employers' Federation, with its vast and heterogenous membership of large and small firms, its traditional basis in the local employers' association, and its lack—like the unions—of a specialist industry structure for the several now distinct sectors of the metalworking economy. These things almost necessarily reduce it to the lowest common denominator of its affiliated membership in formal policy, so that it becomes understandable that its conciliation procedure should be recognizably nineteenth-century in character, and should fail to embody either the actual development of workplace labour organization and relationships of the past generation, or the national integration of separate engineering establishments into giant combines which is now common. We have noted how remarkably this procedure's formal stages have failed to provide for either speedy or definitive settlement of the disputes referred to them. And we particularly noted that a very large proportion of the disputes arising from the 'new' issues in industrial relations are not channelled into the E.E.F.'s formal conciliation procedure at all.

The last situation seems explicable in the light of the Federation's traditional insistence on the sanctity of 'managerial functions' and the exemption of matters other than those related to wages and hours from the unions' bargaining scope (an insistence maintained despite the very real extent to which it is compromised in practice by workplace understandings and agreements). While even within the area of wages proper, the inevitable incapacity of the Federation to devise a national wages structure which would bear some realistic correspondence to the actual states of earnings in the different sectors of its varied interest has deprived its intervention in disputes of effective criteria. At the same time, the Federation's local basis of organization—and to some extent its mere presence—has inhibited the development of positive policies by major individual firms to achieve a settlement of the contemporary issues of labour conflict, either in the wage or the 'non-wage' area.

One major reason for the special concentration of labour unrest in the metalworking industries is thus that the embodiment of new labour expectations into negotiated employment contracts has there encountered a major institutional blockage. Formal union organization has largely failed to express these expectations in concrete bargaining demands: and to the extent that formal employers' organization has encountered these expectations, it has, in the main, been able to offer them only a comparative immobility. One could put the point another way by saying that the traditional collective organization of the old mechanical engineering trades has proven incapable of adapting itself either to the actual development and specialization of the metalworking sector (technological change tends to make all industries engineers' industries) or to the new popular standards created by the achievement of full employment and a steady advance in real incomes. But on the other hand, the same organization has created, in its requirement of workplace bargaining and its shop steward system, an alternative channel for the new expectations' expression.

The structure of the engineering unions—the continued basing of formal union organization in general on the branch, the separation of the latter from the workplace representative system, and, most especially, the fact of multi-unionism at the workplace itself— necessarily gives the joint shop steward organizations within the plant a considerable independence of the official union machines. And with the development and consolidation of a shop steward hierarchy, with a cadre of experienced negotiators, the steward system has in effect become a kind of 'parallel unionism', preoccupied with the assertion of claims to 'fair wages' and 'job property rights' where the national union leaders have been preoccupied with the general advance of wage-levels and with the duties of labour representation in general economic management. At the same time, however, the inability of the shop stewards to maintain effective inter-factory organizations in the absence of managerial recognition or official union assistance, and the limited horizon of the workplace stewards' committee, has made their movement incapable of formulating its concerns in a general negotiating platform, or even of expressing current labour expectations in a generalized way—and thus of promoting a general settlement of the demands they entail. It can only embody them in its detailed response to changing workplace circumstance.

But why, again, has the increased strike-liability of the metal-working sector since the mid-1950s reached a special peak in the car firms? One might, of course, expect that the problems created by the interaction of new labour expectations with technical and economic change would be most severe in the area where change was fastest. And it would seem only natural that the institutional blockage to the reconciliation of those expectations with actual terms of employment should also seem most irksome in the sector where their context was in the most rapid flux. It was noted how the delays and infinalities of formal engineering conciliation procedure had produced their most unsatisfactory result in the car assembly plants. Indeed, in one sense the British-owned car firms' affiliation to the E.E.F. has been a direct cause of their high strike loss, since it involved them—to the extent, again, of some 800,000 working days during and since the 1950s—in general stoppages for increases (which were substantially less than those they were in any case conceding by workplace advances) to wage-rates which were very much lower than those they were actually paying. While on the other hand, conditions in the car firms also provided the strongest stimulus to the development of the 'parallel unionism' to which we have referred: the requirement of continuous workplace bargaining was not only at its most stringent in the face of continuous detailed change, but received an initial reinforcement, at least, from the implicit or open inter-union competition involved in both the growth of the labour force and the rapid expansion of union membership within it. Add to all these things the several effects of the car industry's persistent instability of earnings and employment, and the case would seem virtually complete.

(D) THE FIRMS AGAIN—
AND EXCEPTIONS TO STRIKE-PRONENESS

However, there is one other special circumstance of the industry which has undoubtedly contributed to its particular recent strike-liability. Of almost any other industry, one might say that its relative strike-proneness was determined by its general conditions: individual plants and firms might vary widely on either side of whatever norm those conditions established but, because there are many firms and plants, these variations usually cancel out, so that events in a particular company or establishment have no significant effect on the industry's broad situation. But this is clearly not so of the motor industry; employment is overwhelmingly concentrated in half-a-dozen great firms and a score or so of major worksites—so that the particular policies and special experiences of individual companies have almost certainly made as big a contribution to car manufacturing's

SUMMARIES AND CONCLUSIONS

dispute-propensity as any general circumstance of the industry.

Thus several of the union leaders have attributed the motor industry's strike-proneness to the willingness of individual firms to make concessions, in response to unofficial pressure, which they would not make when these were requested through 'procedure'—thus themselves demonstrating that unofficial strikes paid-off. This view undoubtedly influenced the outcome of the tripartite discussions held between management and union representatives early in 1961; it was interpreted by both the Minister of Labour and the employers as an advice to 'get tough' with unofficial strikers, and successively encouraged the managements' stand in the Pressed Steel, Rootes and Ford affairs of the following two years—a stand we have already noted to have produced somewhat limited results. Its explanatory content, however, seems in fact highly ambiguous. It could hardly be held, for instance, that the contrasting strike-records of Vauxhall and Ford were due either to the former's greater willingness to make concessions through its formal negotiating arrangements with the unions (since its collective agreements offer no significant advantage in wages and conditions over those of Ford) or, certainly, to Ford's having been softer in its response to workplace pressure. And in relation to the 'federated' firms, the view might rather have been interpreted as a criticism of the E.E.F.'s conciliation procedure itself, since its implied suggestion was that the Federation's intervention in disputes led firms to refuse demands that they would otherwise accept.

But what this view also implied was an appeal by union leaders for firms to help them re-establish their authority over their members by making concessions to them rather than to the shop stewards. And it thus seems to infer an incongruously unrealistic view of the nature of collective bargaining. Insofar as the concessions concerned were the result of workplace negotiations which necessarily involved the possibility, and occasionally the actuality, of a strike, it was always open to union leaders to command events for themselves by insisting —as they had the right—on a rapid consideration of grievances in 'procedure' and by themselves calling official and 'constitutional' strikes in at least a considered selection of those many motor industry cases where full procedural treatment ended in 'failure to agree'. To the degree that this criticism of firms' behaviour is valid at all, therefore, it implies as large a comment on union leadership as on the employers' arrangements and attitudes.

Nevertheless, there are clearly respects in which a major contribution to the level of labour unrest in the car firms has been made by the acts and omissions of individual companies. Among the 'acts', for instance, must certainly, in retrospect at least, be included the

Standard Motors early post-war agreements: at the time these might well have seemed in many ways commendable—the 1949 agreement, indeed, was what might now be called a 'premature productivity bargain'; but the disturbance to inter-plant wage-relationships which they set off certainly helped to form the background to the later crescendo of 'wage-structure' disputes in the industry at large. Again, there is the at least strong suggestion that some plant managments have responded to sectional disputes by laying-off uninvolved workers to a greater degree than was inevitable—a reaction that, however understandable, could hardly have encouraged conciliatory relationships. Or again, there was the Ford situation.

Ford's strike-proneness was exaggerated in popular repute by its concentration in a few big stoppages and in the development of an 'endemic conflict' situation in certain key plants in the late 1950s. Nevertheless, in view of the company's size its importation into a British industrial relations environment of elements of managerial policy and attitudes which even in the U.S.A. could not always be maintained in the face of union resistance led to a substantial contribution to the car firms' total strike-incidence. Its acceptance of collective bargaining only under government and T.U.C. pressure committed it to a singularly clumsy bargaining and conciliation arrangement in the first place, and to a system of workplace representation which was exceptionally divorced from union control and guidance. Its insistence that work-loads and efforts were not negotiable particularly invited conflict. A further insistence that the Briggs Bodies workers taken over in the mid-1950s with an established workplace bargaining system adapt to Ford, rather than that the adaptation be mutual, increased the probability of such conflict—a probability which was converted to a virtual certainty by the militant character Briggs' own history of labour relations had helped to develop in its existing A.E.U. steward organization.

However, in general 'omissions' may certainly be more widely attributed than 'acts'. If the British-owned firms' affiliation to the E.E.F. encouraged them to think that their relationships with their workers could be relegated to a secondary function of their works managers and departmental supervisors, from the early 1950s on events themselves must have demonstrated the inadequacy of this assumption. The growing burden that workplace negotiations imposed on factory managements must have been as obvious as the rising frequency of actual stoppages and 'dispute incidents'. And it was open to any company to analyse the overt grievances in the disputes they nearly all experienced and draw the conclusions which would follow from such an analysis: if any one of the major firms had, at this stage, offered the unions a deal involving—say—a reform

Summaries and Conclusions

of its wage structure and system, increased security and more flexibility in the use of labour, the E.E.F. could hardly have resisted. But even the rather elementary lesson of experience—that cars are made by people, and that labour relations are, therefore, a matter for specialist attention and responsibility at Board level itself—has not, at the time of writing, been absorbed by all the firms. Outstandingly, however, there is the failure of B.M.C. to appreciate (or its organizational incapacity to accept) the implications of the Morris-Austin merger for wage-relativities and labour relationships generally, and to develop a labour policy appropriate to an integrated corporation. That the acceleration in the car firms' dispute-frequency should have followed on the amalgamations and 'takeovers' of 1952–53 is clearly more than coincidence.

But one problem we have not discussed directly up to this point is the reason for the apparent exemption of certain firms from disputes—at least, of any consequence, and in the post-war period. Superficially, a number of factors appear to have contributed to Vauxhall's peaceful record. For a motor firm, it had for some time a remarkably low degree of union organization, with probably less than two-thirds of its manual workers in membership up to about 1963. Until recently, at least, it has dealt with only two unions (the A.E.U. and N.U.V.B.), although some of its skilled men belong to other organizations. And this has combined with its effective domination of its industrial locale to enable it to develop an unusually close relationship with the district union officials. Its (in retrospect shrewdly-timed) abandonment of a production-bonus payment system for a comparatively simple time-wage system has limited the appearance of internal anomalies in its wage-rate structure, and avoided the haggling which usually accompanies piece-rate fixing. It has, on the other hand, no arrangement for the formal negotiation of work-loads; but these are not excluded from its grievance procedure, and the Company has not asserted their determination to be a 'managerial prerogative'.

The relative isolation of its main Luton plant from other car factories may, in association with the Company's general personnel policy, have constituted an advantage—and one cannot exclude other local factors, such as the absence of an engineering industry tradition in the district: Rootes's Dunstable plant seems also to have been comparatively dispute-free. While Vauxhall's non-affiliation to the E.E.F. has exempted it from the delays and uncertainties of engineering conciliation procedure, as well as from the inhibitions which an association with employers outside the motor industry might have imposed on its bargaining freedom, and has obliged it to formulate its own attitudes in these matters. And as in the case of Opel in Germany

General Motors seems in any case to have been content to work within and gradually modify an existing organization, rather than—like American Ford—set up satellite companies in its own image.

Above all, Vauxhall seems to have displayed a general sophistication in its treatment of labour problems, and an attitude of going out to meet and anticipate new developments in the labour field, rather than resisting them until it was forced to accept. And there was in any case a long tradition of careful attention to personnel questions in the British company. Its last Vice-Chairman was appointed with a special responsibility for labour matters, and it was among the first companies to include an industrial relations director on its Board. Vauxhall workers themselves rate a prompt response to grievances high among the reasons for the company's low dispute-liability, and the importance it attaches to this response was shown by its appointment, in 1965, of four 'troubleshooters'—including people with experience as operatives—to help handle labour problems raised at the workplace level. Its now well-known Management Advisory Committee, elected by all employees, was preceded before 1942 by an informal consultative arrangement, is not restricted in its discussions to any questions outside the scope of collective agreements, and together with its specialist sub-committees has clearly been taken seriously by the company. Nevertheless, Vauxhall met the sharp increase in union activity about 1962–63 by a grievance procedure operating through the shop stewards' hierarchy at several stages up to top management, and providing for their participation with union officials in discussions at that level. By the mid-1960s it seemed content to allow the M.A.C. system (which the unions have already refused to co-operate with in its Merseyside plant) to recede into the background, and to encourage direct relations with the shop steward system to develop in an integrated way with the official union organization.

All this would be fairly convincing—were it not, perhaps, for the similar recent freedom from strikes of Rolls-Royce's car factory at Crewe. For Rolls-Royce is in almost all respects the opposite of Vauxhall. It is a 'federated firm', which applied the traditional engineering wage-system. Its workers are very solidly-organized, mainly in a variety of engineering craft or ex-craft unions, and with the full panoply of the engineering shop steward system. Its former convener of stewards was said to be a strong left-winger. It has displayed no very notable originality in its labour-management policies. And its car plant's pacific record is especially remarkable in that other sections of the firm—such as its aero-engine and fighting vehicle factories—have been far from strike-free, while the Crewe plant itself was involved in major stoppages during the war and inter-war periods.

Summaries and Conclusions

Of course, Rolls is not a car firm in the same sense as the bigger mass production concerns. Its cars are not made on an assembly line, and its work generally is broken down into 'elements' or 'cycles' which are very much longer than those of cheap mass production. Its processes are, again, much less subject to change—if only because of its stability of design and style—than those of the mass producers. But its techniques are not quite so different in all respects from that of some other major car makers as may be imagined. Daimler—Rolls' historic rival in the prestige limousine market—was, in its days of independence, rather notably strike-prone; and neither a still lower level of mechanization than Rolls and a comparable stability of design has prevented the very small car firms from sharing in the industry's strike-propensity. Between them and Rolls, the main difference appears to be the latter's considerable security of employment and earnings; this in part arises from the stability of the demand for its product. Moreover, the Rolls-Bentley car plant is itself only part of a larger works, which is otherwise engaged in engine and aircraft part manufacture, and this has possibly helped it to maintain steady total employment; while the company has apparently a general policy of contracting out part of its work to absorb demand fluctuations and keep its own labour force stable. This stability is perhaps almost enough to explain the Rolls exception in itself. Otherwise, one is almost left with a dubious psychological interpretation—that working on such aristocratic vehicles imbues their constructors with a feudal mentality!

Between Vauxhall and Rolls, however, the only common factors would seem to be hourly wages which are low—by comparison with other car firms—and geographical isolation from the latter. And these two factors have not saved Ford from making a substantial contribution to the industry's strike-liability. We do not in any case consider that the proximity or otherwise of other car factories explains to any substantial degree the relative dispute-proneness of particular plants —which is why we have made no attempt to set out any analysis of the industry's conflicts on a regional basis. One *might* argue that labour movements in Ford and Briggs at Dagenham affected each other (before the merger of these companies, that is); but the lack of such local infections seems on the whole more remarkable. Even within the highly organized and concentrated Coventry district, for instance, the Rootes plants seemed unaffected by the Standard strikes of the mid-1950s, and Standard appears to have been quite uninvolved by the Rootes movement of 1959–60—while neither of these groups, in their quite long intervals of relative quiescence, responded to the chronic militancy of Jaguar's workers. Particularly, there seems to have been no interaction between labour movements in the linked Oxford plants of Pressed Steel and Morris—though largely organized by the same union. Inter-plant effects appear to occur much more within the firm than the locality—another reason for doubting the contemporary appropriateness of the traditional district collective organization of engineering to the motor industry. And this is also another reason for allowing some weight to managerial policies and attitudes as a causal factor in dispute-proneness: it can hardly be accidental that when both Ford and Vauxhall opened plants in the quite new Merseyside district, the new Ford factory should have experienced more and bigger strikes than the Vauxhall works.

Our inability to suggest any single and conclusive explanation of the Vauxhall and Rolls-Royce exceptions, or to deduce from their experience any simple, cheap and universal nostrum for industrial unrest—or even, for that matter, to forecast with any confidence that their apparent freedom from major disturbance will continue indefinitely—does not, therefore, undermine the evidence that managerial actions and omissions have played a significant part in the contrasting experience of other firms. And in any case, these two companies are only exceptional by comparison with other car-assembly concerns: even in the metalworking complex of industries as a whole, and in the early 1960s, it can be reckoned that less than one in five of establishments experienced in any year a stoppage big enough to be reported either to the Ministry of Labour or the E.E.F. While outside the motor group, too, our evidence is that stoppages tend to be concentrated in particular sectors and, within these, in particular firms and establishments. That two companies should so far have largely evaded or escaped the pressures and circumstances which have made the car industry as a whole unusually strike-prone, therefore, only demonstrates again that there is nothing in the technology or economics of car-manufacture which inevitably predisposes to that condition: it does not reduce the force of the other general factors which have induced it.

(E) THREE APPROACHES: AND A SUMMING-UP

Among these factors, an inadequacy of institutions seems that of the broadest practical significance. And it was, of course, just this one which was least likely to be picked out by the 'official' methods of examination largely adopted. Inquiries such as those into the Austin strike of 1953, the Briggs plant stoppage of 1957, the Ford affair of 1962–63, or the disputes at Morris Cowley and Rover during 1964–65 were in any case necessarily dominated by the specific incidents that preceded them—and these incidents were of diverse kinds: a coherent

Summaries and Conclusions

comparative analysis could hardly emerge from such examinations. But the earlier inquiries were largely conducted by eminent outsiders, agreeable to the major parties to just that institutional apparatus the adequacy of which was really in question; and such people have usually shown a distinct preference for established arrangements. While the later commissions and joint or tripartite meetings were largely composed of professional participants in the same apparatus. Such bodies were unlikely to start by examing closely the assumptions of procedures their members had spent a large part of their lives operating. But it was the failure to do so that made, for instance, the expectations that more training of shop stewards (a specific recommended by the Minister of Labour's official meetings and to some extent applied in the early 1960s) would by itself secure a better conformance to those procedures largely pious. It neglected the question of what—from the shop steward's point of view, say—these institutional arrangements were really supposed to achieve.

It is no part of this study's main purpose to propose remedies for the motor industry's situation. In any case, so far as the general conditions of employment in the car firms are concerned, these almost indicate themselves (indeed, we rather suspect will in any case emerge from the industry's own obligatory self-examinings). On the one hand they would include such things as a 'rationalization' of the wage-structure (perhaps, also, with a greater element of 'fringe benefits'), the explicit acceptance and systematization of 'effort bargaining', more security of employment and earnings, better definition of the individual worker's job entitlement and the shop steward's status, and some effective system of appeal in dismissal and disciplinary cases. But there are alternative ways of doing these things, and to say more here is to invite complication. On the other hand, however, any remedy would certainly involve much more attention by managements, not merely to systematic grievance and consultative arrangements at the factory and within the firm, to relieving engineers of the burden of labour relations, and to more adequate training and induction of new employees, but particularly to better production planning and the avoidance of unnecessary fluctuations in work and earnings. One questions whether even the night-shift working so characteristic of the British industry, or the seasonal cycle with which that is largely associated, are really necessities of which no evasion is possible.

The difficult problem—and the one of widest general significance—is in any case again the institutional one, not merely because of the sundry vested interests (at all levels from the workplace upwards) in existing structures and procedures, but especially because it is impossible to consider this aspect in the context of the motor industry alone, and without regard to broader, national considerations. To some extent, the car industry is already evolving a more appropriate conciliation procedure under pressure of repeated minor crises. At several informal levels—in the relations between shop stewards' committees and local union officials, individual companies and the stewards' 'combines'—relationships are developing which forecast the emergence of a new structure within (and substantially at variance with) the present formal system of collective organization. At a formal level, the Motor Industry Joint Labour Council set up in 1965 has on the one hand brought together both the 'federated' and the American-owned firms with leaders of the main production operatives' unions, and on the other hand indicated its lack of interest in the heavy commercial vehicle and component producers. Its fact-finding commissions, by assuming direct access to the management *and* shop stewards of individual plants, have bestowed a certain recognition on the 'parallel unionism' of the workplace. While if the powers made available to its chairman to act as a Court of Inquiry in specific disputes are actively employed, a new channel of direct reference from the plant to a specialized industry joint panel will be in effect created. But, so far, the new organization has had only an investigatory status. If it proceeds further, in the direction of becoming a negotiating and grievance-settlement agency for the car firms and their workers, it will fall into pretty obvious contradiction with the traditional engineering bargaining and conciliation system. And in that direction there are in any case three possible roads of advance—for the car-making industry as for others.

The first would involve the effective acceptance of the state of 'parallel unionism', and recognition of its consequences. Actual wages and other employment conditions would continue to be determined, effectively, by bargaining at the plant or workshop level; while national negotiations dealt with periodic increases in minimum wages—together with such other general improvements in conditions for which a basis had been established by workplace agreements in a sufficient number of individual firms. Formally, this would necessitate only an explicit recognition of the joint shop steward system's actual elaboration and functions, and a speeding-up of dispute 'procedure'; though to constitute an effective working system of industrial relations it would also involve sundry changes of attitude on the part both of employers (for instance, in relation to 'managerial functions') and union leaderships. The second route would require the virtual dissociation of the British car firms from the Engineering Employers' Federation, and the conclusion by each firm of its own, company agreement with its workers' various unions—which would also have to concert their activities appropriately for this purpose.

Summaries and Conclusions

And the third route would involve the separation of the car firms as a group from the E.E.F. (or as a group within the E.E.F., if the American-owned firms were prepared to join the latter—though we cannot see what advantage that would offer them), and the conclusion of new, industry-wide agreements on wages, other conditions of employment and grievance-settlement for car manufacture.

For each of these three possible lines of development, there are substantial arguments (though one suspects that the second route would very soon veer towards the third).[1] But summarily, we rather think that they are in descending order of potentiality for industrial conflict—both on the particular ground that a common settlement of the major issues of recent dispute within the British automobile industry would provide the best basis for effective and rapid conciliation in individual firms in future, and on the general ground that international comparison suggests that the more centralized an economy's bargaining arrangements the lower its strike-incidence. However, that might very well be regarded as a secondary consideration. We are ourselves sceptical—as we have perhaps indicated—as to the alleged economic waste of strikes: indeed, in the car firms' case we suspect that strikes have to some extent acted as a buffer against recurrent surplus capacity. And it could certainly not be held that the most strike-prone concerns are the least efficient in a productive sense (indeed, Ford's once-high strike-liability might be held in some degree a by-product of its determined competitive efficiency)—or even that a strike-free plant is necessarily the best or most interesting to work in.

The more important considerations seem to us to relate rather to the implications of these alternatives for national economic and social policy. It might, we think, be reasonably argued that the first course—recognition of the state of 'parallel unionism' based largely on active workplace bargaining—would not only yield the most rapid relative material gains to the section of employees involved (at least, in the short run) but that it would be most conducive to an industrial arrangement which was flexible to labour and product market circumstances; in other words, that it would be best suited to an 'open', 'free' or competitive economy. But it would also remove any possibility—for instance—of guiding the development of earnings in accordance with nationally-negotiated 'incomes policies'. To the latter, the risk of an uncontrollable 'wage drift' in the actual wages paid by establishments is one of the major practical obstacles: the metalworking group of industries has in Britain (and in other

[1] At the moment of going to press, the C.S.E.U.'s annual conference has committed itself, in a notable change of stance, to a demand for what seems to be all three things at the same time!

countries) been a principal source of that phenomenon—and there is good reason to think that the car firms in particular have provided one of its key impelling forces. So that the third course—a separate industry-wide agreement, with standing joint representative machinery, for each specialist industrial sector—would provide the best basis for co-operation in national economic and social planning, since it would supply a mechanism both for relating the movement and rationale of earnings and pricings in each sector to national economic requirements *and* for negotiation with the government on that sector's place in the economy. What kind of institutional set-up one favours thus depends largely on what kind of economy one wants.

Whatever the line of development in these respects, however, our analysis in any event indicates a case for substantial improvement in the collective organization of employers and workers themselves. By contrast with the defects and deficiencies (real or otherwise) of the unions, very little attention has in recent years been paid to the effects and working of employers' associations—which are, of course, very much less public in their activities and proceedings. Nevertheless, on our evidence there seems good ground for thinking the present organization, procedures and, in some respects, orientation of the biggest British sectional employers' organization of all—the E.E.F.—to constitute hindrances to progress: in the field of industrial relations, at least. But so far as this study's area of investigation is concerned, the case for an improvement in union organization—for a better integration of the workplace representative system in formal union structures and for closer co-ordination between the separate unions themselves—is at least an obvious one.

Here again, however, we do not think this a problem which can be wholly solved in the context of the car industry alone. Nor does it seem that such minor and gradual improvements as are being introduced by individual unions into their internal organization, or promoted by the T.U.C. for the relationships between unions, are likely to have any substantial impact on it. At the time of writing, for instance, the E.T.U. is about to reorganize itself on the basis of workplace branches and industrial sections, and the N.U.V.B. has already put its shop steward appointments on a more systematic basis in several plants. While over many years the T.U.C. General Council has encouraged amalgamation and closer working between unions, and is (though its detailed initiatives have always avoided the problem presented by the giant unions' overlapping interests in the metalworking complex) at present engaged on another exercise of the same kind. But both the relative autonomy of shop stewards' committees and the lack of positive co-ordination between national

SUMMARIES AND CONCLUSIONS

unions follow inevitably—and the car firms' situation is not untypical in this respect—from the division of the mass of production operatives, at the workplace itself, between three or four big unions which have at the same time large (if not dominating) interests outside the industry affected.

Things like the merger of, say, the metal mechanics' or sheet metal workers' societies in the A.E.U.—or even (at present under earnest discussion) the amalgamation of the N.U.V.B. in either the A.E.U. or the T. & G.W.U.—could not by themselves affect this situation in any fundamental way. At the same time the division referred to also makes any proposal for the creation of an industrial union (for the car workers alone, say) quite impracticable, since no one of the 'Big Three' unions would be willing to sunder itself to facilitate that. Because this is a problem which affects many other industries and occupations, as well as the possibilities of adequate central leadership in British trade unionism as a whole, one of the writers has elsewhere suggested an association of the 'Big Three' unions themselves—within which industrial sections could be established which other unions could then join—as one direct line of attack on the difficulty.[1] But short of such a sweeping approach—or even as one step in such an arrangement—it would be arithmetically possible to arrange an exchange of memberships between the A.E.U., T. & G.W.U., N.U.V.B. and N.U.G.M.W. so that the mass-production operatives in any one car firm were organized by one union only, without involving any one of these unions either in a significant loss of membership or in a firm with which its officers were unfamiliar. The human practicability of such a move is another question.

As regards the other suggestions which are abroad at the present time—for various legal restraints on the power of workers to strike, for the legal enforcement of collective agreements, and so on—we make no detailed comment. These proposals relate to the whole field of industrial relations: but our study of the motor industry—as of others—at least leads us to doubt their practicality and usefulness except in the context of such far-reaching changes in the whole system of British industrial relations that the consequences would be unforeseeable. In the light of this study, however, we would also doubt their relevance and appropriateness. In the car firms, the recent strike waves seem to us to have arisen from authentic causes and grievances—in two senses. First, insofar as they have been stimulated by a background of insecurity, both in relation to employment and particularly to its material rewards. But secondly—and far more generally—in that they express human expectations and aspirations

[1] Turner, 'British Trade Union Structure: A New Approach?' *British Journal o Industrial Relations*, July 1964, II, 2.

which arise naturally in the contemporary social and economic context, and to which there has been a failure of organizations—trade unions, employers' associations and management structures—to accommodate themselves. Fundamentally, we conclude, the recent strike-proneness of the British car industry (and we see no reason to think this conclusion is not more generally valid) reflects a failure of institutions.

INDEX

In principle this index includes detailed references to subjects only to the extent that these are not covered by sub-heads in the *Contents* (pp. 13ff.) and *List of Tables and Diagrams* (pp. 16ff.). Thus the references to 'Accidents' and 'Absenteeism' are broadly to the pages of Ch. IV, Section D, that deal with those subjects, and otherwise to occasional or incidental references outside that Section.

Absenteeism, 75, 167, 184ff., 190, 330ff.
– in other countries, 309, 321
Accidents, 22, 167, 186ff., 330ff.
Adams, R., 105
Alfa Romeo, 314
Allen, V. L., 202
Alvis, 28, 119
Amalgamated Engineering Union (A.E.U.)
– in individual firms, 99, 194, 196, 208, 271, 287, 346ff.
– membership in car firms, 34, 193ff., 201, 347
– organization, 201ff., 217, 341ff.
– role in 'procedure', 252ff.
– recruiting policy, 192ff., 196, 198
– relations with other unions, 88, 198ff., 355
– shop stewards in, 193, 201, 206ff., 211, 340, 346
– in certain strikes, 276ff., 281ff., 284ff.
Amalgamated Society of Woodcutting Machinists (A.S.W.C.M.), 196, 198
American car industry
– collective bargaining in, 297ff.
– labour relations in, 87, 294ff., 323, 339
– production, employment in, 109, 127, 295, 300
– strikes in, 24, 298ff., 328
– wages in, 97, 127, 303ff.
American Federation of Labour (A.F. of L.), 297
American Motors, 295, 301, 304
Anarcho-Syndicalists, 291
Armstrong Siddeley, 28
Assembly-line work, 40ff., 168ff.
Associated Commercial Vehicles (A.C.V.), 29
A.T.C. Ratio (Administrative, technical and clerical employees)
– see *White collar workers*
Austin
– employment, 187, 271

– organization, production, 27, 30, 78, 86, 181, 347
– strikes at, 60, 109, 117, 239ff., 242, 269ff., 282
– unions, shop stewards at, 193, 207ff., 213, 216ff., 272
– wages, conditions, 140, 144, 147, 176, 187
Australian car industry, 318
Automation (see also *Technology*), incidence and effects
– technical, economic, 28, 77ff., 93, 101, 294, 343
– on employment, job-structures, 82ff., 101, 328
– on labour relations, 83ff., 101, 220, 294, 328
– on management, 91ff.
– on impacts of strikes, 95ff.
– on unions, 86ff., 220
– on wages and negotiations, 84ff., 92, 96ff., 328
– on worker's attitudes, job-satisfaction, 82ff., 88ff., 93, 101ff.
Auto Union, 306, 310

B.D.A. (German employers' federation), 307
Bescoby, J., 104, 243, 248
Beswick, F., 55
'Big Five', 27, 119, 121, 230, 231, 233
'Big Six', 27, 230
– shop stewards' association, 220
Birmingham & Midlands Sheet Metal Workers' Society (see also *Sheet Metal Workers' Unions*), 34, 195
Blauner, R., 168
B.M.W., 306
Borgward, 306
Briggs Bodies (see also *Ford*), 27
– labour relations, shop stewards, 208, 215, 287, 346, 349
– strikes, 275ff., 299

357

British Employers' Confederation
(B.E.C.), 36
British Institute of Management
(B.I.M.), 184
British Light Steel Pressings, 284ff.
British Motor Corporation (B.M.C.—
see also *Austin, Morris, Nuffield
Metal Products, Fisher & Ludlow*,
etc.)
- absenteeism in, 185
- employment at, 31, 82, 183
- organization, production at, 11, 27ff., 181, 231, 243, 347
- estimation of strike loss, 25, 53, 74, 237ff., 259ff.
- strikes in, 63, 82, 117, 130, 159, 181, 199, 236, 239, 243, 259ff., 263, 268ff.
- unions, shop stewards in, 195, 199, 218ff., 272, 282, 287
- wages in, 99ff., 140, 142, 144, 153ff., 158ff.
Birmingham Small Arms (B.S.A.), 28

Cameron Report, see *Courts of Inquiry, at Briggs Bodies*
Car factories
- organization of, conditions in, 38ff., 168ff., 329
- size of, 135
Car industry, firms (see also *Big Five, Big Six* and *Production*)
- collective organization of, 33ff., 353ff.
- definition of, 22ff., 28ff., 59
- employment, 31ff.
- geographical concentration, 30, 135, 178
- international comparison, 293ff., 327
- structure, development, 26ff., 30, 135, 175, 327
- work and processes, 38ff., 77ff.
Car workers
- age distribution, 171ff., 329
- attitudes to jobs, 88ff., 93, 102, 168ff.
- numbers, skill-mix, 31ff.
- recruitment, background, 174ff., 321, 329
- social characteristics, solidarity among, 178ff., 291, 328
Census of Production, 31, 33, 80, 94
Central Conference, see *Engineering Disputes Procedure*
C.F.D.T., C.F.T.C., C.G.T. (French union federations), 312

Chinoy, E., 168
Chrysler Corporation, 28, 295, 299, 301, 311
Citroen, 311, 313ff.
Clegg, H. A., 105
Clerical and Administrative Workers' Union (C.A.W.U.), 34
Closed, union shop, 34, 196, 198ff.
Coker, E. E., 203, 340
Collective bargaining, agreements (see also *C.S.E.U., E.E.F.* and *Engineering Disputes Procedure*)
- in engineering and car firms, 22, 75, 134, 200ff., 211, 217, 220ff., 249ff., 257, 334, 341, 353
- in other countries, 294ff., 297ff., 301, 306ff., 311ff., 315ff., 318ff., 322
- workshop bargaining, 205ff., 214ff., 224ff., 252, 255ff., 275ff., 335, 337ff., 340ff., 351ff.
Commercial vehicle industry, 22ff., 29, 160
'Communication' and strikes, 333
Communists
- as agitational body, 290ff., 329
- and industry-wide combine committees, 220
- influence at Austin, 213
- influence at Ford, 213, 277
Communist trade unions, overseas, 311ff., 316
Component firms, 22ff., 29
Confederation of Shipbuilding and Engineering Unions (C.S.E.U.)
- bargaining functions, 22, 217, 249ff., 272ff., 334, 353
- membership, 33
- organization, 33, 200, 207, 217, 248, 341
- relations with shop stewards, 207, 209
Confindustria, 315ff., 318
Congress of Industrial Organization (C.I.O.), 295, 297
Consumers' Association, tests of cars, 25
Contracts of Employment Act. 1953, 337
Consumer demand, 107
Courts of Inquiry
- at Austin, 52, 271ff., 350ff.
- at Briggs Bodies, 52, 117, 215, 276ff., 350ff.
- at Ford, 215, 278, 281ff., 350, 357

INDEX

– use of Motor Industry Joint Labour Council as, 37, 352
Crossman, E. F. R. W., 87, 89, 91, 97

Daf, 318
Daimler
– organization, production, 28
– strikes at, 119, 230, 349
– unions, shop stewards at, 210ff.
Daimler-Benz, 306, 308
Demarcation, 86ff., 198ff., 245, 328
D.G.B. (West-German T.U.C.), 307
Dick, A., 98
Discipline (see also *Strikes in car firms*), 42ff., 351
Dismissals (see also *Redundancy* and *Strikes in car firms*)
– appeals system, 351
– of shop stewards, 61, 212, 214, 267, 271ff., 275ff., 281ff., 290
– in other countries, 297, 305, 307, 322, 339
District Trade Union Officers, 202ff., 209, 211, 215, 221, 228ff., 272ff., 276, 279ff., 284ff., 290, 341, 347, 352
Downgrading, 84ff., 101
Draughtsmen's and Allied Technicians' Association (D.A.T.A.), 34
Department of Scientific and Industrial Research (D.S.I.R.), 8, 88ff., 93ff.
Dutch car industry, 318ff.

Earnings (see also *Wages*)
– of car workers
 – average hourly, weekly, 133ff., 138ff., 257
 – and compulsive comparisons, 142, 234
 – differentials, 133ff., 145ff., 158ff., 324ff.
 – fluctuations, security, 127, 159ff., 331ff., 351
 – at new plants, 144
 – dispersion of, between pay-levels, 152ff.
– of white-collar workers, 136
– and 'fair comparisons', 336ff.
– and size of establishments, 135
– in other industries, 133ff., 257
Effort bargain, 84ff., 92, 96ff., 335, 339, 351
Electrical Trades Union (E.T.U.), 34, 88, 285, 354

Employers, influence of attitudes on strikes, 62, 104ff., 118, 127, 248, 258, 273ff., 277ff., 292, 330, 332, 337ff., 344ff., 353
– in other countries, 295, 297, 299, 301, 314, 316ff., 320, 322ff.
Employers' organization, see *E.E.F.*
Employment in Vehicle Industry, 30ff., 77, 80ff.
Employment in car firms (see also *A.T.C.* and *Strikes in car firms*)
– effect of automation, 82ff., 101, 328
– fluctuation in, 83ff., 118, 127ff., 174ff., 247, 331, 334, 351
– structure of, 31ff., 86ff., 192, 196, 344
Engineering Disputes Procedure
– coverage of, 34
– description of, 250
– functioning of, 206, 217, 251ff., 271ff., 340ff., 344ff., 351ff.
Engineering Employers' Federation (E.E.F.)
– collective bargaining, agreements with C.S.E.U., 22, 249ff., 334, 341
– membership of, 34, 137, 141, 249, 347, 352ff.
– organization, 34, 258, 342ff., 352ff.
– policies of, 34, 141, 196, 249ff., 256ff., 271, 334, 342ff.
– and strikes, 57, 245, 249, 251, 254, 256, 258, 262ff., 285ff., 344ff., 350
Engineering industry (see also *Metalworking industries*)
– collective agreements in, 75, 134, 341
– constitutional strikes in, 251, 254
– employment in, 172, 189
– organization, production in, 339
– national strikes in, 21, 59, 137, 236ff., 334, 344
– wages, conditions in, 133ff., 155ff., 339ff.
Exports, cars, 106ff., 129
Engineering unions (see also *C.S.E.U.*, *Trade unions*, and *A.E.U.*, *N.U.V.B.*, *T.&G.W.U.*, etc.)
– organization, 340ff.
– wage policy, 341

Fact-finding commissions, 37, 212, 240, 244, 248, 288
Faunce, W. A., 89, 93, 168
Feinstein, C. H., 80
Ferrari, 315
Fiat, 311ff., 324ff.

F.I.O.M. (Italian trade union), 316
Fisher and Ludlow (Fisholow)
- absenteeism at, 185
- organization, production at, 27
- strikes, at, 199, 212
- unions, shop stewards at, 199, 212
- wages, conditions at, 146, 154
Ford
- collective agreements and organization at, 35, 194ff., 275ff.
- communist influence at, 213, 277
- employment at, 31, 145, 179, 187, 236
- labour policy of, 92, 102, 194, 215, 275ff., 345
- 'October Revolution', 1962, 216
- organization, production at, 27, 29ff., 78ff., 86, 278ff., 306, 353
- strikes at, 53, 58, 64, 71ff., 85, 109, 117, 119, 126, 179, 213ff., 275ff., 283, 287, 345ff., 349ff., 353
- estimation of strike loss at, 75, 237, 246, 346
- unions, shop stewards at, 193ff., 200, 208, 213ff., 219ff., 276ff., 283, 287, 349
- wages, conditions at, 85, 97, 100, 176, 216
Ford (German), 306, 308, 310
Ford (U.S.), 78ff., 87, 94, 97, 278, 295, 299, 301, 314, 348
'Francis' strike, 281ff.
French car industry, 106, 311ff.
Fringe Benefits, 134ff., 324, 351
- in other countries, 304ff., 310, 317

Galenson, W., 295
General Motors, 27, 295, 299, 301ff., 306, 315, 318, 323, 348
General strike, 109
Germany, see *West German Federal Republic*
Goldthorpe, J. H., 168
Go-slows, 32, 53
Griffiths, F., 78
Guaranteed Wage, 34, 134, 274, 305
Guest, R., 168
Guy Motors, 28

Hill, 136
Hillman, 27
'Hire and Fire' Policy, 127, 271, 337
Holden, 318

Holiday arrangements, 121, 134
- and strikes, 75, 124, 130, 330
Hours of work, see *Working hours*
Humber, 27

Imports, cars, 130
I.G. Metall (German trade union), 11, 308
Incentive payment, in car firms, 97, 100, 155ff., 233, 257, 319ff.
Incomes Policy, 336, 353
International Labour Office (I.L.O.), 97
Italian car industry, 314ff., 324ff.
International Metal Workers' Federation, 11, 318

Jack Report, see *Courts of Inquiry, at Ford*
Jaguar
- employment at, 86
- organization, production at, 11, 28ff.
- strikes at, 73, 119, 213, 230ff., 234, 236, 238, 241, 244, 261ff., 269, 349
- unions, shop stewards at, 195, 210ff., 213, 218, 220
- wages, conditions at, 147, 176
Jensen, 119
Job rights, 199, 336ff.
Joint meetings in motor industry, 24, 35ff., 199, 278, 283ff., 345, 351
Joint Statement by Employers' and Trade Union Representatives, 1961, 35ff., 92, 117
Joint Wages Board for the Vehicle Industry, 35
Jones, R. S., 251ff.
Jowett, 27, 119, 231
Jurisdictional disputes, 198

Kaiser-Willys, 304
Kerr, C., 165
Killingsworth, C. C., 87, 97
Knowles, K. C. J. C., 104, 122, 136, 283, 331, 333

Labour Courts, German, 306ff.
- Swedish, 320
Labour Market Board, Swedish, 321
Labour turnover, 26, 167, 188ff., 247, 330ff.
- in Sweden, 321
Lancia, 315
Lerner, Shirley, 220
Leyland Group, 28, 29

INDEX

L.O. (Swedish union federation), 319, 321
Local Conference, see *Engineering Disputes Procedure*
Lomax, K. S., 80

Management organization, 248ff., 347ff.
'Managerial Functions', 34, 68, 256ff., 271, 282, 334, 342, 347
Mann, F. C., 177
Marsh, A., 34, 203, 251ff., 256, 340
Marriott, K., 168
Maxcy, G., 26, 107
McCarthy, W. E. J., 58
McLoughlin, Q., 177
'McLoughlin' strike, 267ff.
'McHugh' strike, 272ff.
Melman, S., 98, 135, 141
Mercedes, 306, 309, 310
Metal Mechanics, see *National Society of Metal Mechanics*
Metal-working industries, strikes in, 22, 335, 339ff., 343
Miners' Federation, 341
Mining, strikes in, 21, 326, 335
Minister of Labour, see *Joint meetings in motor industry, and Courts of Inquiry*
Ministry of Labour
– classification, definitions of strikes, 23, 52, 55, 63, 236
– role of, 36, 286
– statistics, strikes, 21ff., 25, 51, 56, 114, 129ff., 131ff., 199, 224, 237, 274ff., 335, 350
– statistics, other, 26, 32, 94, 103, 133ff., 152, 158, 160ff., 172ff., 176ff., 182ff., 189ff.
Morris Motors (various plants)
– employment at, 32, 179, 183, 185ff.
– organization, production at, 30, 78, 82, 86, 347
– strikes at, 37, 51, 72, 114, 171, 179, 200, 240ff., 247, 262, 269, 350ff.
– unions, shop stewards at, 193, 196, 200, 207, 217ff., 350
– wages, conditions at, 140, 154, 185ff.
Motor Industry Joint Labour Council, 37, 129, 201, 352ff.
Motor Industry Joint Study Group (see also *Fact-finding Commissions*), 36ff.

Motor Industry Industrial Relations Panel (M.I.I.R.P.), 35
Motor Industry, see *Car Industry*
Motor Show, 107, 130
– and strikes, 122, 124
Motor Vehicles and Cycles Industry (see also *Vehicles Industry*), 135ff., 172, 189
Mott, P. E., 177
Multiple unionism, see *Trade unions*

National Association of Clerical and Supervisory Staffs (N.A.C.S.S.), 34
National trade union officers, 205ff., 211, 220ff., 274ff., 280ff., 285ff., 341, 345, 352
Newspaper printers, earnings of, 133, 135
Night working, see *Shift work*
Nissan, 322
N.S.U., 306
National Society of Metal Mechanics (N.S.M.M.), 195, 285, 355
National Union of General and Municipal Workers (N.U.G.M.W.)
– membership in the car firms, 34, 193, 195
– organization, 342
– recruiting policy, 193
– relations with other unions, 355
National Union of Sheet Metal Workers and Coppersmiths (N.U.S.M.W. & C.) (see also *Sheet Metal Workers' Unions*), 34, 195
National Union of Vehicle Builders (N.U.V.B.)
– in individual firms, 99, 194, 196, 347
– industrial relations policy for motor industry, 204
– membership in car firms, 193ff., 347
– organization, 203ff., 342, 354
– recruiting policy, 192ff., 196, 198
– relations with other unions, 64, 198ff., 212, 282, 355
– shop stewards in, 193, 201, 207, 209, 212
– in certain strikes, 117, 271ff., 282
Nuffield Metal Products, 199, 212

Occupational mobility, 64, 83ff., 198ff.
O.E.C.D., 338
Opel, 306, 310, 347

361

Overtime working, 22, 101, 140, 160
– bans, 52
– in other countries, 307, 313, 321

Panhard, 311
Parallel bargaining, 301
'Parallel unionism', see *Trade Unions*
Pattern bargaining, 301
Pearson, Sir R., 99
Pensions, 134
Peugeot, 311, 314
Plant delegates, in French car firms, 311ff.
Press, as source of strike data, 51ff., 73, 235, 239, 327
Pressed Steel Company
– employment at, 32
– labour policy, 284, 345
– organization, production at, 27ff., 30, 231, 243
– strikes at, 75, 238, 240ff., 244, 262ff., 284, 287, 345
– unions, shop stewards at, 32, 196, 207, 211, 217, 287, 350
– wages and conditions at, 99, 143, 146, 158, 176
Prince, 323
'Procedure', see *Engineering Disputes Procedure*
Production in car firms
– capacity of, 129ff.
– fluctuations in, 69, 83, 105ff., 111ff., 124ff., 331ff., 351
– growth of, 77, 80ff., 205ff.
– processes, 38ff., 77ff., 327ff., 349
– structure of, 27ff., 230ff.
– in other countries, 293ff., 299ff., 306, 315, 322ff.
Productivity
– growth in car firms, 77, 80ff., 101, 205ff., 300ff., 328
– growth in metal working industries, 339ff.

Redundancy (see also *Strikes in car firms*)
– effects of automation and technical change, 82ff., 101, 328
– in other countries' car industries, 307, 321
– Redundancy Payments Act (1965), 337, 339
– in various car firms, 82, 272ff., 281ff., 285ff.

Renault, 313ff.
Restriction of output, by Japanese car workers, 323
Revans, R. W., 167, 186
Roberts, B. C., 202
Rolls-Royce
– employment, production at, 349
– strikes at, 109, 119, 236, 238, 261, 269, 348ff.
– unions, shop stewards at, 348
Rootes
– employment at, 100, 186ff., 285
– labour policy of, 34ff., 284ff., 345
– organization, production at, 27ff., 30, 79, 181
– strikes at, 53, 171, 213, 236, 238, 240ff., 262ff., 269, 284ff., 288, 345, 347, 349
– estimation of strike loss, 246ff.
– unions, shop stewards at, 213, 217ff., 285ff.
– wages and conditions at, 99ff., 141ff., 153, 285
Ross, A. M., 241
Rover
– employment at, 86, 183
– organization, production at, 28, 30, 39, 86, 181
– strikes at, 72, 117, 119, 171, 212, 231, 236, 238, 241, 244, 247, 259, 262ff., 269
– unions, shop stewards at, 212, 217, 220, 288
– wages and conditions at, 147
Royal Commission on Trade Unions and Employers' Associations, 72, 261
Royal Society for the Prevention of Accidents, 186

Saab, 319
S.A.F. (Swedish employers' federation), 319, 321
Scamp, Jack, 37
Scanlon Plan, 99
Severance pay, 117, 125, 337
Sheet Metal Workers' Unions
– membership in the car firms, 34, 195
– relations with other unions, 64, 198ff., 355
– in certain strikes, 285ff.
Shift working
– in car firms, 136, 176ff., 351

INDEX

- and strikes, 64, 75, 101ff., 130, 176ff., 204ff., 329ff.
Shop stewards (see also *Strikes in car firms*)
- conveners, role and activities of, 201, 207ff., 222, 224ff., 272, 330
- dismissals of, 61, 212, 214, 267, 272ff., 276ff., 281ff., 284ff.
- number of, 207, 340
- organization and activities, 34, 205ff., 329ff., 340, 343, 345ff., 348ff., 351ff.
  - combine committees, 261ff., 272, 285ff., 290, 343, 352, 354ff.
  - joint committees, 208, 210, 214, 272ff., 277, 279ff., 343, 352, 354ff.
  - shop committees, 207, 276
  - works committees, 194, 198, 201, 207ff., 224ff., 276ff., 289, 343, 352, 354ff.
- political affiliations, influence of, 212ff., 220, 277, 288ff.
- pressures upon, 34, 214ff., 220ff., 224ff., 272ff., 276ff., 283, 286ff., 345
- recognition and facilities, 36, 207ff., 212, 215ff., 219ff., 251, 272ff., 276ff., 281ff., 351ff.
- relations with unions, full-time union officers, 34, 203ff., 209, 211, 215, 220ff., 228ff., 345, 352, 354ff.
Short-time working, 177ff., 307, 317
Sick pay, 134
Siegel, A., 165
Silberston, A., 26, 107, 300
Simca, 311, 313ff.
Singer, 27
'Size effect', 167, 181ff., 231, 245, 328
Smith, May, 91
Socialist Laboratories, 291
'Socio-technical systems', see *Technology*
Standard Triumph International (S.T.I.)
- collective agreements and organization at, 134, 141, 346
- employment at, 82, 187
- organization, production at, 30, 79, 86
- strikes at, 71, 73, 117, 119, 126, 171, 213, 231, 236, 238, 240ff., 259, 262ff., 269, 349

- unions, shop stewards at, 213, 218, 220
- wages and conditions at, 97ff., 141ff., 147, 234
Stengel, E., 127
Strike ballots, 276ff., 281
Strike pay, 117
Strikes, generally
- and agitators, 283
- and 'conspiracy', 19, 127, 332
- classification and definitions, 51ff., 63, 104ff.
- and economic conditions, 21ff., 24, 104ff., 113, 167, 336
- effects of, 21ff., 326ff.
- and fatal accidents, 188
- in other countries, 297, 308ff., 312, 317ff., 320
- and suicide, 126ff.
- and technology, 166, 327
- trends, 20ff., 326, 335
- in various industries (see also *Engineering, Mining*, etc.), 21ff., 127, 335ff., 339ff.
Strikes, in car firms (see also *Austin, B.M.C., Ford*, etc.)
- and agitators, 283, 287ff., 329ff.
- and attitudes, characteristics, of workers, 171ff., 178ff., 291, 328ff., 331, 333
- average size, length of, 58, 60ff.
- big, 54, 117, 126, 234, 244, 246ff., 265ff., 287ff., 328
- in booms, 107ff., 116ff., 121, 126ff., 331ff.
- cycles of, 241ff., 328
- classification and definitions, 52ff., 57ff., 63ff., 76, 224
- about demarcation, 198ff., 245, 328
- about discipline, 60, 63, 109, 114, 335
- over dismissals, 59ff., 68, 115, 212, 214, 243, 245, 247, 256, 263ff., 272, 276, 281, 320, 334
- and E.E.F., 57, 245, 248ff., 258, 262ff., 285ff., 344ff.
- and employment fluctuations, issues, 31ff., 59ff., 83, 115ff., 124, 127ff., 234, 326, 328, 331ff., 335ff.
- economic effects of, 24ff., 45ff., 54ff., 121, 327, 353
- firms' records of, 53, 72ff.
- and insecurity, 69, 83, 102, 115, 127ff., 164, 199, 247, 331, 336ff.

363

- in major and minor firms, 113, 119, 121, 230ff., 240ff.
- and management questions, attitudes, 68, 114, 118, 127, 182ff., 233, 235, 243ff., 247ff., 256, 262ff., 328, 332
- and market factors, 105, 119, 121, 230, 234, 245, 263
- and other measures of discontent, 75, 185ff., 330ff.
- and Motor Show, 122, 124
- in new plants, 68ff.
- occupational analysis, 170ff., 329
- unofficial, unconstitutional, etc., 56ff., 117, 121, 126, 130, 222ff., 254, 277, 279, 284, 287, 294ff., 307, 324, 345
- in other countries, 24, 298ff., 308ff., 317ff., 320, 322ff.
- and overtime, short-time working, 109, 128ff., 227
- and production, 25, 69, 105ff., 107, 109, 111ff., 118, 126ff., 244, 247, 329, 331ff., 334, 336
- over redundancy, lay-offs, 62ff., 66, 69ff., 114ff., 117ff., 122, 124ff., 127ff., 224, 241, 245, 247, 256, 261, 263, 328, 331ff., 334
- seasonal factors in, 105ff., 111ff., 121ff., 124ff., 332ff.
- and 'secondary loss', 55ff., 73, 236ff., 239, 246ff., 259, 261, 333
- severity of, 116ff., 126
- and shift working, 64, 75, 101ff., 130, 176ff., 204ff., 262, 329ff.
- and 'size effect', 181ff., 231, 245ff., 328
- small, 'downers', 52, 224ff.
- and shop stewards, 211ff., 225ff., 276, 281, 330
- trends, 20, 23ff., 26, 35, 58ff., 64ff., 111, 114ff., 230ff., 261, 326, 331, 333ff.
- about trade union issues, relations, 59ff., 64ff., 109, 114, 116ff., 194, 198ff., 243ff., 248, 256, 259, 261ff., 338
- about transfers of labour, 198ff., 245, 337
- and technology, technical change, 25, 69, 83ff., 96, 99ff., 166, 246, 323, 327ff.
- about wages, wage claims, 59ff., 64, 66, 113ff., 124ff., 133ff., 236, 243, 245, 261ff., 334ff.
- about wage-structure, work-loads, 60, 63ff., 66, 70, 109, 128, 143ff., 216ff., 233ff., 240, 243ff., 247, 256, 259, 261ff., 328, 334, 346, 335ff.
- white collar workers, 182ff., 262ff., 320
- and working conditions, hours, holidays, 59ff., 63ff., 75, 114, 130, 168ff., 240, 243, 247, 262, 329ff., 335
- and work-sharing, work-spreading, 62, 118ff., 127, 130, 332ff.
- workers directly involved in, 55, 180

Studebaker, 304
S.U. Carburettors, 32
Supplementary unemployment benefit (S.U.B.), 305
Swedish car industry, 319ff., 324ff., 339

Technical change, see *Automation*
Technology, as factor in strike-proneness, 25, 93, 95ff., 166ff., 293ff., 323, 325, 327ff., 349ff.
Thrupp and Maberley, 285
Toolmakers' Union, 35
Touraine, A., 90
Toyota, 322
Tractors and Transmissions, 63
Trade unions (see also *A.E.U.*, *N.U.V.B.*, *T.&G.W.U.*, etc., also *Shop stewards* and *Strikes, in car firms*)
- competition, 62, 117, 193ff., 200, 340ff., 344
- full-time officers, 202ff., 209, 211, 215, 220ff. 228ff. 272ff., 279ff., 284ff., 290, 341, 345, 347, 352
- membership, 194ff., 340ff., 344, 347
- organization, 32, 193ff., 196, 335, 340ff., 346ff., 352, 354ff.
  - 'multiple unionism', 198ff., 211, 245, 340ff., 343ff.
  - 'parallel unionism', 222, 343ff., 352ff.
- policy, 64, 105, 117ff., 126, 130, 192, 198ff., 204ff., 273ff., 276ff., 282ff., 332, 336ff., 340ff., 345ff.
- in other countries, 295, 297, 301ff., 308, 310ff., 315ff., 331ff.
Trades Union Congress (T.U.C.), 34, 36, 194, 200, 274ff., 346, 354
Transport and General Workers' Union (T.&G.W.U.)
- in individual firms, 196

INDEX

- membership in the car firms, 34, 193ff., 201, 271
- organization, 201ff., 342
- recruiting policy, 193ff., 196, 198
- relations with other unions, 198ff., 282, 355
- shop stewards in, 201, 206ff., 209, 211
- in certain strikes, 117

Trotskyists, 291
Turner, H. A., 104, 243, 248

United Automobile, Aerospace and Agricultural Implement Workers of America (U.A.W.), 89, 97, 295, 297, 301ff., 305, 318, 323
Unofficial strikes, see *Strikes, in car firms*
United States of America (U.S.A.), American motor industry, 294ff.

Vauxhall
- collective agreements and organization at, 34, 194, 347ff.
- employment at, 31, 86, 145, 179
- labour policy of, 25, 193, 345, 347ff.
- organization, production at, 25, 30, 78ff., 86, 90, 306
- strikes at, 62, 64, 68, 72, 75, 117, 119, 179, 230ff., 236, 238, 245ff., 249, 261, 270, 345, 350
- estimation of strike loss at, 246
- unions, shop stewards at, 194, 196, 200, 208
- wages and conditions at, 85, 98ff., 134, 138, 140, 145, 153ff., 216, 310

Vehicles industry (see also *Motor Vehicles and Cycles Industry*)
- accidents in, 186, 188
- definition of, 22ff., 29
- employment in, 30ff.
- strikes in, 22ff., 29
- wages and conditions in, 136, 160, 176

Volkswagen, 306, 308, 310
Volvo, 319

Wages (see also *Earnings* and *Strikes, in car firms*)
- in car firms
  - and automation, 84ff., 92, 96ff., 328
  - and national rates, 34, 137, 205

- in other countries, 303ff., 308ff., 322ff.
- in other industries, 133ff.
- policies, 97ff., 127ff., 143, 336ff., 351
- drift, 137, 320ff., 353ff.
- structure and work-loads in car firms
  - effect of technical change, productivity, and nature of work, 96ff., 100, 155ff., 328
  - in Sweden, 320ff., 339
- structure and work-loads in engineering, 257ff.
- systems in car firms
  - description, 41, 155
  - and technical change, 96ff.
  - incentive payments, P.B.R., 97, 100, 155ff., 233, 257, 319ff.
  - and merit rating, 100
  - and Scanlon Plan, 99
- systems in engineering and metal trades, 155, 249ff., 339ff.

Walker, C. R., 90, 168
War Labour Board (American), 301
Warwick, D. P., 177
West Germany (Federal Republic), car industry, 306ff., 339
White-collar workers
- earnings of, 136
- proportions of, 32ff., 93ff., 182ff., 187, 214
- strikes by, 262ff., 320
Women in car industry, 31ff., 136ff., 147, 300
Woodward, J., 20, 166
Work-loads, see under *Wages*
Work study, 91ff.
- in Sweden, 321
Working hours, week
- in car firms, 134, 138, 140, 175ff.
- in foreign car firms, 307, 313, 320
Workers' Union, 193
Works Committees, see *Engineering Disputes Procedure* and *Shop Stewards*
Works Conference, see *Engineering Disputes Procedure*
Works Councils (in other countries), 307, 309ff., 315, 319, 321, 324
Works rules, 43ff.
World Federation of Trade Unions, 220
Wyatt, S., 168